Governing the European Economy

edited by Grahame Thompson

SAGE Publications
London • Thousand Oaks • New Delhi

in association with

The Open
University

This publication forms part of the Open University course DD200 *Governing Europe*. The other books that make up the *Governing Europe* series are listed on the back cover. Details of this and other Open University courses can be obtained from the Call Centre, PO Box 724, The Open University, Milton Keynes MK7 6ZS, United Kingdom: tel. +44 (0)1908 653231, e-mail ces-gen@open.ac.uk

Alternatively, you may visit the Open University website at http://www.open.ac.uk where you can learn more about the wide range of courses and packs offered at all levels by The Open University.

For availability of other course components, contact Open University Worldwide Ltd, The Berrill Building, Walton Hall, Milton Keynes MK7 6AA, United Kingdom: tel. +44 (0)1908 858785; fax +44 (0)1908 858787; e-mail ouwenq@open.ac.uk; website http://www.ouw.co.uk

Sage Publications Ltd
6 Bonhill Street
London EC2A 4PU

Sage Publications Inc.
2455 Teller Road
Thousand Oaks
California 91320

Sage Publications India Pvt Ltd
32 M-block Market
Greater Kailash - 1
New Dehli 110 048

British Library Cataloging in Publication Data
A catalogue record for this book is available from The British Library.

Library of Congress catalog record available.

Edited, designed and typeset by The Open University.

Printed and bound in the United Kingdom by The Bath Press, Bath.

ISBN 0 7619 5462 7 (hbk)
ISBN 0 7619 5463 5 (pbk)

1.1

Contents

Series preface

The three volumes that appear in this series are part of the course *Governing Europe* from the Faculty of Social Sciences at The Open University. The course is, in the main, the product of the Politics Discipline within the Faculty, but it has benefited from the participation of a number of academic colleagues from other areas of the University, notably from the Economics, Sociology, Social Policy and Geography Disciplines and from the Arts Faculty. The interdisciplinary approach fostered by this co-operation carries on a long tradition of courses originating within the Faculty of Social Sciences that have tried to preserve a broadly based academic output across the social sciences. The Open University remains almost unique in its ability to foster and preserve such an approach, despite moves toward stricter discipline lines across the academic world more generally. The three books in this series, while specializing in particular aspects of the issue of governing Europe, maintain an interdisciplinary style throughout. The fact that the books still stand together as a coherent series, and work for the course as a whole, is testament to the ability, enthusiasm, and sheer hard work of my colleagues on the Course Team. I thank them all.

To mention all of the people associated with the project by name would create an impossibly long list, but I must record my special thanks to a number of individuals. First, without the other two editors of the books, Simon Bromley and Montserrat Guibernau, life would have been impossible in the three years that it took to prepare the course. Their role has been central to the successful outcome of the project. With clear and penetrating analytical skills and patient attention to detail, they have accomplished the successive drafting and redrafting of chapters with cheery good humour, even while working under impossibly tight schedules. I would also like to extend very special thanks to the course manager for *Governing Europe*, Eileen Potterton. Seldom has someone so new to the OU grasped the tasks at hand so quickly, so firmly and to such good effect. Her expert managerial skills and unflappable manner have calmed the nerves and smoothed the brows of many a fraught academic. Other key members of the course team – Paul Lewis, Richard Heffernan, Mark Smith, Will Brown, Chris Brook and Mark Pittaway – made their own invaluable contribution to the collective discussions that helped frame the books and establish their content. Rob Clifton and Bob Kelly, ably assisted by two OU Associate Lecturers, Brenda Martin and Graham Venters, added the final touches as they constantly reminded us of the primary teaching objectives of these texts. Dianne Cook, Anne Hunt, June Ayres and Fran Ford typed and formatted three drafts of each chapter with their usual good-natured efficiency.

Added to this have been the meticulous editorial skills of Mark Goodwin and Lynne Slocombe, the graphic design skills of Caroline Husher, who designed the striking covers for the books, and Jonathan Hunt and Gill Gowans from the Copublishing Department, who helped to launch the series with Sage. And in this respect I would like to thank Lucy Robinson of Sage, both for her early enthusiasm for the project and for her later support and guidance as the books moved through the production process and into the public domain.

The Open University could not operate as successfully as it does without contributions from academics and others from outside the institution. The *Governing Europe* series has relied upon a wide range of academic input from specialists in European politics and economics from a number of universities in the UK and mainland Europe. This refreshing additional scholarship has only added to the quality of the product. Special mention must also be made of the external assessor of *Governing Europe*, Mike Smith of the University of Loughbrough. As one of the UK's ablest and wisest European Studies academics, his careful and thoughtful assessment of the chapter drafts and his expert advice more generally on matters European have been warmly appreciated.

Finally, two colleagues who have now left The Open University, David Held and Anthony McGrew, were instrumental in getting the course up and running, along with the then Head of the Discipline, Richard Maidment. The fact that I inherited a course structure and a set of book proposals from these colleagues that did not change to any great extent after they had left the project is a testament to the originality and robustness of their early proposals.

Grahame Thompson
Chair, *Governing Europe*
Milton Keynes, August 2000

Book preface

This book was put together over a period of nearly two years. During that time the authors of the chapters worked to very tight deadlines, producing three drafts and responding positively to all the comments made by the course team. This was a learning experience for us all, and I hope the final product, which I edited heavily as the chapters went to press, meet the expectations of both the authors and the readers. The chapters are designed to be read as a collective enterprise so that each follows on from the other and develops themes explored earlier. However, they can also be read separately since each offers a self-contained analysis of the topic under consideration. The areas dealt with here – the evolving characteristics of the European economic space and its governance – are fast moving and rapidly changing ones. But the chapters concentrate on underlying features and structural constraints such that they provide an enduring analysis of the way the European economy is responding to forces for change sweeping across Europe in the early years of the twenty-first century. I would like to thank all the authors, my fellow members of the DD200 *Governing Europe* course team, the secretaries who prepared the final manuscript – Anne Hunt, Dianne Cook, June Ayers and Fran Ford – and the book editors Lynne Slocombe and Gareth Williams.

Grahame Thompson
Editor, *Governing the European Economy*
Milton Keynes, December 2000

Chapter 1
Governing the European economy: a framework for analysis

Grahame Thompson

1   Introduction

The chapters in this book are about the construction and governance of the European economy. As we shall see, these two aspects go together since they have evolved, and are continuing to evolve, in parallel. In large part the European economy has been created by the governance mechanisms generated to regulate and manage it. The process of formation of the European economy cannot, then, easily be separated from the two key aspects of this governance. The first is the way that various public authorities have set about trying to organize that economy, creating the institutions which have served to guide and direct its development over the last sixty or so years. This is the process of *de jure* integration. And the second is in relation to the way private decisions about how to conduct economic activity have also organized the economy in a particular way. This is the process of *de facto* integration.

In examining these processes a number of issues arise. To start with, there is a problem of how far we can yet sensibly talk about an integrated 'European economy' as distinct from the separated national economies of the individual countries that traditionally make up the territory of 'economic Europe'. For the most part the chapters in this book take the post-Second World War period as the main focus for their analyses; this was the period in which the greatest advances were made in constructing a properly functioning European economy (as opposed to the individual economies within it). But there have been other periods when a European economic space of sorts was in place, often focusing on a different area of the continent and involving different territorial boundaries. For the most part we concentrate on the (shifting) boundary defined by that (growing) territory marked out by the European Union (EU) and the countries included within it (see Figure 1.1 below). As we shall see, this has not always been the most sensible way of defining an operational European economic space.

In addition, talk of an operational or coherent European economic space immediately begs the question of the nature of that coherence. For instance, there is a dispute among economists on whether the present boundaries of the EU, or even those of a truly continent-wide European economic territory, could be consistent with what economists call an 'optimum currency area'. Establishing whether an integrating community of nations constitutes an optimum currency area is, for conventional economics, the major indicator of the likely performative outcomes of a process of integration. If the integrating community does not meet the criteria for the establishment of such an area, then it is unlikely, it is argued, to work in an economic sense to maximize the welfare of those who inhabit it – it is *not* an operationally coherent economic space. Indeed, any such lack of coherence could undermine the logic of integration altogether and lead to a collapse of the experiment in constructing a functioning European economic space of the EU type. We return to this issue later in this introductory chapter, and it arises in a less formal way in later chapters of the book.

There is also another important way in which the issue of coherence could be posed. The limits of what we understand by economic activity – and therefore what encompasses a legitimate extent of economic analysis – might seem obvious, but a moment's reflection should indicate that this is less clear cut than at first appears. The extent of the economic domain is a heavily contested one. So, for instance (to cite an example that appears in this book, in Chapter 7), the issues of environmental pollution and environmentally sustainable development have not always been included as legitimate parts of the domain of economic analysis. While it would be nice to think that this resistance has now been overcome, the general point is that what constitutes the legitimate boundaries around what is called 'economic analysis' might just as well be the result of luck, fate or power considerations as the result of some 'natural' economic attributes inherent in economic exchange and the allocation of resources. What is important to recognize is the contested nature of economic Europe at a number of levels. Political and other forces struggle to define this as suits their particular purpose, for instance, or their particular vision for the 'future of Europe' (or, indeed, its past).

The final main issue addressed in this introductory chapter concerns the nature of economic governance. Broadly speaking we can define economic governance as the processes and practices that produce and maintain economic order. In this book we concentrate upon two main mechanisms that, arguably, produce economic order – regulatory activity of various kinds and market activity of various kinds. These are discussed at some length below, and in addition to these a third economic governance mechanism is considered toward the end of this chapter. This is the mechanism of self-organizing networks, which occupies a kind of intermediate position between the two main mechanisms.

2 The history and importance of the European economic space

In trying to define the object of our analysis in this book – that of contemporary 'economic Europe' – the most obvious and conventional way to begin would be to define it as comprising the fifteen member states of the EU in the year 2000. This could then be supplemented by a group of other Western European economies which were not members of the EU in that year but which abutted the EU in a geographical sense (for example, the European Free Trade Association – EFTA – comprising Norway, Iceland, Liechtenstein and Switzerland in 2000), or a set of countries which were part of an eastern European trading bloc (comprising the Central and Eastern European countries of the old Soviet bloc, the Baltic states, and of the 'commonwealth of independent states' (CIS), associated with Russia, which included Belarus and the Ukraine).

Clearly, then, one of the main problems encountered in any analysis of 'economic Europe' is exactly where to draw the boundary around Europe as an economic entity. And this problem is not solved by simply appealing to the EU as representing the logical centre for the European economy. The EU has changed its own geographical boundaries over the years (Figure 1.1), and it could enlarge them again very soon, as we shall see from the analyses in some of the following chapters of this book (Chapters 2 and 8 in particular; see also **Lewis, 2001**). The enlargement of the EU in the early twenty-first century is likely to include a number of the traditional eastern European economies just mentioned.

Section 2.1 focuses upon the changing conception of Europe as an economic entity, and its accompanying character as a political entity. A theme of this section is the multi-dimensional character of 'economic Europe', particularly its political evolution and regulation. How did we get to a point where we can discuss 'Europe' as defined in relation to the list of countries and areas just mentioned? What exactly is the relationship of the 'EU Europe' to other areas that relate to that 'Europe'?

2.1 What is the European economic space?

Is the contemporary economic space of Europe the same as the one which might have been described one hundred years, sixty years or even thirty years ago? Clearly the characteristic features shaping the 'European economic space' in various historical periods are themselves likely to be diverse and contingent.

There are two possible routes to follow in the analysis of the European economic space.

- We could take an overtly *institutional* focus. In this case we would trace the evolution of those institutional mechanisms in which the idea of Europe as an economic unit figured directly, or was implicated by the fact of its geopolitical presence – *de jure* integration.

- The other main way to tackle this definitional problem is to look at the characteristic *patterns of economic interaction* which the European states, or private economic actors residing within them, developed between themselves – *de facto* integration.

The first of these focuses upon a more 'political' approach. It involves charting the definition and redefinition of those typical Europe-wide consultative, regulatory and administrative mechanisms and their practices which implicate some notion of economic Europe in their operations. The second is perhaps a more obviously 'economic' approach. It implies an analysis of the progressive development and reconstruction of market mechanisms to trace growing patterns of trade, investment, production, technological, migration and other economic relationships among the countries of Europe.

While these look to be quite different and separate approaches, a moment's reflection indicates that they represent a different emphasis in a single overall process. As the chapter unfolds, these twin focuses will be progressively drawn together, and we find that they are deployed in combination. But it is still useful to begin our analysis by looking at them separately.

2.2 The *de jure* institutional matrix of economic Europe

Defining post-war 'Western Europe'

Taking a broadly defined 'Western Europe' first, this is largely how the European economic space came to be known over the period from the end of the Second World War until the late 1980s. In that period it was pitched against a perhaps even less clearly demarcated 'Eastern Europe' (discussed later). In an economic sense Western Europe included those sixteen liberal market economies which originally set up the Organization of European Economic Co-operation (OEEC) in 1948, and which later expanded to include the Federal Republic of Germany, Spain and then Turkey (subsequently incorporated and renamed as the Organization of Economic Co-operation and Development, OECD, in 1961), and which were subsequently joined by Finland (1969), the Czech Republic (1995), and Hungary and Poland (1996). In 2000 these made up the European nations in the OECD. The OECD has retained an explicitly economic brief: to foster the development of liberal market economic relations among its members. It does this in the form of an information gathering and consultative institution, carrying out individual country economic assessments, dealing with issues of common economic interests, disseminating the results, and pressing for further liberalization policies among its members.

In addition to this essentially co-operative and consultative institutional mechanism, post-war Western Europe also saw the emergence of a set of more integrationist and co-ordinatory organizational formations. Even while still in exile in London in 1944, the governments of Luxembourg, Belgium and the Netherlands set up a customs union, to be known as Benelux, beginning on 1 January 1948. (In fact, a customs union between just Belgium and Luxembourg, the BLUE, had been in operation since 1921.) This developed into an early prototype for the wider economic unions that were to follow. But as early as the end of the 1950s Benelux achieved the elimination of all remaining trade barriers, the free movement of capital and labour and an important agricultural accord between the countries involved. In March 1948 France and Italy also set up a customs union (Francital) which embodied similar provisions and which by the mid-1950s had achieved much the same result (though not for agricultural activities).

In retrospect, probably the most important of these early co-operative efforts was the European Coal and Steel Community (ECSC) established by the Treaty of Paris in 1951 (becoming operative the following year). Involving France, West Germany, Italy and the Benelux countries (the UK did not join the ECSC), this community eliminated tariff and quantitative restrictions on trade (including subsidies) relating to coal and steel between its members. The ECSC had a considerable symbolic effect on subsequent integrationist tendencies within Western Europe, though its immediate effects upon the coal and steel sectors of the community members themselves were limited.

Rudimentary though they were, the early economic co-operative and co-ordinatory relations fostered by these institutions (and other important organizations that are discussed more fully in a moment) culminated during the second half of the twentieth century in the development of the original EEC of the six, expanding to the EU of the fifteen by 1995 (Figure 1.1). At first this existed alongside the European Free Trade Association (EFTA) which originally comprised nine member states but subsequently shrank to seven (Austria, Finland, Iceland, Norway, Portugal, Sweden and Switzerland) as the UK and Denmark left to join the EU (then the EEC) in 1973. Portugal followed in 1986, and Austria, Finland and Sweden in 1995. Although formally EFTA still exists, its effectiveness is minimal and to all intents and purposes it has been absorbed into the EU's *de facto* integrative process (though not its *de jure* one) by being a part of the wider European economic area (EEA). This EEA also extends to the Visegard countries in central eastern Europe (Poland, Hungary, the Czech Republic and Slovakia) and many more besides. Since 1980 the EEA has become the main EU institutional mechanism for the extension of 'free trade' to associate member countries that negotiate bilateral trade agreements with the Union. An important adjunct mechanism to this was the EU–Mediterranean partnership agreement negotiated from 1992 and signed in November 1995 at the Barcelona Conference. This brought together the EU plus the MED 12 (Algeria,

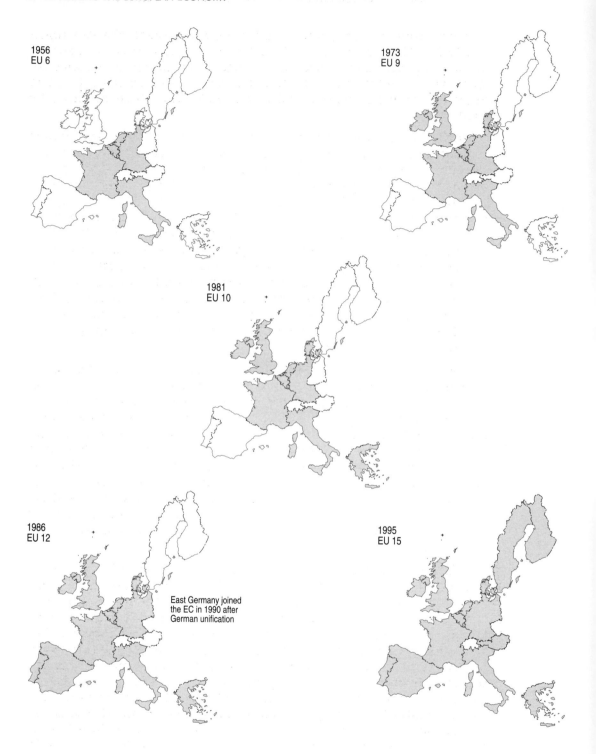

Figure 1.1 The evolution of the European Union

Morocco, Tunisia, Egypt, Jordan, Lebanon, Syria, Israel, the Palestinian Territories, Cyprus, Malta and Turkey) in a wide-ranging associate membership agreement covering a range of economic and social co-operative and integrative activities. The aim of this agreement was to negotiate complete comprehensive free trade with these countries by 2010.

Broadly speaking, these developments represent the main institutional contours of the Western European economic space after the war. Clearly, this integrating institutionalized economic space of the post-war period did have a certain geographical continuity and logic, being initially centred on the industrial heartland of Northern Europe bounded by the Saar and Ruhr and stretching southwards to Northern Italy. For much of the pre-1914 period Germany occupied a pivotal position within central Europe, producing the manufactured goods which were then exchanged for agricultural produce from Eastern and other Central European countries. Thus it was the processes of industrialization in the latter half of the nineteenth and early part of the twentieth centuries that forged the modern industrialized states of Europe, which were responsible for securing one of the main economic foundations for the integrationist moves of half a century later.

How different this was to the previous 'European' economic spaces of the Mediterranean basin in the time of Antiquity, or the North Sea and Atlantic Ocean (maritime states of the sixteenth and seventeenth centuries, England, the Netherlands, Spain, Portugal and France). These earlier periods of European pre-eminence established their own typical regimes of economic relationships where in a sense the European economic space was extended to areas and regions far beyond the borders of continental Europe itself. In a way then, the European economic space has for much of its history not been confined just to the countries of the European continent. And this is reinforced in the contemporary period by the Euro-MED agreement with the North African countries just mentioned.

Indeed, the period since the Second World War has seen a further way in which the European economic space could be defined, at least in part. This involves the role of the USA in particular, and the institutional matrix it was instrumental in developing and supporting after 1945. The term 'Western Europe' as an economic conception, for instance, owes much to the USA and to its sponsored developmental agencies, especially those established immediately after the war. Originally these had in mind a broader Europe, conceived by the UN as part of its plan for post-war reconstruction for the entire continent. But the intensification of the Cold War during the late 1940s left this wider conception moribund. The work of the US-sponsored UN Economic Commission for Europe would have included what subsequently became known as 'Eastern Europe and the Soviet Union' in that reconstruction package, but it required those benefiting from assistance to agree to promote a system of liberalized multilateral free trade as they recovered, something the USSR could not accept. Thus although the eastern European countries were offered Marshall Aid (as it came to be known), this was more or less vetoed by the USSR.

Instead, the main institutional instrument of US-led reconstruction efforts centred upon those sixteen countries that set up the OEEC in 1948 to administer the European part of the Marshall Plan (named after the American Secretary of State in the 1940s, General George Marshall, who was responsible for administering the programme). By most accounts the Marshall Plan was a great success, though this is controversial (for a positive assessment see Hogan, 1989; for a sceptical view see Milward, 1984). The Plan was a specially formed programme with its own separate institutional apparatus. Originally it was intended to operate for only four years (1947 to 1951), but it continued with a second phase until well after the Korean War ended in 1953. The Plan involved US$ 3 billion of official (World Bank) loans and US$ 17 billion of direct US government gifts – not loans – in total amounting to some 3 per cent of US gross domestic product (GDP) in 1948 and 1949. The Marshall Plan significantly contributed to a modernization of European infrastructure and the reconstruction of its productive industries, but it also enabled rearmament to take place at the same time. It provided for the 'dollar shortage' at a vulnerable time for Europe, helping the European OECD countries to finance their severe balance of payments deficits. In addition, the Plan, particularly in its second phase, envisaged increasing intra-European co-operation as quota and tariff barriers to trade were to be lifted. In this the immediate outcome was less successful. Thus to some extent the stimulus for post-Second World War European integrative co-operation originated from an organized centre, although that centre was not a part of Europe as such.

It is clear, then, that US concern with European economic reconstruction and integration was very much set within the framework of its wider strategy of containment. The Cold War and a hostile attitude toward the Soviet Union's presumed expansionary intentions in Europe (and elsewhere) were what drove the policy. But there was another if secondary reason, involving relationships *within* Western Europe, between France and Germany in particular. It was anticipated that the form of economic and political reconstruction in Europe after the war would solve once and for all the 'German problem' – it would lock (West) Germany into a system of liberal market relationships *and* into a system of constitutional arrangements with its neighbours that would prevent a repeat of the inter-war experience in continental Central Europe. This is a theme we return to in later chapters of this book (Chapters 2, 3, 5 and 8).

Defining post-war 'Eastern Europe'

We have seen the difficulties in trying to define the western European economic space, constituted as it was by a number of different determinations and overlapping institutional frameworks – and defining the eastern European economic space turns out to be nearly as problematical. As a response to the rejection of the US initiatives in Eastern Europe in the context of the Marshall Plan, the Soviet Union set up its own reconstruction package, the Cominform and the Molotov Plan (1947). These were later extended to become the Council of Mutual Economic Aid (CMEA or COMECON, set up in Moscow in 1949), which assumed the role of premier instrument for the construction of an integrated economic system among the centrally planned economies (CEPs) under Soviet tutelage.

After Stalin's death the COMECON developed as a mechanism for national and sectoral economic specialization among its members (a kind of socialist international division of labour), though the extent of intra-COMECON trade remained relatively weak as the basic autarkic national development strategies of the socialist countries failed to break down fully. However, in certain key sectors effective country specialization did emerge (for instance, the case of bus construction, which was centred on Hungary). In addition, within the Soviet Union itself a highly integrated specialization emerged. The republics of the USSR evolved to trade a very high proportion of their output among themselves. These interdependencies proved a major problem as the Soviet and Eastern economic bloc began to disintegrate in the late 1980s/early 1990s.

The European institutional framework: summing up

To sum up this section, we have seen how the idea of a European economic space is not easy to define in a consistent institutional sense. It has been the subject of a number of determinations and transformations. A complex overlapping framework emerges, especially for the area of Western Europe and the old Soviet Union. In addition, 'Europe' as an economic object should not necessarily be confused with the geographical limits of what is normally understood as Europe (for instance: Greenland and the Faeroe Islands had associated status as members of EFTA; the USA and Canada almost operated as an adjunct to Europe immediately after the War; the seventy African, Caribbean and Pacific states signing the Lomé Convention had a privileged associate status with respect to the EU). What is more, 'Eastern Europe' presents another set of definitional problems, the characteristic limits of which are equally ambiguous (during the 1950s Mongolia, the People's Republic of China, North Korea, and North Vietnam became associate members of COMECON – and Mongolia, Cuba and Vietnam later became full members). In geographical terms, where exactly does economic Europe end in the east and Asia begin? Turkey has candidate membership of the EU but is it really a part of Europe? What is more, can the UK be counted as part of a genuine European economic project given its well known stand-offishness and generally sceptical position? Bearing these points in mind we can now move on to review briefly the pattern of economic interactions that have characterized the institutional spaces of Europe since the Second World War.

2.3   Patterns of *de facto* European economic interactions

In an influential analysis of the reasons for the post-Second World War 'long boom' in economic activity, Matthews (1968) argued that this was less the result of a (publicly inspired) Keynesian demand management of the European and American economies, and more the result of the (privately inspired) dramatic increase in investment and trade among the countries of the 'West'. It is on the importance of trade and investment that we concentrate in this section.

The crucial impediment to the rapid re-establishment of international trade among the main capitalist countries after the Second World War was the 'dollar shortage', particularly among the countries of Europe. This was solved by a combination of (a) the Marshall Plan and its associated aid and loan arrangements (discussed above), and (b) the inauguration of the European Payments Union. This latter body acted to conserve the available dollar and other official reserve holdings used by the European countries to settle international payments among themselves. It also enabled a more effective use of these reserves in financing the trade and balance of payments of the participants with the outside world.

With the immediate crisis of the dollar shortage easing, it was the devaluations in 1949 that set the western European countries on the route to their dramatic increases in international trade. This major realignment of twenty-six, mainly European, currencies against the dollar (they depreciated by about 30 per cent) secured a dramatic competitive advantage for the European countries vis-à-vis the USA, the benefits of which lasted until the early 1970s. The European economies were effectively transformed into export-oriented economies almost overnight by this move.

The historical record of European economic growth shows that there was a period of rapid growth up to the early 1970s, but from the mid-1970s the growth rate fell, and it was particularly poor during the first half of the 1990s (Chapter 2, Table 2.2). In addition, it should be noted that over the period up to 1990 Europe demonstrated a marginally better growth record than the USA, but a remarkably worse one compared to Japan. From 1990 onwards however, the US growth rate surged ahead of both Europe and Japan.

The post-war economic success of Europe is also demonstrated if we look at trade. Western Europe as a whole increased its importance in total world trade, and within this total the EU significantly increased its own importance relative to that of the rest of Western Europe. Along with this went a significant growth in trade interdependence between the European economies. In 1997, for instance, nearly 70 per cent of West European (WE) imports were from other WE economies, and most of these were intra-EU trade. The growth of integration of the EU economy was particularly marked in the run-up to the single market programme of 1992. By 1998 about 18 per cent of WE GDP (gross domestic product) was trade with itself, the highest proportion of any of the main trading blocs in the global economy.

Thus WE, and the EU in particular, has been rapidly integrating in terms of trade. But WE countries have also been integrating in terms of foreign direct investment flows (FDI). As noted in Chapter 2, FDI relates to how much production is becoming internationalized as multinational corporations (MNCs) invest abroad to set up production facilities overseas. The flows of FDI into, out of and within the EU show that the degree of 'internal' integration within the Union expanded rapidly in the years prior to the 1992 SMP in particular (Chapter 2, Figure 2.1; see also Dunning, 1997), but levelled off somewhat after that. A big question is whether the 2001 EMU programme will see another increase in the intra-EU FDI.

These issues of the development of an interdependent and integrated European economy based upon the EU raise two further considerations. How far is this due to *de jure* public policy to encourage it, and how much is due to *de facto* decisions of private agents acting independently of official policy (Chapters 2, 4, 6 and 8)? Second, it raises issues of whether the EU is an 'optimum currency area', or is moving toward becoming one. An optimum currency area would have a sufficient degree of underlying structural convergence between the economies involved to make the establishment of an economic union between them, and the introduction of a common currency, a viable proposition. Only if there is a significant degree of actual convergence does it make sense to establish an economic union and impose a single currency on it.

The question of whether the EU can be considered an optimum currency area is a difficult one to answer. An optimum currency area depends upon the economic circumstances facing the economies that are integrating and there are several criteria to be considered.

- First, what are the relative inflation rates between the countries? Only if there are similar inflation rates is it sensible to introduce a common currency because otherwise governance of the system would be more difficult after the union than before it.

- Second, what are the countries' relative monetary policy stances and interest rates? The imposition of a common currency implies a single interest rate, but if interest rates already differ significantly, this will be difficult to establish.

- Third, where are the counties in terms of their business cycles? If the business cycle pressures are divergent rather than convergent ones, again the system is unlikely to operate effectively.

- Fourth, what is the degree of exchange rate variability among them? The establishment of an economic union requires the fixing of exchange rates (indeed their elimination) among the countries involved, so if there is considerable volatility in these this is another signal that monetary union is unlikely to work.

- Fifth, what is the state of the bilateral trade intensities between the economies involved? A high degree of trade between countries indicates that they are already effectively integrating, so a union is more likely to be successful.

- Finally, what are their relative labour market conditions (unemployment rates), and how far is labour mobile between them? This is a very important criterion, since only if unemployment is low and labour mobility high will there be enough flexibility to make a union work.

What these criteria amount to is a signal as to the potential effectiveness of a monetary union in terms of its economic governance. The issues involved are represented in Figure 1.2.

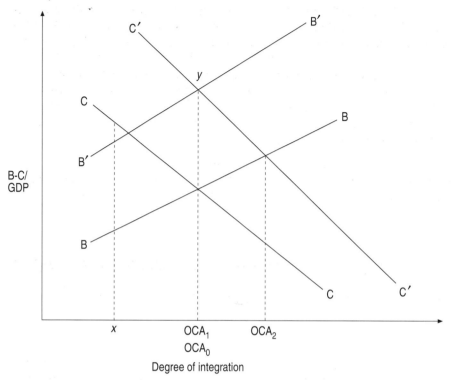

Figure 1.2 An optimum currency area (OCA) and the EU (B = benefits and C = costs)

Along the horizontal axis is measured the degree of integration between the European economies, while up the vertical axis is measured the net benefits of the move toward further integration (B – C) divided by GDP. The curves CC and BB express the cost and benefit schedule respectively; costs involved with the creation of a union decrease as the degree of integration increases, while the benefits associated with the union increase as the degree of integration increases. Where they cross we have the position of an optimum currency area (OCA), let's call it OCA_1.

Figure 1.2 can be used to analyse two important aspects of the European integration project current in the early years of the twenty-first century. One is enlargement and the other is the move toward economic and monetary union (EMU). Any move to enlargement might actually 'undo' some of the criteria mentioned above, making the economic position worse; this would reduce the degree of integration between the existing members, resulting in moving the level of integration back towards the origin and leading to a disequilibrium position, say at point x. Here costs are greater than benefits.

Alternatively, we can use the diagram to analyse EMU. This time let's assume that OCA_1 represents the position of the EU after the 1992 single market programme. But a move toward EMU would change the position of the curves CC or BB. If the EMU involves costs then this could push the cost curve out to $C'C'$ and require a greater degree of integration to establish a new OCA at OCA_2.

If, on the other hand, the 1992 programme has already established an advanced level of integration, in effect this means that OCA_1 also becomes the optimum OCA as designated by OCA_0. It represents the best outcome that can be anticipated in terms of integration. In effect, then, any further move toward EMU merely registers as an outcome of the interaction of changed cost and benefit schedules associated with the creation of EMU, shown at point y (where $C'C'$ and $B'B'$ cross). There is no further integration necessary, merely an enhanced net-benefit position for the EU (if EMU is a success).

As we will see in the chapters that follow, both of these processes are fraught with dangers and difficulties, and there are great uncertainties in making judgements about what will actually happen in each case.

3 European economic governance: the nature of regulation and the market

Given that the European economies have evolved in the manner suggested above, by what principles has their governance been organized? The key concept is economic governance. Here two broad analytical approaches can be identified, which can be described in terms of 'a regulatory order' and 'a market order'. (As we noted earlier, we leave aside for the moment the third option, that of governance by self-organizing networks.) Any discussion of these two main approaches means that first we have to say in rather abstract terms what 'regulation' means and what 'the market' means.

3.1 Regulation

The key feature of regulation is that it requires some form of overt design and direction. It requires an explicit 'intervention' with an objective or outcome in sight. Broadly speaking we can call this 'administration' or 'management'. Bear in mind that this could be an activity of both the private and the public sectors as usually understood. Private organizations or institutions, like firms, require administrative practices to organize their activity, and they rely on management to direct their operations. This applies in a similar way to public agencies like the UK's National Health Service or the European Commission.

Clearly, however, there are major differences between private and public forms of regulation or management. Most private sector economic organizations sell goods and services within a competitive marketplace, so their 'internal' managerial activity is geared up to, and constrained by, the need to perform effectively in that respect. If they fail they will eventually go out of business. Thus their 'external' environment is quite different from most traditional public sector authorities. The latter do not have to meet the same 'commercial' criteria or constraints as private sector firms. They will not go out of business so readily if they fail in the regulatory task. Private sector firms are therefore better considered as 'governed' or co-ordinated by the market system as a consequence, as discussed in Section 3.2.

Under 'regulation', then, we are mostly concerned with public sector activity; this is relatively autonomous, free from the direct constraint of being co-ordinated by a market system and of being subject to market-comparable 'commercial criteria' (though, as we shall see in the chapters in this book, there have been growing pressures within Europe for the public sector to behave in this way – to try to 'mirror' the way the private market sector conducts its business). But for our purposes regulation can be considered as governance by *political means*. It requires political decisions and action in the first instance, which are then followed up by administrative action to implement those decisions. This administrative action often takes the form of hierarchical co-ordination and bureaucratic measures.

Hierarchy is a structured mechanism of control, designed to run large and complex organizations. It requires a layered or tiered organizational structure, with divisions or departments that are ordered in a sequence of the superordination and subordination of authority or power. By such bureaucratic mechanisms as supervision, scrutiny, auditing, the issuing of orders or directives, monitoring of activities and behaviours, and the like, the attempt is made to *control* the institution or organization so that all its parts act together for the collective purpose of producing the desired end result. The image here is one of a top-down command structure, where the flow of direction is 'downwards' from higher to lower tiers in a pyramid-type matrix.

In many ways this particular type of hierarchical organizational form for governance is considered to be 'old fashioned' and is somewhat discredited, at least rhetorically. A popular alternative would be co-ordinative governance by non-hierarchical means. The flows of information and decision making would be more two-way here, requiring adaptation and mutual accommodation between different parts or divisions of the institution that were conceived as being equal in power and authority. A 'flat' or 'level' organizational arrangement would typify this structure, where it is co-operation and consensus-building mechanisms that constitute the means for regulation and control.

These governance arrangements, whether hierarchical or non-hierarchical, can pertain to *intra*-organizational forms (that is, as between the 'internal' parts of a single organizational unit) or to the *inter*-organizational level (that is, as an 'external' structure co-ordinating the activities between separate individual organizational units).

Thus far we have considered regulation in a highly abstract man\
order to provide the clearest account of its basic characteristics. We
see how this operates as a genuine governance mechanism in Europ
respect to specific economic issues as the chapters progress. The r
lation approach is summed up in Figure 1.3.

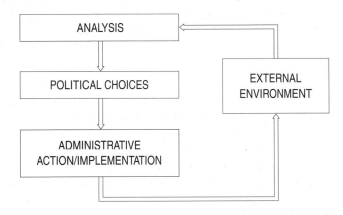

Figure 1.3   The regulation approach

Beginning in the top left-hand corner of the figure, on the basis of an
analysis of the problem under consideration, political choices are made
between the policy options that such an analysis offers. This results in
administrative action to implement the decision. The external environment then provides the testing ground and the constraints for the policy,
which leads back to a further round of analysis. The cycle can then be
repeated.

3.2   The market

The key feature of a market is that it claims to be a mechanism that
secures economic order and the co-ordination of economic activities
without any conscious organizing centre directing it. It is based upon
'decentralized' decision making, involving a competitive process between
dispersed economic agents who make their decisions according to the
price mechanism. So, it is an information gathering and dissemination
process based upon prices, where no single agent controls things but
which arrives at an *ex post* optimum outcome that best satisfies social
needs and maximizes social welfare. These, at least, are the strong *claims*
made for this mechanism.

How exactly, then, does the price system work to provide the necessary
information that leads to these virtuous outcomes? In fact there are two
fairly well developed but distinct approaches to how all this operates.
These are known as the 'neo-classical approach' and the 'Austrian
approach'. Both of these approaches claim a common lineage with
Adam Smith's pioneering analysis of the market economy in his *An
Inquiry into the Nature and Causes of the Wealth of Nations* (1976, first
published in 1776), but they derive somewhat different forms of analysis

and conclusions from this heritage. Let us start with the neo-classical approach, which is the one that dominates contemporary economic analysis.

The neo-classicals

The pioneering theorists from within the neo-classical tradition are the influential English economists Alfred Marshall (1842–1924) and Arthur Pigou (1877–1959). They set about analysing what goes on in the act of exchange. They considered how a set of self-interested individuals, who were assumed to have a clearly defined set of *personal preferences,* would go about maximizing their own well-being. They put aside the rather bothersome question of how production might actually be organized to concentrate upon exchange. Given that each participant has a different bundle of consumption goods, how would these be distributed or allocated between them? Here the key move was to appeal to the notion of individual utility, and the rationality of the participants in assessing the gains they could make in satisfying their preferences and gaining the maximum utility by engaging in *mutual exchange*. They would *trade* among themselves, and such a trade would result in mutual gains to each party. Here, then, is the origin of a founding notion in economics: the mutual gains from trade. And this is the basis of the benefits thought to arise from the formation of an economic entity like the EU, as long as the 'artificial' barriers to trade are eliminated within that entity.

As soon as we start to think about bundles of goods being exchanged and thereby re-allocated or distributed around the system and between the parties involved in it, it is a short step to arrive at the notions of a supply and a demand for the different sets of goods. For the neo-classical economists this interaction between someone's willingness to supply goods and another's willingness to demand them constitutes the key moment in the construction of the notion of a *market*. A market, then, is where suppliers (and supplies) and demanders (and demands) are brought together. How does the interaction take place?

It does so through the medium of the *price* for the good or service in question. In fact, that market price is precisely established by the interaction of supply and demand in the marketplace. Suppose I come to the market with my goods in the hope of meeting your demands and I pitch my opening offer of a selling price at a level which is too high for you to be willing to engage in trade with me so as to realize your desires, driven as they are by your attempt to maximize your utility, based upon your preferences. Under these circumstances you will not buy. So I am faced with the option of withdrawing or lowering my offer price. My initial price is too high to induce you to trade with me, so if I am to sell anything and thus recoup my outlay in producing the goods, I have to lower my price. This sends a signal to you. It provides information on the 'state of the market', and is the basis for the idea of markets being an information producing and disseminating process.

In the next round, if I were to pitch my offer price too low then I would find that I was faced with an 'excess of demands'. Lots of people would want to buy from me and trade with me. I would take this as a signal that I could raise my price a little to try to clear the market. In addition, it would send a signal to my competitors that they could enter this market with their own supplies to meet the unfulfilled demand. Eventually, after a number of rounds of toing and froing like this, an *equilibrium price* will be established which will just clear the market. All demands will be satisfied, and all supplies will be taken up. The market will (temporarily) come to rest. It is in an (ordered) equilibrium.

Now we could easily generalize from this little story based upon a single transaction in a single market. In practice, there are assumed to be multiple buyers and sellers, no single one of which is able to exercise a control over the process. (Indeed, if there were such a single operator who could exercise control we would say that it exercised a *monopoly position* in the market, and could potentially manipulate the market to its own advantage and against the interests of the majority.) In addition to multiplying the number of agents operating in a single market, to make it more realistic we can also multiply the number of distinct markets themselves to create a *market system* of interacting individual markets.

Finally, the way the market works in bringing supply and demand into an equilibrium not only sends the correct information to consumers about the state of the market, but it also sends this information to producers as well and therefore integrates them explicitly into the process. On the basis of the 'conditions of exchange', suppliers are provided with incentives to increase or decrease their own production, and to reduce their costs to a minimum consistent with them being able to stay in business. The lower their costs, the more likely they are to entice consumers to demand their particular goods as against their rivals because they can offer their goods at lower prices. Hence this generates *competition* between producers to supply the market. Such competition will drive costs down to make the system more efficient. Thus producers are linked to consumers' preferences; they are provided with an incentive to satisfy these consumer preferences as made manifest through the price consumers are willing to pay for their goods or services. But note how it is 'consumer preferences' that drive this system, and provide the links back to the producers.

Clearly, this is a very abstract presentation of the way the neo-classical system is claimed to work, and it begs as many questions as it answers. But I have tried to give you a basic idea of how the market might work. For good or ill this is a very powerful and logical analytical approach, and as a result one that attracts strong and determined support.

The Austrians

We can now move on to look at the Austrian approach to the market, but in a little less detail since it shares some of the characteristics of the neo-classical model. Here I stress the differences between the two models, and the criticisms levelled at the neo-classical approach from this Austrian alternative. As its name implies, the Austrian approach is most closely associated with a group of Austrian economists including Friedrich von Hayek (1899–1992), Carl Menger (1840–1921), Ludwig von Mises (1881–1973) and Joseph Schumpeter (1883–1950). There are two key characteristics of the Austrian approach. The first is to stress the market as 'a process of creative destruction'; the second is to stress the signalling and information aspects of the market.

The Austrians were concerned with *innovation and the creation of new products and processes*. They therefore focused more on the *production side* of economic activity. Market competition works to promote the introduction of new products and new processes of production. Thus the market is a constantly changing and adaptive system. New rivals continually challenge established producers. This sets up a process of *creative destruction*. Note how the emphasis here is upon the market as an *evolving process*. It is always in a state of dynamic flux and adaptation. So there is no 'static equilibrium' where prices act to co-ordinate supply and demand and establish a point of rest. The market is continually restless, in a constant state of *disequilibrium*. The neo-classical system has a difficulty in dealing with how new products and processes are introduced into the market and avoids tackling this problem head on.

If we think of the market as dynamically innovating, then those firms that fail to keep up with the competition will fall by the wayside and go out of business, *however large they are*. Thus, among (some of) the Austrians, there is not such a concern with 'monopoly' and large-scale production. Indeed, monopoly is something to be expected – a reward for innovation – but which will only be temporary anyway since the 'gales of destruction' will blow away any (temporary) advantage it confers. But there is a clear policy implication here. It is up to the public authorities to make sure that the possibility of entry into the market is not stifled.

The other feature of the Austrian approach is to stress the information generating and disseminating activity of the market. Again, the emphasis is on the market as a process, but one of competitive price changes. Instead of concentrating on a process of adjustment involving price-taking behaviour that equilibrates existing supply and demand, the Austrians look to a process of adjustment where supply and demand are *continually out of equilibrium*. Here prices act as the incentive to guide the system forward and to innovate. The competitive market is thus akin to a 'machine' for sending out information to those who need it. Vital information about consumers' tastes and production possibilities is continually transmitted by the market system, a lot of which will be redundant because it may be out of date by the time it can be used; nevertheless some will prove useful. The 'secret' is to remain nimble in relation to such 'excesses of information' so as to gain an advantage over one's competitors. It is to seize and use the available information, to sort through it quickly and precisely, before it goes out of date.

Summing up the market approach

Clearly, there are many points of similarity between these two images of the market. They are not totally opposed to one another, though they do emphasize different interpretations of its effectiveness. Despite their differences, these two approaches would both support the spontaneous and non-actively designed outcome emanating from the operation of the market system. Both the approaches support an ordered and co-ordinated outcome from the 'non-governance' offered by the market. We can sum up the market model overall in terms of Figure 1.4.

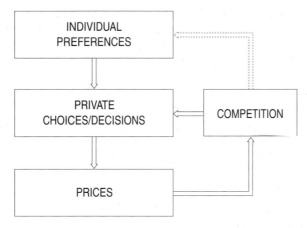

Figure 1.4 The market approach

Beginning again at the top left-hand corner of the figure, market traders' individual preferences lead them to make choices about what to demand (and how much to supply). On the basis of these private choices and decisions, prices are formed. The process of competition then returns the system to private choices and decisions again, or to re-evaluation of preferences. The model is a little ambiguous here, since most versions stress that preferences are the 'given' in a system and do not change. In this case there is no re-evaluation of these as the market cycle continues. On the other hand, other versions allow for there to be a re-evaluation of these as prices and competition take their course, which is indicated by the dashed line in the figure.

3.3 A regulatory order and a market order

Having discussed the notion of regulation and the market in abstract terms we need to investigate how these translate into actual governance regimes. Let us call these regimes a 'regulatory order' and a 'market order'. For the purposes of this book we can say that a regulatory order constitutes a consciously constructed and established attempt to generate a system or regime of governance mechanisms and practices that organize economic activity according to some objective or design. In contrast to this we can specify a market order as one that operates 'spontaneously', so to speak, to produce economic 'order' without the conscious intervention of a guiding presence that organizes economic activity. A market order, then, operates 'naturally' without overt guidance. The outcomes of its operation constitute an ordered system, which from the point of view of the advocates of this system produces the 'best' outcomes in terms of economic welfare, but without any obvious public presence to plan it. The classic example of such a market order would be the idea of the 'market system' of free competition, organized by the price mechanism, in which individual economic agents make their own decisions on what to do based upon their preferences and constraints in an attempt to maximize their individual benefits. If this system works according to how it is supposed to, these initially *ex ante* unco-ordinated individual activities will eventually produce the optimum outcomes of maximum welfare for the collective unit as a whole. The 'unseen hand' or 'guiding hand' of the market system leads to an *ex post* co-ordination or economic order that maximizes participants' satisfactions and welfare.

Clearly, what is being outlined here under the title of a market order is something that does not conform to the idea of a consciously constructed governance system. Indeed, it is the very opposite of such a consciously guided governance system, since market order is a spontaneously generated one. So it really represents the 'other' of a constructed, established and designed economic 'regulatory order', the one promoted by official edict and planned organization. For our purposes, a regulatory order and a market order are, in effect, opposites. They are perhaps better described as non-commensurable co-ordinating mechanisms, since one is a genuine governance system (a regulatory order), while the other rejects the idea that designed governance is needed to secure satisfactory economic outcomes (a market order). Both look toward 'order' as their desired *ex post* outcome, but they see that order as arising from quite different social and economic processes.

But why the emphasis on order? By order we mean an outcome that is not completely incoherent. It is a system that is genuinely co-ordinated, where all the parts fit together in a reasonably consistent way. In contrast, a disordered system would be one in which complete fragmentation ruled, one which lacked co-ordinative governance and a systematic configuration of its parts. Interestingly, both the regulatory order and the market order see each other as producing precisely these (opposite) outcomes: from the point of view of the regulatory order idea, a market system left to its own devices will actually produce disorder; from the point of view of those advocating market solutions to economic activity, it is any regulation or intervention that leads to the disordered outcome.

Thus the main consciously ordered governance mechanism considered in the chapters that follow has to do with the broad category designated by the term 'regulation'. But in this book this category of regulation, and the associated term 'regulatory order', encompass a number of different forms of regulation. These are associated with terms such as public scrutiny, management, policing, intervention, monitoring, institution building – in fact any activity that involves public authorities attempting to design things with an objective or outcome in mind. Thus economic practices and policies like 'Keynesian demand management' (Chapter 4), 'corporatist bargaining' (Chapters 3, 4 and 5), 'tariff reductions' (Chapters 2, 8 and 9), 'EU institution building' (Chapters 3, 5, 6, 7, 8 and 9), as well as more obvious and straightforward regulatory initiatives, are all considered to be part of the grander term 'regulatory order'. And this extends to the idea that the EU might be considered as a 'regulatory state', a separate category of state, different from, say, the 'Keynesian Welfare State' (Chapters 3 and 7 in particular; see also **Bromley, 2001a**). Thus regulatory order is something of a catch-all category, designed to indicate all those practices and mechanisms associated with the overall governance of European economic activity which are not organized in the first instance by market, price or competitive considerations.

A summary of the two main economic orders can be found in Table 1.1.

Table 1.1   Types of economic order

Basic attributes	Regulatory order	Market order
Type of order envisaged	designed and consciously organized outcomes	spontaneously generated outcomes
Behaviour of agents	active public authority inputs	private competitive decisions
Mechanisms of operation	hierarchically organized/bureaucratic administration/monitoring, scrutiny, interventions	price mechanism, competition, self-interest, self-regulation
Type of overall 'governance'	overt, active guidance and 'proper governance'	unseen 'guiding hand' and 'non-governance'

4   The evolution of European capitalist market systems

If the distinctions outlined so far were not enough, when we come to examine them in practice another level of complexity has to be introduced. Clearly, in the case of the actual European economies, we are dealing with capitalist market economies in the main (apart from the communist command economies of the Soviet era, but these are now dead). However, these capitalist market systems are not all the same. In this section we outline the evolution of the overall market systems in Europe, which we divide into two main types: an 'organized capitalist' variant and a 'decentralized capitalist' variant. These two forms capture the basic differences between the governance of actual economies in Europe, and they involve a *combination* of the regulatory order and the market order just discussed. Indeed, these would also involve elements of our third governance mechanism, self-organizing networks, although again here we concentrate first upon the two main governance forms.

4.1 Organized capitalism versus decentralized capitalism

It is important to remember that many of our present-day attitudes toward the market system were forged in the latter part of the nineteenth and the early years of the twentieth centuries. Of particular importance in this evolutionary understanding was the rapid surge of industrial growth toward the end of the nineteenth century, occurring in the USA and Germany, in particular, and to a lesser extent in the UK. The dynamic growth at this time was accompanied by waves of mergers, which accelerated the growth of industrial concentration and led to a widespread concern with the 'process of monopolization' and a new age of giant enterprises that seemed to herald the advent of the twentieth century.

Interestingly the reaction to this common process was different in the USA and in Germany, the two newly emerging key economic powers at the time. In politically conservative Germany, protectionist sentiment was widespread, which at the domestic level manifested itself in the common, restrictive practice of striking price and sales agreements between firms. In Germany these cartel agreements were given protection in law by a landmark decision of the *Reichsgericht* of 1897. Cartel agreements became legally binding contracts, which if broken by any of the signatories rendered them liable to action by the remaining signatories. This arrangement gave German industrialists and financiers a large degree of stability that persisted in this form until well into the mid-twentieth century in some cases. It reflected a widespread attitude in Germany, and perhaps more importantly encouraged an institutional configuration to support it, that accepted *regulation and management* of the market system – an arrangement not only whereby large corporations were tolerated and even officially fostered, but which also implicated organized labour and governmental bodies in a more general accommodation towards what became known as 'organized capitalism'.

In contrast in the USA, and to a lesser extent the UK, such cartels were viewed as inimical to the public welfare and against the public interest. In the USA they quickly became the object of judicial review. But in both the USA and the UK, market dominance by large corporations was thought to eliminate the beneficial effects of free competition – product and process innovation, low and stable prices, open labour and financial markets. This served to define a prevailing sentiment among Anglo-American economists and policy makers toward 'big business' and a continuing commitment to the virtues of the free market and perfect competition. In Europe, this typical attitude has informed the UK approach to the EU institution building, and the economic policies associated with it.

Thus was established one of the earliest configurative differences in the understanding of the market system. The German form of regulated, bureaucratically driven, 'organized' market capitalism *versus* the Anglo-American system of 'decentralized', competitively based, free and 'unorganized' market capitalism. Each of these models has demonstrated considerable durability and economic success. Both have performed well in the twentieth century, if with difficulty at times and as subject to changing policy fashion. Thus, contrary to popular belief perhaps, the Anglo-American model of free markets and economic competition has not proved the only one able to stimulate the essential dynamic properties needed for capitalist success. Capitalism based upon a codified and regulated structure has performed just as well, and possibly better at times. Nevertheless, these two images have tended to dominate the ideological battles fought over the meaning of the capitalist market system that have haunted economic analysis ever since the turn of the twentieth century. And they continue to do so even in the Europe of the early years of the twenty-first century.

still debated.

4.2 Consequences and implications

Interest groups

One important consequence of this different manner in which the market system has been historically organized has to do with the significance afforded to interest groups. Take the 'unorganized capitalist' market-driven variant first. In this system interest groups are analysed as akin to self-seeking individual agents out to maximize their own personal advantage. These interest groups either maximize their particular interest at the expense of the majority or act like monopolists, extracting economic advantage by lowering output, forcing up price and restricting competition.

The classic examples of interest groups conceived in this manner are trade unions, seen as organizations that act akin to monopolists by restricting the supply of labour and pushing their own prices up above the competitive level. Thus the way to deal with such interest groups is to ignore them, dismantle them, or even ruthlessly suppress them, so restoring the benefits of a competitive outcome. In principle all organized interest groups can be conceived in this way – as seeking their own particular advantage – and in a society with a proliferation of such groups the problem becomes one of predicting the general outcome.

What happens in a system where interest groups are so embedded that they constitute a major constraint on adaptation and change? In an influential analysis Olson (1982) argued that the social embeddedness of interest groups inhibits the domestic response to any exogenous shocks. This is an argument about the economy becoming inflexible because of the proliferation of interest groups that are only looking to protect their particular advantage. Once such coalitions become established they are very difficult to shift, and society as a whole suffers as a result. For those countries with long traditions of plural government and continuity in social structure, cultural outlook, and the like, this becomes ossified in a loss of dynamic energy for change. Such was the case in the UK and the USA, Olson argued, with the resulting inability to respond effectively to a productivity slow-down occasioned by the impact of the oil price shocks in the 1970s (Olson, 1988).

On the other hand, those societies in which interest groups are less developed (not so extensive or powerful) retain their dynamic and innovative ability to respond positively to shocks and thus remain internationally competitive. In Olson's view these national differences in the configuration of interest groups explained why some countries remained successful economically and socially while others did not in the post-Second World War period up to the 1980s. It is a view which animated much of the analysis and public discussion of the supposed malaise hanging over the European economy as it struggled to rekindle growth and flexibility in the 1980s and 1990s. But the terms of this debate changed somewhat. Now it was the main continental economic powers like Germany, Italy and France that, arguably, had succumbed to the sclerosis effect of organized interest groups, while the UK (and the USA) had thrown off these constraints through a vigorous embrace of a neo-liberal market-oriented policy agenda. Here again was another example of the 'organized-capitalism-equals-bad-capitalism' *versus* the 'decentralized-capitalism-equals-good-capitalism' argument.

However it is a slightly different view of the role of organized interest groups which tends to pervade the analysis offered by the 'organized capitalism' variant of the market system. As might be expected, an element in the regulated and organized nature of its economic order is an accommodation with social interest groups. In many continental European countries for instance, the stakeholders, or 'social partners' as they are known, continue to play a key role in the conduct of economic activity and its management. The main 'social partners' would be the organizations of labour, those of employers (perhaps divided between large and small companies) and the governmental authorities (but in principle these could also be extended to encompass agricultural interests, perhaps consumers, and even environmentalists). These stakeholding social partners bargain between themselves in various arenas, usually alongside the traditional channels of representative democracy, over economic objectives and the means to achieve them. This approach emphasizes co-operation between the social actors rather than competition between them in the conduct of economic activity. It is designed to reach a broad social consensus on economic objectives and the means to achieve them. As the chapters below indicate, this is one of the main and most widespread forms of a regulatory governance order to have emerged in continental Europe during the post-Second World War period. It is known as 'social corporatism' and its economic variant as 'neo-corporatism' (Chapters 3, 4, 5 and 7 in particular).

This discussion of interest groups serves to introduce the more general analysis of what the consequences are of such 'neo-corporatist' bargaining arrangements, and particularly the impact they have on the wage formation process and inflation. It is through the institutional organization of the labour market that neo-corporatism is thought to have its main impact (Chapters 4 and 5). Broadly speaking, this draws a distinction between highly *centralized* bargaining (regulated neo-corporatist arrangements) and *decentralized* bargaining (neo-liberal market-based arrangements). Centralized bargaining of a neo-corporatist type implies that the peak organizations of labour and employers are brought together at a national or regional level, usually under government auspices, to decide systematically on wage levels, and often other aspects of economic activity. Decentralized bargaining tends to leave it to individual employers and their workers to bargain over work and conditions according to local circumstances, without the intervention of government. Thus no overall nationally considered outcome emerges (Flanagan et al., 1993). One other advantage claimed for neo-corporatism is that it enabled *real* economic variables to be targeted by governments (employment, investment, output, training, etc.), not just monetary ones, like inflation, the money supply and interest rates (Rowthorn et al., 1993).

Economies like that of the UK have traditionally been most hostile to neo-corporatist forms of interest group governance along these lines, particularly in the context of labour market co-ordination. They have gone furthest down the route to decentralize their wage bargaining approaches, driven by a strong adherence to neo-liberal economic ideology. On the other hand neo-corporatist forms of organization have traditionally typified many of the continental countries, as mentioned above. However, despite this, there has been a definite intellectual and policy turn against centralized neo-corporatism at the European level, as the supposed advantages of a decentralized neo-liberal intellectual and policy programme have gained ground. And as the European economy integrates further, the specific role of the *individual* economies in the EU – whether neo-corporatist or not – will tend to lessen in the face of whatever new central mechanisms of regulation at the European level emerge. Since there is no reason why these common institutions of economic management will be neo-corporatist in nature, this particular 'regulatory' model may be on a long-term decline in Europe. The debate and struggle between those two contemporary positions is highlighted at length later (Chapters 2, 3, 4, 5, 7 and 8).

Consumers' and producers' preferences

A second feature of the organized versus decentralized model of the market system is to note that it is 'producers' preferences' and large-scale production which are thought the most appropriate in driving the first variant, while the second is much more sensitive to the key role played by 'consumer influence' in the economic mechanism and small-scale production.

For the decentralized variant the economy works in the interests of consumers in the first instance. Producers (or workers) must adapt to the incentives provided for them by consumer preferences as registered through the market. Monopolization must also be clarified. From the point of view of this approach, as the object of regulation and public scrutiny (rather than as the object of an academic debate) monopoly does not so much imply large, even dominant firms measured in respect to the size of the market, but more their behavioural dispositions – how they *act* under particular circumstances. Are they behaving in a manner that is inimical to the full operation of the market system in terms either of engaging in unfair competition or of deliberately inhibiting the entry of new competitors into the market? The growth of large firms in the name of efficiency (say through the operation of economies of scale) has often been actively encouraged by the public authorities. Indeed, this was one of the strongest economic rationales advanced by the advocates of further integration during the debate about the development of the single market in the EU during the late 1980s. The single market programme was predicated on the advantages that were calculated to arise for the European economy as a whole from the process of the concentration of production across Europe. This would stimulate economies of large-scale production, which would result in greater efficiency and lower prices to domestic consumers and more internationally competitive European products and services on the global market (Cecchini, 1988; EC, 1988).

In the case of the organized variant of capitalist development a greater tolerance can be seen in relationship to large, even monopoly-type firms and organizations. The regulated or organized economies, the clearest examples of which in the EU are Germany and France, have seen the emergence not only of cartel agreements as mentioned above, but also of integrated conglomerate-type holding companies and networks of corporate governance which display a strongly oligopolistic form of organization (Chapter 3).

Table 1.2 provides a summary of the main features typifying the variant forms of market capitalism examined in this section.

Table 1.2 Typical features of organized capitalism and decentralized capitalism

Typical sentiments	Organized capitalism	Decentralized capitalism
Attitudes toward interest groups	accommodating with interest groups	heavily suspicious of interest groups
Type of economic bargaining	centralized neo-corporatist 'stake-holding' encouraged	decentralized bargaining favoured
Objectives of economic policy	real economic variables stressed	monetary economic variables stressed
Organization of economic activity	virtues of co-operation stressed	virtues of competition stressed
Type of preferences favoured	emphasis on producers' preferences/interests	emphasis on consumers' preferences/interests
Attitudes toward market forms and outcomes	acceptance of large-scale productive organizations and networks – cartels and oligopoly tolerated	rhetorical hostility to monopoly and large-scale production organizations – a stress on the virtues of 'free competition'

The organization of public policy for integration

In this section we look at a further consequence for the European economic space of the division between an organized and a decentralized approach toward the market system. This has had important implications for the way integrative public policy has actually been operationalized, mainly by the political élites that run the EU. Here I introduce a key distinction between *negative integration* and *positive integration*, a distinction first explicitly posed by the Dutch developmental economist Jan Tinbergen in the mid-1950s (Tinbergen, 1954). This has had an enduring impact on how the European economy is governed (Scharpf, 1999). In the first instance at least, this distinction is not associated with the *de facto* processes of integration driven by market forces and the economic decisions of private competitive actors, but with the *de jure* activity of governmental authorities in their attempts either to foster and engineer a more integrated economic space already in existence or to enlarge that space itself beyond national boundaries.

Negative integration has to do with the removal of so-called 'barriers' to trade, capital flows and integration – like tariffs, quotas, capital controls and other quantitative and qualitative restrictions on the free movement of economic factors, goods and services. It is 'purgative' in form; it involves public policy that seeks to *remove* barriers to a process of integration which it presumes is the norm of a competitive and market oriented system. On the other hand we have the idea of positive integration which seeks to reconstruct a system of economic regulation at the level of the integrating system or its enlargement. Thus this approach to integration sees the need to 're-regulate' the economic space of integration as the old barriers to integration are removed (Majone, 1996). Its approach is to consciously design integration – not leave it to the dictates and outcomes of an uncontrolled market system. It could perhaps be expressed in the rather awkward terms of a 'de-regulatory re-regulation' of economic Europe, an oxymoron that effectively describes much of the activity that might actually go on in the process of constructing an integrated European economy.

This distinction overlaps, but is not completely synonymous with, a further distinction in these governance matters: that between 'market-making' and 'market-correcting' policies. Clearly, negative integration is closely aligned with a market-making policy sentiment. It implies an emphasis on the beneficial operation of the market process in driving integration. But measures of positive integration might also imply a market-making element, as well as its main emphasis on market-correcting policies. This would be the case, for instance, when divergent national product standards are 'harmonized' across Europe in order to eliminate those product standards which act as a non-tariff barrier to integrative trade. In this case, the approach is market making in form (it eliminates what is considered to be a barrier to trade across European national borders), but it still supports some kind of (now common) regulatory standards, so it is also market correcting in this sense. This example of positive integration can be contrasted with other examples which are more obviously market correcting in character, like the adoption of regulations on working conditions across Europe, or of pollution controls.

Scharpf (1999, pp.44–7) argues that this latter distinction (the one between market-making and market-correcting policy stances) expresses the key ideological conflict between anti-interventionist – for example, neo-liberal marketeers – and interventionist regulators – for example, social-democratic or Keynesian (and, we might add, neo-corporatist) theorists, political parties, interest groups and policy makers at the pan-European level.

> From an anti-interventionist point of view, what matters is negative integration, whereas positive integration is acceptable only in so far as it serves market-making purposes (e.g. through the adoption and implementation of rules of undistorted competition). From the interventionist perspective, by contrast, negative integration should be considered problematical unless it is accompanied by the creation of political capacities for market-correcting positive integration.
>
> (Scharpf, 1999, p.46)

Thus at the level of European public policy with respect to economic integration we have another complex array of terms, categories and distinctions centred on the organized versus decentralized approach to the market system. These are identified in Table 1.3.

Table 1.3 Forms of integrative public policy

Issues	Organized market capitalism	Decentralized market capitalism
Type of integration favoured	positive integration	negative integration
Attitudes toward 're-regulation'	market-correcting	market-making
General policy stance	pro-interventionist	anti-interventionist
Ideological outlook	social-democrat, Keynesian, neo-corporatist	neo-liberal marketeer, conservative monetarist

As we shall see in the chapters that follow, the current debate in Europe over its integration and the form of governance that will typify the economy of the twenty-first century very much involves the issues discussed in this main section. Broadly speaking, the EU has found it very much easier to go down the route of negative integration than positive integration. This is aided by the way the European Court was set up to guarantee the 'four economic freedoms' outlined in the Treaty of Rome (the freedom of trade without restrictions, the freedom of capital flows and investments, the freedom to establish and provide services, and the freedom of movements of labour) and the way it has interpreted its brief in establishing case law. Given the competence of the Court over national legal provision in these respects, as far as economic integration driven by the EU is concerned, this has proceeded very much in the image of negative integration. Precedence has been given to negative integrationist moves, much of the momentum for which has emanated from the deliberations of the Commission and the Council, as against any more positive integrative moves that might have come from the pressures of national sentiment or the inertia and tradition of economic management residing there. Whatever residual commitment to a more positive integration there might have been at the national or local level, this has been pushed aside by the onward march of both the neo-liberal policy turn adopted by political élites at the pan-European level and the founding constitutional provisions written into the Treaty of Rome (to which the Court eagerly responded). Of course, this competence of the European Court over national legal provisions in respect to economic activity is only guaranteed by dint of a political decision to allow it to be so, agreed and passed at the national level (see **Bromley, 2001b**).

4.3 European capitalist market systems: summing up

To sum up this section, the form of 'organized capitalism' discussed here clearly sits most easily with the 'regulatory order' discussed in the previous section, while the 'decentralized capitalism' discussed in this section maps most easily onto the idea of a 'market order'. In addition, these clearly connect to the ideas of a positive integration on the one hand and a negative integration on the other. Broadly speaking, under the heading of the 'regulatory order' approach we can gather the terms and characteristics of positive integration, market-correcting activity and an interventionist sentiment, while under the 'market order' approach we can gather the terms and characteristics of negative integration, market-making and anti-interventionist sentiment.

5 Self-organizing networks as an additional governance mechanism

In this section we introduce another mechanism for economic governance which complements the two main ones we discuss in the chapters of this book. This third governance mechanism is termed 'self-organizing networks', and it constitutes a genuine governance form. It is not like the market, which, as we have seen, at best constitutes only a 'negative' governance system since it eschews any overt and conscious attempt to impose order.

Self-organizing networks have proved a useful additional conception in analysing how the European economy is organized and governed at a number of levels.

- First, this is so in the case of the way that public policy is formulated in respect to economic decisions which affect the *de jure* governance of the economic system. It involves the way that 'policy networks' are formed across Europe and how political élites form relatively cohesive groups which set the agenda for policy discussions and guide decision-making processes within the institutional structure of pan-EU economic management (Chapter 7 in particular).

- Second, it appears in the form of local networks of firms and public and semi-public organizations that have had an important impact on the innovative capacity of different economies. This therefore affects the technological capability of the European economy overall, raising issues of how this particular type of economic activity both is, and can be, fostered and governed (Chapter 6 in particular).

These networks are neither organized like a market, nor officially sanctioned in the form of a regulatory structure. This is why they are described as 'self-organized'. They arise 'spontaneously' so to speak, but they are not co-ordinated solely by the price mechanism according to the dictates of purely competitive and commercial criteria, nor solely by a consciously designed administrative or management structure. They may involve these mechanisms in part, but they are distinctive enough in their own right to constitute a separate governance system, albeit a limited one. These mechanisms are also important for understanding the 'bottom-up' type of organizational arrangement that characterizes much of civil society (**Guibernau, 2001**). They connect to 'private interest governance' that is strongly present in the sphere of non-governmental organizations (NGOs).

One problem with these mechanisms is that they are not so clearly definable as the other two we have been discussing so far. They are a variable and intermediate form, in many ways falling between the market and regulation as discussed so far. They sometimes involve and combine elements of these other two systems, but they are also often defined as much by what they are not as by what they are, by how they differ from either market or regulation. So in some ways they are a 'hybrid' organizational and governance form. But what are their specific attributes, in as much as these can be coherently isolated and elaborated?

Networks are above all 'informal' practices of co-ordination. They rely upon direct personal contact. They tend to be localized as a result, or confined to a particular clearly defined group with similar concerns, interests or aspirations. They display a systematic orientation, working through attributes like loyalty and trust rather than administrative orders or prices. Thus these mechanisms have implications for how economic behaviour might be conceptualized. They provide a critique of market-driven self-interested instrumental rationality on the one hand, and of bureaucratic rationality on the other. Governance of an activity is achieved through the identity of a common purpose or interest, for which all will work for a collective result. These tend toward a 'flat' organizational structure, where at least there is a great deal of formal equality between the participants (though in practice there may be very real and significant differences of power and authority). We can sum up the self-organizing network model as in Figure 1.5.

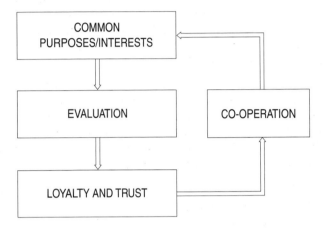

Figure 1.5 The self-organizing network approach

Beginning in the top left-hand corner, based upon a presumed common purpose and interest, isues or problems are evaluated. Loyalty and trust serve to drive the network, which relies on co-operation to co-ordinate the activity. This reinforces common purposes and interests.

6 Relationships between regulation, the market and self-organizing networks

As the following chapters will show, there are complex relationships between the three modes of governance as they operate in the European economic context. These modes of governance could operate at the micro level: in the context of how the firm or corporation is governed (Chapter 3); in the context of how social welfare and the labour market is governed (Chapter 5); how technology and innovation are governed (Chapter 6); or how environmental policy is organized (Chapter 7). Alternatively, they could operate at the more macro level: in the context of the formation and implementation of macroeconomic policy (Chapter 4); how the overall economic mechanism is organized and co-ordinated (Chapter 8); or how the EU fits into the wider international context (Chapter 9).

A way of understanding the possible relationship between these govern-ance mechanisms is illustrated in Figure 1.6. Supposing we thought of the three mechanisms as separate analytical torches which throw a different beam of light on any one object of analysis. They could thus illuminate only part of that object, or all of it, depending on the appropriateness of that particular torch for the analysis being undertaken. In theory, then, it is possible that any single conceptual torch could illuminate or explain the whole of one discrete issue or object under investigation. But this is unlikely, since in the social sciences we are dealing with complex objects of analysis which do not lend themselves easily to a single conceptual schema. We are much more likely to find that there is a combination of conceptual torches that either illuminate different aspects of the overall object of analysis or highlight one part more strongly than another. Thus, the three 'spotlights' of the conceptual torches are partly separated but also partly overlap.

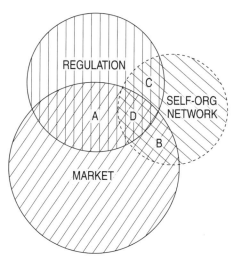

Figure 1.6 The governance approaches compared

In the context of European economic activity it may be that the market governance mechanism illuminates more than the regulation mechan-ism, which itself illuminates more than the self-organizing network mechanism. This is shown by the different sizes of the spotlights, and the fact that the self-organizing network model is less clearly formulated than the other two is indicated by the broken line acting as its boundary (Figure 1.6).

If it is more a combination of regulation and market that better illustrates the problem under investigation, we are in zone A; if regulation and networks are the better guides, we are in zone C; and if networks and the market are the appropriate combination, we are in zone B. On the other hand, if all three of our governance mechanisms in their own way, but operating in combination, offer some illumination on the issue or problem, then we are in zone D.

The task of the following chapters, in large part at least, is to 'unpick' precisely the objects of their investigation along these lines, to see which one of the governance mechanisms, or what combination of them, best illuminates the activity they focus upon. And as we will see, this is not a static approach. An important issue for the chapters, and one that we will return to in the concluding chapter, is the evolution of the governance regimes operating in Europe, to see how the shifting balance between them has moved historically.

Finally, we should be cautious about attributing too much to our three conceptual tools, the governance mechanisms. Like all conceptual tools they are not designed to be (nor could they be) suitable for explaining everything: in practice economic life is too complex for this to be possible. While they provide a comprehensive package of conceptual tools to begin an analysis of the European economic space, there will inevitably be areas of economic life that will resist or escape them, those aspects of economic life that are not captured by the three governance mechanisms.

7   The chapters that follow

This introductory chapter has provided an overview of the issues tackled in the rest of the book and, importantly, has concentrated on clarifying the conceptual apparatus used in the chapter analyses, which deploy the governance mechanisms outlined here.

The next chapter (Chapter 2) builds on this introduction to outline the overall evolution and trajectory of the European economy since the ending of the Second World War. It concentrates on the way trade and investment integration have developed, and the relative convergence of the EU economies as they have moved further towards an integrated economic space. The chapter charts the successive phases and waves of integrative initiatives characterizing the evolution of the European economy, looking at the role of the early common policies adopted by the EEC, the factory mobility associated with the four freedoms, and the early moves toward monetary integration. Finally, the chapter opens up the analysis of the European economy in its international context and looks at the size and importance of the EU in its role as a world economic actor.

After the large canvas depicted in Chapter 2 there is the much narrower focus of Chapter 3, which concentrates on the way 'corporate Europe' is governed. Chapter 3 looks at the typical modes of corporate governance that have characterized the individual European economies, particularly those of the UK and Germany, which offer the strongest contrast, and then at the way the pan-European corporate governance structures are evolving as the EU begins to address issues of a common approach. This chapter thus serves to open up a central issue tackled in subsequent chapters, namely the way in which, and the extent to which, individual country governance structures are being transformed by pan-European ones. Like many other chapters this one stresses the variety of economic governance structures in Europe and their resilience to, or weakness in the face of, pressures for change and reform arising from both exterior and interior factors. In this chapter we see a range of private *de facto* and public *de jure* forces exerting pressure for change.

While Chapter 3 deals with a more micro aspect of European economic governance, Chapter 4 moves back into the macro world of economic management. What have been the typical approaches to macroeconomic management that have characterized the post-war European economies? The chapter concentrates on the evolution of the Keynesian approach to this issue, then looks at the move toward a more neo-liberal approach, and also at the fate of other mechanisms of macroeconomic management that have been important at the European level. The chapter then poses the question of why the individual economies should be prepared to give up some of their 'economic sovereignty' in favour of a European-level regime. This issue is confronted in a preliminary analysis of the role of EMU as a new economic governance regime, and what it might mean for individual EU economies.

Chapter 5, like Chapter 4, also concentrates on a key element in the overall economy, in this case the issue of what has come to be known as 'Social Europe'. The idea of 'Social Europe' encompasses the governance of labour relations and welfare provision – these are linked together by this term and the way that the labour market works in Europe. The chapter sets up the notion of a typical regime of governance based on this term and then shows how this was modified and embodied in particular national practices. The chapter then raises the issue of a 'crisis' in this regime of governance, and what has happened to it both at the national level and at the wider European level. Once again we see the variety and heterogeneity of responses to, and patterns of adaptation to, the common pressures for change.

After these two chapters dealing with overall economic governance, Chapters 6 and 7 move back into the more micro territory of particular aspects of economic activity. Chapter 6 looks at the technology and innovation record of Europe, set very much in an international context, and asks how this activity has typically been governed. The historical evolution of the 'national system of innovation' that has characterized economic Europe is the focus of discussion, followed by a review of whether such systems are being superseded by a European, or indeed a 'global', innovation system. This chapter serves to open up the complex relationships between all three of the governance mechanisms reviewed above, and shows how the network model has proved a significant additional analytical tool in understanding how this particular area of economic life is governed in Europe.

Networks are also important for an understanding of how environmental policy has been organized and governed in Europe, which is the subject of Chapter 7. The chapter shows how environmental management and the promotion of 'sustainable development' have become key areas for European governmental practices since the mid-1970s. This is nowhere more so than in the context of the enlargement of the EU, as a range of new environmental problems emerge with the accession of countries to the east of the traditional EU heartland. But the chapter also shows how that heartland itself has confronted the authorities with somewhat intractable environmental problems, ones they have sought to address with innovative governance initiatives involving a complex mix of all three of the models described earlier in this chapter.

With Chapter 8 the book turns again to the aggregate level. Here, however, the chapter brings into focus the range of areas and levels that have been partially analysed elsewhere, and builds them into a picture of how the EU economy overall might be characterized in governance terms. Thus the chapter looks at the European integration project as a whole, at the policy governance issues that will arise under EMU, and at the way business systems and corporate governance relationships fit into this evolving picture. The forces for harmonization and divergence are assessed, and developments in the relationships between national economies and Europe-wide economic actors and authorities highlighted.

The national or European levels discussed in Chapter 8 lead on in Chapter 9 to an examination of how the European economies and the EU have operated in an international context. This penultimate chapter is concerned with the mechanisms of international governance, how these have evolved over the post-Second World War period and how they are being recast as the EU becomes a more important player in the international system, claiming competence over policy issues on behalf of the individual EU countries. The complex developments in international governance in the light of the three models deployed throughout this book are reviewed more generally in the context of increased internationalization of economic relationships.

Finally, Chapter 10 offers a concluding review of the issues raised in the book as a whole. It returns to the three models of governance to assess the relative importance of each in the explanatory story that the chapters tell. It is particularly concerned to summarize the overall trajectory and changing role of their relative importance in the evolution of economic Europe. The chapter also provides a review of the main themes that have arisen in the analysis of the preceding chapters.

References

Bromley, S.J. (ed.) (2001a) *Governing the European Union*, **London, Sage/The Open University**.

Bromley, S.J. (2001b) 'The nation state in the European Union' in Bromley, S.J. (ed.) *Governing the European Union*, **London, Sage/ The Open University**.

Cecchini, P. (1988) *The European Challenge: 1992*, Aldershot, Wildwood House.

Dunning, J.H. (1997) 'The European internal market programme and inbound foreign direct investment', *Journal of Common Market Studies*, Parts I and II, vol.35, no.1, March, pp.1–3, and vol.35, no.2, June, pp.189–223.

European Commission (EC) (1988) 'The Economics of 1992', *European Economy*, no.35, Luxembourg, Office for Official Publications of the European Communities.

Flanagan, R.J., Moene, K.O. and Wallerstein, M. (1993) *Trade Union Behaviour, Pay Bargaining, and Economic Performance*, Oxford, Clarendon Press.

Guibernau, M. (ed.) (2001) *Governing European Diversity*, London, Sage/The Open University.

Hogan, M.J. (1989) *The Marshall Plan*, Cambridge, CUP.

Lewis, P. (2001) 'The enlargement of the European Union' in Bromley, S.J. (ed.) *Governing the European Union*, London, Sage/The Open University.

Majone, G. (1996) *Regulating Europe*, London, Routledge.

Matthews, R.C.O. (1968) 'Why has Britain had full employment since the War?' *The Economic Journal*, vol.78, pp.556–69.

Milward, A.S. (1984) *The Reconstruction of Western Europe 1945–1950*, London, Methuen.

Olson, M. (1982) *The Rise and Decline of Nations*, Newhaven, CN, Yale University Press.

Olson, M. (1988) 'The productivity slow-down, the oil shock, and the real cycle', *The Journal of Economic Perspectives*, vol.2, no.4, pp.43–69.

Rowthorn, B. (1993) 'Corporatism and labour market performance' in Pekkarinen, J., Pohjola, M. and Rowthorn, B. (eds) *Social Corporatism: a Superior Economic System?* Oxford, Oxford University Press.

Scharpf, F. (1999) *Governing in Europe: Effective and Democratic?* Oxford, Oxford University Press.

Smith, A. (1976) *An Inquiry into the Nature and Causes of the Wealth of Nations*, Oxford, Oxford University Press.

Tinbergen, J. (1954) *International Economic Integration*, Amsterdam, North Holland.

Chapter 2
The development of the EU and the European economy

Valerio Lintner

1 Introduction

Chapter 1 raised some basic issues pertinent to the analysis of the European economy after the Second World War, notably the extent to which we can talk sensibly of a European economy rather than separate national economies, the extent and limits of 'economic Europe', and the essential nature of, and the choices implicit in, economic governance in Europe. What is clear, however, is that the development of the European economy in the post-war period has been conditioned to a considerable extent by the emergence and development of the European integration project.

The immediate post-war scenario consisted of a (Western) 'Europe of the nations' comprising a number of small and medium-sized states essentially operating as discrete economic and political entities and pursuing broadly independent and often distinct policies. Yet, within less than half a century the majority of these same nation states are on the very verge of monetary union, have succeeded to an extent in establishing a common market among themselves, are pursuing common policies in a number of important areas, and are well on the way to collectively becoming major economic and political actors on the world stage. The locus of many aspects of economic governance and economic policy making has shifted from the nation state to the supranational level in the form of the European Union (EU), and we have moved to a situation in which there is every prospect that a truly integrated European economy will emerge in the early part of this century. This chapter discusses the salient aspects of this process, analysing the nature and development of the various functions of the EU as an economic actor. As such, it builds on Chapter 1 and it can be seen as laying the ground for much of what follows in the remainder of the book.

Section 2 traces some broad aspects of the development of the European economy in the post-war period, and Section 3 discusses some essential issues surrounding the emergence and development of the European economy and of the EU. Subsequent sections of this chapter consider the common policies of the EU, the trade and factor (labour and capital) mobility arrangements of the integration process, the central contemporary issues of monetary integration, and finally the EU's role as an international economic actor.

Since this chapter is centrally concerned with the 'process of economic integration' it will be useful to define this before we proceed. As the term implies, this is an ongoing process – it is a developing programme; indeed, integration implies the progressive development of inter-dependency between the nations and economic actors that make up the EU economic space.

2 The development of the European economy

We begin by briefly outlining the development of the European economy in the post-war period, during which the EC/EU emerged and developed. For convenience and brevity this can be divided into three 'phases':

1 A period of *reconstruction* from 1945 until around 1950, during which the various economies of the victors and the vanquished were reconverted to meet civilian requirements.

2 A period of *sustained growth* and increasing prosperity, the 'Keynesian boom' from about 1950 until approximately the mid-1970s.

3 The emergence of *neo-liberalism* from about the late 1970s onwards.

There is debate surrounding the turning point which marks the end of the 'Keynesian consensus', but the unrest of 1968 is seen by many as being particularly significant.

Two key points about these developments are of particular significance. First, although there was considerable *unity* in the way in which economic governance developed in the various Western European states – they all adopted a mixed economy of public and private activity, and were faced with broadly similar internal and external challenges, for example – there was also much *diversity* in their experiences. (Central and Eastern European States, CEES, were of course absorbed into the Soviet bloc and established planned economies.) Western European states adopted different interpretations of the mixed economy and, along with it, different forms of economic governance based on varying mixes of *regulatory order* and *market order*. It was, therefore, a somewhat disparate group of states coming from different traditions that engaged in the move toward integration. Second, there was a fundamental shift in the mid-1970s in the broad approach adopted toward economic governance, from a Keynesian interventionist and proactive view of markets and economic policy, which generally emphasized *regulatory order*, to a neo-liberal laissez-faire stance based more on *market order*. The latter, it should be added, was embraced with much more enthusiasm in the UK than in other countries, which have attempted (sometimes in vain) to hold on to as much as they could of the social aspect of the single market (see Chapter 5) in the face of the growing power of deregulated global capitalism.

2.1   Relative size and importance of the European economy

Some of the main aspects of the development and importance of the European economic space that has emerged can be seen from the data reproduced in Table 2.1. At the most basic level, we can see from the table that the economy of the EU 15 is roughly of the same dimension as that of the USA in terms of share of world GDP, but that it is much more dependent on trade, a significant proportion of which consists of intra-EU trade. We shall return to this. Per capita GDP in Europe is significantly lower than in the USA, but high in world terms.

Table 2.1   Shares of world aggregate GDP, exports of goods and services, and population, 1996

	GDP (%)	Exports (%)	Population (%)
EU 15	20.4	40.0	6.5
USA	20.7	13.0	4.6
Japan	8.0	7.2	2.2
Newly industrialized Asian economies	3.4	10.1	1.3
Developing countries	39.2	17.3	77.1
Transition economies	4.2	4.2	7.1

(adapted from International Monetary Fund, 1997, p.135)

But how has the growth rate of Europe fared since the 1960s? Table 2.2 clearly demonstrates that the high rate of growth during the Keynesian boom period has slowed following the crisis of Keynesianism and the shift toward forms of economic governance based more on a market order than a regulatory order.

Table 2.2   Real European GDP growth (average annual percentage change) 1960–1998

1960–7	1968–73	1974–9	1980–90	1991–5	1996–8
4.7	4.9	2.6	2.2	1.5	2.3

Note: Figures are for OECD Europe, except for 1991–5 and 1996–8 which are for the EU 15.

(adapted from: OECD *Historical Statistics*; OECD *Main Economic Indicators*)

2.2 Trade integration

The growing interdependence of the European economy, and in particular of the EU member states, is evident from the data in Table 2.3. It can be seen how import trade between Western European (WE) countries, and in particular intra-EU trade, has increased significantly since the establishment of the EEC in the 1950s, though there was a slight slow-down in this growth over the mid-1990s. In 1997, intra-WE trade (that is imports just between these countries) comprised 67.6 per cent of total WE imports, and that of the EU was 62.3 per cent of this total.

Table 2.3 Merchandise trade (imports) of Western Europe by region (1958–1997): percentage share in total Western European imports 1958, 1963, 1973, 1983, 1993 and 1997

	1958 (%)	1963 (%)	1973 (%)	1983 (%)	1993 (%)	1997 (%)
Developed countries of which:	57.4	70.9	76.1	74.0	80.9	79.6
Intra-WE (total)	45.3	56.1	64.3	61.8	68.2	67.6
EU 15	**35.2**	**51.8**	**59.8**	**56.2**	**62.6**	**62.3**
Other WE	10.1	4.3	4.5	5.6	5.6	5.3
USA	11.4	13.9	9.6	8.9	8.2	8.5
Japan	0.7	0.9	2.2	3.3	4.5	3.5
Eastern bloc	3.8	4.2	3.9	5.4	3.7	4.7
Other developing countries	–	24.9	20.0	20.6	15.4	15.7

Note: The 'Eastern bloc' comprises the Central and Eastern European States (CEES) of the old Soviet bloc, the Baltic states and the Confederation of Independent States (CIS).

(derived from World Trade Organization, 1998, Table II.2, p.14)

2.3 Investment integration

The EU has thus been rapidly integrating in terms of trade. But it has also been integrating in terms of foreign direct investment (FDI) flows. FDI is a measure of the way production is becoming internationalized as multinational corporations invest abroad to set up production facilities. The flows of FDI into and out of the EU, into and out of the USA, and between EU countries are shown in Figure 2.1. It is intra-EU flows that show the degree of 'internal' integration within the Union. This expanded rapidly in the years prior to the 1992 programme to complete the single market (see below).

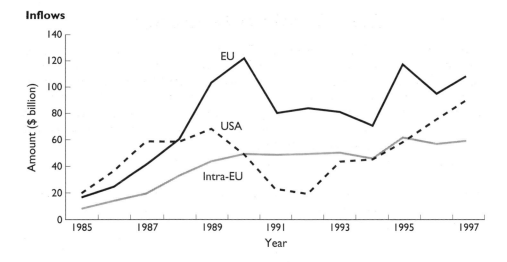

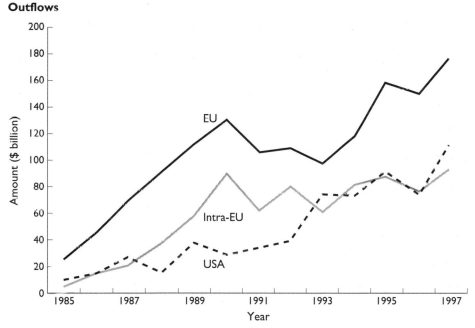

Figure 2.1 EU, intra-EU and USA FDI inflows and outflows, 1985–1997

Note: Intra-European investment was estimated by using the share of the EU in the total EU investment provided in *Eurostat*, 1997 and 1998.

(United Nations, 1998, pp.154, 156)

2.4 Convergence

Up to now we have been looking at the development of the degree of integration of the European economy, particularly the EU part of it. But has there been any evidence of a *convergence* between these economies as they have been integrating? From Figure 2.2 we can see how rates of inflation in the EU have converged and fallen in the 1990s as EU countries have adopted tight macroeconomic stances in order to meet the Maastricht Treaty's (1992) convergence criteria (see Box 2.3 in Section 6). This figure also shows how inflation increased following the oil and political crisis that ended the Keynesian consensus after the late 1960s. The steady convergence of inflation since the 1970s contrasts with the continued growth of fiscal deficits up to the early 1990s.

Fiscal deficits
(general government balance,
excluding Greece)

Inflation

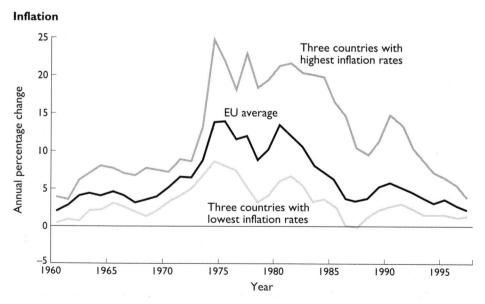

Figure 2.2 The EU: fiscal deficits (general government balance) and inflation (International Monetary Fund, 1997, p.66)

2.5   EU relative economic performance

While standards of living in the EU have risen enormously since the foundation of the EEC in 1957, the performance of the EU economy in terms of the labour market has been less favourable than that of the USA and some other countries such as Japan. This can be seen from Figure 2.3.

Unemployment rates

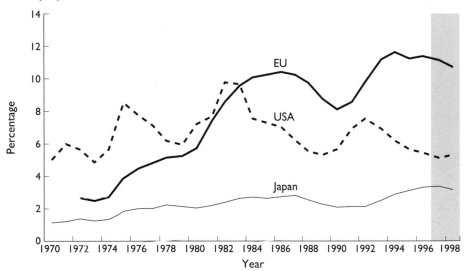

Employment

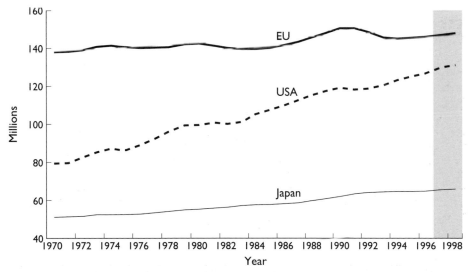

Figure 2.3   Unemployment and employment in the EU, USA, and Japan
Note: Shaded areas indicate IMF staff projections. Rates are based on national definitions.

(International Monetary Fund, 1997, p.39; unemployment rates based on national definitions)

Unemployment in the EU has been significantly higher than in the USA since 1990, increasing rapidly in the early 1990s as a result of a recession exacerbated by the tight macroeconomic stances that came with German unification and with the need to meet the Maastricht convergence criteria (see Box 2.3). The number of people in employment in the EU has remained broadly static, in contrast to the significant increase that has occurred in employment in the USA and Japan. The EU's labour market performance compared with the USA and Japan has been particularly weak since the mid-1990s.

Summary

- There has been a move from a regulatory order toward a market order among the EU economies.

- The EU growth rate has fallen since the 1960s.

- There has been an increase in trade and investment integration among EU economies.

- The EU economies have converged toward a common position in a number of economic areas.

3 The emergence of European integration

The starting point in our analysis of the integration process is to outline some of the fundamental forces that caused the EEC to be set up in the first place and propelled its development since. Many of these are essentially political:

1 A basic desire, in the immediate post-war period, to prevent another war in Europe.

2 The desire, up to the late 1980s, to establish a capitalist bloc in Western Europe as a bulwark against Soviet Communism – sometimes referred to as the 'Cold War' aspect of European integration.

3 The possibility of a continental-sized economy collectively wielding greater power in international relations.

4 Later, the wish of the newly established democracies in Greece, Spain and Portugal to anchor their political systems by linking them to established democratic states – an objective now pursued by applicant countries from the former Soviet bloc.

5 The fundamental internationalist idea that co-operation, interchange, mobility and access on a Europe-wide scale was eminently desirable.

Others are more economic, for example:

6   The desire to benefit from whatever rewards might be available from internal trade liberalization and access to a vast market (gains in economic welfare as a result of better allocation of resources, economies of scale, greater efficiency resulting from increased competition, and so on – these issues are taken up below).

7   A wish to obtain any gains in efficiency that might result from increased intra-union labour and capital mobility.

8   The benefits to be had from co-ordinating policies in various areas (despite the losses inherent in the Common Agricultural Policy, CAP, discussed later).

9   The desire to protect the European economy from external challenges, for example from the newly industrialized countries (NICs) in the Pacific Rim and elsewhere.

10 The wish to follow 'best practice' (that is, often German practice) in macroeconomic management (which in Germany resulted in historically low levels of inflation).

11 Latterly, the desire to recapture collectively some of the economic power and influence which has been lost by individual nation states as a result of increased economic interdependence, and in particular the vastly increased power of deregulated global markets (that is, regarding the EU as a logical response to globalization, discussed later). This was arguably of particular significance in the case of the accession of smaller countries – such as Sweden (in 1995) – which had been accustomed to exercising considerable autonomy in economic decision making, but which now felt the need to anchor their economic systems within a larger grouping.

Britain was not an original signatory of the 1957 Treaty of Rome, preferring to found the European Free Trade Area (EFTA) instead. However, the success of the EEC and Britain's own relative economic decline precipitated a UK application under Harold Macmillan in 1961. This was vetoed by French President de Gaulle in 1963, who was then instrumental in delaying UK entry until the early 1970s under Edward Heath. The UK's relationship with the Community and the Union has been a difficult one ever since, as is testified by two referendums, the disputes of the Thatcher years, the opt-outs from Economic and Monetary Union (EMU) and the Social Chapter of Maastricht, and the emergence of 'euroscepticism' in the 1990s.

The various past enlargements of the Union (Chapter 1) have all been logical and largely successful from an economic perspective, since, with the partial exception of the southern enlargement, they have all involved countries at similar stages of economic development. In future we may be looking at further expansion that poses more serious problems, since it will involve small countries with less developed economies (Lintner, 1996). Since its inception, the European integration project has principally concerned economic arrangements, although political aspects have naturally always been present, and indeed have increased in importance in more recent years especially in the context of the *Maastricht Treaty* of 1992 and the *Amsterdam Treaty* of 1997.

We turn in the next three sections to an examination of the development of the EU in each of the main policy areas with which it has been concerned. The arrangements which form part of the *acquis communautaire*, the range of legislation and regulations contained in the Treaty of Rome and developed since then, can be conveniently divided into three categories: the various common policies of the EU (Section 4); the trade arrangements in the customs union and the free movement of labour and capital within the common market (Section 5); and monetary integration (Section 6). The object here is to introduce and place into context these arrangements, many of which are dealt with more fully elsewhere in this book. A central point that should be noted throughout is that the process of integration in its several guises fundamentally alters the locus of decision making and thus the essential nature of the governance of the European economy.

Summary

- The momentum for the European economic integration project has come from a variety of political as well as economic factors.

- Britain has often displayed an enigmatic attitude toward European integration.

- Enlargements have been generally successful but greater problems will loom in the next round.

4   Common policies

There are a number of common policies established by the EU, of which the most important are the Common Agricultural Policy and the policies associated with the structural funds.

4.1   The Common Agricultural Policy

By far the most significant of the EU's common policies has been the Common Agricultural Policy (CAP) which came into operation in 1964. The objective of the CAP was to provide a system of agricultural protection and subsidy designed to promote the development of an industry that was both strategic and very basic, particularly following the aftermath of the Second World War when food was in short supply. This was to be done on a pan-European level by creating a single market in food, partly to promote integration and partly to mediate potential tensions between France and Germany, both of which possessed large and influential farming sectors. The method chosen to achieve this was to operate directly through the price mechanism: setting minimum prices above world market prices for most agricultural products. These are maintained at the desired level by a tariff, the Variable Levy. Prices are often set without much regard for what people actually want to buy, and so frequently they have been above the level required for intra-Union equilibrium between supply and demand.

The result has been not only expensive food but also surpluses, which have been mopped up by the EU's 'intervention buying'. These surpluses have sometimes been stored, generating the infamous 'butter mountains' and 'wine lakes' which scarred the public image of the EU for much of the 1970s and 1980s. Alternatively they have been 'dumped' (exported at below cost price) on world markets, to the detriment of food producers elsewhere. In addition, the CAP has redistributed resources between states and individuals in member countries in a generally regressive fashion. It has also arguably contributed to the continent's ecological degradation by promoting the indiscriminate use of chemical additives, since the subsidy system rewards quantity of production rather than the quality of what is produced (Chapter 7).

The CAP has resulted in some benefits to Europe since it is now a substantial net exporter of food where once it was a net importer. Food is plentiful, if you can afford it; agricultural incomes have been increased, however inefficiently and inequitably this may have been done; and there have been vast improvements in agricultural technologies and in agricultural productivity, even at the cost of the environmental damage referred to above and of the threat to the purity and integrity of what we eat. Above all, perhaps, the CAP is the example *par excellence* of an area of economic activity the management of which has been transferred from the national to the supranational level, and of the EU acting as a *regulatory state* (see Chapters 1, 3 and 7). The consumer, however, has had to pay heavily and twice over for the policy, mainly through high food prices, but also via the EU budget, 50–75 per cent of which has typically been swallowed up by the CAP.

There have been numerous attempts to modify the excesses of the policy, such as: production quotas, set-aside and price cuts during the 1980s; in 1989 in the wake of the budget reforms that doubled the size of the structural funds (see below) following the establishment of the '1992' programme; and through the McSharry Plan and the General Agreement on Tariffs and Trade (GATT) Uruguay round of multilateral negotiations aimed at reducing barriers to trade.

Reform from inside has proved to be difficult because of the numerous vested interests involved. The obvious other approach to agricultural protection is through some system of direct cash transfers on the model of the former UK 'deficiency payments' system, which would probably be politically unacceptable because of its tax implications and because of the transfer of direct spending power to the EU that it would involve. As a result, most change has been precipitated by external forces, for example pressure from the USA and others in the GATT international trade negotiations, although Agenda 2000 (agreed by the EU in 1999) envisages cuts in prices and subsidies in order to accommodate future enlargements. Nevertheless, over the last few years prices have fallen, surpluses have been reduced, and the budgetary cost of the CAP has to some extent been moderated. The fundamental problem lies, however, in the very nature of the policy, which is based on millions of consumers paying to protect the interests of a minority of large farmers. Such regulation has been distinctly unavailable to other industries such as steel and coal mining, which, despite some national protection, have increasingly had to live (and die) in the free market.

4.2   Structural funds

The CAP is of course not the only common policy to be pursued at the supranational level, although one could be forgiven for thinking that it is, given the adverse publicity that it has generated and the huge proportion of the budget that it has accounted for. Other major policies have been operated at the EU level through the 'structural funds': the European Regional Development Fund (ERDF), which has become the main instrument of the EU's regional policy, and the European Social Fund (ESF), the principal means of implementing the Union's social policy. The operation of these structural funds has been substantially reformed as part of 'Agenda 2000', which has been driven by the imperatives of the future expansion of the EU.

4.3   Other policies

Important aspects of European industrial and competition policy, fiscal policy, transport policy, environmental policy, and fisheries policy have been increasingly conducted at the EU level. In addition, the common regulatory frameworks established by the 1992 programme affect a wide range of aspects of economic and political life – from employment contracts to the quality of drinking water, and from local economic development to industrial subsidies.

Common policies, apart from promoting convergence in the European economy, also change the nature of economic governance in Europe, edging important aspects of this toward the supranational level. These EU policies are financed from the EU budget, and the budget itself has frequently been an issue of contention, particularly for the UK, which has resented its position as a net contributor to the financing of the EU's policies and administration. It is financed from customs duties (about 20 per cent of total EU income), from the first 1.4 percentage points of VAT receipts (about 40–50 per cent of total EU income) and from a (limited) GNP-based 'fourth resource' (see **Laffan, 2001**).

Summary

- The EU has established a number of 'common policies', ... important of which have been the CAP and the structura...

- Common policies change the nature of EU governance and ... significant budgetary implications.

5   The 'four freedoms': trade arrangements and factor mobility

In this section we move on to review some of the core elements in the European economic integration process. The 'four freedoms' embodied in the Treaty of Rome – freedom of trade, investment, labour movement and service provision within the EU – have provided the key framework for subsequent integrationist developments.

5.1   Trade: the customs union

We begin with the customs union, which is the most basic of the EU's economic arrangements. This involves establishing and policing internal free trade between members. EU members have to remove all tariff, as well as substantial non-tariff barriers (NTBs) such as quotas or preferential trading arrangements, to intra-Union trade in goods and services. This is an example of what is sometimes referred to as 'negative integration', in the sense that it involves promoting integration by reducing barriers to exchange in sympathy with the market order of economic governance discussed above (and in Chapter 1).

The customs union was established in a *de jure* sense by the Treaty of Rome, and explicit tariffs on trade between EU members were removed relatively soon after the Treaty of Rome and the various accessions. The six had removed all intra-tariffs by the end of 1969, while new entrants were allowed transition periods of five years (but seven years for Spain and Portugal). In the case of the latest EFTA enlargement, no period of transition was required since the entrants had previously been, to all intents and purposes, members of the Common Market through their membership of the European Economic Area (EEA).

The transition from *de jure* liberalization to *de facto* liberalization has been more complex. The importance of tariffs as sources of trade distortion has greatly diminished on a global scale since the Second World War, and NTBs have become more important impediments to trade. Some of these have been removed or reduced as a result of the EU's ambitious and remarkably successful '1992' programme (discussed below). Membership of the customs union also necessitates adopting a common external trade policy vis-à-vis the rest of the world. This involves both common external tariffs (CET) and common NTBs, as well as adopting a common stance in trade negotiations such as the various rounds of multilateral trade negotiations conducted since the 1950s under the auspices of GATT and its successor since 1995, the World Trade Organization (WTO). The introduction of the EU's CET was completed by 1968.

The rationale for creating and then completing the customs union in Western Europe was provided by the development of *customs union theory*. The arguments involved here can be divided into two categories, often referred to as 'static' and 'dynamic' theory, which we now examine in some detail.

Static effects

Static customs union theory seeks to examine the 'once and for all' effects of the customs union on trade flows, economic welfare, and the international distribution of production. It does so by a comparative static analysis of the position 'before' and 'after' the formation of the union. Previous analysis had suggested that customs unions were unambiguously a step toward free trade and therefore necessarily desirable in their effects, because of the internal tariff elimination to which they lead – in the neo-classical economic model, free trade optimizes economic welfare by promoting a more efficient allocation of resources. But early customs union theory showed that this view is simplistic, since a customs union with its discriminatory tariff changes represents both a move toward free trade (the removal of internal trade barriers) and a move toward potentially greater protectionism (the common external trade policy). This leads to two separate effects: trade creation and trade diversion. Trade creation improves the international allocation of resources and increases economic welfare; trade diversion has the opposite effect. Thus, the trade effects of a customs union can be evaluated by comparing the relative dimension of the two effects. The analytical sequence is set out in Box 2.1.

Trade creation occurs when changes in tariffs and other trade impediments that result from the formation of a customs union lead to consumers purchasing relatively more efficiently and cheaply produced goods and services provided by other members of the union, instead of less efficiently produced and more expensive products made domestically. Trade diversion, on the other hand, occurs when the tariff changes following the creation of a customs union result in prices changing in a way that leads consumers to buy goods and services produced relatively less efficiently in partner countries in place of those produced more efficiently and cheaply in other non-member countries. The transmission process between tariff changes and welfare changes that these bring about is summarized in Box 2.1.

Box 2.1   The relationship between changes in protection and the location of production which result from a customs union

TARIFF/NTB CHANGES

result in

CHANGES IN RELATIVE PRICES

which, in turn, result in

CHANGES IN CONSUMPTION PATTERNS

which, in turn, result in

CHANGES IN PRODUCTION PATTERNS

Trade creation toward cheaper and more efficient sources/areas = increase in overall economic welfare

Trade diversion toward more expensive and less efficient sources/areas = reduction in overall economic welfare.

This model gives us some insights into the effects of customs unions, but it also has serious limitations. It ignores issues such as intra-industry trade (trade of products from within the same industry) and the effect of imperfect competition on trade (the fact that there might be gains from a larger scale of production, for instance – discussed below). It also takes no account of issues of the distribution of the gains between different groups of consumers. Furthermore, the empirical studies which were carried out on the dimension of trade creation and trade diversion suggested that these were likely to be of relatively modest dimensions.

It must be noted at this point that empirical investigation of the economic consequences of a customs union is extremely difficult and problematic. Apart from anything else, it is virtually impossible to separate out the impact of the customs union itself from the plethora of other factors that influence trade flows, not least the tariff reductions that have resulted from the various rounds of the GATT. In many cases, researchers have to estimate a counter-factual, that is, what would have happened to, say, trade flows between the countries in the absence of the EU. In essence this must consist of a guess, even if it is an informed guess made by highly competent people. Nevertheless, the studies that have been carried out (notably by Truman, 1969, 1975; Williamson and

Bottrill, 1971; Kreinin, 1972, 1981; Aitken, 1973; Balassa, 1975; Mayes, 1978) do suggest that the EU customs union significantly altered trade flows and was, on the whole, trade creating. Trade creation was greatest in manufacturing, and outweighed the trade diversion that occurred, particularly in the agricultural sector. The best estimates suggest that net trade creation may have increased national income in the EU by something like 0.1 per cent – a small amount and certainly less than the estimated impact of dynamic factors. Partly because of this, the emphasis in recent years has therefore been increasingly on analysing the so-called dynamic effects of customs unions.

Dynamic effects

This area of customs union theory concentrates on the effects of a customs union over time, rather than on the once-and-for-all effects outlined above. There is some debate among economists as to what exactly constitutes a true dynamic effect. However, the following are usually mentioned in this context: economies of scale, increased competition, improvements in the terms of trade and increased growth, which we shall now look at in turn.

Economies of scale

The increased internal specialization that results from the formation of a customs union leads to efficient firms and industries in a union expanding production and growing in size as they service a larger market. In many cases this allows unit costs of production to fall, thus increasing the welfare of consumers, who can enjoy lower prices as a result. This process occurs as a result of the following:

- *Internal economies*, which are advantages that result from the growth of firms. Examples of this might be the more efficient use of machinery, with large production runs, and increased scope for the division of labour within the firm, as well as scale economies in respect of research and development (R & D) expenditures.

- *External economies*, which result from the growth of industries as a whole. For example, large industries can be serviced by specialist and efficient manufacturers of components. *Economies of agglomeration* may result when the growth of an industry in a particular area leads, for example, to the development of a pool of suitably skilled labour in the area. Both of these could also lead to lower prices.

It is very difficult to quantify scale economies. However, in the run-up to the 1992 programme the EU Commission estimated, perhaps rather optimistically, that the potential welfare gains available from the fuller exploitation of scale economies in the Union might amount to as much as 2.1 per cent of Union GDP (Cecchini, 1988; Emerson et al., 1998). However, the quest for scale economies is one of the factors that have influenced the spate of cross-frontier mergers which occurred in the run-up to 1992 and thereafter (as indicated by the intra-EU FDI data plotted in Figure 2.1 above).

Increased competition

The opening up of internal markets that results from the formation of a customs union can expose firms to increased competition from rivals in partner countries. Single-firm national monopolies may become competing European oligopolies within a customs union, thus reducing the degree of monopoly power in the union overall. This may force firms to improve techniques, cut costs, and generally increase efficiency in order to remain or become competitive. In the long run, this process will increase welfare and benefit all. Politicians have often referred to it as 'a bracing cold shower'. It is of course a phenomenon that is very difficult to verify empirically.

Improvements in the terms of trade

A country's or an area's terms of trade can broadly be seen as the price at which it buys its imports in relation to the price it obtains for its exports. If the formation of a customs union leads to a fall in demand for imports from the rest of the world as a result of trade diversion, then the international price of these imports will tend to fall (since demand for them is now lower) and the union's terms of trade will improve. This effect may mitigate or even outweigh the negative effects of trade diversion, but it is important to note that any gains are made at the expense of the rest of the world. Petith (1977) suggests that terms of trade gains may be substantially more significant than static gains in the EU customs union.

Increased growth

It follows from the static and dynamic gains outlined above that, overall, the effects of a customs union should be to increase the rate of economic growth in the area concerned. This extra growth might in turn precipitate greater investment spending and stimulate even further growth. Empirical studies in this area should be treated with a good deal of caution. Nevertheless, in the case of the EU, the growth effect has been traditionally estimated to be, overall, equivalent to about an extra 1 per cent GNP. More recent estimates (for example, Marques-Mendes, 1986) are more optimistic, suggesting that in 1972 the Union's GDP had been increased by 2.2 per cent by the European integration process, and that by 1981 the GDP of the enlarged Union was as much as 6.9 per cent higher than it would have been without any integration.

5.2   Factor mobility: the common market

A common market (sometimes referred to as an 'internal market' or 'level playing field'), as we have seen, involves the free movement of labour and capital between member states, as well as the free movement of goods and services. Again, in the neo-classical economic model the rationale for the free movement of labour and capital was provided by the argument that these measures improve economic welfare. In the comparative static terms used above, the free movement of the factors of production can, under certain (albeit restrictive) assumptions, be shown to lead to improved resource allocation and thus result in welfare gains for the participants. The principle is that in a free market environment capital moves to where it is most productive in response to differentials in the rate of return. Again, it results in a change in the international location of production. The establishment of the free movement of labour between partners in a common market can similarly be shown to result in welfare gains. There may also be dynamic gains arising from the free movement of the factors of production. These are extremely difficult to analyse, but what literature does exist very tentatively suggests that they may broadly work in the same direction as the static effects discussed above. We thus have the broad theoretical rationale for promoting the free movement of labour and capital, and for creating and completing a common market, although one should bear in mind the familiar health warnings relating to the assumptions on which the model is based.

One of the conclusions from the above analysis is that the free movement of capital tends to equalize factor earnings between participating countries or regions, and thus leads to economic convergence between the countries within the common market. However, we should note that the radical critique of neo-classical theory in this area suggests that no such convergence will necessarily take place; instead, the free movement of capital in particular could lead to the exacerbation of national and regional differences in real income and welfare, with well-off areas gaining at the expense of less well-off countries and regions. This critique is largely based on the work of the Swedish economist Gunnar Myrdal (see Myrdal, 1957). He essentially held that the free movement of capital leads to 'polarization' effects through a process of 'cumulative causation'. Broadly, the inflow of capital into areas where the increase in its productivity is likely to be greatest sets in motion dynamic processes that reinforce the attractiveness of these host areas, which grow in prosperity, and thus attract more and more capital from the other source areas, which gradually decline relatively. The free movement of labour may lead to similar effects, since it may drain source areas of the workers with the greatest amount of human capital and enterprise. There may be a limited flow of capital from the prosperous economic centre to the less well-off periphery as a result of factors such as low labour costs and congestion, but this is unlikely to be sufficient to compensate for the polarization effects referred to above.

Thus instead of there being convergence and equitable growth within a common market, we may see the emergence of cumulative unevennesses between partners. It is very difficult to test this hypothesis empirically, although it is arguable that countries such as the UK and Greece may have suffered from it in the context of the EU. To the extent that it does exist, at the very least it provides a strong case for an active and well-resourced regional policy within a common market. Indeed, the fact that there seems to have been a convergence toward a common position among the EU countries – at least up to the late 1990s (Figure 2.2) – is generally recognized to have been the result of deliberate public policy at the EU level to use structural funds to enhance the growth prospects of those countries at the periphery.

5.3   The completion of the internal market?

As we have seen, the Treaty of Rome established the EEC common market in a *de jure* sense, but *de facto* the internal market was still far from complete even by the mid-1990s. The convergence of consumer prices that one would expect in EU countries if the customs union were in fact complete simply had not materialized. Just to take one example, there had been the much publicized difference in new car prices (as well as many other goods) between the UK and the Continent. This is an instance of the continuation of NTBs within the EU.

Thus, in the area of trade, important NTBs still existed, and in many cases grew in significance hand in hand with the elimination of tariff barriers to intra-EU trade. In principle an almost infinite number of factors can distort trade and thus act as NTBs. However, the most important ones which were relevant to the EU are the following:

- *National preference in public procurement*
  The EU Commission suggested (Cecchini, 1988; Emerson et al., 1998) that the value of member-government contracts that might have been deemed suitable for competitive allocation was between 7 and 10 per cent of GDP in the mid-1980s, and of these only a tiny fraction (0.14 per cent of GDP) was placed abroad. The same Cecchini Report (see Box 2.2) suggested that telecommunications, power generation, railways, and defence are the sectors worst affected by these discriminatory practices. Opening up public procurement to Union-wide competition would have resulted, the Commission and Cecchini suggest, in a saving of about 0.5 per cent of 1986 Union GDP.

- *Differences in indirect taxation*
  Rates and coverage of VAT still differ considerably in EU countries. This distorts prices and requires elaborate bureaucratic procedures at frontiers. Additionally, there are even wider differences in excise duties in the EU, often discriminating according to country of origin.

- *Monopolies and restrictive practices*
  Large dominant firms or firms acting in collusion can distort trade by indulging in unfair practices such as price fixing or market sharing. Examples of this include the persistently high UK car prices mentioned above, and the airline industry, which arguably has operated a route-sharing and fare-fixing cartel.

- *Differences in technical regulations and standards*
  Specifically, these have included differences in the areas of technical regulations, standards, testing and certification procedures. These differences were identified by European companies as one of the most serious aspects of the incomplete customs union (Cecchini, 1988). Particularly significant, from the UK's point of view, have been the

often severe obstacles to trade in services, and in particular insurance, banking, and other financial services. The Cecchini Report estimated that, in total, the gains from the integration of banking, insurance and securities brokerage could amount to 22 billion ECU (European Currency Unit).

- *Frontier formalities*
  The Cecchini Report estimated that the total cost of customs formalities was over 3 per cent of trans-border sales in the mid-1980s. The average total cost of formalities was claimed to be 1.5 per cent of the average consignment's value.

- *State subsidies*
  These probably vary between something like 5 and 10 per cent of domestic income in EU countries in the 1980s. A particular problem is regional aid, which was permitted by the competition clauses of the Treaty of Rome.

- *Differing trade and aid policies toward third countries*
  An example of this is tied aid. In addition, despite the CET, EU countries frequently concluded bilateral deals with countries outside the Union. For example, Britain, Italy and France have at various times restricted the quantity of Japanese car imports, and the International Multi-Fibre Trade Agreement set national quotas for textile imports. Article 115 of the Treaty of Rome allowed national governments to discriminate in favour of non-EU goods coming into a country via a partner country.

- *Different currencies*
  At the most basic level, this increases the cost of trading by forcing importers to pay the price of changing currency on the foreign exchange markets. More important, currency fluctuations increase the risks involved in trade and thus render it a less attractive proposition. Furthermore, the presence of a multitude of different currencies reduces the transparency of price differences between different countries, thus reducing the possibility of rational consumer choice. EMU will, of course, eliminate these distortions.

- *National quotas*
  It was estimated that there were about 1000 of these in existence in the Union in the mid-1980s. A variant to these national quotas was the Voluntary Export Restraint agreements (VERs) which several EU countries negotiated with potential exporters from outside the Community, whereby they agreed to export only a certain quantity of goods to the EU countries. These are, of course, anything but voluntary.

Box 2.2   The Cecchini Report 1988

The Cecchini Report is named after the Italian Special Advisor to the Commission, who chaired the Committee that assessed the economic benefits and costs associated with the creation of a single internal market for the EU. The Report was called 'The Costs of Non-Europe'.

The freedom of movement clauses of the Treaty of Rome also ⟨
de jure integration in this area right from the outset, but in prac⟨
EU labour migration has been limited during most of the post-wa⟨
The main internal migration took place between the Italian Mezz⟨
and Germany, France and Northern Italy, in the years imme⟨
following the Treaty of Rome. Thereafter, labour shortages in the ⟨
of Europe were tackled by importing extra-EU workers. In recent ⟨
high unemployment has meant that intra-EU migration has been ⟨
limited. Furthermore, exchange controls provided a barrier to *de fi*⟨
capital mobility until the late 1980s. More recently, deregulated markets
and advances in technology have rendered vast amounts of capital highly
mobile throughout the world, rendering governments' delivery of
democratically expressed preference in economic policy very problematic.

5.4   The 1992 single market programme

The '1992 programme' to complete the internal market (also known as
the single market programme, SMP, or single european market, SEM)
represented a major development of the EU as a *de facto regulatory state* in
the sense that it promotes *positive integration* by further removing barriers
to trade but based on proactive measures. It also marks a shift in emphasis
from the earlier *quantitative* removal of barriers (see above) toward
qualitative liberalization (for example, the elimination of NTB's). It was
established in 1986, with the Single European Act (SEA) of the same year
providing the enabling legislation. It is probably fair to say that the '1992
programme' kick-started a period of rapid 'intensification' of the integration process, which eventually led to the Maastricht Treaty.

The major thrust of the original programme for '1992' consisted of a series
of measures and a 'timetable for action' published by the EU Commission
in a White Paper in June 1985 (European Commission, 1985), which was
followed closely by the key Cecchini Report discussed above. This
included over 300 legislative proposals (directives), subsequently reduced
to 279, aimed at removing what the Commission saw as being all the
technical, physical, and fiscal barriers which prevented the internal
market from functioning properly. As a result of the modifications to the
Treaty of Rome made by the SEA, these required a qualified majority in
the Council of Ministers in order to be approved (except for directives
relating to taxation and professional qualifications, which still required
unanimity). All this was supplemented by a series of seemingly ad hoc
measures aimed at other NTBs and obstacles to factor mobility. The whole
was supplemented by the so-called 'Social Charter'.

The content of the '1992' programme can thus be summarized as follows:

- *The removal of physical barriers to trade and factor mobility*
  The Commission set the objectives of simplifying administrative
  checks and moving them away from borders, eliminating all internal

frontiers and controls by 1992, and developing a common transport policy.

- *The elimination of barriers to trade and factor mobility*
  Essentially, the strategy here has been, wherever possible, to move toward harmonization: that is, to introduce common standards and practices that are acceptable throughout the EU. Where this has not been possible, then the principle of mutual recognition has been adopted; that is, countries must agree to accept technical regulations and standards that are recognized in other member states, even if they do not meet their own domestic standards. (A key legal ruling supporting this move was the famous *Cassis de Dijon* case that came before the European Court of Justice (ECJ) in 1979; see **Wincott 2001**.) The principle of mutual recognition goes well beyond the elimination of nation preference, and may in some instances actually result in foreign goods and services being treated more favourably than domestic ones. The specific objectives included adopting Union-wide standards for health and safety, food, pharmaceuticals and electrical goods, creating a common legal framework for cross-border activities by enterprises, reforming intellectual and industrial property law, creating a common market for services, and removing exchange controls.

- *The reduction of fiscal barriers to trade*
  The Commission originally decided that, in line with experience in the USA, a variation of about 5–6 per cent in VAT rates is the most that would be consistent with the customs union. It therefore proposed that there should be only two bands of VAT in the Union: a standard rate of between 14 and 20 per cent, and a lower rate of between 4 and 9 per cent for food, books, medicine, children's clothes, etc. Even more radically, it proposed that rates of excise duty be exactly the same throughout the Union. Subsequently, the Commission was forced to abandon, for the time being at least, the bulk of its plans in this area.

- *Opening up public procurement*
  In the UK, perhaps the most significant impact has been on the purchasing policies of local authorities, with the secondary effect of restricting the possibility of local government using procurement policies to create local multiplier effects as part of economic development strategies.

- *A firmer application of competition policy*
  The Union operates a competition policy which focuses on the trade effects of dominant firms, mergers, and restrictive practices, to the extent that these affect trade. It also deals with the abuse of subsidies by the governments of member states. This was used more vigorously, for example in the case of the merger between British Airways (BA) and British Caledonian in the 1980s, with BA being forced to give up several routes. There is considerable evidence, however, that the completion of the single market has spawned a big increase in these cross-frontier mergers, and thus in the level of industrial concentration in Europe.

● *The 'Social Charter'*
   This was later incorporated into the Maastricht Treaty as its Social
   Chapter (see Chapter 5 of this book).

The Commission has, on the whole, adopted a pragmatic approach to the
internal market, pressing forward where possible and modifying its
proposals where it meets strong resistance from member states. There
have been various obstacles to success, some technical, others practical
and philosophical, the majority involving political will. Nevertheless,
considerable steps have been taken along this road since the mid-1980s,
perhaps propelled by the feeling that there is a considerable amount to
gain from the process. This is borne out by the empirical work carried out
on the potential and actual benefits of the single market.

The potential benefits were estimated in the Cecchini Report discussed
above, which acted as the key background source for the push toward the
'1992 programme'. This was in essence an *ex ante* study of the potential
benefits of completing the internal market in the context of realities such
as imperfect competition and economies of scale. As such, it involves all
of the serious methodological problems associated with attempting to
predict the future. Nevertheless, Cecchini estimated that the benefits
from reducing market entry barriers alone in the EU would range between
5.8 and 6.4 per cent of EU GDP in total. Of this, removing frontier
controls would increase GDP by between 0.2 and 3.0 per cent, removing
technical and regulatory barriers would increase GDP by 2.0–2.4 per cent,
removing obstacles to scale economies would increase GDP by 2.0–2.1 per
cent, and removing barriers which restricted competition and allowed
monopoly to continue would increase GDP by 1.6 per cent. The
macroeconomic benefits of the SEM would increase GDP by 4.5–7.5 per
cent, cut prices by 4.3–6.1 per cent, and increase employment by between
1.8 and 5.7 per cent. These were clearly very substantial numbers, and
they suggested that the single market would bring considerable changes
to the structure of the European economy.

5.5   Reviewing the single market programme

The Commission itself has carried out what is to an extent a retrospective
study of the effects of completing the single market in 1996 in the form of
its Single Market Review (European Commission, 1996a, 1996b, 1996c;
European Economy, 1996; Monti, 1996). This Review covered the period
between 1987 and 1994, and it focused on the way in which the single
market had affected the efficiency of how resources were utilized, the
growth effects of the single market, and its effects on the location of
economic activity within the EU. The broad findings of the Review were
that the failure to harmonize VAT rates and excise duties had meant that
the establishment of totally free frontiers has yet to be achieved, and the
potential benefits of harmonizing technical standards and regulations
through the principle of mutual recognition remained to a considerable

extent under-exploited. The impact of the public procurement regulations had likewise been limited.

There had been a very significant increase in intra-industry trade, which grew from 35 per cent to 42 per cent of total manufactured trade between 1987 and 1994. This indicates that the more developed EU states, such as Germany, had tended to specialize in high price and high quality products, whereas the less developed states, such as Spain and Portugal, had tended to specialize at the lower quality, lower price end of the spectrum. The UK, France and the Benelux countries were positioned in the centre, but the poorest areas, such as Greece and Southern Italy, had not managed to develop any significant specialization in the area of intra-industry trade (European Economy, 1996). There had also been a substantial increase in mergers and acquisitions, many of which had been cross-frontier. Substantial price differences persisted within the EU, but these were lower in the case of longer-term members. The price dispersal was most significant in industries such as telecommunication services, airlines, and energy, where liberalization had been slow and where state aid had been greatest (Monti, 1996). The Review estimated that the single market had increased GDP by between 1.1 per cent and 1.5 per cent, creating between 300,000 and 900,000 jobs. It is interesting to note that these estimates are significantly lower than those produced in the *ex ante* Cecchini Report.

As far as the distribution issue is concerned, the Review concluded that the single market had promoted *convergence* among EU states. Spain, Portugal and Ireland had fared best here, narrowing the gap vis-à-vis the core of the EU. Greece and Southern Italy had, however, made little progress, possibly because of their reliance on low-wage inter-industry trade (Monti, 1996). All this is to an extent borne out by other work in this area. There is evidence (Allen et al., 1998) that the larger and more developed economies, such as Germany, France and the UK, have benefited more than smaller and less developed economies from the direct liberalization effects of the single market, at least as far as manufacturing is concerned. However, the less developed countries seem to be experiencing large increases in competition that in the long run may be of greater significance. Extrapolating the Allen et al. findings to the whole economy would suggest that the single market will result in overall welfare gains in the region of 4 per cent of GDP for the larger EU economies and more for the smaller ones.

An interesting feature of the Review, and indeed of the Cecchini Report is the relatively low profile afforded to the impact of the single market on the rest of the world. The Cecchini Report concluded that this was likely to be of modest proportions, a view reiterated in the Review. Some have claimed that any negative effects on the rest of the world were likely to be outweighed by the increased exports to the EU that would result from the income-increasing effects of the single market (Winters, 1992, pp.104–8).

Partly as a result of this Review, the Commission has put forward a series of proposals aimed at further improving the way in which the single market operates (European Commission, 1996c), although this has naturally taken a low profile in comparison with EMU. It is important to note that the choices the EU has made regarding the governance of the European economy have been firmly rooted in what is essentially a free market (market order) framework, even if the nature of the economic liberalism that has been adopted has had a distinctly European 'social market' feel to it, in the tradition of the models of the mixed economy and 'organized capitalism' which Germany and France have preferred.

Summary

- The EU integration project has been supported by static and dynamic customs union theory and by the factor mobility benefits argued to derive from the creation of a common market.

- The 1992 single market programme marked a move away from *quantitative* reductions in tariffs between members and toward the removal of *qualitative* restrictions on trade.

- Significant economic benefit, it was argued, resulted from both the reduction in tariffs and the removal of NTBs.

- The empirical estimates of the benefits, while not as generous as expected, nevertheless indicate substantial gains.

- The SMP was one firmly rooted in the move toward a more market-friendly form of governance for the EU.

6   Monetary integration

In recent years monetary integration has become the single most important issue facing the EU and it represents the strongest example of *positive integration* (Chapter 1). It was not originally an explicit aim of the then EEC, and there was no mention of it in the Treaty of Rome. However, we have now reached the point where there will almost certainly be a single currency for Europe, or at least for most of it, during the early years of this century. Since EMU is discussed at some length elsewhere in this book (Chapters 4, 8 and 9) its development and significance is only outlined here. As an aid to the discussion, Box 2.3 sets out the history of monetary union in the EU.

Box 2.3   History of monetary union

For convenience, this history can be divided conveniently into three phases: the Werner Plan, the European Monetary System, and Maastricht.

1   The Werner Plan

The issue of monetary integration first appeared on the European agenda at the Hague summit in 1969, partly as a strategy aimed at restoring stability after the political events of May 1968. The debate at the time centred on the extent to which Europe was in fact an 'optimum currency area', that is, an area in which it is possible and beneficial to maintain fixed exchange rates (see Chapter 1), and on the best strategy for constructing a monetary union. On the latter issue, there were two points of view, which came to be referred to as the 'economist' approach and the 'monetarist' position (*not* Milton Friedman's monetarism). The former, mainly supported by the Dutch and the Germans through the *Schiller Plan*, favoured a gradualist approach to EMU, concentrating on the promotion of harmonization and convergence necessary to prepare the ground for the single currency. The latter position, canvassed by the Commission, France and Belgium through the *Barre Plan*, may be regarded as a 'shock theory' approach, involving the introduction of fixed exchange rates as a fait accompli, leaving countries to adjust to their effects.

The outcome was predictably a compromise between the two, in the shape of the *Werner Plan* of 1970, most of which was adopted by the Council of Ministers in March 1971 and which came into effect in March 1972. It provided for efforts to harmonize economic policies, but also created the 'snake in the tunnel' system of fixed exchange rates. The 'snake' consisted of fixing the exchange rates between the nine participants (the original six, plus Britain, Denmark and Ireland who were in the process of joining the then EEC) within bands of + or − 2.25 per cent. The 'tunnel' was the fixed parity of the snake currencies against the dollar and other world currencies within the 4.5 (2.25 × 2) per cent bands established by international agreement in December 1971 (the Smithsonian Agreements). The overall objective was a 'monetary union by 1980', so it is easy to see that the plan failed, collapsing in the wake of the economic disarray which followed the oil crisis of 1973.

2   European Monetary System (EMS)

The impetus toward monetary integration was revived in 1977 by Roy Jenkins and Helmut Schmidt, and the EMS was set up at the Bremen Council of 1978, coming into operation in March 1979. Its original objectives were somewhat more modest than those of the Werner Plan, based on a return to more fixed exchange rates as a means of stimulating intra-EU trade. The EMS had two main features:

- The European Currency Unit (ECU), which was the Eur... 'parallel currency' and around which the ERM was structure... was based on a 'weighted basket' of all the currencies involved.

- The ERM, which attempted to fix the exchange rates between the participating countries and between these currencies and the ECU within a band of + or – 2.25 per cent (+ or – 6 per cent for weaker currencies such as the lira and sterling). There was thus a 'snake', but this time no 'tunnel', since the ERM currencies could float vis-à-vis world currencies. The mechanism for maintaining exchange rates within the system consisted of agreements for supportive central bank intervention in foreign exchange markets, a limited reserve-pooling obligation, and a largely redundant divergence indicator. This was backed up by some measures to promote policy convergence.

Prospects for the EMS did not seem particularly rosy at the time of its launch, and it encountered early instabilities. But, to many people's surprise, from the mid-1980s it proved to be a considerable success. It promoted exchange rate stability in Western Europe. There were only eleven realignments altogether (twelve, if the exit of sterling and the lira in late 1992 is included), and none at all between January 1987 and the exit of sterling, while currencies outside the ERM experienced considerably greater instability. Furthermore, it contributed to lower and increasingly convergent rates of inflation in Europe, although it must be said that price stability was also facilitated by the neo-liberal consensus on economic policy in this period. Finally, it established an increasing role for the ECU as a private sector currency in the course of the 1980s.

However, the EMS was weakened by the UK's refusal (until October 1990) to join the ERM when 'the time was right' (although sterling was always part of the ECU basket), and arguably by excessive reliance on German leadership. Its partial disintegration in 1992 represents a good example of the relative impotence of modern nation states in the face of powerful and deregulated capital markets. Nevertheless, it paved the way for what was to follow.

3   Maastricht

The very success of the EMS provided the stimulus in the late 1980s for a debate on how the system should develop. The Commission's response was to set up the Delors Committee which produced the Delors Report in April 1989, advocating a full monetary union to be established in three stages. This spawned two Intergovernmental Conferences (IGCs): one on the subject of political union, which now came onto the agenda; and afterwards the Maastricht Treaty, which was eventually ratified in EC member states following an often difficult process. It is important to note that the Maastricht Treaty deals with more than just monetary union, for it constitutes a wide-ranging reform of the Union and a significant step forward for European integration on a number of fronts.

The so-called 'Maastricht model' is the one that has been chosen by the EU for its monetary union. This fundamentally consists of the EMU provisions of the Maastricht Treaty and of the set of agreements and arrangements that have been agreed since then, the most important of which is the Stability Pact on fiscal policy. They have remained largely unaffected by the Treaty of Amsterdam of 1997. The specific Maastricht proposals and timetable are summarized now.

First of all, EMU was to be achieved in three stages:

- *Stage 1* consisted of the completion of the single market, increased co-ordination and co-operation in the economic and monetary fields, a strengthening of the EMS, an extended role for the European Currency Unit (ECU) and an enhanced profile for the Committee of Governors of EU members' central banks. This stage began in 1990 and should have been completed by January 1993. In fact it was thrown into disarray by the currency crisis of late 1992.

- *Stage 2* involved the groundwork for the single currency: all members were to be included in the narrow band of the ERM, and the European Monetary Institute (EMI) was to be set up to promote the co-ordination necessary for EMU. This stage began in January 1994, but turmoil in the ERM meant that it was arguably never really completed.

- *Stage 3* consists of complete monetary union, with the introduction of what has been named the 'euro' as the single currency for the EU, or most of it. A specific agenda was developed for this, with deadlines and convergence criteria to be met.

The timetable for *Stage 3* involved – by December 1996 and if the Council of Finance Ministers decided by a qualified majority that a critical mass of seven states (six with the UK opt-out) had met the convergence criteria – setting a date for introducing the euro in qualifying states. Failing this, by December 1997 there should be the start of an automatic process leading to complete monetary union among a minimum of five states by January 1999. Additionally, 1998 was to see the start of the creation of the European Central Bank (ECB), which replaces EMI and is seen as the independent issuer of currency, and of the European System of Central Banks (ESCB), the independent body responsible for the conduct of monetary policy and foreign exchange operations. National central banks have to become independent at this time. The Maastricht convergence criteria consist of:

    a maximum annual budget deficit of 3 per cent of GDP;
    a maximum total public sector debt of 60 per cent of GDP;
    no realignments within the ERM;
    a rate of inflation not more than 1.5 per cent above the average of the three lowest inflation countries in the year before decision, this rate to be judged as 'sustainable';
    long-term (government bond) interest rates to be no more than 2 per cent above the average.

6.1   Monetary union considered

The limiting case of monetary integration is a complete monetary union. This is popularly conceived as consisting of a situation in which countries agree to replace their own national currencies with a single common currency, in this case the euro. However, the important point is that EMU will thus have far-reaching implications for the conduct of economic policy in general, and monetary and fiscal policies in particular, for it will involve these being determined and conducted to a large extent at the supranational level. This naturally involves a very fundamental change in European governance in the area of economic policy.

Monetary union will be impossible to achieve and maintain at an acceptable political cost without substantial economic convergence among EU states, and this in turn is impossible to achieve without an appropriate amount of joint policy making and implementation. If there is not an appropriate level of convergence, then it is likely that the union will lead to the rich members benefiting at the expense of poorer participants. Broadly speaking, countries or regions with a relatively high level of competitiveness will tend to attract economic activity and employment at the expense of areas which are less well off. Without a monetary union, countries might hope to bridge competitiveness gaps by devaluation. Countries which are relatively uncompetitive can devalue their currencies, thereby reducing the costs of their exports and increasing the cost of their imports. In this way they can stimulate domestic demand and increase their international competitiveness. Other more competitive countries should revalue their currencies, but, in practice this has rarely been done as a matter of policy. This also assumes that revaluations actually work in practice in anything but the short run.

But if there are no different currencies, their values cannot of course change, and in the absence of devaluation, differences in competitiveness must be balanced either by falls in living standards (if there are flexible labour markets which permit wages to fall in response to a decline in the demand for labour) or by unemployment and a decline in the level of economic activity and thus in material prosperity. Thus it will be seen that the costs of the monetary union will tend to fall disproportionately on weaker areas in such a scenario. Here we have a clear case of potential conflict over the future of EMU.

6.2   The Maastricht model: for and against

There are different definitions of what should constitute economic convergence. As we have seen, the Maastricht model of EMU has adopted a definition which is based almost exclusively on financial variables. It can be argued that this definition is an excessively narrow one, and that it would be more appropriate to include 'real' variables such as the level of employment, social variables and living standards in the definition of onstitutes convergence. The inclusion of real variables in the on of convergence would imply different economic policy targets uld therefore significantly alter the types of policies adopted by in the economic arena.

essity, EMU will also have a huge bearing on the myriad of policy that are financed from the public purse in EU countries. For example, the Maastricht model of EMU, and in particular the Stability and Growth Pact which now forms part of it (involving limited fiscal redistributions – see Box 2.4), will entail public finances operating under constraints that are determined at the supranational level. And, of course, interest rates and other monetary variables would be determined outside the nation state, with obvious implications for inflation, growth and employment. This throws up a number of important issues, many of which are associated with basic principles of democracy.

The view taken here is that some form of EMU, although not necessarily one based on the Maastricht model, is fundamentally desirable. Basically, this is because it offers the possibility of increasing the effectiveness of economic policy making in the context of the decreasing national control over macroeconomic policy that has resulted from globalization, and in particular from the emergence of vastly powerful and deregulated international capital markets. In other words, EMU is argued by its proponents to be a necessary response on the part of European nation states to the process of globalization. The experience of economic problems in Europe during the 1980s, it is suggested, provides evidence of the declining macroeconomic sovereignty of individual medium-sized nation states. Global capitalism is increasingly more and more out of democratic control, and EMU, and the centralization of macroeconomic policy making that goes with it (the pooling of 'economic sovereignty'), offers at least the possibility of recapturing some of this lost control on a 'unity is strength' principle, particularly by medium-sized European states. The 'Euro bloc', if it in fact emerges, will be a powerful actor on the international economic stage and will afford its participants collective policy options not open to individual states (recall Table 2.1 above).

In addition, EMU might also offer vulnerable states the advantage of similar stability and credibility to that which has been enjoyed by Germany and others over recent years, thus instantly providing a credible anchor for the economy. EMU offers a number of other potential advantages mainly associated with making the common market work better, but the view taken here is that the issue of national economic (and political) sovereignty is paramount in this context. Needless to say, this is a controversial area which throws up many issues which are not testable from a rigidly empirical point of view, but it is important to note that sovereignty fundamentally involves an issue of democracy, for loss of economic sovereignty to international capital markets means that citizens are deprived of the possibility of having their choices on economic policy implemented. The determination of important aspects of economic policy has effectively been transferred to capital markets, which are, of course, not democratically accountable. The experience of Italy and the

UK during the ERM crisis of September 1992 represents a particularly good case study of this.

On the other hand, critics of EMU have argued that participation in the project and the consequent transfer of policy-making powers to the supranational level erodes national sovereignty. This is based on a belief in the effectiveness of the residual economic powers still retained by nation states. Some critics also point out that the proposed EMU might increase regional disparities, and would be certain to carry substantial risks, especially in its initial stages. Others point to the costs and uncertainties of the transition period.

Thus the Maastricht proposals can be seen as being halfway between the 'gradualist' and 'shock' theory approaches to EMU, which have dominated the debate on how best to achieve EMU within the EU. The driving force behind EMU may be (partly) economic, but the establishment of EMU under the Maastricht model involves a definite political choice.

Britain under the Major government negotiated an 'opt-out' from the monetary union provisions of Maastricht. Under the Blair government in 2000, the rhetoric was considerably more positive, but the decision to join was put off once again 'until the time is right'. There were plausible economic reasons for this delay in joining in 2000, including the famous lack of synchronicity between the economic cycles of the UK and those of other EU states, and the advantages of avoiding early problems with the new arrangements. There were also dangers, such as being excluded from the formulation of the 'rules of the game' for EMU, as well as the effects on sterling of remaining outside. But one suspects that the real motivation was political.

The Maastricht proposals had a distinctly bumpy ride. The 1992 currency crisis undermined the ERM and this has arguably never been fully restored, despite the fact that, until the end of 2000 at least, currencies have remained largely within the original bands. Above all, meeting the convergence criteria was rendered very problematic by German unification and by the early 1990s recession in the European economy. German unification meant high continental interest rates, and this exacerbated the European recession. The consequent downturn in economic activity cut government tax receipts and increased expenditure on welfare. In this context, meeting strict public debt and borrowing criteria meant bringing further deflationary bias into economies by big tax increases and severe cuts in public spending, further exacerbating the recession. The net result was record European unemployment of 17 million or more in the late 1990s, which proved very hard to reduce.

The original Maastricht proposals were supplemented in the overall EMU model by a number of agreements, the most notable of which is the Stability and Growth Pact (outlined in Box 2.4) which seeks to control post-EMU fiscal policy by projecting the Maastricht fiscal limits into the future.

Box 2.4   The Stability and Growth Pact

The essential features of the Stability and Growth Pact were agreed at the Dublin Summit of December 1996, and its final version was included in the Amsterdam Treaty of 1997. It basically aims to ensure fiscal rectitude in EMU by codifying the 'excessive deficit procedure' in the Maastricht Treaty. Countries will be free to conduct their own fiscal policy, but national budgets are to be controlled by limiting government borrowing to the Maastricht level of 3 per cent of GDP per annum, with a maximum public debt of 60 per cent of GDP. Countries will be free to spend more, but will have to raise taxes to do so, de facto severely limiting public spending in the context of a common market with its free movement of labour and capital. There will be quasi-automatic fines for those who deviate from this position.

There has been a substantial amount of political will to make the Maastricht project work, no doubt reinforced by the amount of personal political capital invested in it by former Chancellor Kohl of Germany, and the EU was heading full steam for the complete introduction of the euro in 2002 in the eleven (and perhaps as many as fourteen in the future) participants. This would itself be a momentous achievement.

Nevertheless, there are reasons for questioning the extent to which the Maastricht model provides the basis for a successful EMU which is appropriate to the needs of the European economy in this century. These concern the limited coverage and potential deflationary effects of the convergence definitions, the lack of a credible redistribution mechanism, and a 'democratic deficit' in the political control of economic policy.

Summary

- The key to the future of the European integrationist process now lies with monetary union.

- The 'Maastricht model' adopted by the EU emphasizes monetary convergence among the members, but rather neglects 'real' variables like employment and growth.

- Monetary union will be severely tested by the vagaries of the global system of financial relationships.

- Monetary union is argued to enhance economic prospects by enabling the EU countries to 'pool' their sovereignties.

7   Conclusion

In this chapter we have discussed how the economy of the EU has developed from one organized essentially around the economic governance provided by a number of discrete small and medium-sized nation states, into an increasingly integrated economy which is regulated by an EU whose influence has grown more rapidly in the economic arena than in the political fields, leaving it open to accusations of 'democratic deficit'. This economy is rooted in the free market order, but also in a concept of the free market which draws on the European social market regulatory order traditions – to the extent that this is possible in a world dominated by deregulated global capitalism.

In particular, the chapter has examined the unity and diversity in the nature and development of the European economies at the level of the nation state, the relationship between national and supranational competencies in economic governance and the relationship between European integration and national economic sovereignty, the relationship between 'globalization' and European integration, the essential dynamic features of the integration process, and the political economy of the approach by the EU and its institutions to economic governance.

The key to the future of the European integration project in the immediate future is EMU, which was proceeding within something like the conditions and timetable set out in the Maastricht Treaty. This represented both a truly momentous historical development, and an enormous challenge for the EU, since (as we have argued) the Maastricht model may pose problems for the European economy and for European citizens. Nevertheless, EMU is likely to have enormous effects, precipitating a truly integrated European economy under the aegis of a common regulatory framework provided by the EU. The position of the UK and the prospect of enlargement to the East mean that various outcomes are possible in the future, including a two-speed or even a 'variable geometry' Europe (**Lewis, 2001**).

The EU of the future could take a number of forms, for example a Europe of independent but interrelated nation states. This is the model favoured by those on the right (and a few on the left) of UK politics. Alternatively one might envisage a Europe based on some sort of federalism, which is the model favoured by many others. It is clear that the globalization of world economic relations and, in particular, the vast increase in the international mobility of capital have ushered in an era in which the ability of European citizens to exercise control over the economic aspects of their lives through the democratic process now requires certain economic policies to be conducted at a level above that of the nation state. This in many ways provides the essential rationale for economic integration in Europe (see Chapter 9).

However, there are still many imponderables concerning which policies should be pursued at which level of government. The principle of *subsidiarity* (that is, policies should be pursued at the lowest level of government compatible with their efficient implementation in order to maximize democratic accountability) calls into question the future of the current EU nation states. This is emphasized by the desire in many parts of Europe to exercise more power at the sub-national or regional level. Other questions concern the size of the EU, its relationship with other major international actors, whether the EU is in fact the appropriate level for supranational policy making, and how democratic control over EU actions can be established.

One thing that seems certain, however, is that the EU of the future will be a major economic bloc and will thus exert a great deal of influence on the world stage. To an extent, this has already been the case for some time. We have seen how the customs union (and the CAP) result in the EU acting as a trading bloc, with internal free trade and the joint management of external trade relations through the CET, and joint representation in international bodies such as GATT and the WTO. We have also seen how the common market has created the logic for common stances on internal and external labour and capital mobility. In addition, the EU has pursued a common approach toward the developing world by means of the Mediterranean policy as well as the Lomé Conventions (Chapter 1). The latter are trade and aid deals with a selected group of developing countries.

However, EMU, by cementing the internal market, by precipitating the common determination of many aspects of economic policy and governance, and by creating a major world currency, will undoubtedly enhance the EU's position as a world economic actor. So will enlargement, which will of course increase the size of the EU bloc, perhaps to about 400 million people. This holds many potential benefits for EU states, for example greater power in international bodies and negotiation, and the possibility of greater control over Europe's terms of trade. It also involves risks. There is a 'nightmare scenario' in which the world is divided into regional economic blocs which vie with each other in an increasingly aggressive and protectionist fashion. Some embryonic signs of this can be noted in the trade disputes that have broken out with the USA over the CAP and over differing regulatory frameworks in, for example, the use of hormones in meat production. This kind of tension is something which will have to be carefully defused.

References

Aitken, N. (1973) 'The effects of the EEC and EFTA on European trade: a temporal cross section analysis', *American Economic Review*, December, no.63, pp.881–92.

Allen, C., Gasiorek, M. and Smith, A. (1998) 'The competition effects of the single market', *Economic Policy*, no.27, pp.439–86.

Balassa, B. (1975) 'Trade creation and trade diversion in the European Common Market: an appraisal of the evidence' in Balassa, B. (ed.) *European Economic Integration*, Amsterdam, North Holland.

Cecchini, P. (1988) *1992: The Benefits of a Single Market*, Report on the Cost of the Non-Europe Steering Committee, Aldershot, Wildwood House.

Emerson, M., Aujean, M., Catinat, M., Goybet, P. and Jacquemin, A. (1998) *The Economics of 1992*, Oxford, Oxford University Press.

European Commission (1985) *Completing the Internal Market*, White Paper from the Commission to the European Council, Luxembourg, Office for Official Publications of the European Communities.

European Commission (1996a) *The Single Market Review, 38 Reports*, London, European Commission/Kogan Page.

European Commission (1996b) *The Impact and Effectiveness of the Single Market: Communication from the Commission to the European Parliament and Council*, Luxembourg, Office for Official Publications of the European Communities.

European Commission (1996c) *Action Plan for the Single Market: Communication from the Commission to the European Council*, Luxembourg, Office for Official Publications of the European Communities.

European Economy (1996) *Economic Evaluation of the Internal Market*, Reports and Studies No. 4, Luxembourg, Office for Official Publications of the European Communities.

International Monetary Fund (1997) *World Economic Outlook: October 1997*, Washington, DC, IMF.

Kreinin, M.E. (1972) 'The effects of the EEC on imports of manufacturers', *Economic Journal*, vol.82, September, pp.897–920.

Kreinin, M.E. (1981) 'The effect of EC enlargement on trade in manufacturers', *Kyklos*, December, pp.215–35.

Laffan, B. (2001) 'Finance and budgetary processes in the European Union' in Bromley, S.J. (ed.) *Governing the European Union*, London, Sage/The Open University.

Lewis, P.G. (2001) 'The enlargement of the European Union' in Bromley, S.J. (ed.) *Governing the European Union*, London, Sage/The Open University.

Lintner, V. (1996) 'The economic implications of enlarging the European Union' in Healey, N.M. (ed.) *The Economics of the New Europe*, London, Routledge.

Marques-Mendes, A.J. (1986) 'The contribution of the European Community to economic growth', *Journal of Common Market Studies*, XXIV, June, pp.261–77.

Mayes, D. (1978) 'The effects of economic integration on trade', *Journal of Common Market Studies*, XVII, September, pp.1–25.

Monti, M. (1996) *The Single Market and Tomorrow's Europe*, London, Commission/Kogan Page.

Myrdal, G. (1957) *Economic Theory and Underdeveloped Regions*, London, Duckworth.

Petith (1977) 'European integration and the terms of trade', *Economic Journal*, vol.87, pp.708–13.

Truman, E.M. (1969) 'The European Community: trade creation and trade diversion', *Yale Economic Essays*, no.9, Spring, pp.201–57.

Truman, E.M. (1975) 'The effects of European economic integration on the production and trade of manufactured products' in Balassa, B. (ed.) *European Economic Integration*, Amsterdam, North Holland.

United Nations (1998) *World Investment Report 1998: Trends and Determinants*, New York, United Nations.

Williamson, J. and Bottrill, A. (1971) 'The impact of customs unions on trade in manufacturers', *Oxford Economic Papers*, 23, pp.323–51.

Wincott, D. (2001) 'Law, order and administration in the European Union' in Bromley, S.J. (ed.) *Governing the European Union*, London, Sage/The Open University.

Winters, L.A. (1992) 'The welfare and policy implications of the international trade consequences of 1992', *American Economic Review*, Papers and Proceedings, May, pp.104–8.

World Trade Organisation (1998) *Annual Report 1998: International Trade Statistics*, Geneva, WTO.

Further reading

Brower, F., Lintner, V. and Newman, M. (eds) (1994) *Economic Policy Making and the European Union*, London, Federal Trust.

Edye, D. and Lintner, V. (1996) *Contemporary Europe*, London, Prentice-Hall.

Lintner, V. (2000) 'Controlling monetary union' in Hoskyns, C. and Newman, M. (eds) *Democratizing the European Union*, Manchester, Manchester University Press.

Lintner, V. and Church, C.H. (2000) *The European Union: Economic and Political Aspects*, Maidenhead, McGraw-Hill.

Strange, S. (1996) *The Retreat of the State*, Cambridge, Cambridge University Press.

Young, H. (1998) *This Blessed Plot: Britain and Europe from Churchill to Blair*, London, Macmillan.

Chapter 3
Governing European corporate life

Michael Moran

1 Introduction

At the millennium most of us, if only for superstitious reasons, expected the year 2000 to mark an important turning point. But in the field of corporate governance the early months of that year did indeed see momentous events. At the start of the year the German telecommunications giant Mannesmann was taken over, against the initial wishes of its management, by the British telecommunications firm Vodafone. Not only did the take-over amount to a huge change in the nature of a key high-technology industry, it was reportedly the first example in Germany of what is common in Britain, a successful hostile take-over. In March of the same year several thousand Rover car workers in Britain woke one morning to find that, without any public warning, the German owners of their firm, BMW, had negotiated a sale of Rover with a group of British businessmen of whom the workers had never heard. And within a few days many of these same workers realized that, as a result of the sale, they would soon be unemployed.

What do these two headline issues have to do with this chapter? The answer is that both the take-over and the sale raise issues about corporate governance. And as the examples make clear, the dry phrase 'corporate governance' involves some very important social issues concerning how corporations should be run, how ownership rights should be organized, and what interests should be taken into account when those rights are disposed of. As we shall see shortly, these issues are also at the centre of wider questions about the governance of European economies.

This chapter examines these matters, first by explaining what we mean by corporate governance. It then sketches some important national styles of corporate governance and explains how they are changing. It summarizes what we presently know about the role of the European Union (EU) in corporate governance. Finally, it links the subject to the wider themes of this book by asking how far the development of corporate governance in

Europe is strengthening either a 'market order' or a 'regulatory order' (Chapters 1 and 10).

2 Corporate governance

The economies of the member states of the EU are all, in their different ways, market economies, and the business firm is probably the single most important institution in such economies. Most of the things that make an economy tick happen through firms, big and small: investment in buildings and machinery; turning that investment into goods and services; employing and organizing the workforce; and marketing the goods and services produced by that workforce. It is no exaggeration to say: no business firms, no market economy. That alone explains why understanding corporate governance is important to understanding how the economy is governed in Europe. But what is 'corporate governance'? The question is easy to pose but difficult to answer.

2.1 Why 'governance'?

In recent years a tremendous amount of ink has been spilt in establishing the distinctiveness, supposed or otherwise, of the 'governance' approach to the study of institutions (Chapter 1; **Bromley, 2001a**). In essence, 'governance' refers to a process by which institutions are linked in complex, mutually dependent networks, thus ruling out the possibility of governing through the simple exercise of governmental authority in a hierarchical manner. There is consequently one particular way in which the language of 'governance' hints at something important about how firms are governed in a market economy. Firms can often run their affairs in ways that make them highly independent of their surroundings, including that part of their environment that consists of the state. They can also be run in a very hierarchical, authoritarian way. A whole sub-industry in business studies is devoted to examining exactly these kinds of leadership styles in firms. But authority in the firm cannot, in the last analysis, be generated solely from within the firm itself. Ultimately, it rests on the legal standing of the enterprise and that legal standing is conferred by the state – whether sub-national, national or supranational. In other words, the firm is embedded in a network of institutions, among the most important being the legal and administrative institutions of states. Authority in the firm reflects its place in this network, and that place is typically the result of a complex historical evolution involving both the development of legal and institutional forms and the development of notions about the purposes of firms.

In looking at how the corporation is governed we are therefore looking at something different from government in the modern state: we are looking partly at how the firm relates to the state, and partly at debates about the purposes of the corporation. In so far as the specialized use of 'governance' has a point here, its purpose is to hint at this distinctiveness in the governing of the firm.

2.2 Defining corporate governance

If the firm is the linchpin of the market economy, then potentially almost every aspect of government intervention in an economy impinges on its governance. After all, everything from the biggest decisions about tax policy to the most minute details about health and safety legislation affects how firms run themselves internally. If we adopted this expansive notion of corporate governance, however, almost everything that happens in a market economy – and certainly virtually everything done by government to influence a market economy – would be relevant to this chapter. For our purposes we need a more precise definition of the subject.

The task of definition is not a straightforward one. Indeed, the way different people, and, more importantly, different nations, define corporate governance actually reveals a great deal about how they think the corporation should be run. Consider the following example of a definition from a very good survey of corporate governance in Europe: 'Corporate governance refers in essence to the organization of the relationship between owners and managers of a corporation' (Lannoo, 1999, p.271). The most striking feature of this definition is what it omits. It says nothing about the wide range of groups other than managers and owners whose interests are affected by the activities of the corporation, especially the big corporation. To highlight the most obvious omission of all: the definition is silent about the role of workers. Yet we shall see that some national systems in Europe formally include workers or their representatives in the governing institutions of firms, while others make no such provision. The example illustrates how any definition we apply affects not only the range of institutions and groups that we study, it also, by implication, conveys a view about who should, and who should not, have a claim to a say in corporate governance. If corporate governance were indeed about the relations between owners and managers then we would take no interest in worker participation, and would not expect systems of corporate governance to include provision for employee representation (see Chapters 4 and 5).

The issue of defining the proper domain of corporate governance is actually just a special case of a wider problem already raised in the Introduction to Chapter 1: how to define the 'economic' domain. We saw there that 'what constitutes the legitimate boundaries around what is called "economic analysis" might just as well be the result of luck, fate or power considerations as the result of some "natural" economic attributes' (p.2). Likewise, there is nothing 'natural' about the domain of corporate governance; how it is defined – in particular, how narrowly or widely it is defined – has important consequences for deciding who is 'included' and who 'excluded' in the struggle for control of the corporation. As in all political struggles (and, in essence, this is what lies at the root of arguments over corporate governance), people, interests and issues can be admitted into the arena, or kept out, by the very way the subject is defined.

Our purpose here is to understand how firms are governed, not to advance some particular set of prescriptions about how they should be governed. We need to avoid any particular view of who should be included, and who excluded, from corporate governance. That suggests we should err on the side of an inclusive, rather than exclusive, definition. Corporate governance, as used here, is therefore defined as follows: the organization of the relationship between the most important interests affected by the activities of corporations – owners, managers, workers, consumers and the state.

Some systems of governance will try to include all these interests; others will not. Our definition is particularly useful for what we are trying to do here – to make a comparative examination of corporate governance in different countries – since it alerts us to look for differences in how nations conceive of the proper scope of corporate governance. At the same time, it does not commit us to the view that all these interests should be formally included in the institutions of corporate governance, still less to any view about how the institutions should be run. It offers us a broad, rather than narrow, approach; but the focus on the way firms are organized for purposes of governance means that we do not have to look at the whole picture of how government economic intervention impinges on the internal running of firms.

2.3   Issues in corporate governance

Why are issues to do with corporate governance so important? We can begin to understand why if we appreciate something about the historical development of the large modern corporation. When modern industrial economies of the sort that we are familiar with in Britain first developed, the structure of firms was by modern standards fairly simple. The typical firm was 'owner controlled'. In other words, the individual or small group of individuals who owned the enterprise also controlled day-to-day management. But even by the beginning of the twentieth century a different pattern had emerged, notably in the biggest firms that soon dominated advanced industrial economies.

These firms were mostly 'joint stock' concerns of some kind. This meant that ownership was usually divided among large numbers of holders of stock in the firm, the ownership of shares often being traded on stock exchanges. Meanwhile, specialized strata of managers took the daily decisions in the firm. These managers might own – though they did not need to own – a significant chunk of the firm. The key point was that they owed their importance not to ownership but to the authority that came from the managerial positions they occupied in the firm and to the specialized expertise they possessed. There had thus occurred, in the most important firms, a separation of ownership from daily management. This explains why corporate governance is indeed so centrally concerned with the relations between owners and managers. For instance, some of the classic studies of the rise of managers argued that there had actually taken place a *separation of ownership from control*. In other words, the power in firms was no longer exercised by the legal owners but by a specialized élite of managers. That suggestion – if true – obviously had very wide implications for the distribution of power in capitalist economies, implications going well beyond even the important matter of who controlled firms.

The historical setting of the rise of managers in firms explains two important features of discussions of corporate governance, features that recur in the rest of this chapter.

- First, the discussion about the governance of corporations applies particularly to the biggest corporations. In the simplest sense, any enterprise, even the smallest garage that employs a couple of mechanics, has to be governed because there has to be someone who directs how it will run and be responsible for the lawful conduct of its affairs. But the complexities of corporate governance only really emerge with corporations where owners become separate from managers. It is precisely these corporations that are typically the biggest, and therefore the most influential, firms in modern market economies.

- Second, this separation between ownership and management means that how ownership is organized is a critical matter in corporate governance. In addition, the way ownership is organized (whether it is widely dispersed or controlled by a small circle, whether it changes frequently through sale in the market) is deeply affected by the nature of the financial system in any economy. This is because it is the financial system – and in particular the way banks and stock exchanges operate – that has a vital effect on the way corporate ownership is organized. This is why, as we shall see later, many of the important national differences in corporate governance are tied in with national differences in the way financial systems are organized.

Summary

- The firm is embedded in a network of institutions, among the most important being the legal and administrative institutions of states; authority in the firm reflects its place in this network.

- There is no 'obvious' definition of corporate governance.

- Corporate governance inevitably raises issues of inclusion and exclusion, and conflict and consensus over the form of governance.

- We need a definition which does not commit us to any particular view of who should be entitled to a say in governing the firm.

- The origin of corporate governance issues can be found in the historical separation of ownership from control.

- The question of *ownership* and its entitlements is at the heart of issues to do with corporate governance.

3   Corporate governance and European competition

We have seen, then, why corporate governance is so important within individual countries. Since the firm is probably the single most important institution in a market economy, how it is governed is a key matter for the functioning of the economy. This also begins to explain why the subject is so important for the wider government of the European economy: if we want to understand what sort of economic government is being established in the EU and beyond, we have to get some sense of what the Union is doing, if anything, about the governance of firms.

There is also an important analytical reason for getting to grips with the governance of firms, and it links to the wider themes of this book. This reason is connected to the kind of judgement we make about the sort of economic order the EU is creating (see also **Bromley, 2001a**). The inspiration for the original 'Common Market' (a phrase actually used in the founding Treaty of Rome in 1957) was to free the separate national economies from barriers to competition. That involved a commitment to remove all tariffs and other restrictions on trade within the new market, and a commitment to prohibit practices that stood in the way of competition between member states: in short, both removing barriers to competition and then making sure there was a level playing field between the competitors. That aim was reaffirmed in the Single European Act (SEA) of 1986, which was designed to rejuvenate the process of economic integration by completing the creation of a single internal market between member states by 1992. The revised treaty that came out of the SEA included a commitment to an 'internal market, [which] shall comprise an area without internal frontiers in which the free movement of goods, persons and services is ensured'.

Notice a feature of this commitment that turns out to be vital to understanding what is happening to corporate governance. Free movement of goods and services is not going to happen automatically; nor will it happen just because of the removal of barriers to trade, opening up to competition firms that have developed in very different national economic environments. Some positive intervention is needed to ensure that these very different national environments do not result in competitive advantage for some at the expense of others. In Chapter 1 we saw that there is an established debate between observers of the modern economy about whether it would be best organized as a 'regulatory order' or a 'market order': in other words, whether markets should be built and shaped by the conscious development of regulations and institutions or whether they can emerge spontaneously. Whatever the outcome of this general debate, however, there can be no argument about the present state of corporate governance across Europe: it is a complex mosaic of unity and diversity produced by long histories of regulation, shaped by different national legal traditions, state structures and economic institutions. Removing barriers will simply expose to competition firms that have to operate in very different national regulatory environments. That is why the notion of making a 'level playing field' is so often used in discussions about how to create a single internal market in the EU.

A level playing field could be created by two very different means. One way is to 'level down' by establishing as free and equal as possible a competitive environment for everybody through deregulation. That way would involve strengthening a *market order* across the European economy. An alternative is to 'level up': to create equality of competition by obliging those with lower regulatory standards to match those with higher. The effect of creating a single internal market in this way is to strengthen a *regulatory order*; the paradoxical effect of creating a single competitive market would therefore be to increase controls over economic life. (This is a theme we shall return to later.)

One of the most striking features of the EU is that its member states have very different traditions of corporate governance. Thus, issues of corporate governance go to the heart of the problem of creating the level playing field because the rules by which firms have to live can have a profound effect on their ability to compete in markets. In the next section we sketch some of these national differences.

Summary

- The original mission of the Common Market implied a reduction of controls over the corporations.

- However, 'creating a level playing field' in practice often involves an increase in controls.

4   National systems of corporate governance

There are (currently) fifteen member states of the EU. All, to some degree, have their own distinctive histories of economic government – which also means that all, to some degree, have distinctive histories and institutional arrangements as far as the government of the firm is concerned. It is impossible here to summarize all these different systems. How might we choose which are useful for us to concentrate on? Two grounds are particularly appropriate: those suggested by the wider themes of this book, and those to do more immediately with corporate governance. Fortunately, choosing these grounds makes our task a little easier since both point us in the same direction: to a concentration on two cases, the German and the British.

- *Germany and the new Europe*
  Recall from the opening chapter of this book a critical point made about the historical origins of the movement to create a single economic and political space in Europe: 'It was anticipated that the form of economic and political reconstruction in Europe after the [Second World] war would solve once and for all the "German problem" – it would lock (West) Germany into a system of liberal market relationships, *and* into a system of constitutional arrangements with its neighbours, that would prevent a repeat of the inter-war experience in continental Central Europe' (Chapter 1, Section 2, p.8). We can assume that for Britons, the critical matter is how the UK fits into the project for European integration. But from the viewpoint of the wider integration project the critical question is what is happening in the German context? It is how Germany is fitted into the new Europe, and how Germany shapes that new Europe, that is the critical matter – both because of the historical origins of the whole integration project and because the German economy is the biggest in the Union. So when we look at corporate governance we need especially to understand the German system.

- *The special nature of corporate governance in Germany and the UK*
  The actual system of corporate governance in Germany gives us our second important reason for focusing on the German case and makes clear why the British case is also so important. We shall see that the two systems spring from two very different philosophies of economic life and in many respects these two philosophies have been struggling for ascendancy in the EU over the last three decades.

However, this focus on Germany and the UK needs to be understood in the light of two cautionary thoughts. First, we should remember that Germany and the UK do not set the pattern for the whole of Europe. Indeed, the British system is something of an oddity viewed from across the Channel. The German system, by contrast, has been a pioneer, imitated by a small family of nations, mostly those historically connected to the Germanic world, such as Austria. In addition, many of the candidate EU member states to the east are being encouraged to follow a German style of corporate governance as they prepare for entry into the EU. Thus the German system receives special attention here because it has been important in debates about how the EU itself should organize corporate governance. What is more, one of the outstanding features of the *style* of German governance – the tendency to document things as law – strongly resembles other national styles, notably the French. Second, like national systems everywhere, the German and British ones are constantly changing – a particularly important point in these two large and complex national economies, exposed as they are to forces for change both within the EU itself and in the wider international economy. Indeed, as we shall see in the final section of the chapter, this whole question of the relationship between tradition and transformation and the meaning of change turns out to be critical to how we characterize corporate governance in Europe now.

4.1 Corporate governance in Germany

We turn to the German system first, viewing it from the vantage point of Britain. Viewed thus, it looks highly distinctive in four important ways: its institutional structure; its philosophy concerning the range of interests entitled to be represented in the governing of corporations; the role of law in corporate governance; and its patterns of ownership and control.

- *Institutional structure*
  The institutional structure of corporate governance is easily the most distinctive feature that strikes any outside observer of German economic life. The most important firms have a dual-board system – best interpreted as a distinctively German solution to the problems created by the historical separation of management and ownership (referred to above). I call it 'dual' rather than 'two-tier' to avoid the suggestion that there is a 'lower', less influential, tier. The two parts of the system are a 'supervisory board' (*Aufsichtsrat*) and a 'management board' (*Vorstand*). The supervisory board is chosen from a mixture of groups – shareholders, employees, and externally nominated trade unions. The formal functions of the supervisory board are wide and potentially important: authorizing the company accounts and dividends to shareholders; approving decisions about major capital expenditures and acquisitions; and, maybe most important of all, appointing the management board. The management board is drawn from the senior managers of the enterprise and is responsible for the daily operational control of the firm.

- *Philosophy of representation*
  Although it leaves open the vital question of what is the balance of power between the two aspects of corporate governance, the institutional structure just described does make absolutely clear the distinctive German philosophy about the range of interests that are entitled to a say in governing firms. This distinctiveness is encapsulated in the German idea of 'co-determination'. Ownership (of shares in the concern) is one important basis of entitlement; but, as the position of trade unions and employees on supervisory boards shows, it is not the only one. When added to a widespread (and legally enforced) system of works councils within enterprises obliging managers to consult widely with employees, these institutional arrangements all add up to the distinctive philosophy of 'co-determination'; that is, to the idea that the main 'social partners' should all have a right to be consulted in the business of management. The widely used phrase 'social partners' indicates the German philosophy: that firms

are to be seen as coalitions of interests between a range of partners, not as the sole property of shareholders who hire labour for the business of production (also discussed in Chapters 1, 4, 5 and 8).

- *The importance of law*
  It is a matter for debate how far these ideals of partnership actually shape decision making in firms. What is undeniable is that they are embodied, in a special way, in the legal system itself. The institutional arrangements summarized above are enforced in law, and this legal enforcement is rooted in a distinctive philosophy of property embodied in the most fundamental German law of all – the so-called 'Basic Law' (the German constitution). The constitution's commitment to an explicit philosophy of property ownership is found in Article 14: 'property imposes duties. Its use should also serve the public weal'.

  The importance of law is further reflected in wider features of economic life, which bear in important ways on corporate governance. For example, much of the work of economic regulation in Germany is done by institutions like stock exchanges (there are several) and, at local level, by chambers of commerce, the latter having a much more prominent role in regulation than is the case with their counterparts in Britain. Both stock exchanges and chambers of commerce are examples of a very characteristic German institution, the Public Law Body. Public Law Bodies, though run by private interests, are regulated by statute, and wield powers over their members which are legal in character. In short, the system of corporate governance in which law plays a central role is just part of a wider economy in which legal regulation plays a central role.

- *Patterns of ownership and control*
  A good deal of what we have summarized thus far does not necessarily tell us much about the everyday practical realities of corporate governance – it bears on formal institutional arrangements and social philosophy. But this fourth and final feature of governance in the German system concerns not matters of legal form or institutional structure but practical patterns of ownership and control. The history of shareholding and investment in big firms in Germany has been highly distinctive. Historically, dealing in the shares of firms on stock exchanges has been comparatively unimportant.

  The centrepiece of the system has been the dominant position of a comparatively small number of banks as holders of substantial chunks of ownership in various guises. This is connected to historically distinctive features of the German financial system, and reinforces a point made earlier – that the nature of the financial system has a profound effect on corporate governance. Three historically established features of the financial system should be highlighted: banks have been unusually important as sources of investment capital for German industry; banks have, partly in consequence, been unusually important in the daily government of firms, reflected in part in their presence on the supervisory boards of corporations; and ownership of corporations has typically been controlled in large blocks, either by banks directly or by banks acting on behalf of other owners.

The overall pattern that this suggests is one where power and control in big firms are in the hands of a fairly small number of groups, with the biggest banks exercising a very important role, directly in making critical decisions and indirectly in co-ordinating the activities of the biggest owners. Table 3.1 illustrates this with an analysis of the holdings of two major German banks and an insurance company; the figures show not only the importance of holdings in leading industrial economies but also how important in turn are cross-holdings between leading financial institutions.

Table 3.1 The web of ownership in German corporate governance (percentage of stock held in selected firms at 31 December 1999)

Deutsche Bank	%	Allianz Insurance	%	Dresdner Bank	%
Daimler Chrysler	11.9	Dresdner Bank	21.7	Allianz	10.0
Allianz	7.0	Deutsche Bank	5.0	BMW	5.0
Münchener Rück	9.6	Münchener Rück	25.0	Münchener Rück	9.3
Heidelberger Zement	8.7	Hypo and Vereinsbank	17.4	Karstadt	10.0
Linde	10.0	Karstadt	14.2	Heidelberger Z.	20.8
Continental	8.0	RWE	10.1	Continental	5.3

(*Evening Standard*, 18 January 2000, p.45)

The German system summarized here might be described as the 'classical' German mode: dual-board corporate governance; an inclusive philosophy of representation; extensive legal regulation; and a bank-dominated system of financial control. As we shall see later, there is evidence that it is changing, but we postpone examining this for a moment to describe the very different system in the UK.

4.2 Corporate governance in the UK

As an alternative to the German case just discussed, we can now look at a somewhat different case, that of the system in the UK. This in many ways demonstrates features which are in direct contrast to those just outlined.

- *Institutional structure*
  Institutionally, the British system prescribes only a unitary-board structure in which there is none of the formal separation between a supervisory board and a management board that marks the German system. In the 1970s there was an extended debate about the possibility of worker representation on boards, but proposals for worker representation that might eventually have led to a dual-tier structure were decisively rejected and have never been resurrected. In practice, the largest companies usually have boards that are made up of executive and non-executive directors. The latter, as outsiders to the full management of the enterprise, might be expected to play some of

the roles of a supervisory board, but this is not something that is prescribed in the formal institutional rules.

- *Philosophy of representation*
  As the reference to the failed attempt to introduce worker representation on boards in the 1970s shows, there is an obvious connection between institutional design and the underlying philosophy of representation. This philosophy gives primacy to ownership of a legal stake in an enterprise (usually in the form of share ownership) as the basis of entitlement to a say in governing the firm. Of course in practice, in the daily struggle for control in firms, a wide range of interests get their voices heard; and even in law some interests (for example, creditors of a firm) have legally enforceable entitlements. But in the critical issue of corporate governance – who gets a place on the board of directors – shareholders are the sole interest with entitlement. Ownership is thus the only legitimate basis for a claim to an established say in the governing structure of the firm.

- *The role of law*
  There is a long-established legal framework governing the internal affairs of enterprises. Indeed, historically the most important kind of company – that incorporated with limited liability – is the result of major innovations in legal form during the nineteenth century. The most important British enterprises are thus creatures of the law. But the law has traditionally practised a light touch as far as control is concerned. Britain has no written constitution so there can be no question of the sort of commitments relevant to corporate governance that are embedded in the German constitutional system. A couple of examples make the point. Until recently many of the most important rules governing the biggest enterprises arose because of the need to comply with those required for a listing on the London Stock Exchange – and the Stock Exchange was an independent body that regulated its own affairs independent of the law. (This contrasts with what we noted earlier about the public law status of stock exchanges in Germany.) As we shall see, the law became much more important than hitherto in corporate governance in the UK in the 1980s and 1990s, but a second example from the 1990s shows the continuing marginality of the statute book in governance issues. Probably the biggest single governance issue in Britain in the 1990s concerned the role of non-executive directors, because of their potential importance in checking the power of full-time managers. But discussion of this issue in Britain in the 1990s largely took place in a series of committees and working parties convened by the business community itself, and was designed both to develop a self-regulatory code governing the conduct of directors and to head off any legal intervention in this aspect of corporate governance.

- *Patterns of ownership and control*
  The most commonly noticed feature of the practice of ownership and control in the British system is, in short, that banks have enjoyed nothing like the central role that has historically marked the position in Germany. The British system has been stock-market driven. Stock-

markets emerged early as important sources of finance for capital investment. The London Stock Exchange in the years after the Second World War gained a role as a major international exchange. Dealings in the shares of firms (and the actual or potential threat of takeovers leading to more takeovers) are a critical influence on corporate decision making – especially when we recall that this is combined with the philosophy of representation which gives shareholders the primary entitlements in corporate governance.

- *Comparison with the German system*
  Table 3.2 summarizes the contrasting features of the 'classic' German and British models.

Table 3.2 The classic German and British models of corporate governance

	Germany	*UK*
Governing structure	dual-board	unitary-board
Philosophy of representation	inclusive	exclusive
Role of law	pervasive	marginal
Ownership	bank dominated	stock-market dominated

Summary

- The German system of corporate control is something of a paradigmatic case for the way continental European corporate governance is organized.

- The British system, while something of an oddity in Europe, represents an alternative pole of governance.

- German corporate governance represents a ' highly organized' and regulated system, with a good deal of networked interdependence and legal underpinning.

- The UK system is more antagonistic in structure, with light-touch legal regulation and 'decentralized' ownership and control.

5   Patterns of change in national systems

Sketching the German and the British models in this way helpfully illuminates the range of national styles of corporate governance 'on offer' in the EU. It bears repeating that these two systems do not exhaust the variety of national possibilities. They do, though, helpfully crystallize the range of choice open in trying to build a system of corporate governance for the EU as a whole. But no national system is static and changes at the national level are reworking corporate governance in ways that have big implications for the wider European pattern. What are the most important changes taking place at national level?

5.1 Privatization

The first change concerns the impact of privatization. Although there is a European (indeed global) wave of privatization its impact is most significant in the UK. At first glance the impact of privatization on corporate governance looks straightforward: it seems to shift enterprises that formerly were under various kinds of public control to the realm of the private corporation, and thus to strengthen traditionally established national systems of corporate governance. But the effect is more ambiguous than this superficial expectation suggests. It has been extremely rare for a public enterprise simply to be transformed into a private company. A wide range of devices has been developed to ensure that public authorities retain a significant say in governing the enterprise. In the UK these have included, for instance, the retention in some cases of a 'Golden Share' by the state – a stake in the equity of the privatized enterprise which allows the state a large say (typically a right of veto) over corporate decisions. In some cases (the privatization of railway services is a good example) privatization consists of 'franchising', in that the state awards a licence to enterprises to provide a service for a designated period, but stipulates in close detail a large number of conditions that the franchisee must obey. Finally, and most significantly, the state has almost universally developed a distinctive model of regulation for the newly privatized industries that involves a much more intrusive control of internal corporate affairs (stretching from oversight of institutional structures to detailed control of pricing policy) than has hitherto been the case with private enterprises.

The growth of this regulatory sphere is by no means trivial: the regulated sector in the privatized industries covers some of the most dynamic parts of modern economies (such as telecommunications) and the most fundamental parts (such as energy, water and transport). What is more, the rise of this kind of regulation has begun to spill over into areas where more traditional kinds of corporate forms once dominated. For example, in the financial services industries (banking, securities, and insurance) there has occurred in virtually every member state of the Union a growth in the extent of regulation of the internal institutional structures and many of the management practices of enterprises.

In short, there is a connection between the rise of a regulated privatized corporate sector and the second major change identified in this section, that of the growth of legal controls.

5.2   The rise of legal controls

The 1980s and 1990s were often spoken of as the age of deregulation. This would lead us to expect that these decades saw a lightening of legal controls over corporate governance. The reverse was actually the case, especially in respect of enterprises in financial markets – a key sector, as we have already seen, for the wider pattern of corporate governance. Two linked developments took place.

First, in those systems (like the UK) where markets had historically been ruled by self-regulatory bodies largely independent of the law and the state, comprehensive legal changes were instituted, transforming the self-regulatory bodies into institutions that were both subjected to legal controls and exercised such controls over their own members. One way of viewing this is to see it as a trend across the EU for systems to converge on the German model of a legally pervasive system of corporate control.

At the same time, a second set of changes altered the significance of Public Law Bodies in the German system: the law began to take a much closer interest in their workings and constitution, in part attempting to force them to reform in an 'Anglo-American' direction. In the 1990s, for instance, the German stock exchange system was obliged to undergo wholesale reform in order to encourage many of the trading practices that had made London such a successful international financial centre. The result was to encourage a convergence in the culture and organization of financial markets, whereas historically the differences between nationally organized financial markets had been one of the key sources of national differences in systems of corporate governance.

5.3   Convergence in ownership and control

The stark contrast between bank domination and stock-market domination has begun to reduce. If there is some evidence of a convergence on a system of more legally controlled corporate governance, there is also some evidence of a convergence on patterns of ownership and control that resemble the British pattern. Probably the most important source of this is changes in the character of financial systems that, as we noted at the beginning, are critical to the practical workings of corporate governance. The distinctiveness of national financial systems is being eroded in three ways.

- First, the increasing organization of financial markets on an international scale (a scale that typically, indeed, transcends the EU) is eroding the distinctiveness of separate national systems, and in the process is destroying one of the key factors that gave national systems of corporate governance their distinctiveness (discussed in Chapters 6,

7 and 8). When big firms begin to have their shares listed on exchanges outside their country of origin they obviously begin to be exposed to sources of influence other than those from their own national traditions.

- Second, the linchpin of distinctive systems of corporate governance – the national financial system – is showing signs of convergence. For example, in Germany until quite recently many of the methods and practices that marked out stock-markets in the UK and the USA (for example the invention of a wide range of new financial instruments) were strongly resisted. That resistance has crumbled as the German system (and especially the leading financial centre, Frankfurt) has tried to reorganize so as not to lose business to foreign competitors, notably London.

- Finally, this de facto process of integration has produced pressure to align standards of regulation between centres. For example, until quite recently there were very different standards governing insider trading in different financial centres. (Insider trading is dealing in stock on the basis of information acquired as a privileged insider, for instance as a member of a corporate board.) In the last decade there has been great pressure to apply common standards governing insider trading to the different centres in Europe.

One big source of pressure for regulatory change of this sort is the institutions of the EU itself. This brings us naturally to the direct role of the EU in corporate governance.

Summary

- National systems of corporate governance are being reshaped by a mixture of public policy and economic forces.

- Privatization, the rise of the law and changes in ownership structures are the most important reshaping forces.

- The progressive internationalization of financial activity, in particular, is having a profound impact on national and European systems.

6   The EU and corporate governance

Corporate governance in the EU is an intensely political matter, but the politics happens in many different arenas. Some of these are arenas of *high politics* and some are of *low politics* (**Heffernan, 2001**). This is a crude distinction but one that alerts us to something very important.

Many critical issues are argued out at the very highest and most public levels of the Union's institutions, the most obvious example being the bargaining that produces results in the meetings of the European Council of Ministers, or in the meetings of heads of government. These products of high politics, even when they do not focus on issues of corporate governance, nevertheless will 'spill over' to the government of the firm in important ways. Consider an important motive of the SEA: to increase co-operation between big firms across Europe, not just to promote integration but to make the European economy more competitive internationally against the other big trading groups in the world economy, like the USA and Japan. This sort of co-operation – for instance on research and technology policy (Chapter 6) – also has extensive implications for corporate governance, for example in influencing the legal basis of joint ventures between firms from different legal jurisdictions. Similarly, the decision of the new Labour Government in Britain in 1997 to sign up to the 'social' provisions of the Maastricht Treaty gave a sharp push to the increased regulation of the workplace across the Union.

High politics is the sort that dominates news headlines. But the Union is a complex political arrangement with many layers involving large numbers of institutions, and most of its business – and most hard negotiating – is done in the routines of these institutions. The politics of corporate governance in the EU, like the politics of most policy areas, is thus a form of *low politics*. What that phrase conveys is not that the politics is in some way discreditable, but that it tends to take place mostly beyond media and public scrutiny, typically concerns highly technical issues that are beyond the understanding of people other than those well versed in a particular subject, and often involves bargaining and argument within the institutions whose job it is to deal with the daily business of the Union, of which the two most important supranational bodies are the Commission and the European Court of Justice (**Bromley, 2001a**).

The role of the Court introduces another important distinction in the political process. The Union can be considered a system of government that – unlike the British system, for instance – has its own written constitution. The 'constitution' consists of the original founding Treaty of Rome and the successive amendments made at important historical moments in the life of the Union, for instance that marked by the Single European Act of 1986. The provisions of the Treaty, and of rules made under the Treaty, are binding on members, and the role of the Court is to adjudicate on whether particular practices conform to these. But the Court's job is not a mechanical one. Constitutional adjudication is a business that leaves much room for discretion and interpretation (**Bromley, 2001b**; **Wincott, 2001**). As a result, adjudications by the Court – often on highly abstruse questions – can have an important effect. One result is that there is a tendency for policies to develop in two (linked) channels: in a *de jure* way, meaning that they are the result of a binding legal process; and in a *de facto* way, meaning that they take place beyond these legal channels. In respect of corporate governance, high and low politics and *de jure* and *de facto* processes are all at work.

The single most striking feature of the high politics of corporate governance in the Union is its slow and tortuous nature. The most obvious place for 'high politics' to begin is by addressing the central issues of corporate governance of the sort that we saw earlier: issues to do with the legal personality of corporations and with their internal governing structures. This is exactly what has so far, after over thirty years of negotiation, proved to be impossible. The most important proposal in this respect is the so-called draft fifth Directive on company law, designed to create a Europe-wide statute regulating the structure of the company and the terms of employee participation. Negotiations started as long ago as 1966 and have yet to be concluded. The most important sticking points will by now be familiar to us: they involve a clash between the different philosophies of representation discussed in our account of national systems. The early discussions (which of course took place before the UK's accession in 1973) were heavily influenced by Germany and so reflected the German commitment to co-determination as a model of corporate governance; it is precisely this model that the British, since their accession, have consistently refused to accept.

This example shows the obvious difficulty with high politics in this area. Issues that involve the high principles of corporate governance inevitably draw in the most senior political actors, representing national governments. These naturally defend well-established national principles, and the rules of decision in the Union – notably the emphasis on unanimity in making critical decisions – mean that opposing member states with deeply opposing interests or philosophies can veto each other. The clash of 'conflict' and 'consensus' drives this particular dynamic.

The sensitivities of high politics have produced a number of responses. The most important way the Council of Ministers makes 'law' for the whole Union is by agreeing Directives. But Directives, like any other laws, can be drafted in many different ways. They can, in particular, either lay down with great precision what member states must do, or they can lay out general principles and allow member states a large amount of freedom as to how they put those into practice in their own national laws. The latter has been the characteristic course taken with Directives regulating company affairs – the institutional reform of stock exchanges, the reform of laws dealing with insider trading and the effort to create Union-wide rules governing the reporting of company accounts all have these features. In other words, the response is to push the policy-making process down to the domain of 'low' politics.

The roles of the Court and of the European Commission in issues of corporate governance illustrate well how the routines of 'low politics' fill the gaps that high politics leave. The creative use of the Court's famous *Cassis de Dijon* judgement of 1979 provides a good illustration of how abstruse legal rulings can be employed (**Wincott, 2001**). The judgement (which ruled that a good or service produced legally in one member state could be legally produced and sold in any other member state even if it was produced to standards different from those enforced domestically in the latter) meant that free movement of goods and services was possible without harmonization of standards across the Union. Perhaps the most creative use of this judgement for corporate governance is in the banking sector, where the reasoning has been used to create a 'passport' system allowing banks accredited in one member state of the Union to gain recognition across the entire Union. On the part of the Commission, perhaps the most creative expansion of power has been in the field of competition policy, where an expansive interpretation of powers conferred by the Treaty of Union has allowed the directorate concerned with competition policy to intervene against collusion in markets by firms, levying substantial fines on some big corporations (Chapter 8).

Summary

- The key institutions of the Council of Ministers, the Commission and the Court have helped shape the EU's approach to corporate governance.

- The EU, however, reshapes corporate governance as much through the 'low' politics of root and detail as through 'high' politics of ministerial negotiation.

- The 'low' politics of judicial change is a particularly important influence.

7 Sources of change in European corporate governance

We saw earlier that national systems of corporate governance are changing. The same is true, of course, at the level of the Union itself. What are the key developments that affect how corporate governance evolves?

Changes in the scale and scope of the Union itself

The original Common Market consisted of six members; in 2000 there were fifteen members of the single market and negotiations were already beginning for the accession of a number of others from the former Communist bloc in Eastern Europe. Increasing the size of the Union in this way has two consequences, one obvious and one less obvious. Unless there is some significant change in decision rules to weaken the ability of small minorities to veto policy proposals, it makes agreement on change more difficult. There is indeed a long-term tendency in the Union to widen the area of decision making by majority rule and this pattern may in future extend to company law. But the less obvious consequence is much more important. There are already Union states with very different traditions of corporate governance. The likely addition of former Communist bloc members will bring in states which have radically different histories, and only since the end of the 1980s have they begun to build a system of law appropriate to a market economy where the firm is a key institution.

Changes at national level

As far as corporate governance is concerned the most important consideration is the future of the German system, both because Germany is the biggest economy in the Union and because the German system has provided one of the most influential 'models' for European corporate governance. But the German system is in question. There is now a sustained debate in Germany about the ability of the wider economy to perform effectively, and many of the features criticized in that debate – extensive legal regulation of economic life, and emphasis on consensus between the main 'social partners' – are also central to the German system of corporate governance.

Changes at firm level

The future of corporate governance is not just a matter of what happens to the law and to the framework of public institutions; it is also affected by what happens in practice to the structure of firms. Here, huge changes are taking place, partly as a result of forces within the Union and partly in response to wider international forces – changes that are described in other parts of this book (Chapters 5, 6, 7 and 9). The most important consequence for corporate governance arises from the continuing spread of the multinational corporation, which naturally organizes itself internally in a way very different from firms that operate within national boundaries. Multinational corporations are important influences in breaking down the distinctiveness and the unity of national systems. Some observers believe that in respect of the management of the workforce, for instance, the divide within national systems between multinationals and the rest is just as important as the divide between different national systems.

Changes at global level

It will by now be obvious that the EU is not sealed off from the rest of the global economic and political system: in part that wider system is shaped by what is happening to the EU, and likewise what is happening in the European economy is shaped by the global economy (Chapter 9). This is hinted at above in our discussion of the importance of multinational corporations, for the mergers and alliances that reshape corporate governance are not confined to the EU. We only have to think of the patterns of ownership in an industry like automobiles to see that the borders of the Union often bear little relationship to patterns of multinational activity. But the impact of the global system goes well beyond the mergers and more informal alliances that multinational firms create. We have seen that the reshaping of financial markets, especially of stock exchanges, is important within the EU as far as corporate governance is concerned; but that reshaping is only part of wider global reshaping of both stock-exchange practices and structures. For instance, one important area of business that has been reformed in recent years within the Union concerns the regulation of 'insider dealing' (as we noted earlier, this is share trading by people who possess information by virtue of their privileged position as insiders in firms). Yet one of the most important sources of pressure to reform the law on insider trading comes from outside Europe, notably from regulators in the USA intent on raising regulatory standards to American levels.

Summary

- Changes in the scale of the EU put great pressure on its abilities to make authoritative decisions about corporate governance.

- Changes within member states are altering the terms of debate about the likely future path of corporate governance.

- Economic changes are producing corporate sectors ever more dominated by firms attuned to global markets and influences.

8 Markets, regulation and the regulatory state

How are we to understand the process that has reshaped systems of corporate governance in Europe, and in particular how can we understand it in the light of the major themes of this book – notably, the contrast between a *market order* and a *regulatory order?* Are we seeing the strengthening of one at the expense of the other? Actually, it is possible to interpret the story in two very different ways, one consistent with the market order thesis, the other with the regulatory order thesis.

The story that suggests the ascendancy of the market order in the sphere of corporate governance starts, appropriately, with the impact of change in markets, especially in financial markets, on patterns of ownership and control in firms. It will have been clear from our earlier summary of the historical contrasts between the German and the British systems, for instance, that a key source of those contrasts lay in differing forms of financial system organization. But the last quarter century has seen a competitive revolution in financial markets. That competitive revolution began in the financial markets of the Anglo-American world, especially in its stock exchanges and, in turn, spilled over into the traditionally more tightly regulated financial systems of the mainland of Europe. As far as corporate governance is concerned the single most important impact of increasingly competitive stock exchanges is that the key to corporate control – property rights embodied in stock ownership – is the subject of aggressive trading. Perhaps the most striking symbol of this is the take-over battle, particularly the hostile take-over: high-profile struggles for ownership of large corporations which have been a characteristic feature of the British system for a generation, but which were until recently unheard of in most other European systems, especially in Germany. For many commentators, therefore, the triumph of the market-order model was signalled in 2000 by the landmark event mentioned at the beginning of this chapter: the take-over, against the initial wishes of its management, of the German telecommunications giant Mannesmann by the British telecommunications firm Vodafone.

What this episode made clear was just how far corporate governance is embedded in the wider system of financial markets. Viewed in this way, what seems to have happened is not simply a straightforward triumph of a market order over regulation. An alternative explanation of the triumph of the market order can be told in the following terms. Systems of corporate control which are stock-market driven – particularly by innovative and competitive stock markets constantly looking for ways of wringing the maximum value out of corporations for shareholders – give primacy to one set of interests in the corporation over others: they elevate shareholders over employees. It is not coincidental that where the stock-market driven systems dominate, as in Britain, there also exist very distinctive systems of industrial relations – different from the German emphasis on integrating the workforce into decision making in the firm (see Chapter 5). Similarly, it is no accident that the changes in the market for corporate control in Germany have been accompanied by soul searching about that other key feature of the German model, its consensual industrial relations system.

We can see, then, that struggles about corporate governance represent something more complex than the triumph of a spontaneously generated market order over systems of regulation. In effect, they represent the ascendancy of one system of regulation over another – a system that privileges one set of stakeholders in corporations over others. Ownership of property rights in the form of shareholdings is itself a regulatory creation; indeed, its legal character means that it is necessarily a creation of the state. What is more, we know that, while financial markets have become more competitive and innovative, they have also been subject to more detailed regulation, including legal regulation. In part at least this is due to the impact of the EU, a 'law driven' political creation in which the equivalent of a constitutional court – the European Court of Justice – is a key institution in clarifying the character of the legal creation which is the EU.

The issue of where the development of corporate governance leaves us in the debate over the *market order* versus *regulatory order* is therefore complicated. One way of simplifying this complexity can be found in the work of Majone (1996), who has offered perhaps the single most important interpretation of the character of the EU as a political creation (see also Chapters 1, 2 and 7). Majone sees the EU as a new sort of creature, at least in Europe: a 'regulatory state'. The rise of the EU as a 'regulatory state' involves a change in historically established systems of control over markets. Across Europe until recently, governments regulated markets through the device of public ownership, but much of the public sector has been dismantled by waves of privatization. Regulation is a shift to indirect control via rules imposed on private enterprise. It is a response to two developments: a general disenchantment with the effectiveness of traditional systems of direct public ownership, and – in the case of the EU – a response to the perceived impossibility, given the limited financial and administrative resources of the supranational institutions of the Union, of operating direct 'hands-on' control from Brussels. In its reliance on indirect control via national and sub-national institutions, the regulatory state anticipates the third system of governance which is sketched in the opening chapter of this book, that operating via self-organizing networks.

The regulatory state nevertheless demands active government because there are powerful pressures demanding regulation. Three are particularly important.

First, the scale and complexity of modern economies – think of the scale of the EU – means that a traditional reliance on custom and trust to govern markets is no longer adequate. That impinges directly on corporate governance: it is perhaps the single most important reason for something that figured large in this chapter, the rise of regulatory controls in big financial markets.

Second, the complexity of the big corporation itself means that there is intense pressure to regulate the relations between the big interests which it contains. This is why there has been, despite the concern with extracting value for shareholders, a sustained debate about incorporating other stakeholders, notably workers, into corporate governance.

Finally, big corporations operate in societies where there exists a widespread popular perception of vulnerability to risk – from environmental damage, from dishonesty and fraud, from failings in health and safety controls. Corporations are by no means the only institutions that pollute the environment, perpetrate fraud or endanger the health and safety of workers. But precisely because of their importance in the modern economy they are seen as important potential sources of these risks; hence part of the history of the corporation over the last generation is a history of the growth of regulatory controls – over environmental standards, over internal accounting rules and over health and safety at work (Chapter 7). The regulatory state, therefore, is not just a response to particular features of the EU; it reflects deep-seated features of the EU. It also reflects deep-seated features of modern industrial societies, and these features constantly shape and reshape how the corporation is governed.

Summary

- A new order for the corporate sector is being slowly recreated in Europe.

- That order is deeply influenced by the competitive forces of a market economy.

- The impact of competitive forces, however, is not unambiguously strengthening free markets; it is also producing a growth in the scale and complexity of regulatory controls over the corporation. This may even involve the creation of a form of 'regulatory state' body.

9   Conclusion

Two linked ideas have dominated this chapter. First, because the big firm is the centrepiece of capitalist economies in Europe, understanding how the big firm is governed is a critical clue to understanding the governance of these economies. Second, various changes in institutional practices, law and the actual workings of markets have in recent decades drastically reshaped what were once highly distinctive national systems of corporate governance.

We related these changes to the main themes of this book and concluded that they cannot be interpreted as a simple triumph of market order over regulatory order. Rather, the changes that are taking place reflect a transition from one system to another – one that involves more indirect control over the activities of private enterprise. This is reflected in suggestions that the EU can be characterized as a 'regulatory state'.

References

Bromley, S.J. (ed.) (2001a) *Governing the European Union*, London, Sage/The Open University.

Bromley, S.J. (2001b) 'The nation state in the European Union' in Bromley, S.J. (ed.) *Governing the European Union*, London, Sage/The Open University.

Heffernan, R. (2001) 'Building the European Union' in Bromley, S.J. (ed.) *Governing the European Union*, **London, Sage/The Open University.**

Lannoo, K. (1999) 'A European perspective on corporate governance', *Journal of Common Market Studies*, vol.37, no.2, pp.269–94.

Majone, G. (1996) *Regulating Europe*, London, Routledge.

Wincott, D. (2001) 'Law, order and administration in the European Union' in Bromley, S.J. (ed.) *Governing the European Union*, **London, Sage/The Open University.**

Further reading

Charkham, J. (1994) *Keeping Good Company: A Study of Corporate Governance*, Oxford, Clarendon Press. A study of corporate governance with a traditional emphasis on national differences.

Clarke, M. (2000) *Regulation: The Social Control of Business between Law and Politics*, Basingstoke, Macmillan. A good account of the wider social forces producing the demand for regulation.

Lannoo, K. (1999) 'A European perspective on corporate governance', *Journal of Common Market Studies*, vol.37, no.2, pp.269–94. Gives an overview of corporate governance issues.

Majone, G. (1996) *Regulating Europe*, London, Routledge. The definitive statement of his regulatory state thesis.

Marginson, P. and Sisson, K. (1998) 'European collective bargaining: a virtual prospect', *Journal of Common Market Studies*, vol.36, no.4, pp.505–28. Traces the changing regulation of the workplace and stresses the importance of the divide between multinational firms and the rest over national distinctiveness.

Pagoulatos, G. (1999) 'European banking: five modes of governance', *West European Politics*, vol.22, no.1, pp.68–94. Examines comparatively a key sector, banking.

Parkinson, J. (1993) *Corporate Power and Responsibility: Issues in the Theory of Company Law*, Oxford, Clarendon Press. This is now a classic on Britain and is particularly useful on the key historical development leading to modern corporate governance – the separation of ownership from control.

Scharpf, F. (1999) *Governing in Europe: Effective and Democratic?* Oxford, Oxford University Press. Issues of economic governance are discussed in an up-to-date setting, and are fixed in the context of wider European developments. Chapter 3 is particularly useful.

Young, D. and Metcalfe, S. (1997, second edition) 'Competition policy' in Artis, M. and Lee, N. (eds) *The Economics of the European Union: Policy and Analysis*, Oxford, Oxford University Press. Pages 118–38 provide an overview of both theory and practice of competition law and Europe.

Chapter 4
Governing the European macroeconomy

Graham Dawson

1 Introduction

The objectives of macroeconomic policy are to achieve certain outcomes with regard to unemployment, inflation and the balance of payments. These are ways of measuring the performance of the whole economy for which policy makers are responsible, whether it is a national economy such as the UK economy or a supranational one such as the economy of the EU. In order to try to achieve their preferred outcomes for unemployment and so on, policy makers have made use of three macroeconomic policy instruments: monetary policy, which is concerned with setting interest rates and controlling the money supply; fiscal policy, which involves decisions about government expenditure and taxation; and exchange rate policy. These policy instruments are not completely independent of each other; for example, interest rates affect the exchange rates as well as the money supply and inflation. Macroeconomics is the branch of economics that analyses the effectiveness of these policy instruments.

When the current phase of European integration, and in particular the project of Economic and Monetary Union (EMU), was announced, many economic commentators argued that its impact on the macroeconomic policies of member states would be greater than that on any other aspect of policy. 'More than any other great issue the European Community has faced, Economic and Monetary Union raises questions of national sovereignty – real and imagined [it] calls for a transfer of national power to the Community that goes beyond anything the EEC has known' (*Economist*, 22 April, 1989, p.45).

It is clear now that monetary union is a reality for many EU member states, that it has entailed a loss of national economic sovereignty over two of the three macroeconomic policy instruments. Those who are taking part in the single currency have necessarily relinquished their capacity for a national exchange rate policy. In another core commitment to monetary union, the same member states have transferred formal authority over monetary policy to the European Central Bank, the ECB (which is at the head of the European System of Central Banks). True, they continue to be in nominal command of their fiscal policies. However, as Valerio Lintner pointed out in Chapter 2, the qualifying criteria for participation in monetary union imposed stringent constraints on the budget deficit and on public sector debt, curtailing national governments' freedom to pursue expansionary fiscal policies (see also Chapter 8).

The main aim of this chapter is to clarify the issues surrounding the apparent willingness of national governments to share macroeconomic policy instruments that had been considered their own inalienable prerogative only twenty years earlier. There are three main issues to be examined here: events, theory and institutions.

- Part of the explanation for the transfer of macroeconomic sovereignty lies in the unfolding of macroeconomic events. The elevation of the fight against inflation to the top of policy makers' priorities occurred in response to the sharp and unanticipated increase in inflation in the early 1970s. Was this the predictable long-term outcome of targeting full employment, which required a revision of the Keynesian theoretical perspective that dominated the orthodox macroeconomics textbooks of the time? Or was it an external shock that would have happened whatever policy regime had been in force during the preceding years?

- Another part of any explanation lies in the evolution of macroeconomic theory from a Keynesian approach dedicated to maintaining full employment to a neo-liberal emphasis on defeating inflation so that markets can work properly (explored in Section 3). From a neo-liberal perspective national autonomy in macroeconomic policy is as much a threat as an opportunity. The argument is that national policy makers in many member states had repeatedly revealed themselves to be unable to resist the temptation to pursue policies that aimed at full employment but succeeded only in raising the rate of inflation. One way of understanding this transition from Keynesianism to neo-liberalism is as a shift in the form of economic governance from a regulated order to a market order (see Chapter 1).

- The third part of the explanation, examined in Section 4, concerns economic and political institutions and their variability across member states. Understanding the importance of institutions and their cultures adds a further layer of complexity to the theoretical narrative of evolution from Keynesianism to neo-liberalism. On both sides of the theoretical watershed, policy decisions and outcomes were influenced by cultural assumptions and by institutional arrangements. It is a matter of controversy whether all the major European economies actually followed Keynesian policies throughout the 1950s and 1960s. It is also disputed that the policies implemented, for example in the UK, under the auspices of Keynesianism were in fact true to the prescriptions of Keynes himself. Whatever view is taken on these debates, there is no doubting the influence of national cultures such as the egalitarianism of the Scandinavian model, and of national institutions, such as wage bargaining arrangements and the electoral system, on the making of macroeconomic policy. The cultural and institutional pressures that shaped macroeconomic policy in three European economies – France, Germany and the UK – will therefore be examined.

The chapter is predominantly historical in approach, as befits the discussion of a project such as economic and monetary union that is the recent culmination of a process of European economic integration sustained over half a century. In Section 5 the focus shifts to the new framework for EU macroeconomic policy that was established in 1999. A critical examination of the terms on which the participating member states agreed to launch the single European currency reveals their bias toward convergence on financial criteria such as inflation and interest rates, to the exclusion of 'real' economic variables such as unemployment rates. This appears to confirm the view that Maastricht embodies a neo-liberal orthodoxy on macroeconomic policy.

However, a review of the actual conduct of monetary policy in the first eighteen months or so of the single currency suggests otherwise. The policy of the ECB has been more pragmatic and eclectic than anticipated, mixing rules and discretion in a way that reflects a 'Keynesian' sensitivity to economic growth and unemployment as well as a 'neo-liberal' concern with the control of inflation. This might be interpreted as a qualification to the apparent willingness of participating member states to relinquish national autonomy, in that the ECB policy stance might be taken as a serious attempt to balance their different needs, traditions and preoccupations. Perhaps 'the story so far' is that national governments have not in reality had to converge on the new anti-inflation orthodoxy that seemed to be the guiding spirit of the Treaty of Maastricht.

2 Macroeconomic performance and European integration

The early stages of European integration took place against a background of strong macroeconomic performance, marked by full employment, low inflation and rapid growth. In many countries this 'golden age of capitalism' was associated with the Keynesian approach to macroeconomic policy, which was presented as a major component in the construction of a regulatory order designed to 'soften the edges' of capitalism, that is, to govern the market order in the interests of social justice. There was a broad consensus to remove the capacity of unregulated markets to cause persistent mass unemployment, by creating a framework for maintaining aggregate demand at a level sufficient to guarantee full employment. Keynesian demand management in European economies flourished in the context of an international regulatory order, Bretton Woods, which fixed exchange rates for the major currencies. Its collapse in 1970 was soon followed by a crisis in the Keynesian policy-making framework, which was to lead eventually to its replacement by monetarism.

The goal of monetarism was to eliminate inflation by controlling the money supply, as a precondition of a return to growth and full employment in the long run. Monetarism was the macroeconomic component of the larger neo-liberal policy regime based on the 'free' or relatively unregulated market. The neo-liberal revolution has had the effect of relegating macroeconomic policy to a rather less important role than it had enjoyed in the 1950s and 1960s. Demand management gave way to supply side reforms, which tackled inefficiency and uncompetitiveness in particular markets, essentially a microeconomic project. An increased degree of central bank independence has further curtailed the scope of government intervention. In this context the persistence of high unemployment in many EU countries highlights the difficulties facing macroeconomic management in an internationalizing world.

2.1 European integration and the curtailment of national macroeconomic autonomy

In the early years of post-war European integration, including the formation of the Common Market, macroeconomic policy did not figure among the main subjects for negotiation. There was no suggestion at this stage that the national autonomy of member states over monetary, fiscal and exchange rate policies would be compromised in any way. One reason for the relative neglect of macroeconomic policy may have been a consensus among member states in the prioritizing of macroeconomic policy objectives and an awareness that the macroeconomic performance of most European economies was satisfactory and needed no special attention. Gregory and Weiserbs (1998) argue that '[m]ember countries shared the same macroeconomic agenda: full employment and rising prosperity' (p.47). In this context rising prosperity can be understood as increasing GDP (gross domestic product) per head of the population; in terms of the objectives of macroeconomic policy, the member states shared a commitment to full employment and economic growth. This consensus 'was given formal expression in Article 1 of the Treaty of Rome with its explicit commitment to enhancing the prosperity of member states' (Gregory and Weiserbs, 1998, p.47).

Macroeconomic performance was exceptionally good in the years 1950–1973, not only in European economies but throughout the industrialized world, surpassing both the inter-war years and the period after 1973. The level of GDP per head increased substantially in most economies; on average the populations of these economies became significantly better off in material terms. The best performer was Japan, which reached tenth place in the GDP per head 'league table' as its level of GDP per head in 1973 was almost six times greater than in 1950. The decline of the UK from second place in 1950 to seventh in 1973 was even more striking. In the process of overtaking the UK, most European economies had also narrowed the gap with the most prosperous economy, the USA.

It is important to bear in mind, however, that GDP-per-head data gives no indication of changes in the distribution of income. The rising prosperity of the golden age was not spread evenly across all sections of society; many inequalities and injustices remained. As Sforza Pallavicino put it in 1644, in a very different context, 'the Golden Age is for those that have gold' (quoted in Andrews, 1999, p.92). Nevertheless, it was soon to appear to be a period of relative tranquillity.

It was not until the establishment of the European Monetary System (EMS) in 1979 that European integration significantly impinged upon the national economic sovereignty of member states in the macroeconomic sphere. The first macroeconomic policy instrument to be given up by the member states was the freedom to manage their own exchange rates. Their willingness to do so was largely explained by the turbulence of exchange rates during the 1970s. In this they reflected the general macroeconomic turmoil of that decade. Moreover, the freedom to manage national exchange rates had been only a recent experience, following the collapse of the Bretton Woods system of fixed exchange rates that had provided a stable framework for international trade during the 1950s and 1960s. European policy makers believed that the experiment with floating exchange rates had been one of the causes of the ensuing macroeconomic instability and sought to recreate a fixed exchange rate system, but this time in the context of the European Community.

[margin handwriting: global system had collapsed.]

[margin handwriting: regional solution.]

The virtual collapse of this system (the Exchange Rate Mechanism of the European Monetary System) in 1992 left European policy makers at both national and EU levels with a dilemma. Two fixed exchange rate systems had now collapsed, either side of a period of floating exchange rates marked by a slow-down in growth, rising unemployment and an upsurge in inflation. Furthermore, after the years of poor macroeconomic performance across the industrialized economies of the world, a much quicker recovery had been seen in the USA and Japan than in the EU. This unsatisfactory macroeconomic record relative to the European economies' main international competitors raised doubts about the whole process of European integration.

The response of the European Commission to this crisis in European integration was radical and imaginative. In 1985 the Commission published a White Paper, *Completing the Internal Market* (Commission of the European Communities, 1985), proposing nothing less than the accomplishment of a further stage of integration. From a Common Market with no formal implications for member states' sovereignty over monetary and fiscal policies, the EC would move on to economic union entailing monetary union, which would deprive member states of monetary and exchange rate policies. The Treaty of Maastricht of 1992 signalled another fundamental change in European macroeconomic policy. In place of the Treaty of Rome's neglect of macroeconomic policy instruments (on the assumption of there being a consensus on growth and full employment as the primary objective of macroeconomic policy), there was to be a European Central Bank with the duty of controlling inflation. In effect, low inflation had displaced full employment as the avowed aim of the macroeconomic authorities.

This change of priorities was driven by both events and developments in macroeconomic theory. The theoretical revolution will be discussed in Section 3. The acceleration in inflation and the policy responses to it that brought to an end the relatively untroubled prosperity of the 1950s and 1960s are discussed next.

2.2 The macroeconomic performance of European economies since 1960

Economic and monetary union, with its transfer of much macroeconomic policy making from the national to the European level, was in part a response to the inflationary 1970s. It was not simply that inflation rose; so too did unemployment, while growth slowed down. These disturbances to the unproblematic trends of macroeconomic variables in the preceding two decades occurred with differing intensities across the main European economies. The aim of this section is to track these changes and foreshadow issues for theory and institutions to be taken up in later sections.

Let us consider economic growth first. The size of a national economy is measured in terms of GDP. By the 1960s it was generally assumed that in capitalist economies GDP grows year on year with a cycle of years of faster growth succeeded by years of slower growth and so on. The wise application of macroeconomic policy instruments, however, would prevent the recurrence of major depressions in economic activity.

The growth performance of selected economies is shown in this way in Table 4.1, which shows the average annual percentage change in GDP for each period. The current EU economies are divided into four groups according to the date of their accession. This acknowledges the long-standing integration of the 'original six', while recognizing the potential for differential macroeconomic performance among the other groupings. France and Germany are among the 'six', the UK was one of the countries that joined in 1973, the Southern European countries joined in the 1980s and those representing the Scandinavian model (including Austria even though it is not geographically part of Scandinavia) in 1995. The USA and Japan are shown as benchmarks against which the performance of EU economies can be compared.

From Table 4.1 we can see that virtually all economies achieved their highest rate of growth during the period 1960–73. The lowest growth rates occurred during 1974–9 or 1980–5. Most of the economies experienced a recovery in 1986–90, but nowhere does growth return to the rates attained

Table 4.1   Economic growth in selected economies 1960–1997

	Average rate of real GDP growth				
	1960–73	*1974–9*	*1980–5*	*1986–90*	*1991–7*
Belgium	4.9	2.4	1.2	3.0	1.5
France	5.4	3.2	1.5	3.0	1.3
Germany	4.3	2.4	1.6	2.9	1.6
Italy	5.3	2.7	1.9	3.0	1.1
Luxembourg	4.0	1.5	2.2	6.5	4.9
Netherlands	4.8	2.5	1.2	3.1	2.5
Denmark	4.3	1.9	2.2	1.3	2.7
Ireland	4.4	4.1	2.5	4.8	7.1
UK	3.1	1.3	1.4	3.4	1.8
Greece	7.7	3.8	1.4	1.9	1.7
Portugal	6.9	2.9	1.7	5.5	2.2
Spain	7.3	2.6	1.4	4.5	1.8
Austria	4.9	3.0	1.4	3.2	2.0
Finland	5.0	2.4	3.2	3.4	1.0
Sweden	4.1	1.9	1.7	2.3	0.8
Japan	9.7	3.7	3.7	4.6	1.9
USA	4.0	2.8	2.1	2.8	2.9

(derived from OECD Economic Outlook, *Historical Statistics*, 1960–80, 1960–94, 1960–97, Table 3.1)

during 1960–73. Denmark and Finland are the exceptions to the general pattern of a recovery in 1986–90. Denmark was alone in seeing a brief (and very limited) recovery in 1980–5. There is a significant divergence between the 'original six' and the 'Scandinavian' economies, with the 'original six' undergoing a deeper recession in 1980–5 but bouncing back in a sharper recovery in 1986–90. While there is not a great difference between the average growth rates of the two groups for the whole period, the 'Scandinavian' economies seem to have been more stable.

Other things being equal, economic growth tends to be higher during the early stages of industrialization and hence it is no surprise that the Southern European economies enjoyed above average growth during the 1960s. Another source of diversity is size. In fact, the top three economies for growth over the period 1970–95 are Ireland, Portugal and Luxembourg (Artis and Lee, 1997, Table 2.4, p.39); all three are small and the first two began the 1970s relatively unindustrialized.

Even so, the greatest difference is not between one European group and another, but between Japan and all the other economies – the Japanese growth rate being consistently higher than the rest. (This enabled Japan to achieve the fourth highest level of GDP per head by 1989.) Japan was clearly the 'star' performer. The other benchmark economy, that of the USA, might claim second place for a relatively stable growth rate through the troubled 1970s and early 1980s, although most European economies, as well as Japan, were 'catching up' during the 'golden years' of 1960–73. Denmark's post-1973 growth performance is the worst, while the UK was extremely volatile in moving from the lowest growth during both 1974–9 and 1980–5 to one of the stronger recoveries in 1986–90. To sum up, it is clear that there was a common watershed around 1973 but that there were also differences among the economies in the severity of recession and the strength of recovery. More recently, however, it is the US economy that has been the 'star performer' – economic growth there in the late 1990s being on average over 4 per cent – while Japan languished with low and even negative growth rates.

We turn now to unemployment rates. Unemployment data are chosen here in preference to employment figures because unemployment is the standard measurement of how far a government committed to full employment has fallen short of its target. Table 4.2 shows standardized unemployment data, which means that efforts have been made to remove distortions caused by national differences in the administration of unemployment benefits.

Table 4.2 Unemployment in selected economies 1960–1997*

| | *Average rate of unemployment (%)* | | | | |
	1960–73	*1974–9*	*1980–5*	*1986–90*	*1991–7*
Belgium	2.2	5.6	11.3	10.2	11.8
France	2.0	4.6	8.3	9.7	11.4
Germany	0.8	3.5	6.5	7.2	7.9
Italy	5.3	6.6	9.1	11.5	11.5
Luxembourg	*	0.0	0.1	1.1	2.0
Netherlands	1.1	4.9	10.4	9.0	6.5
Denmark	1.3	6.1	9.2	6.8	8.1
Ireland	5.2	7.6	12.6	16.2	13.7
UK	1.9	4.2	9.8	8.4	8.7
Greece	4.6	2.0	6.1	7.4	9.5
Portugal	2.4	6.0	7.9	6.1	6.0
Spain	2.5	5.8	17.1	18.6	20.8
Austria	1.7	1.6	3.0	3.4	3.9
Finland	2.0	4.4	5.3	4.3	14.3
Sweden	1.9	1.9	2.8	1.8	6.9
Japan	1.3	1.9	2.4	2.5	2.8
USA	4.8	6.7	8.0	5.8	6.1

* no data for Luxembourg for 1960–73

(derived from OECD Economic Outlook, *Historical Statistics*, 1960–84, 1960–97, Table 2.15)

With various qualifications in mind, it is reasonable to expect unemployment rates to mirror economic growth (approximately at least), rising as growth rates turned down in the 1970s. Equally, it is likely that individual economies and groups will show some interesting variations around this general trend. The growth slow-down was indeed mirrored in an increase in unemployment up to 1980–5. This is a common feature among all the economies. Once again, among the larger economies Japan was the star performer, confirming the connection between growth and unemployment, with an unemployment rate in 1986–90 that would have been perfectly satisfactory during 1960–73. While Japan cannot be said to buck the trend, the rise in unemployment from a very low base was well below the average.

Throughout the whole period the rise in unemployment was less marked in the 'Scandinavian' economies than in the 'original six', perhaps reflecting the greater stability of their growth record. The increase in US unemployment was closer to that of the 'original six' economies in this period. However, when growth recovered in 1980–6, 'original six' unemployment failed to respond in line with US unemployment, which fell back below its 1974–9 rate. Unemployment in the 'Scandinavian' economies did not change much from 1980–5 to 1986–90 but this largely reflected their disappointing growth performance. Perhaps the most striking anomaly is the unemployment rate in Spain, the highest in the EU by a considerable margin in the mid-1990s despite a long-run growth record that was better than average.

The extent of the variations around the general trend in European unemployment raises a further issue for investigation. Why did unemployment follow such different trajectories in these European economies? Do the differences in macroeconomic theories and policies or in economic institutional culture hold the key? Perhaps the most striking result is the 'original six' unemployment rate during the growth recovery of 1986–90. Here the link between growth and unemployment seemed to break down, raising another issue. Was it the macroeconomic theory informing policy, or the institutions that conditioned it, that was responsible for the failure of 'original six' unemployment to fall in 1986–90?

Section 2.1 concluded with the thought that the acceleration in inflation in the 1970s, and the policy responses to it, brought to an end the relatively untroubled prosperity of the preceding two decades. To turn from the growth slow-down and accompanying rise in unemployment to the inflation experience of the 1970s is to move from the symptoms of economic disorder to its cause. It is important to keep in mind the distinction between inflation and the policies designed to contain or eliminate it, since it may not always be clear which is doing the damage. Anti-inflationary policies are widely, although not invariably, acknowledged to cause a slowing of growth and a rise in unemployment in the short term; they are undertaken nevertheless in the belief that without them inflation is likely to wreak a far greater havoc in the long term.

The measurement of inflation is no less problematic than that of growth and unemployment. The figures in Table 4.3 are based on annual changes in consumer price indices, abstracting from the diversity of consumers by imagining a 'typical' household and the basket of goods it buys. The years 1960–73 were characterized by low or moderate inflation, typically in the middle single digit range; prices were rising but not at a sufficiently rapid rate to cause serious problems. The inflation rate then approximately doubles in the 1970s before falling back over the next two 5-year periods to reach its lowest point for the period as a whole in 1986–90.

Table 4.3 Inflation in selected economies 1960–1997

| | *Average rate of inflation* | | | | |
	1960–73	*1974–9*	*1980–5*	*1986–90*	*1991–7*
Belgium	3.6	8.5	6.9	2.1	2.3
France	4.5	10.7	10.3	3.1	2.1
Germany	3.3	4.7	4.2	1.4	3.0
Italy	4.7	16.4	15.3	5.7	4.5
Luxembourg	3.2	7.4	7.2	1.7	2.4
Netherlands	4.8	7.2	4.6	0.7	2.6
Denmark	6.3	10.8	8.7	3.9	2.0
Ireland	5.9	15.1	13.4	3.3	2.2
UK	5.1	15.7	9.0	5.9	3.2
Greece	3.3	16.2	21.4	17.4	11.9
Portugal	6.1	23.8	22.2	11.4	5.9
Spain	6.8	18.4	12.8	6.5	4.5
Austria	4.2	6.3	5.1	2.2	2.7
Finland	5.6	12.8	9.0	5.0	1.9
Sweden	4.6	9.8	9.8	6.3	3.4
Japan	6.0	10.2	3.6	1.4	1.2
USA	3.2	8.6	6.8	4.0	3.0

(derived from OECD Economic Outlook, *Historical Statistics*, 1960–80, 1960–94, 1960–97, Table 8.11)

It is striking that there was a greater uniformity of inflation experience than was the case for growth and unemployment. Only the USA can be said to diverge from this common sequence of events, though it did not post its lowest inflation rate in 1986–90. The amplitude of the differences between the groups of economies was also less for inflation than for growth and unemployment. However, it is worth noticing that the greater stability of the 'Scandinavian' economies in comparison with the 'original six' is maintained; inflation there peaked at a lower rate than in most of the 'original six' in 1974–9 but had fallen back less sharply by 1986–90.

The identification of a star performer is not difficult. Japan is once again the easy 'winner' with 3.6 per cent in 1980–5, 1.4 per cent in 1986–90 and 1.2 per cent in 1991–7. Once again, as with unemployment, Germany was the best 'original six' performer and even had a lower inflation rate throughout the period 1960–90 than any of the 'Scandinavian' economies.

2.3   Some implications for macroeconomic theory, policy and institutions

What clues does this comparative survey of the macroeconomic performance of EU economies provide toward explaining their transfer of major macroeconomic policy decisions up to the European level? There are two main issues to be followed up in the next two sections on macroeconomic theory and institutions – the two principal influences on policy makers as they respond to events or try proactively to shape the future course of their economies.

The first arises out of the sequence of decline and recovery in macroeconomic performance that all the industrial economies experienced in the 1970s and 1980s, and the greater uniformity of their inflation records. The relative homogeneity of their inflation experiences is consistent with the causal role that has been widely attributed to the upsurge in inflation. This was apparent in all economies and was experienced as a double external shock as oil prices rose in 1973 and again in 1979. However, it has also been questioned whether the 1973 oil price rise really was a bolt from the blue, even if it was widely perceived as such at the time. What led up to it? Would the chain of events that resulted in a quadrupling of oil prices between 1973 and 1974 have occurred whatever policy regime had been in force during the preceding twenty years? Or did the macroeconomic policy framework generate conflicts and tensions that the economic institutions of the time could not dissipate or control? Did the golden age of capitalism carry within itself the seeds of its own destruction?

There is no universally accepted answer to these questions but an account of the explanations of the oil price rise offered by competing macroeconomic theories will clarify the issues and introduce the theories. It will become clear that one theoretical perspective, monetarism, exerted a decisive influence over policy makers in many, although not all, EU member states. This excursion into macroeconomic theory in Section 3 will therefore be a step toward understanding why the national governments of many EU member states have acquiesced in the loss of economic sovereignty over macroeconomic policy instruments that is entailed by European economic and monetary union.

The second issue arises out of the differences among economies in the way they were affected by and reacted to the increase in inflation. After catching up with the USA during the 1950s and 1960s, European economies seem to have been outperformed by the USA, as well as by Japan, in adjusting to and recovering from the inflationary shock of the 1970s, at least up to the early 1990s.

Within Europe the European Free Trade Area (EFTA) economies plus Germany fared better than the rest in terms of the stability of unemployment and, to a lesser degree, inflation. Why were these economies able to adjust more effectively to the oil price rise that befell all economies? The reception of macroeconomic theory and the formation of policy alike are mediated by culture and by institutions. Perhaps the greater stability of unemployment in the former EFTA economies plus Germany reflects cultural factors and institutional arrangements in those economies that are not found elsewhere. In Section 4 this hypothesis will be examined as part of a survey of national differences in macroeconomic policy regimes, cultures and institutions among EU member states.

Summary

- Macroeconomic performance throughout Europe (and in the USA and Japan) deteriorated sharply in the 1970s, as growth declined and both inflation and unemployment increased.

- Inflation in most European economies fell during the 1980s and 1990s but the recovery of growth and unemployment was uneven.

- The Scandinavian economies and Germany exhibited greater stability in economic growth, unemployment and inflation throughout the period 1960–1997.

3 The revolution in macroeconomic theory – and policy?

The main aim of this section is to explore the contribution made by developments in macroeconomic theory to the apparent change of heart by policy makers toward prioritizing the elimination of inflation, or in other words the achievement of price stability, thereby sacrificing the goal of full employment. The macroeconomic objectives set out in the Treaty of Maastricht state that 'the primary objective of the ESCB [European System of Central Banks] shall be to maintain price stability'. The European Central Bank, at the head of the ESCB, has not been 'burdened with other duties and obligations that might [be] incompatible with the control of inflation' (Artis, 1997, p.365). The ESCB should support the general economic policies in the Community, provided that it can do so 'without prejudice to the objective of price stability' (Article 2). This is a long way from the consensus on full employment that was expressed in the Treaty of Rome. To what extent can the revolution that occurred in macroeconomic theory illuminate this re-ordering of priorities?

3.1 Keynesian macroeconomics: full employment and demand management

Until the mid-1970s, macroeconomic policy in Europe was based on the assumption that the principal objective of policy makers was to run the economy as close as possible to full employment. There was a general confidence that this would be very close indeed, given the appropriate deployment of monetary, fiscal and exchange-rate policy instruments. This confidence was grounded in the macroeconomic theory of John Maynard Keynes, which is illustrated in Box 4.1.

Box 4.1 Keynes's theory of unemployment

In *The General Theory of Employment, Interest and Money,* first published in 1936, Keynes attacked the view that unemployment occurs because wages are too high: if firms and workers can agree on a wage rate at which everyone who wants to work can find a job, the labour market clears and there is no unemployment. The implication of this seemed to many economists and policy makers to be that unemployment could occur only if wages were too high to clear the labour market. In that case, trade unions and unemployment benefits were responsible for unemployment: trade unions used their monopoly power to push wages above the market-clearing level, while unemployment benefits set a floor beneath which wages could not fall because no one would work when they could achieve the same income without working. This was the 'orthodox' view.

Against this, Keynes argued that the cause of unemployment lay outside the labour market in the macroeconomy. If aggregate demand, the demand for the total output of goods and services produced by the economy, was too low, stocks of unsold goods would build up and production would therefore be reduced. This implied that wage cuts would not solve the unemployment problem. Even if unemployed people were willing to work for nothing, they would have no hope of finding a job if employers believed that they would be unable to sell the goods the new workers produced.

The central concept in Keynesian macroeconomics is aggregate demand (AD), the demand for the macro-economy's output of goods and services. The basic component of aggregate demand is the expenditure of consumers (C), which is funded by wages and other sources of income such as interest and dividends. This explains why cutting

---

wages was in Keynes's view so misguided a response to persistent large-scale unemployment. It would actually make the problem worse, by reducing the most important component of aggregate demand, when it was already too low to support full employment. However, it is not only households or consumers who buy goods and services from firms – other firms do so too when they invest in capital equipment (I). The government is another major source of aggregate demand, when it in effect buys the services of public sector employees such as nurses and teachers and provides their services free to its citizens (G). The government also purchases goods such as defence and medical equipment. Finally, overseas consumers and firms buy domestically produced goods and services exported to them (X). There is another side to international trade: domestic consumers spend a proportion of their incomes on imported goods and services, which is thereby diverted from adding to aggregate demand in the home economy (M). Aggregate demand can therefore be expressed as:

$$AD = C + I + G + X - M$$

If one component of aggregate demand, AD falls, or is predicted to fall, any adverse effect on AD can in principle be averted by a compensating adjustment in another. If investment I, is predicted to fall, policy makers can increase government expenditure, G, to offset it. Keynes thought that investment was indeed the most volatile element in aggregate demand, since decisions about purchasing capital equipment intended to increase productive capacity (rather than simply replace obsolete or worn-out equipment) were essentially a gamble. Business leaders in the 1930s had very limited information on which to make such decisions. Relying on their subjective feelings or 'animal spirits' in Keynes's phrase, they were prey to waves of confidence and caution.

This focus on the volatility of investment is in fact closer to Keynes's own beliefs than is 'Keynesian' demand management. The main policy recommendation of the *General Theory* is not demand management but the 'socialization of investment', by which he meant the encouragement of both private and public investment through whatever policy instruments were appropriate (Smithin, 1990, p.25). The aim of demand management should not be the constant adjustment or 'fine tuning' of the economy to diminish fluctuations as they arose, but the long-term stability of investment and *hence* aggregate demand.

Keynesian macroeconomic policy

If an expected fall in investment was for Keynes the typical cause of a reduction in aggregate demand, a compensating increase in government expenditure was the standard Keynesian policy response. In principle, three policy instruments were available: fiscal, monetary and exchange rate policies.

- Fiscal policy concerns changes in government expenditure and in government revenues from taxation and borrowing. Adjustments to government expenditure are, in a sense, the most direct of the three policy instruments, relating to the one component of aggregate demand that is under the government's immediate control.

- Monetary policy operates mainly through interest rates. A cut in interest rates has a dual effect. First, the lower cost of borrowing increases the take-up of loans, among which mortgages are particularly important, and also leaves households that already have a mortgage with more 'spending money'. Second, the lower return on savings deposits makes savers more likely to withdraw (part of) their savings and increase their spending. A similar logic holds for borrowing and saving decisions by firms. The lower the interest rate the more likely firms are to borrow and invest, and vice versa.

- The effects of the exchange rate on the macroeconomy have important implications for unemployment. A fall in the exchange rate means that exports are cheaper on world markets and imports more expensive on the home market. If overseas consumers respond to this change in relative prices by increasing their demand for exported goods and domestic consumers switch from imported to domestically produced goods, domestic aggregate demand will increase. (See also Box 4.2.)

Box 4.2 Bretton Woods to EMU

An important role in making possible the 'golden age' of capitalism is generally attributed to the Bretton Woods system of fixed exchange rates. Under Bretton Woods, named after the conference location in New Hampshire, USA, where it was negotiated in 1944, each currency's exchange rate was in effect fixed against others. Only if there was sustained pressure on a particular currency could this rate be readjusted by a devaluation. If the exchange rate remained under downward pressure in the long run this reflected a lack of competitiveness in the national economy. The Exchange Rate Mechanism (ERM) and now EMU itself can be seen as attempts to recover the stability of exchange rates for EU currencies that was maintained by Bretton Woods for over two decades.

Keynesian macroeconomics and inflation

It is therefore clear that the Keynesian model of the macroeconomy had the theoretical and policy resources to cope with inflation. The pre-war inflationary danger against which Keynes had warned was labelled 'demand pull' because it was caused by an excessive growth of aggregate demand. The policy instruments simply had to be put into reverse;

aggregate demand could be made to go down as well as up. Nevertheless, the experience of inflation in the 1970s was a major problem for Keynesian macroeconomics. In the 1950s and 1960s a new type of inflation emerged.

As the 'golden age' of the 1950s and 1960s wore on it came to be widely believed that the 'factor mainly responsible for rising prices in the post-war period has not been excess demand, but something quite different – rising costs' (Stewart, 1967, p.176). This was 'cost-push' inflation, which was initiated by an increase in firms' costs and disseminated through the whole economy when firms passed on the cost increases to their customers in the form of higher prices. The largest element in firms' costs of production is wages, and rising wage settlements were in fact perceived as the main source of inflationary pressure in the more inflation-prone European economies. It was against this already inflationary background that a sudden eruption of cost-push inflation occurred. Between 1973 and 1974 the oil price rose from $3 to $12 per barrel, and after a brief respite the oil price again rose sharply between 1978 and 1980 from $13 to $31 per barrel.

Keynesian demand management was not well equipped to control inflation on the scale that ensued. The difficulty was political rather than theoretical; 'to reduce inflationary pressure by fiscal means would require either spending cuts or increases in taxes', the unpopularity of which implied that 'in the real world Keynesian policies are biased in an inflationary direction' (Smithin, 1990, p.14).

A similar reluctance on the part of policy makers to risk unpopularity among voters inhibited the use of monetary policy. The elimination of inflation through monetary policy required interest rates significantly in excess of the inflation rate; in the mid-1970s this would have necessitated interest rates at politically imprudent levels, which would have potentially very undesirable unemployment consequences.

There were, however, critics of Keynesian demand management who had other ideas. Monetarists argued that the problem with monetary policy was not that it had been tried and had failed, but that it had not been tried. The rise in unemployment would only be temporary; in the long run, inflation – if left unchecked – would actually cause more unemployment. The conjunction, from the mid-1970s, of higher inflation and higher unemployment than had prevailed during the previous two decades led monetarists to argue that the Keynesian policy framework, far from being part of a possible solution to the problem of inflation, was itself the major cause of inflation. The apparent dismantling of Keynesian demand management in macroeconomic theory goes some way toward explaining the willingness of European policy makers to relinquish national sovereignty over the techniques of macroeconomic policy.

3.2   The neo-liberal revolution: price stability and competitive markets

The first stage of the neo-liberal revolution was 'the monetarist experiment', which sought to tackle the conjunction of inflation and unemployment that had precipitated the collapse of Keynesianism. The policy objective of monetarism was to eliminate inflation by controlling the money supply and to do this by raising interest rates. Where monetarist policies were implemented with the greatest conviction, in the UK and USA, policy makers believed that a tight monetary policy, that is, high interest rates, would cause only a moderate and temporary rise in unemployment. In practice, monetarist policies appealed to policy makers on the political right who advocated the withdrawal of the state from large tracts of the economy and favoured market solutions to economic problems. This is the political ideology that came to be known as neo-liberalism. While it was no more than an interlude in policy regimes, monetarism bequeathed its anti-inflationary stance to the neo-liberalism that succeeded it as a major theoretical influence on macroeconomic policy. The relationship between these is explained in Box 4.3 (overleaf).

The neo-liberal macroeconomic strategy (described in Box 4.3) was followed more wholeheartedly in the UK than in other large EU economies. However, it was reflected in the deflationary bias of the Maastricht agreement. The requirement to converge on the inflation rates and interest rates of the best performers and the constraints imposed on government borrowing and public sector debt are clearly deflationary. They are also policy rules that prohibit the exercise of discretion in pursuit of growth at a time of persistently high unemployment. The EU macroeconomic agenda still hovers over the labour market reforms that make up the other plank of the neo-liberal platform. From a neo-liberal perspective the social chapter of the Maastricht treaty is a declaration of resistance to a competitive EU labour market and the UK government is among those urging reform (see Chapter 5).

Policy implications

The conclusion of the monetarist analysis was that it was possible for the government to drive unemployment below some technologically defined natural rate by expanding aggregate demand, but only temporarily while inflation was accelerating. Thus, in addition to the rejection of demand management in pursuit of full employment, two policy implications were drawn from the monetarist analyses.

- First, the high inflation of the mid-1970s could be eliminated relatively painlessly, that is, at the cost of only a moderate and temporary increase in unemployment. The key to this was to readjust expectations in the economy so that agents no longer *expected* inflation to rise.

- The second, and connected, implication was that policy ought to be guided by rules rather than left to the discretion of policy makers. Governments will improve the performance of their economies if they relinquish the right to exercise discretion and follow fixed rules. Only by tying their own hands in this way can governments avoid the temptation to misuse macroeconomic policy instruments for electoral purposes and alter the pattern of expectations among economic agents.

Box 4.3   The relationship between monetarism and neo-liberalism

The monetarist experiment was postulated on two ideas about inflation. First, inflation was a more serious problem than unemployment, threatening the profitability of investment on which capitalist accumulation was based. Second, it was an entirely monetary phenomenon in the sense that it was caused, not by cost-push factors traceable largely to trade union militancy, but solely by an excessive increase in the money supply and could be eliminated simply by bringing the money supply back under control. This could be done by raising interest rates, without adversely affecting the 'real' side of the economy (by which is meant output, employment and unemployment).

In the event, the monetarist experiment conducted in the UK and the USA demonstrated beyond reasonable doubt that monetary policy could control inflation but only by causing adverse effects on the real economy (Smithin, 1990, pp.34–5; Dawson, 1992, pp.167–71). Inflation fell as a consequence of recession caused largely by monetary tightening. But it became increasingly difficult to draw a line around something called 'the money supply'. This was firstly because it proved difficult to construct a reliable measure of what the money supply actually was, and secondly because it became very difficult to detect a reliable relationship between the money supply, however it was defined and measured, and the rate of inflation. Targeting the money supply gave way to targeting the exchange rate (using a high exchange rate to keep import prices low and hence bear down on inflation) and eventually to targeting the inflation rate itself.

Neo-liberalism has since developed a macroeconomic policy framework from its monetarist roots. The first principle of neo-liberal macroeconomics involves making price stability the main policy objective and consequently disengaging from the commitment to use aggregate demand expansions whenever necessary to keep the economy operating at full employment. The second focuses on the 'supply side' of the economy, and in particular on the efficiency with which it supplies goods and services. This entails a drive to increase incentives and to make markets, and especially the labour market, more competitive.

Since a demand expansion raises inflation without accomplishing a sustained decline in unemployment, governments should announce and adhere to a rule to use demand management policy instruments only in a deflationary direction. This has usually taken the form of setting price stability as the objective of macroeconomic policy. A solution to the problem of unemployment lies outside macroeconomics. Governments should reform their labour markets in order to make them more competitive and thereby reduce the 'natural' rate of unemployment.

The classic example of such rules in the European context is the Maastricht convergence criteria, which display the influence of monetarist economics very clearly. Maastricht represents the triumph of monetarism in establishing a new consensus on European macroeconomic policy. As one economist puts it: 'There is wide agreement in Europe ... on the importance of price stability [and] the need to dedicate monetary policy to that aim' (Kenen, 1995, p.13). In terms of monetary policy the convergence criteria remove the discretion of national governments over the choice of policy instrument, namely the interest rate, as well as the selection of the policy objective, namely price stability.

However, this consensus conceals deep differences on the wider neo-liberal macroeconomic agenda and it is in any case of only recent construction. On the first point, the social chapter of the Maastricht agreement does not envisage labour market reform in a neo-liberal direction. This does not necessarily reflect the convergence of EU member states on a shared alternative model of the labour market. It is possible that the social chapter is a compromise that acknowledges the difficulty of reconciling disparate national labour market institutions (see Chapter 5). National differences in policy preferences, shaped by the distinctive institutional structure of the economies of the EU member states, are also apparent in connection with the second point. Boltho (1998, p.148) argues that 'EMU really only became conceivable once France abandoned in the mid-1980s its earlier policies ... and switched to a German-inspired macroeconomic stance'. Not only does this indicate the agreement on an anti-inflationary agenda to have been difficult to engineer but it also hints at the possibility of longer-term differences in macroeconomic policy. For many years the German macroeconomic stance has indeed tempered adherence to Keynesian demand management with an anti-inflation rule, in the form of an independent central bank charged with the task of maintaining price stability. This reinforces the potential for macroeconomic policy to be modulated by the economic institutions and cultures of the EU member states.

Summary

- Until the 1970s the main objective of macroeconomic policy was generally agreed to be the maintenance of full employment; since then the control of inflation has taken over as the principal goal of macroeconomic policy makers.

- Keynesianism sought to provide the theoretical understanding and the practical policy instruments for sustaining aggregate demand at the level required for full employment.

- Monetarism was a short-lived attempt to eliminate inflation by controlling the money supply.

- Neo-liberalism also prioritizes the control of inflation and emphasizes improving the competitiveness of markets, especially the labour market.

4   European macroeconomic institutions: from diversity to unity?

As noted in the Introduction, the main aim of this chapter is to clarify the issues surrounding the willingness of EU member states to relinquish national economic sovereignty over most of the instruments of macroeconomic policy. We have seen that the cataclysmic events of the 1970s together with the neo-liberal turn in macroeconomic theory undermined confidence in demand management. The third factor, which we look at now, concerns economic and political cultures and institutions and their variability across member states. One way of acknowledging the diversity of institutional structures across EU member states is through the concept of corporatism.

4.1   Corporatism

The perception by economic agents of events or 'external shocks', and hence their impact on macroeconomic performance, is mediated by theory and by institutions. In Section 2 we saw that the 'Scandinavian' and German economies enjoyed greater stability of growth, unemployment and inflation during the turbulence of the 1970s than the other EC economies. One explanation is that the institutional structure of the Scandinavian and German economic models predisposed them to greater resilience in the face of adverse economic events. The Scandinavian economies, and more controversially the German economy, are sometimes identified as 'corporatist' on the basis of similarities in their institutional arrangements. Corporatism is a multi-dimensional concept covering economic, social and political institutions, which was raised in Chapter 1 and which will be further examined in Chapter 5. The focus here will be on the relatively narrow definitions that are employed in the macroeconomic literature.

Corporatism refers to a mode of economic organization in which interest groups rather than individual economic agents participate in the process of policy formation and implementation. For example, in a corporatist economy collective bargaining between trade unions and employer organizations covers a significantly larger proportion of the workforce than in non-corporatist economies. It is also likely that the government participates alongside the trade unions and employer organizations in negotiations aimed at achieving a consensus on the future trajectory of wage rates and profits. Economists have investigated the effect of corporatist institutions on macroeconomic performance and there is a body of opinion that supports the impression given by the data in Section 2 about EU economies that the unemployment record of corporatist economies is superior to that of non-corporatist ones. For example, Henley and Tsakalotos (1993, p.2) suggest that 'corporatist institutional features appear to have enabled a more prolonged achievement of full employment than where such corporatist features were absent'.

In an influential study, Calmfors and Driffill (1988) link the degree of centralization of wage-setting institutions to the 'natural' rates of unemployment. They adopt a narrow definition, corporatism being understood as the degree of centralization of the formal institutions of wage bargaining. Economies are grouped as centralized, decentralized or intermediate and their unemployment performance compared. The result for the average of unemployment rates for 1985 and 1989 for eleven economies is a hump-shaped relation between unemployment and the bargaining structure (see Figure 4.1). Somewhat paradoxically, centralized

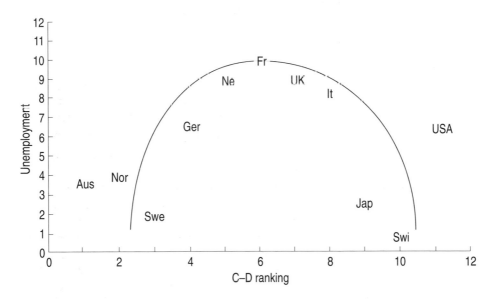

Figure 4.1   Corporatism and unemployment 1985–1989

Note: C–D ranking refers to zero being completely centralized and 12 being completely decentralized. Unemployment is as a percentage rate.

(Soskice, 1990, Figure 3, p.40)

and decentralized economies both outperform intermediate ones. The implication is that there are two very different routes to low unemployment: corporatist economies such as Sweden and Austria were able to keep unemployment low through consensus, while decentralized economies such as the USA achieved the same result through a competitive or flexible labour market. Perhaps intermediate economies such as France and the UK were less successful in the 1980s because they were unable to secure the benefits of either co-operation or competition. Thus, adopting the terminology used in Chapter 1, an 'organized capitalism' on the one hand and a 'decentralized capitalism' on the other were both able to secure lower unemployment than those systems that fell between these two ends of the spectrum.

Although the Calmfors and Driffill study has been very influential, it has also received some criticism. For example, Soskice (1990) argues that Calmfors and Driffill underestimate the degree of co-ordination in two of the putatively decentralized economies, Japan and Switzerland. If valid, this is enough to weaken, although not to demolish, the hump-shaped relation between unemployment and the bargaining structure. Henley and Tsakalotos (1993, p.83) suggest that Calmfors and Driffill rely on an excessively narrow definition of corporatism. In focusing exclusively on the formal structure of wage bargaining, they risk overlooking the wider political and cultural context that may help to explain how wage bargaining centralization is made workable (see Chapter 5). Nevertheless, the superior performance of the economies at the corporatist and decentralized extremes remains clear.

At the very least the hump-shaped relation between unemployment and corporatism captures quite dramatically one 'take' on the policy dilemma facing European economies in the late 1980s when the early plans for EMU were being drawn up. Most EU member states belonged to the intermediate group of economies with an inferior unemployment record in the late 1980s. Which way should they jump? Should they try to deepen co-ordination in their economies along corporatist lines, or deregulate their economies, and in particular their labour markets, according to the US model? Are cultural shifts, changes in the accustomed ways of making decisions, even feasible on this scale? In the UK, Thatcherism was a step in the direction of the decentralized or neo-liberal model. Elsewhere in the EU a third alternative took shape: since purely *national* macroeconomic strategies had in many cases failed to produce satisfactory outcomes, a 'pooling of sovereignties' might offer a way out of the dilemma.

Three differences in cultures and the institutional configuration of modern European capitalisms are represented in the intermediate group of poorly performing economies – those of France, Germany and the UK – although it is worth remembering Germany's above average record on inflation and growth, and even unemployment until the late 1980s. The different attitudes of policy makers in these economies to EMU implies that macroeconomic policy is shaped not only by events and theories but also by nationally specific institutions.

4.2 The diversity of national macroeconomic institutions in the UK, France and Germany

A greater awareness of institutional diversity among EU economies suggests that there is more to the standard narrative of post-war European economic history than a cataclysmic shattering of faith in a universal Keynesian paradigm and its replacement everywhere by neo-liberalism. An alternative interpretation is put forward by Thompson (1992), who proposes four ideal types of European market economy: the French planning model, the German social market, UK liberal Keynesianism and Scandinavian consensus Keynesianism. Aspects of the institutional structures of the UK, France and Germany will be briefly examined to ascertain the extent to which they contribute to an explanation of the different attitudes among these three member states to the loss of macroeconomic sovereignty inherent in EMU.

The UK

The standard interpretation of post-war economic history is perhaps least disturbed by the development of macroeconomic policy in the UK. Until the mid-1970s 'demand management remained the main short-term means of achieving the four objectives of full employment, stable prices, balance of payments equilibrium and economic growth' (Peden, 1985, p.166). Monetary and fiscal policy instruments were routinely used to fine-tune the economy, expanding aggregate demand if unemployment was predicted to rise (or a general election loomed?) and contracting it when an upsurge in inflation seemed to be the most immediate danger. Nevertheless, the maintenance of full employment was the predominant long-term objective (Hopkin, 1992). However, it does not follow from this that demand management was important in initiating and sustaining the 'long boom' in economic activity. For much of this period in UK economic history the government ran a budget surplus; private investment was sufficiently high to ensure full employment without government borrowing to finance an increase in public investment.

This has led some economists and historians to conclude that full employment during the 'golden age' was the consequence of a long-term increase in private investment, not of the judicious management of aggregate demand (Matthews, 1968; Tomlinson, 1981). On the other hand this may be to miss the point. The enduring significance of the *General Theory* may be that it demonstrated that governments had the means to achieve full employment if it was not delivered by the autonomous working of the economy. In view of the importance that Keynes attached to business confidence in motivating investment decisions, the knowledge provided by Keynesian theory and policy – that the government was, as it were, always the investor of last resort – may itself have been a crucial factor in the sustained increase in investment. An economic advisor in the 1960s, Cairncross, suggests that 'the boom itself owed something to demand management: the confidence that sustained investment throughout the period was nurtured by a conviction that the government would, if necessary, act to sustain demand' (Cairncross, 1992, p.8).

There is little doubt that the convulsive events of the 1970s were followed in the UK by a radical change in 'economic philosophy' (Cairncross, 1992, p.234). Under the Thatcher administration the main objective of macroeconomic policy was to achieve and then maintain price stability. A sustainable reduction in unemployment could be accomplished only through microeconomic policy, that is, trade union and social security reform to make the labour market more competitive or flexible. The neo-liberal revolution in macroeconomic policy had arrived.

The commitment of successive UK governments to a broadly neo-liberal economic strategy goes some way to explaining the reluctance of the UK to participate in EMU. In terms of the hump-backed relation between corporatism and unemployment considered in Figure 4.1, the UK can be seen to have sought to move from the intermediate group in the direction of the decentralized edge. The neo-liberal case for the efficiency of competitive markets extends to the foreign exchange market and highlights the perceived advantages to the UK economy of a flexible exchange rate for sterling. This confirms the influence of macroeconomic theory on UK policy toward the euro, although nationally-specific microeconomic institutions such as the housing market have swayed policy in the same direction.

France

The course of French planning further illustrates the temporal variability of economic policy, which adds another layer of complexity to its diversity across countries. Under French indicative planning, government agencies designed strategies for industrial modernization, on the assumption that this was a more reliable route to faster economic growth than leaving industry to modernize itself within a framework of Keynesian demand management. Indicative planning could thus be seen as a centralized approach to improving the supply side of the economy, which pre-dated the neo-liberal supply side reforms based on the competitive market. The decline of French planning in the 1970s coincided with the promotion of an explicit fiscal policy (Thompson, 1992, p.133).

In fact it was the French government under President Mitterand that undertook the last major Keynesian fiscal expansion in Europe. In an effort to redeem its 1981 electoral pledge to reduce unemployment, the Mitterand government not only embarked on a Keynesian expansion, but also 'reactivated the tools which had served France so well in the post-war reconstruction effort, namely planning and nationalizations of large industrial groups and financial institutions' (Reland, 1998, p.87). The collapse of this strategy in the face of repeated currency and public sector financial crises marked the end of the French attempt to 'go it alone' at a time when other industrial countries were prioritizing the control of inflation.

From 1983 French governments have followed a *franc fort* policy, seeking to emulate German experience in using a strong currency to keep costs down and thereby enhance the competitiveness of its exports on world markets. So the willingness of French governments to accept the loss of sovereignty over macroeconomic policy instruments entailed by participation in EMU is in part explained by the fact that such economic sovereignty had already been forfeited. It is clear that 'France's desire to maintain the parity of the franc in a D-mark-dominated EMS has limited its ability to follow an independent economic and monetary policy' (Reland, 1998, p.103). The forces depriving French governments of effective control of macroeconomic policy instruments were not confined to Europe: global capital movements in response to short-term speculative pressures as well as long-term shifts in competitiveness were also responsible. French policy makers believed that EMU would 'help governments regain some of the tools of economic policy making which they have lost to the markets' (Reland, 1998, p.103). Some commentators went further: 'EMU is not only a way for European countries to recover a lost sovereignty, but also a way to gain a new one' (Fitoussi, 1995, p.281). It was thought that a European central bank would exert a more powerful influence in global financial negotiations and on world interest rates than the French central bank alone had done.

The post-1983 French policy of using monetary policy to maintain the value of the franc against the Deutschmark, as a safeguard against inflation and the consequent loss of international competitiveness, set an example that other EU economies followed. This confirmed the ascendancy of the German approach to macroeconomic policy, with its traditional anti-inflation stance.

Germany

In this anti-inflationary respect at least, the German social market model represents a wider departure from Keynesian demand management, and one that was largely unchanged by the events of the 1970s. One important aspect of the German model has already been noted: the corporatist orientation toward social order and consensus. The corporatist welfare settlement entailed a comprehensive social security system and an active labour market policy, enabling unemployed people to return to the workforce through retraining. The consensus on economic policy among the government, trade union leaders and employer organizations facilitated a high degree of wage restraint, which contributed to both low inflation and low unemployment. This represented a key element in the 'regulatory order' that typified German economic governance through to the 1990s.

It is the other aspect of the German social market and its 'regulatory order' that poses the sharpest challenge to the hegemony of Keynesianism. The German central bank, the Bundesbank, was charged with the sole objective of maintaining price stability and was granted independence from political control. The independence of the Bundesbank was a safeguard against accelerating inflation caused by repeated demand expansions undertaken for political reasons (Section 3); it was able to 'insulate monetary policy from interest groups' (Theil and Schroeder, 1998, pp.105–6). In this respect the German macroeconomic policy framework eschewed the monetary policy route to demand management, overriding the discretion of policy makers with a rule. The German approach has exerted a substantial influence on European economic and monetary union, in part by providing a model for maintaining price stability and in part by establishing the terms on which German participation can be expected. For example, Theil and Schroeder (1998) suggest that '[t]his stance has been ... internalized by the German people to the extent that an equal level of independence for the European Central Bank is a necessary condition for German acceptance of EMU' (pp.105–6).

Towards unity?

This brief review of aspects of the institutions and recent history of three EU economies adds further insights to the explanation of the readiness of most EU member states to 'pool their economic sovereignty' in macroeconomic policy (Chapters 2 and 8). For most of the EU economies that are neither unequivocally corporatist or decentralized, moving toward either type of institutional structure was unthinkable. To replicate in the short-term institutions that have evolved over generations in another country and been moulded by its own history and culture would require, if feasible at all, a change of national identity. Only the UK might be thought to have attempted this, in seeking to import elements of the competitive, decentralized US model. To conform to the German macroeconomic policy model, with its pursuit of price stability entrusted to an independent central bank, was, however, a realistic – if still ambitious – project.

Monetarist theory advocated price stability and policy rules and the German macroeconomic stance furnished an institutional exemplar of the beneficial effects of those policy recommendations on economic performance. The internationalization of capital markets reinforced the lesson that the French government had drawn about the enhancement of macroeconomic autonomy that monetary union could deliver. As Henley and Tsakalotos (1990) suggested, '[t]he EC, as a large monetary area, will have some monetary independence because it will be able to influence the world interest rate' (p.160). It was in this theoretical and institutional context that EMU was conceived.

Summary

- Differences in economic and political cultures and institutions affect the relative macroeconomic performance of national economies.

- There is some (contested) evidence to suggest that corporatist and decentralized economies have outperformed intermediate ones.

- The German macroeconomic policy framework was more influential on the design of EU macroeconomic policy and institutions than those of the UK and France.

5   Before and after Maastricht: European macroeconomic policy under EMU

On the surface, the Maastricht convergence criteria and the policy framework stipulated for the European Central Bank reflect the new anti-inflation orthodoxy on macroeconomic policy. The likelihood of a severely deflationary policy stance was a source of misgiving about the prospects for the macroeconomic performance of the countries participating in EMU. In particular, attention was drawn to the narrowly monetary nature of the convergence criteria. Was EMU desirable among countries that displayed highly disparate unemployment rates?

In the event, the European Central Bank showed itself prepared to exercise discretion in the interpretation and application of policy rules. It seems reasonable to understand this approach as an attempt to balance the needs and interests of the various member states, perhaps in recognition of the strenuous efforts they had made to satisfy the convergence criteria. The theoretical foundations for such a policy stance can be seen as eclectic rather than wholly anti-inflationary, in that weight was given to considerations other than price stability.

5.1   EMU and unemployment

Given the diversity of nationally-specific macroeconomic traditions and institutions, participation in EMU entails an endeavour toward convergence. We have seen elsewhere in this book that an adequate degree of convergence on certain aspects of macroeconomic performance is a necessary condition of participation in EMU (Chapters 1, 2 and 8 in particular). The reason is that a single interest rate and exchange rate will be appropriate for different economies only if they resemble each other in relevant ways, for example, only if they have similar inflation rates and are approaching on 'optimum currency area'. An important question that the convergence criteria raise is whether the dimensions of macroeconomic performance on which convergence was required were sufficient. In particular, should the convergence criteria have been supplemented by the addition of a criterion on unemployment? Should economies have been permitted to take part in EMU only if their unemployment performance was sufficiently close to that of the economies with the lowest unemployment rates?

If the Maastricht convergence criteria had included one on unemployment, framed in similar terms to those on interest rates and inflation, it is clear that some major players would have been debarred from taking part. For example, it is difficult to envisage a meaningful degree of convergence when French and Italian unemployment, for instance, was much higher than in most other EU economies in the middle 1990s (see Table 4.4). It is therefore easy to understand the absence of an unemployment convergence criterion.

Table 4.4 Unemployment in the EU 1994–1995

	Unemployment rate (percentage of labour force)
Belgium	10.1
France	11.9
Germany	8.3
Italy	11.6
Luxembourg	3.7
Netherlands	6.8
Denmark	7.5
Ireland	15.0
UK	9.0
Greece	8.9
Portugal	7.1
Spain	23.3
Austria	4.5
Finland	17.8
Sweden	9.4
Weighted average of 3 lowest	4.6

(adapted from Boltho, 1998, p.151)

However, the decision to omit such a criterion may have been ill-advised. Some economists, for example Boltho (1998), argue that the prospects for EMU are put at risk by the lack of convergence among participants on unemployment. In signing up to Maastricht, EU economies are in effect adopting a German-style macroeconomic policy framework. The anti-inflation and rule-bound German policy stance has produced satisfactory macroeconomic outcomes for Germany, but it has done so in conjunction with a distinctively German labour market and industrial relations system. In economies with markedly different labour market and industrial relations institutions the unemployment consequences of maintaining price stability may be higher than they have been in Germany. It is also possible that Germany's own labour market, industrial relations and social security systems will require reform – the German advantage on unemployment was already crumbling in the approach to EMU (see Table 4.4).

If wide divergences of unemployment performance emerge among economies participating in EMU, the anti-inflation consensus could collapse. Different policy preferences could lead to conflict among national representatives, not least on the board of the ECB, which takes majority decisions. In retrospect, Boltho may be seen to have summed up the risks facing EMU from the limited range of convergence criteria required for participation: 'Use of an unemployment criterion may thus actually help in preventing a union that could prove to be undesirable on economic grounds, and thereby maintain a degree of policy autonomy for individual countries that they could find both welcome and necessary' (Boltho, 1998, p.151).

5.2   EMU's first steps

External shocks and internal disputes may lie ahead but the first eighteen months of EMU have seen the emergence of a more pragmatic monetary strategy than had been expected, and one that goes some way toward maintaining a balance between the control of inflation and the reduction of unemployment. The Eurosystem's monetary strategy was announced late in 1998, and after its first year of implementation the Organization for Economic Cooperation and Development (OECD) concluded that 'the strategy has been relatively eclectic and has been applied rather pragmatically' (OECD, 2000, p.4). Monetary strategy, as demonstrated in the ECB's judgements about the timing and scale of interest rate changes, has been informed by wider concerns than a single-minded commitment to price stability. The conduct of monetary policy has been pragmatic in reflecting a willingness to exercise discretion in the application of policy rules. This is far from what had been generally expected.

The euro had been widely expected to assert itself on world financial markets as a 'hard' or anti-inflationary currency, one that by holding its value against other currencies would keep import prices low and so diminish inflationary pressures. In this way the euro would inherit the role of the Deutschmark and, no less than the independence of the ECB noted above, a strong euro was a condition of German popular support and hence participation. Yet the euro exchange rate's dramatic fall against sterling and the US dollar throughout the first year of its existence did not provoke the defensive increase in the EMU interest rate that was expected (see also Chapter 8). Why was the Eurosystem's monetary policy stance more relaxed than expected? Why did policymakers show such alertness to deflationary risks?

To some extent the strategy can be seen to have emerged as a response to the particular circumstances of the launch of the single currency. Two factors seem to have been important.

- First, the collapse of economic growth in the South East Asian 'tiger' economies caused an adverse demand shock on the EMU economies. Lower consumer demand in SE Asia led to a fall in European exports to the area and hence a fall in aggregate demand in the eleven countries participating in EMU. From a broadly Keynesian perspective this was a reason for keeping interest rates low in order to offset the fall in AD. If policy had been motivated solely by the commitment to price stability most closely associated with neo-liberalism, interest rates would have been raised in an effort to buttress the euro exchange rate and avert any risk of 'importing' inflation.

- Second, by the end of 1998 interest rates and inflation rates in the participating economies were already low because of the efforts to meet the Maastricht convergence criteria. A period of 'relaxed monetary conditions rewarded the convergence efforts made in the run-up to the single currency' (OECD, 2000, p.4).

The pragmatic strategy of the Eurosystem is reflected in its interpretation of the objective of price stability that was set for it by the governments of the participating economies. The objective of the strategy is to maintain price stability over the medium term, defined as an annual increase in consumer prices of less than two per cent. However there is some evidence, inferred from the documents and practice of the Eurosystem, that the definition of price stability is being interpreted symmetrically. This means that an inflation rate below some minimum or floor level would be regarded as just as much a failure of monetary policy as an annual inflation rate in excess of 2 per cent. Ultimately 'it may become easier to consider moving to a more explicitly symmetric inflation objective, possibly centred somewhere in between one and two per cent' (OECD, 2000, p.6).

The implication is that a reduction in unemployment, if not necessarily the achievement of full employment, has entered the Eurosystem by the back door. The relaxed monetary conditions of the early stages of EMU 'contributed to sustained domestic demand, limiting the extent of the deceleration' (OECD, 2000, p.1). So the commitment to price stability has been tempered by an alertness to the need not to overdo things but to keep in mind the importance of sustaining growth and reducing unemployment. The 'story so far' therefore offers some support to the view that the neo-liberal orthodoxy of the years leading up to EMU was more apparent than real. For example, it was predicted that 'once states have qualified there is a possibility that they will attempt to rewrite the rule book, undermining the strong commitment of the arrangements to price stability' (Menon and Forder, 1998, p.183). The Keynesian orthodoxy of earlier times has not been entirely forgotten. The Eurosystem seems to have moved on from the stark choice between Keynesian and neo-liberal horns of the macroeconomic policy dilemma to a more pragmatic blending of theories, where 'discretion' and 'rules' coexist in an uneasy combination.

Summary

- The Maastricht convergence criteria were narrowly monetary in nature, including inflation, interest rates and government finances but excluding unemployment.

- There is an issue about the long-term prospects for successful economic and monetary integration among economies with disparate unemployment rates.

- The experience of economic and monetary union so far suggests that EU macroeconomic policy is based on a pragmatic blending of Keynesian and neo-liberal elements.

6   Conclusion

This chapter has sought to explain why many EU member states were willing to transfer control of macroeconomic policy instruments from national governments to the EU. National policy makers believed that through sharing decision-making power economic and monetary union would improve macroeconomic performance. Three lines of explanation for this view have been considered: events, theory and institutions. The decline in macroeconomic performance in the 1970s, the displacement of Keynesianism by neo-liberalism as the ruling macroeconomic orthodoxy, and the particular histories and institutional structures of individual EU economies all have some explanatory power. The outcome of the interplay of these factors was a policy stance embodied in EMU that favoured the curtailment of discretion by policy rules. The renunciation of discretion in the use of macroeconomic policy instruments for the purposes of demand management has already begun at a national level, for example in the granting of independence to the French central bank. Maastricht was the culmination of a process already under way at a national level.

A comparison of the treaties of Rome and Maastricht suggests a shift from a consensus around one macroeconomic orthodoxy to a consensus

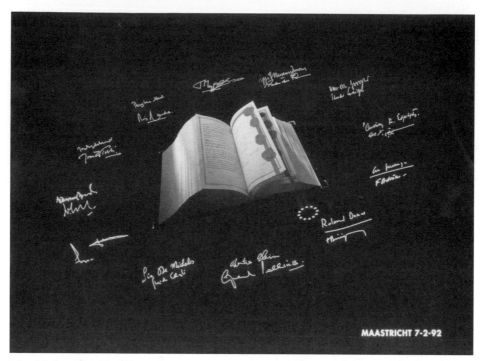

The Maastricht Treaty 1992

around another, marking the displacement of full employment by price stability as the principal objective of macroeconomic policy. The exclusion of unemployment from any formal role in guiding macroeconomic policy in the Maastricht convergence criteria and the EMU regime mirrors the exclusion of unemployed people from social and economic life across the EU. However, this focus on formal statements of agreement masks the conflicts that have enlivened macroeconomic policy debates, as well as the institutional differences among member states. While 'there may be troubles ahead', monetary policy in the first phase of EMU has been less dogmatic in its pursuit of price stability than generally expected and more open to considerations of growth and unemployment in exercising discretion in the application of policy rules.

References

Andrews, M. (1999) *Landscape and Western Art*, Oxford, Oxford University Press.

Artis, M. (1997) 'European Monetary Union' in Artis, M. and Lee, N. (eds) *The Economics of the European Union: Policy and Analysis*, Oxford, Oxford University Press.

Artis, M. and Lee, N. (eds) (1997) *The Economics of the European Union: Policy and Analysis*, Oxford, Oxford University Press.

Boltho, A. (1998) 'Should unemployment convergence precede monetary union?' in Forder, J. and Menon, A. (eds) *The European Union and National Macroeconomic Policy*, London, Routledge.

Cairncross, F. (ed.) (1992) *The British Economy Since 1945*, Oxford, Blackwell.

Calmfors, L. and Driffill, J. (1988) 'Centralization of wage bargaining and macro economic performance', *Economic Policy*, no.6, pp.13–61.

Commission of the European Communities (1985) *Completing the Internal Market*, Com (85), 310, Luxembourg, Office for Official Publications of the European Communities.

Dawson, G. (1992) *Inflation and Unemployment: Causes, Consequences and Cures*, Aldershot, Edward Elgar.

Fitoussi, J.P. (1995) *Lé Debat Interdit*, Paris, Arléa.

Gregory, M. and Weiserbs, D. (1998) 'Changing objectives in national policy making' in Forder, J. and Menon, A. (eds) *The European Union and National Macroeconomic Policy*, London, Routledge.

Henley, A. and Tsakalotos, E. (1993) *Corporatism and Economic Performance: A Comparative Analysis of Market Economies*, Aldershot, Edward Elgar.

Hopkin, B. (1992) 'The development of demand management' in Cairncross, F. (ed.) *The British Economy Since 1945*, Oxford, Blackwell.

Kenen, P.B. (1995) *Economic and Monetary Union in Europe*, Cambridge, Cambridge University Press.

Keynes, J.M. (1936) *The General Theory of Employment, Interest and Money*, London, Macmillan.

Matthews, R.C.O. (1968) 'Why has Britain had full employment since the War?', *The Economic Journal*, vol.78, September, pp.556 69.

Menon, A. and Forder, J. (1998) 'Conclusion: states, the European Union and macroeconomic policy' in Forder, J. and Menon, A. (eds) *The European Union and National Macroeconomic Policy*, London, Routledge.

OECD (2000) *Policy Brief: EMU One Year On*, Paris, OECD.

Peden, G.C. (1985) *British Economic and Social Policy: Lloyd George to Margaret Thatcher*, Oxford, Philip Allan.

Reland, J. (1998) 'France' in Forder, J. and Menon, A. (eds) *The European Union and National Macroeconomic Policy*, London, Routledge.

Smithin, J.N. (1990) *Macroeconomics after Thatcher and Reagan: The Conservative Policy Revolution in Retrospect*, Aldershot, Edward Elgar.

Soskice, D. (1990) 'Wage determination: the changing role of institutions in advanced industrialized countries', *Oxford Review of Economic Policy*, vol.6, no.4, pp.36–61.

Stewart, M. (1967) *Keynes and After*, Harmondsworth, Penguin.

Theil, E. and Schroeder, I. (1998) 'Germany' in Forder, J. and Menon, A. (eds) *The European Union and National Macroeconomic Policy*, London, Routledge.

Thompson, G. (1992) 'The evolution of the managed economy in Europe', *Economy and Society*, vol.21, no.2, May, pp.129–51.

Tomlinson, J. (1981) 'Why was there never a "Keynesian Revolution" in economic policy?' *Economy and Society*, vol.10, no.1, pp.72–87.

Further reading

Forder, J. and Menon, A. (eds.) (1998) *The European Union and National Macroeconomic Policy*, London, Routledge.

Henley, A. and Tsakalotos, E. (1993) *Corporatism and Economic Performance: A Comparative Analysis of Market Economies*, Aldershot, Edward Elgar.

OECD (2000) *Policy Brief: EMU One Year On*, Paris, OECD.

Smithin, J.N. (1990) *Macroeconomics after Thatcher and Reagan: The Conservative Policy Revolution in Retrospect*, Aldershot, Edward Elgar.

Chapter 5
'Social Europe' and the governance of labour relations

John Grahl

1 Introduction

This chapter takes a broad view of labour market governance in Europe by stressing the close relationship between industrial relations systems on the one hand and social protection systems on the other, as two sides of what is often known as the 'European social model'. Both aspects of the social model are at present under severe pressure, but it may be too soon to argue that they are in terminal decline.

The chapter addresses a number of associated issues. It begins with a general consideration of the employment relation and the specific nature of the governance problems to which this relation gives rise (Section 2).

The 'European' response to these problems, which involved a high degree of politicization, is then discussed and the emergence, after the Second World War, of European social models in a developed form is described (Section 3). The chapter goes on to assess the differences across nations in the two key domains of industrial relations and social protection (Section 4).

Section 5 reviews the nature of the crisis in European social models, with stress on the structural factors behind macroeconomic disturbances; the 'free market' critique of the models which emerged is also introduced. The responses to this crisis are then described (Section 6): while a certain decentralization took place everywhere, governance mechanisms became at this point a key factor of differentiation among countries. Divergence prevailed over convergence during the 1980s and 1990s.

The focus then moves from national systems to the European Union (EU). The increase in interactions among different national systems raises the issue of the emergence of transnational governance systems within the EU. Although nothing like a single, Europe-wide system of labour market governance is emerging, there are increasing spillover effects among national systems which has led to a certain development of EU institutions (Section 7).

The final section (Section 8) raises the theoretical question of corporatism in its relation to labour relations governance. It is suggested that corporatism in the strict sense has become increasingly less important in Europe, but that a move to more pluralist governance systems, reflected in an increasing prominence of network relations as against hierarchical authority, is compatible with the basic values which underpin the European social models.

The chapter concludes by suggesting that a new balance of forces is emerging within Europe, which will propel a reorganization and a reshaping of the governance structures deployed to regulate and monitor labour relations.

2   The employment relation

In terms of the three main governance mechanisms discussed in this text – markets, regulation through hierarchies and self-organizing networks – the employment relation in capitalist societies is necessarily a *hybrid*: it must involve both markets and hierarchies. Its function, however, has been the subject of debate.

2.1   Employment as a hybrid relationship

In an economy where labour services were provided by purely market arrangements one would not observe employment as it is usually understood but only *self*-employment, where specific labour services were directly marketed to customers concerned immediately with the product or outcome of the labour. The *employment relation*, in contrast to self-employment, is usually understood as involving first a *market transaction* which places workers at the disposal of an employer or employing enterprise, then a relation of *subordination or control* where the efforts of the workers are directed by these employers. Thus it is a combination of 'market' and 'hierarchy'.

2.2   What is the function of employment?

The function of the employment relationship is a matter of long-standing dispute. Since Marx, one view has been that the essence of the relation is the subordination itself, which permits the exploitation of workers unable to provide their own capital equipment. Other writers, in what is known as the 'transaction cost' tradition (Coase, 1993; Williamson, 1985), have argued that the subordination of the employee, who is subjected to hierarchical managerial control, arises from the efficiency brought about by this form of economic organization. Hierarchy has some efficiency advantages over market forms of organization. These efficiency gains resulting from employment (as against some hypothetical alternative where there would only be self-employed producers) are viewed in various ways. Sometimes the gains are seen as arising from more effective monitoring of workers than is possible where they are independent; at other times the gains are traced more to the possibility of redirecting workers to different tasks as product markets require it without the need to alter contractual relationships. According to this second approach the employment relation makes it easier to deal with uncertainties than would be possible if labour contracts specified the outputs which are needed rather than establishing the general readiness of the worker to follow instructions. In both these views, however, employment relations are traced to *transaction costs*, that is, to the costs of relying completely on the market to bring about organizational change in the productive system. Such market-based transaction costs are eliminated if employment relations are brought within the ambit of the firm and subject to a hierarchical organization. Thus in both views there is a very close connection between the *business enterprise* as a specific form of economic organization and the employment relation. The enterprise is a hierarchical institution, an 'island of planning', in the midst of a market economy.

Summary

- The employment relation is necessarily a hybrid – it involves elements of a market mechanism and a regulated hierarchical one.

- The function of the employment relation is to economize on the costs of pure market transactions by bringing it within the ambit of the enterprise or firm.

3   The European response

In very broad terms it is possible to detect a divergence in the evolution of modern employment relations between Britain and the USA on the one hand and continental Western Europe on the other.

3.1   Free contract: Anglo-Americans and Europeans

Developments in Britain, especially through the first industrial revolution, ran ahead of full social awareness. In both Britain and the USA, employment relations and the modern business enterprises to which they are linked, had already become the predominant form of productive activity before they were generally perceived as posing a key social problem. In France, Germany and other European countries the full emergence of modern industrial systems out of more traditional, largely rural, economic systems was a later development and one more subject to political debate and systematic investigation. From the start, the conditions of existence of the new urban workforce tended to be seen as a social and political issue.

This contrast between 'Anglo-American' and 'continental European' patterns of development can be seen in the divergent approaches which were taken to *employment law*. In Britain, employment relations were at first governed by the archaic law of master and servant, which related to the ubiquitous ties of personal dependence that existed in pre-modern and early modern society. From the late eighteenth century onwards, the highly prescriptive provisions of this code – which took a fixed social hierarchy and differences in status as given – were gradually dissolved into a purely contractual interpretation of the employment relation. Every aspect of employment – wages, working conditions, hiring and firing, specification of tasks, workplace discipline – was seen as a matter to be left to free contract between worker and employer (and this within a context where the combining of workers in an attempt to alter these contractual terms collectively was fiercely repressed). Since, by the nature of employment, many of these factors are not clearly specified in advance but are variable and at the discretion of the employer, this minimalist employment law left workers with very few formal rights.

Now the treatment of employees as market agents like any others, free to dispose of their own capacities and subject only to the discipline of the market, raises fundamental difficulties. The employee is treated as a fully independent participant in the market economy, while the substance of the employment relation entails his or her dependence on the employer as a stronger agent, with more complete powers of decision. Inside an existing employment relation the actual subordination of workers may threaten both their interests and their autonomy, while failure to enter employment, or the loss of employment, may be insupportable to individuals not capable of independent, self-initiated economic activity.

In Britain and the USA these problems were gradually addressed through a long, conflictual, social learning process which, in pragmatic and experimental ways, moved employment away from the complete rule of free contract toward a social recognition of the inequality of the employer and the employee and some attempt to compensate for this inequality. Thus, in nineteenth-century Britain the first industrial legislation limited the hours which could be worked and imposed safety inspections on factories. Limited unemployment and old-age insurance schemes were introduced before the First World War without either of these developments undermining the basic interpretation of the employment relationship in terms of free contract. (It is significant that the first legislation concerned the employment of children, who cannot plausibly be seen as fully independent market agents, and of women, for whom the same was true in nineteenth-century societies.) Similarly, the employment legislation and social security legislation which reformed employment relations from the American New Deal era of the 1930s onwards left the essentially contractual nature of employment in the USA unchanged.

In continental Europe the social problems inherent in the growth of modern urban workforces were, from the start, perceived in a more complete way, and they elicited a range of responses which involved organized political programmes. These responses came from all standpoints – socialist, conservative (often Christian) and liberal – but they had in common a recognition of the profound challenge to the social system which was presented by new masses of employees who were juridically free but economically at least partially dependent on the initiatives of employers.

Two dimensions of the contrast between the Anglo-American and continental European responses can be emphasized. The first concerns the law, and the second relates to trade union organization.

The law

In Anglo-American society a large body of labour market and employment law gradually developed, but this mostly takes the form of specific departures from or additions to the contract and company law which govern economic life in general. In France and many other continental countries, in contrast, there is a specific labour code: once an economic interaction is identified as involving an employment relationship ('dependent' labour) it is removed from standard economic law and becomes subject to a separate corpus of statute and case law with explicit social objectives.

Thus, British workers do not possess a 'right to strike'. Rather they enjoy a derogation from civil action for breach of contract when pursuing certain kinds of 'trade dispute'. In France and Germany, labour law promulgates a positive right to strike and specifies the conditions under which this right may be legally exercised.

Trade union organization

In Britain and the USA, trade unions emerged first as *networks* of (usually skilled) workers who combined in an increasingly systematic way in order to counteract the asymmetries of the individual employment relationship. Only slowly did organized labour begin to constitute itself as a political force. In Britain this politicization took place first within the existing Liberal Party and then took the form of a separate Labour Party just prior to the First World War. In the USA the political agenda of organized labour was never successfully embodied in the programme of a distinct mass political party and remained a more or less important component of the coalition of interests grouped in the Democratic Party.

In France, Germany and elsewhere in continental Europe such networks of workers certainly emerged. But modern trade union organization resulted to a much greater extent from the deliberate strategies of existing political formations. In the first instance these tended to be anti-capitalist – such as anarcho-syndicalism in France and Spain or social democracy in Germany – but more conservative unions, often inspired by confessional political formations, Catholic or Protestant, were developed to represent a more gradualist and less contestatory response to the 'social question'. These ideological divisions – overlaid by many subsequent realignments and reorientations – led to competing trade union centres which persist to this day in several countries, notably France, the Netherlands, Spain and Italy, although in other countries such as Germany and Sweden unified trade union structures emerged by agreement among rival tendencies or by the domination of one tendency over the others.

3.2   The flowering of the European social models

Until the period following the Second World War, the practical impact of European conceptions of the 'social question' on the polities and economies of Western Europe was limited. Structural reasons for this included the numerical weakness of the urban working classes as well as the very weaknesses derived from their economic status, such as their subordinate political position and restricted access to education. Historical reasons comprised war, depression and political upheavals (which frequently included the violent suppression of working-class organizations and the crude assertion of proprietorial interests). In the post-Second World War era, however, in the context of politically stable democracies and continuous industrial expansion, the social question was finally addressed in a comprehensive way. The basic conditions of existence of urban employees were less and less simply an outcome of the functioning of market forces and enterprise hierarchies. Instead, these conditions became central matters of political concern, and both labour markets and employment conditions were deeply influenced by elaborate systems of wider regulation.

It is important to stress that the social models that emerged were national – they developed within the nation states, which were the key form of political organization, and differed markedly from one country to another. Nevertheless there existed both important similarities among national models and a real tendency for these models to converge in functional if not in institutional terms. This convergence resulted from the presence of similar economic and social trends across Western Europe so that one can speak, if not of a European social model in the singular, then at least of a *family* of European social models with many shared characteristics.

To summarize these characteristics of the European social model one can make a simple but realistic distinction between the *industrial relations* and *social protection systems*. The former governed the working conditions and remuneration of those actually in employment, while the latter provided for those not in employment through sickness, unemployment or old age. The two structures were linked by the widespread use of the social insurance principle, whereby entitlements to social protection are tied to contributions from employees and employers and thus depend on a worker's employment record. Social provision was completed by the massive expansion of health, housing and education services so that almost every aspect of the working and living conditions of the urban masses was subject to political intervention and control.

During the period of its strongest influence (the 1950s through to the late 1970s) the European social model was both economically functional – it contributed to growth – and socially integrative. It stabilized social tensions.

Summary

- The organization of employment relations can be conveniently divided into two broad types: the Anglo-American version and the continental European version.

- These differ in their approaches to employment law and trade union organization.

- In the post-Second World War period, however, there was a real tendency for a single European social model (or family of models) to emerge, involving similar industrial relations systems and social protection systems.

4   Differentiation of social models

Up to now the chapter has concerned itself with some basic and rather abstract definitions and differentiations which served to lay the groundwork for a fuller and more concrete analysis. In this section we develop those earlier preliminary and exploratory discussions. The three key definitional terms used so far are outlined in Table 5.1 (overleaf).

It was suggested that since the end of the Second World War a broadly common pattern (or family of models) of governance of employment relations had emerged within Western Europe more generally – the 'European social models'. These involved *some* aspects of the British version of the Anglo-American model modified by distinct continental European political developments.

In this section we discuss some important differences in the detail of these European social models in different European countries. Thus the approach adopted here is on the one hand to insist that there have been important common trends, and sometimes convergence, in European social models, but on the other hand to emphasize the differentiations that have recently made for significant divergence.

Table 5.1 Some key terms summarized

Terms	Features	
Employment relation	(i) market transaction – work of employees put at disposal of employers	
	(ii) hierarchical relation – workers subordinated to employers' control	
Types of employment relation	*Employment law*	*Trade union organization*
Anglo-American	free contract between worker and employer plus ad hoc labour market and employment law	loose, networked structure evolving into political force
Continental European	strict labour code defining enforceable statutory rights	deliberate strategy of political organization based upon ideological divisions
European social model (social insurance principle)	(i) industrial relations system governing conditions and remuneration in work	
	(ii) social protection system governing sickness, unemployment and old-age protection	

Clearly other approaches could be adopted for this type of analysis. We could, for instance, suggest that each social model was different and entirely nationally specific within the European context. This would be to downplay some of the important general forces at work within Europe as a whole. A somewhat different type of theory is adopted by Esping-Andersen, who discusses three European models under the heading of 'welfare state regimes', which he calls the 'liberal welfare state', the 'corporatist state', and the 'social democratic state' models (Esping-Andersen, 1990). The outline features of these three models are given in Table 5.2. This analysis has been very influential in opening up a discussion of matters similar to those discussed in this chapter, though not necessarily confined to just the European arena as analysed here.

The account given here is less systematic than that of Esping-Andersen. But as we shall see, some of these features also come into play in the analysis that follows. The categories of Table 5.2 help to provide some additional background features for our own account.

Table 5.2   Esping-Andersen's models of 'welfare regimes'

	Traditional main features
Liberal welfare state	means tested; non-universal transfers; modest social insurance benefits guaranteed minimum benefits only; supplements to private welfare schemes
Typical country examples: USA, Canada, Australia	
Corporatist state	statutory provision of guaranteed social insurance; mixed provision regimes with 'social partners' and churches often heavily involved; differentiation on the basis of membership of organized associations and groups
Typical country examples: Austria, France, Germany, Italy	
Social democratic state	principle of universalism widely adopted; 'generous' benefits; emphasis on social reform as objective of system; graduated benefits according to employment status and social expectation
Typical country examples: Scandinavian countries, the UK until the 1980s	

(derived from Esping-Andersen, 1990, pp.26–9)

4.1   Industrial relations

Although it is possible to make a general characterization of Western European welfare states and industrial relations systems, it is equally important to specify the significant differences among national systems. We can take as a benchmark the British system, where the pattern of governance is very clearly defined. The British social system displays a very clear-cut dichotomy: wages and, for the most part, working conditions are negotiated between unions and employers on an industrial and/or occupational basis; social protection and social services are the responsibility of the state. This structure comes closest to reconciling the tradition of free contract with the expansion of social provision. Buyers and sellers of labour retain their autonomy, although this is increasingly exercised in a collective way, yet social entitlements do not lead to new obligations on private agents but rather on government so that, once again, the freedom of individuals and enterprises is not impaired by direct social obligations. However, there are a number of other features that serve to differentiate industrial relation approaches.

Decentralization and centralization

In European countries other than the UK the same dichotomy underlies the development of the social model but it is often less well defined. Everywhere the determination of wages and working conditions is separate from the state and remains essentially a matter for negotiation between organized labour and employer interests. Were this not the case, then one would have been moving a long way from a core relation of the capitalist economy, which is a *labour market*. However, we observe a great deal of variation in the structure of these bargains: the degree of *centralization* is an important variable (Sweden offers a good example of highly centralized industrial relations) but it should also be recognized that somewhat less centralized systems, where negotiations take place on a regional or industrial basis, are capable of more or less *co-ordination* among the distinct bargaining processes (Soskice, 1990). For example, most accounts of wage bargaining in Germany note a high degree of co-ordination among the separate industry-wide wage settlements, with the powerful engineering workers' union, IG-Metal, acting as pacemaker for the unions as a whole.

The articulation of levels

The *articulation of levels* in industrial negotiations is another important dimension of differentiation in industrial relations systems. Some division of responsibility among national, industrial (in larger countries often also regional) and enterprise-level negotiations is a functional necessity and can be seen virtually everywhere, but the way in which these levels relate to each other varies considerably from country to country. Britain exemplifies a decentralized system: there is hardly any negotiation which applies to all or even a substantial majority of employees; wages are in principle determined by employers' organizations and unions according to an incoherent set of industrial and/or occupational groupings but many other issues, often in practice including earnings, are a matter for bargaining at the level of the enterprise or even the establishment (that is, the individual plant or other workplace). At the apogee of British trade unionism in the late 1970s there were nearly one million shop stewards and other workplace trade union representatives able to monitor wages and conditions on a local basis and to challenge managerial decisions on a very wide range of issues.

Elsewhere, the articulation of levels was more coherent and 'organized'. In post-war Germany enterprise-level structures were introduced which tended to stabilize employment relations at workplace level and to focus potential conflicts at the level of the industry. Works councils (formally distinct from trade union representation even if most of those elected were in practice active trade unionists) acted as a channel through which managements communicated with and consulted employees, while in the larger companies employees were accorded minority representation on company boards. The aim, and to a great extent the result, of these arrangements was to preserve social peace within individual companies – even at times when industrial wage bargaining was a matter of intense conflict. These structures, especially the works councils, were subsequently adopted, in varying forms, by most other continental countries (Chapter 3).

Ideological differences

Subjective or *ideological* differences were equally as important as institutional ones. In most Latin countries the strongest trade union centres were aligned on explicitly anti-capitalist political projects. For example, in France the CGT, the largest and most influential of the trade union confederations, was led by communists from the Second World War onwards; another powerful centre, the CFDT, held to an *autogestionnaire* (workers' self-management) philosophy. Communists were also influential in Italian and, even before the end of the Franco regime, Spanish trade unions. In Britain, trade union leaderships, while less concerned with ideological positions, were equally or even more adversarial in their approach to company managements. In Germany and Sweden, although in somewhat different ways, unions were more inclined to accept the legitimacy of capitalist employment in practical terms, although this does not mean – far from it – that they did not succeed in constraining managerial decisions in the interests of their members.

Common features

None of these patterns of differentiations, however, prevents us from finding a certain broad functional equivalence in European industrial relations systems during the period from the 1940s to the 1970s. Whatever their governance structure, and despite the presence of Marxist and other contestatory ideologies on the workers' side, European industrial relations were in practice both economically functional and socially integrative. Collective bargaining tended to make the evolution of wage costs more stable and predictable and may also have tended to promote a steady expansion of aggregate consumption demand for the growing output of durable goods. At the same time millions of recently urbanized workers were able, under the auspices of the social models, to find their place in the modern world.

This functionality helps to explain the residual role of the state in wage bargaining. The aim of direct interventions, such as the minimum wages promulgated in France, Britain and elsewhere, was to compensate for the *absence* of institutionalized collective bargaining, above all in small-scale enterprises not effectively organized by the unions. State intervention in the other direction – to *correct* rather than to *generalize* the outcome of collective negotiations – was usually a later development which only arose when the European models were already in the throes of inflationary crisis.

4.2   The welfare state

It was suggested in the last section that direct government responsibility for social protection (typically pensions, unemployment indemnities and sickness benefits) and social services (such as housing, education and health care) supports the basic relations of the market economy by preserving enterprise autonomy. To the social rights accorded to workers there correspond not social obligations on employers, who retain their freedom of action in the market sphere, but *governmental obligations*, making the state, not the employers, the social counterpart of the workers outside the field of employment itself. This logical division is seen most clearly in Britain (and in the USA) where the values of free contract and the autonomy of market agents are most deeply rooted in political culture. In Britain this autonomy of market agency was fiercely defended not only by the employers but also by the unions, although the latter always insisted in interpreting this autonomy in collective terms (as in the slogan of 'free collective bargaining').

The same logic applies to continental Europe, but in a much less clear-cut way. As a result of the specific European conception of the 'social question', organized private interest groups are frequently present not only in industrial relations but in one or more organs of the welfare state. Certainly the government is omnipresent in welfare state institutions – as co-ordinator and as paymaster – and social services and social protection are, and are perceived to be, governmental responsibilities. However, these responsibilities are in varying ways and to varying degrees *delegated* to non-state or para-state agencies within which employers, workers, and other groupings, such as churches, are represented. Thus in France, the standard provision of unemployment indemnities is jointly managed by employers and trade unions and is to some extent a matter for negotiation between these 'social partners' (the same is also true, for example, in Denmark). Across Western Europe, 'social' (in practice, subsidized) housing is entrusted to a host of non-state agencies, profit-making and otherwise. Health insurance and health care systems are sometimes organized along industrial or occupational lines, rather than being the direct responsibility of the national government. In Belgium, even public education is provided, not directly by the state, but by agencies linked to either the Catholic Church or the workers' movement. In consequence, welfare state institutions are governed not by the pure governmental hierarchies, but by relatively autonomous para-state hierarchies involving a strong admixture of networking relations among the interest groups involved.

Once again, these institutional differences were of limited pertinence so long as the general industrial expansion of the 1950s and 1960s made for economic and social stability – at the same time limiting the demands on the welfare states and making them relatively easy to finance.

Evolution of welfare state development

During the 'long boom' or 'golden age' of the European economies, which saw the full elaboration of social models, the most significant factor of differentiation was a matter not of governance, but of temporality. The models were developed early in the northern countries at the heart of the long industrial expansion: Scandinavia, Britain, France, Germany, Belgium and the Netherlands. In Italy, which started from much lower levels of industrial development and urbanization, many of the structures of the social model – as concerning both industrial relations and the welfare state – only emerged in the 1970s. Developments in Spain and Greece were, for the same reasons, even later. However, until the sharp economic crises of the 1980s these southern countries tended to take the northern social systems as the model for their own future development: the Italian national health service instituted in the 1970s, for example, was influenced by the British precedent.

More recently this pattern of evolution has been called into question. A perception that the developed, expensive social models of Germany or Scandinavia are in crisis has prompted the question of whether the southern systems – Portugal, for example – represent a distinct and in some ways more advanced form of social model rather than being incomplete versions of the northern systems. Conservative commentators, in particular, have pointed to the role of the family in providing support for people like the young unemployed, who would be clients of welfare agencies in the north. The role of private voluntary groups (often linked to the Church) that operate at the local level is also sometimes now seen as an important strength of these southern social systems, which are not only clearly much less costly to taxpayers but also, it is asserted, more flexible in meeting the needs of individuals and in adapting to their specific circumstances than are the standardized procedures of the big hierarchies, state or para-state, which implement social policy in Britain or France. What is asserted in this type of argument is the superiority of informal networks over strongly institutionalized, hierarchical forms of governance.

Summary

- Despite there being a general and distinct social model for Europe, there have been considerable variations in its form within different countries.

- These differences arise in the context of features of centralization and decentralization, the articulation of levels of bargaining, historical and ideological differences, and the evolution of systems.

- Whether the traditional patterns of evolution have now become dysfunctional is the subject of intense contemporary debate.

5   The social crisis in Europe

In this section we examine some of the factors behind the crises in the European social models, and discuss a free-market critique of these models.

5.1   Macroeconomics

We need to recognize that the primary source of the crises is economic. It is very difficult to find in Western Europe anything analogous to the 'taxpayers' revolts' which eroded popular support for some aspects of the US welfare system. The European systems of social protection and social services in particular, but also the notion of social partnership in employment, remain popular in European countries; they have not suffered any serious loss of legitimacy and indeed are probably still regarded by most people as more legitimate than the business enterprises which are officially promoted as the only source of economic and social salvation.

Inflation

The profound deterioration of economic performance in many European countries, however, certainly led to unprecedented pressures on European social models. In the first instance these were macroeconomic pressures. In the 1970s, rising levels of inflation encouraged direct state intervention in wage determination in several countries. At this stage it appeared as if the development of the European social models might work to erode the market element in employment relations by further politicization. For example, with attempts to introduce incomes policies it seemed as if income formation, even within employment, might be increasingly determined by direct political forces and less by supply and demand in the market. Again, waves of nationalization – in systems as diverse as those of Italy, France, Sweden and Britain – seemed to call into question the continuation of capitalist employment relations as such.

But these expectations were rapidly dispelled. As it became clear that deep structural transformations of European economies were becoming necessary, and in a climate where external financial and economic pressures on European countries were becoming more intense, policy shifted toward a reassertion of market mechanisms and market disciplines. This shift was itself differentiated – radical and early in Britain, long delayed and attenuated in Sweden, very gradual in Germany, and so on. But the pressures and the direction of change were quite general, corresponding to a new set of macroeconomic circumstances.

Unemployment

Most prominent of these circumstances was the return of mass unemployment, which destabilized European social models in several ways. The balance of forces between employees and employers tilted in favour of the latter, while unprecedented pressure developed on social protection systems. Because unemployment fell most heavily on particular groups and categories of workers it also had the effect of sharpening differentiations within workforces and making it more difficult for trade unions or political parties to aggregate employee interests. At the same time a *fiscal crisis* undermined the ability of European governments to finance ambitious extensions of social protection and social services. A key factor here was a transformation of global financial conditions from late 1979 onwards. The introduction of restrictive monetary policies in the USA drove up real credit costs, so that governments which did not move promptly to narrow public sector deficits were faced with a spiral of public indebtedness; throughout the 1980s, interest payments on public debt were the most dynamic component of public expenditure.

5.2 Structural factors in the crisis

Behind and alongside the macroeconomic deterioration, a complex of structural factors also tended to destabilize the European social models. In industry, facing more mature markets for many consumer goods and subjected to intense external pressures in both product and financial markets, strategies had necessarily to be reoriented. The volume of production that could be achieved became less significant: control of costs and a rapid adaptation of the product mix to the changing requirements of customers became key priorities. These shifts favoured a radical decentralization of governance mechanisms and a new emphasis on the enterprise itself as the locus of decision making.

There were also strong centrifugal forces at work among employees. Important groups of highly qualified workers, with a key role in the restructuring and reorientation of business enterprises, tended to perceive a widening differentiation between their own interests and those of other groups. The rapid feminization of European workforces, the increasingly salient distinction between those exposed to and those sheltered from direct international competition, the concentration of unemployment in particular localities and among workers of certain industries all acted as further factors of disaggregation on the side of employees.

Similarly, systems of social protection and of social provision (for instance in housing) had to deal with an increasing differentiation of needs and of circumstances. Throughout the 1980s and 1990s average incomes in Europe continued to rise rapidly, although no longer at the breakneck rhythm of the previous decades. Higher incomes permitted the expression of more complex and differentiated preferences. At the same time there emerged pockets of acute disadvantage – in housing, incomes, educational and employment opportunity – which posed acute problems for the standardized routines and procedures of the European welfare states. In particular, the lengthy exclusion from stable employment among some disadvantaged social groups tended to undermine the principle of social insurance which had been the link between working and non-working life. Thus in both spheres of the European social models a structurally determined pressure for differentiation combined with macroeconomic factors to call the existing institutional framework into question.

5.3 'Free market' critique of the European social models

Through the 1980s and 1990s, European employment and welfare systems were subjected to a fundamental critique, which held that they worked to blunt market processes and to obstruct economic adaptation. In the labour market and employment relations, the governance mechanisms which were inherited from the long boom were accused of introducing manifold rigidities. A flexible labour market, it was asserted, required a thoroughgoing deregulation of employment contracts, a shift of decision making back to the enterprise and wage structures giving stronger incentives to workers to acquire valuable skills and to promote the profitability of their employers.

In a similar way, social protection systems were blamed for raising the cost of labour and for weakening market-led adaptation of the workforce to structural change. In addition, of course, it was claimed that the costs of the welfare state, met either by taxes and other charges or by public borrowing, imposed heavy burdens on the private sector.

Such thinking did not prevail everywhere and immediately. The 'flexibility agenda' was endorsed most enthusiastically by the British government and by the organizations of (especially large-scale) employers, but elsewhere it encountered more or less determined resistance. The first big waves of labour shedding in European industry, from the early 1980s, were in fact often accompanied by measures to increase state protection of employees and to mitigate the impact of unemployment on some social groups, such as the young. Thus these years saw a reduction in the official retirement age in France and the state funding of early retirement in much of German industry – in both cases the aim being to shield younger people from the collapse of employment opportunities.

However, as slow growth and high rates of unemployment persisted in Western Europe, the thinking behind labour market 'flexibility' and welfare reform became increasingly influential and began to condition the political programmes of most governments including those of the left. In the 1990s, the long, continuous upswing of the US economy was seen as evidence for a more market-determined model of employment. The kind of reforms which were advocated tended, besides, to correspond to the most pressing need of government to limit budget deficits and to the need for enterprises to control costs. Even those most deeply committed to the values expressed in the social models – solidarity, equality, social cohesion – began to search for ways to make governance structures more efficient and more compatible with these economic imperatives.

Summary

- The 'crisis' in the European social model arose in the context of a number of macroeconomic changes, among which were a sudden increase in inflation and a severe increase in unemployment.

- In addition a series of structural changes – leading to a long-term decline in the efficiency of the model – emerged in the 1970s and 1980s.

- This led to a call for 'reform' in the name of the need for greater all-round 'flexibility' in the labour market and welfare provision.

6   Governance and the response to crisis

It was suggested above that specific models of governance were of limited significance during the period of rapid post-war growth, which had been characterized by strong tendencies to convergence among social institutions, essentially for functional reasons. However, as social institutions came under pressure, governance structures became an important factor of differentiation both because these structures reflect the political culture of different European countries and because they are a key strategic constraint on reform agendas. The negotiation of radical change is a very different matter according to whether or not there are strongly institutionalized industrial relations systems and to whether organized private interests are present or absent within the welfare agencies themselves.

6.1   Britain: drastic and rapid change

Consider first the British example: the welfare state and industrial relations were governed, as we have seen, by government agencies and collective bargaining respectively, and the governance mechanisms involved were sharply delineated. This reflected a political culture in which conceptions of agency emphasized freedom of contract and a clear distinction between public and private responsibilities. During the 1980s it proved possible to effect radical changes in the British social structure. On the one hand, government had a direct purchase on welfare state systems such as housing or unemployment indemnities; on the other, enterprise managements, facing trade union interlocutors radically weakened by unemployment and industrial restructuring, were able to reshape industrial relations toward an enterprise-centred system, dominated by labour market pressures on the one hand and managerial initiatives on the other.

Ultimately, of course, all Western European governments are able to require reductions in social entitlements and to enforce other reductions in social expenditure; they can use both market pressures and hierarchical power structures (the power of the purse and legislation) to constrain the options of other agents. But the kind of revolutionary upheaval in social protection systems which took place in Britain in the 1980s – for instance the straightforward abolition of income-related benefits, or the virtual cessation of investment in social housing – is inconceivable in most continental European countries where powerful private interest groups are directly present in welfare structures. (In France an amendment to the Constitution was needed in 1996 to prepare the way for a reassertion of governmental control over social security.) Thus differences in governance certainly help to explain differences in the scope and speed of change in European social models, even if the direction of change – toward less universal and less generous provision – is common to them all.

6.2   Sweden: stubborn defence of full employment

In contrast to Britain, the Swedish social model resisted fundamental restructuring throughout the 1980s. This is not because the model was functioning well. The macroeconomic strategies put into place in the 1960s combined centralized wage bargaining with inflation targets designed to protect the competitiveness of exports. In addition, wage setting had a strongly egalitarian character and tended to limit differentials for skills and qualifications; to preserve full employment, 'active' interventions in localities with employment deficits were preferred to any general loosening of macroeconomic policies. Although the Swedish model did not originally involve additional constraints on enterprise autonomy (the 'right to manage'), structures of worker representation influenced by German practice were gradually introduced.

In practice, *network* relationships were central to the functioning of the Swedish employment system. Governments, until 1979 invariably dominated by the Social Democrats, were intimately connected to the leadership of the main industrial workers' union, LO (*Landsorganisationen i Severge*), who shared this political allegiance. Between the 'social partners', network relations were also important in a small country with a homogeneous population, so that industrial negotiations, in principle highly centralized and formalized, had in practice a great deal of flexibility. So, informal connections, probably inconceivable in large economies such as Britain, France or Germany, were an essential element of employment relations.

By the beginning of the 1980s, many factors were working to dislocate and disorganize all these Swedish employment governance systems. On the side of employees the growth of a massive service sector that was shielded from international competition and thus without a direct and immediate interest in international competitiveness created serious divergences, as did the emergence of highly organized unions of graduate ('academic') workers disinclined to accept the hegemony of the largely blue-collared LO. Among enterprises, the differentiations of consumer markets and of production technologies provoked increasing dissatisfaction with centralized bargaining and repeated attempts to break free of it by pulling out of bilateral negotiations at national level, while the larger companies now had opportunities to transfer production out of Sweden. Meanwhile, an overall macroeconomic balance became much more difficult to achieve within an increasingly volatile world economy.

At the same time, enterprise governance became a hotly contested political issue. A project for employee pension funds, to be controlled by the unions and intended to build up big equity stakes in Swedish companies, was originally intended as a system-preserving measure which would reconcile workers to the increase in profits which even LO economists perceived to be necessary. It was bitterly resisted by the employers' organizations who succeeded in reducing its implementation to a relatively trivial exercise.

However, popular commitment to the goals of full employment and distributive justice prevented any drastic reorientation of national policy objectives. Devaluations – sometimes very aggressive ones – and a rapid expansion of public-sector payrolls were used to secure the very high levels of employment which could no longer be brought about by the macroeconomic mechanisms of the previous era.

When Sweden finally did abandon full employment it was a forced move in the context of a huge financial crisis. At the end of the 1980s the collapse of a real-estate boom and the failure of an attempt to peg the krona to the Deutschmark made it virtually impossible to go on absorbing workers displaced from the private sector into the public sector. Accumulated weaknesses on the supply side of the economy, which had led to stagnant incomes and productivity over two decades, were finally addressed through the kind of reforms that had taken place elsewhere in Europe many years previously. Market disciplines on employees were tightened; some reduction in levels of welfare provision was unavoidable. Nevertheless, even as Sweden moved back toward more standard European employment practices in the 1990s, high levels of employment remained an exceptionally high priority in political and social life.

These two examples illustrate that different governance mechanisms – Britain and Sweden are almost polar opposites in their approaches to employment relations – can play an important role in the pace and direction of labour market change. This is particularly so because differences in governance are not arbitrary variations but tend to be rooted in the political cultures of European countries.

6.3 Italy: unstable governance mechanisms

Two other brief examples can be used to reinforce this view of the influence of political culture on governance mechanisms, Italy and Germany. In Italy, industrial relations remained largely a matter for the enterprise, and the welfare state was very undeveloped until a vast wave of industrial unrest in 1969 led to a drastic revision of employment regulation and to a rapid expansion of public services. Concessions to trade unions in the governance structure of large enterprises were then made in the form of both collective agreements and legislation to strengthen participation procedures. Also, a very generous system of compensation for laid-off workers, financed by employers and the state, protected the incomes of employees in large-scale industry when they became unemployed.

Outside of the large-scale employers of the Turin–Genoa–Milan triangle, however, things remained much as before, with few restrictions on the autonomy of small and medium-sized companies. This dichotomy in employment governance had the most profound effects on the subsequent economic development of the country. In the big industrial enterprises, constraints on managerial decision making in general and on labour shedding in particular blocked major reorganizations and restructuring throughout the 1970s, and their performance deteriorated sharply. In contrast, the performance of Italy's small-scale enterprises – often loosely networked in 'industrial districts' in the 'third Italy' of the centre and the north-east – became one of the most celebrated economic phenomena of contemporary Europe. The ability of very small businesses to deploy advanced technologies, to respond rapidly to changing market conditions and to export a very high fraction of their output rescued the Italian economy from crisis over an entire decade (see Chapter 6).

In the 1980s the withdrawal of the concessions previously granted to organized workers gradually moved Italy back toward more typical Western European modes of governance. One step in this process was the defeat of the unions in a major strike at Fiat in Turin in 1982; this signalled a change in the balance of forces in industry and a restoration of control by managerial hierarchies. Another aspect of the same 'normalization' of the Italian model was the gradual erosion and ultimate abolition of the *scala mobile* wage indexation system which had compensated industrial employees for price increases, drastically squeezed wage differentials and accelerated the inflationary process. But although the exceptional dysfunctional character of Italian labour relations governance was in the end largely eliminated, this was a lengthy process which was very important for the political and economic evolution of the country through the 1980s and into the 1990s (Sassoon, 1997).

However, perhaps against all expectations, since the early 1990s Italy has seen the conclusion of a series of relatively successful and robust agreements between industry, organized labour and the state on wage determination, industrial relations and welfare state reform. A new set of effective 'social pacts' were negotiated and a semi-corporatist social accord established as a result (Negrelli, 1997; Regini and Regalia, 1997).

6.4 Germany: gradualism and stability

German governance structures also conditioned the process of industrial restructuring and the pattern of reform of the social model. There are certainly other factors making for a gradualist approach to change – the sheer industrial strength of Germany and the solidly based competitiveness of its industrial companies meant that it was seldom necessary to undertake change in a climate of emergency. It is true, however, that the governance systems of large enterprises, with prominent representation of employee interests, worked against crude exercises in labour shedding (Chapter 3). German industry certainly restructured away from production which made intensive use of less-skilled labour, but it did so without (until the shock of German reunification) suffering the rates of unemployment experienced in France, for example (Giersch et al., 1992). Thus until the mid-1990s at least the German system of industrial relations and welfare provision remained largely intact.

6.5 General patterns of reform

Although European employment systems came under pressure almost everywhere, and although there are clearly common elements in the kind of changes that occurred both in enterprises and more widely, the extent and the nature of reform therefore varied considerably. Perhaps only in Britain can one find an attempt at complete reversal of the previous social model toward essentially market-determined labour markets. Elsewhere, change was slower and more limited, and it often combined attempts to lighten and modernize employment and social protection systems with measures to preserve the core of the social advances achieved between the 1950s and the 1970s.

Employment regulation and social protection

The actual content of reform varied considerably. In Britain, only a few measures of direct employment deregulation were enacted (notably the suppression of minimum wages in those industries where they applied), because trade union reform, together with a drastic loss of trade union membership and strength, sufficed to free managements from the constraints which had limited their powers of decision. In Germany and Spain, in contrast, an important dimension of reform was the widening of access to short-term employment contracts, because these were significantly less regulated than 'indefinite' contracts. For example, one effect of this was the ease with which employees could be dismissed. In Spain this measure led to an explosion of short-term employment which became, by the late 1980s, the typical path of entry into the labour market for young workers. Such a pattern of reform only made sense because of the close regulation of 'standard' indefinite contracts.

Similarly, social protection systems were modified in different ways and to different degrees. In Britain the principle of social insurance was compromised to the point of virtual disappearance, because the income-related welfare benefits to which contributions by employees gave entitlement were eliminated, making minimal means-tested benefits originally designed for those without contribution records all that was available for most claimants. In France and Germany reforms pressed down on the level of social security benefits and curtailed access to the most generous levels of provision, without moving away from the two-tier (social insurance plus 'safety-net') organization of the system as a whole. It is true, however, that the social insurance principle came under general pressure because of the increasing importance of groups (the long-term unemployed, school-leavers and other marginalized groups) without adequate contribution records. In France this pressure led, for the first time, to the introduction of a standardized minimum income (the RMI) for those without other resources.

Delegation

In terms of governance, a very important aspect of the reform programmes is *delegation*. In Britain the erosion and attenuation of collective bargaining procedures and welfare entitlements were presented explicitly as a system change which would substitute market disciplines for the aggregative, politically influenced determination of the incomes and living conditions of employees. This radical conception of reform was not generally accepted elsewhere. Instead, a certain decentralization of industrial relations, moving many substantive questions from national or industry-wide bargaining back to the individual company, was often viewed as a way of reforming, rather than suppressing, the existing structure of social control, with 'framework agreements' still negotiated at higher levels acting as a constraint on company-level decisions.

Working time and flexibility

The ambivalence of the 'flexibility agenda' is well illustrated by the different approaches adopted to the question of working time. In Britain there were few limits on working hours or shift patterns and only minimal entitlements to holidays beyond those enforced in 'free collective bargaining' by the unions. The relative eclipse of union power then left managements free, within very wide limits, to impose the work-time arrangements they found most advantageous. In Germany, in contrast, trade unions, retaining a great deal of their power, saw generalized reductions in the work week as a socially progressive response to high levels of unemployment. Through the 1980s the German unions negotiated substantial reductions in the standard working week. These were traded off against a flexibility in working time which accorded to the enterprises, within the new overall constraints, greater control over the distribution of working hours from week to week and over the organization of shift patterns. In France the unions themselves were not powerful enough to impose such reductions, but on two occasions socialist-led governments legislated for substantial reductions in working time, leaving it then to the 'social partners' themselves to cement the implementation of new maxima. This kind of initiative by no means blocked the drive toward more flexible employment practices, but it situated the flexibility drive in a context where social priorities could still be asserted in economic life.

6.6 Crisis and differentiation

It was suggested above that the 1960s and 1970s saw a significant convergence in the social models of different European countries, and this was related to the functional value of these models in stabilizing social and economic relations during the long European upswing. How did the long crisis of unemployment relations affect differentiation?

Clearly, many of the pressures on European labour relations were universal – this is true of both the macroeconomic and the structural factors which have been identified. For example, all countries experienced rising inflation in the 1970s and rising unemployment in the 1980s (Chapter 4); everywhere it became more important to adapt employment relations to the increased diversity of the workforce and to the circumstances of the enterprise. But these general pressures certainly did not result in uniform change.

How did change differ from country to country? Two factors above all seem to be critical: *economic performance* and *political traditions* (the latter expressed in specific governance structures).

On the one hand, stronger economies were under less pressure to undertake drastic and immediate reform. In Spain the collapse of employment at the turn of the 1980s led to attempts at root and branch change; Germany's industrial strength enabled it to undertake much more measured and gradual reform. On the other hand, aspects of governance structures – the degree of organization and cohesion of interest groups, the autonomy of employers and employees vis-à-vis the government, and patterns of state intervention – filtered the general pressures for change into very different outcomes. The impact of governance is more pronounced because differences in governance mechanisms are not arbitrary – they encapsulate important differences in political cultures and political value systems.

However, divergence in a situation of crisis carries the risk that social inequalities will increase. Specifically there is the danger that workers in stronger economies, industries and enterprises will continue to enjoy highly regulated employment conditions and high levels of social protection while their colleagues in less advantageous conditions will suffer more or less acute insecurity. This is the danger of *social exclusion*, which exists in contemporary Europe both within and between countries, and which tends to generate structures of privilege in the labour market. In its international form it has led to an increasing interest in the social dimension of the EU, which will be examined next.

Summary

- The reaction to the economic downturn in Europe after the mid-1970s was a highly differentiated response in the main economies, dependent upon specific economic performance and political traditions.

- In this context the governance mechanisms embodied in industrial relations and welfare provisions became a crucial variable in determining trends for change.

- Bearing these issues in mind, there has been a common pressure for more flexibility and an erosion of the social model in the name of market incentives.

- These trends embody serious dangers concerning inequality and social exclusion.

7 The EU in labour relations

The argument so far has presented the governance of employment and labour markets as essentially a national question, albeit a national question strongly influenced by wider social and economic trends. This is justified by the fact that the main decisions have been taken by governments and other actors within an essentially national context. This is most obviously true of social protection systems and other social services, for which primary responsibility falls on national governments, but it is also true for the interactions of employers and employees at enterprise, industry and economy-wide levels. Although some rudimentary transnational structures exist to deal with industrial relations issues, they are dominated in practice by structures of governance rooted firmly in individual countries. However, it is also necessary to examine the impact of European integration on the evolution of national social models.

7.1 The 'social dimension' of the EU

Since the very start of the integration process in the Schuman Plan of 1950, the leaders of European construction have given explicit recognition to social objectives; so the European Social Fund, originally designed to compensate workers who were adversely affected by the integration process, dates back to the European Coal and Steel Community of 1951.

The temporality of EU social development is somewhat different from that of the member states. Apart from the Social Fund itself there were few initiatives until the 1970s, when the powerful dynamic toward more comprehensive and ambitious social models in the majority of member states started to influence European-level developments with the first directives to promulgate minimum standards in employment practice throughout what was then the EEC. For the most part these concerned equal treatment of female employees, health and safety at work and (a sign of the impending restructuring of industry) the handling of mass dismissals.

7.2   Stagnation of European social policy

In the 1980s, social policy at European level was blocked by the resistance of the British government to any measures which would counteract its own drive to reinforce market disciplines in the labour market and by the determination of the main European employers' organization, UNICE, to avoid any new constraints on management. This stagnation involved the abandonment of an ambitious project to harmonize European employment relations by means of a European company statute which would impose common industrial relations procedures as a condition of company registration.

Both the European Parliament (dominated by Social Democrats and Christian Democrats committed to the development of social models, albeit in somewhat different ways) and the European Commission (led from 1985 by the French socialist Jacques Delors) attempted to relaunch European initiatives in employment regulation. In the Single European Act of 1986, for the most part a matter of further economic integration based on the removal of barriers to the free movement of goods and resources, majority decision making on health and safety legislation was reinforced. In the late 1980s, Delors sponsored negotiations on new technology and other themes between the representatives of labour and business at European level (the 'social dialogue'), but these were without any concrete result. In 1989 all member states except Britain endorsed a Charter of Employment Rights, which, although without legislative force in itself, envisaged an 'Action Programme' aimed at reinforcing and generalizing the rights of individual employees.

7.3   Relaunch of 'social Europe'

The Treaty of Maastricht, signed in 1992, was once again concerned primarily with economic integration, in this case through monetary union, but it also pursued the logic of the Charter and Action Programme.

A 'Social Protocol', from which Britain was granted a derogation, allowed labour market legislation across a wide range of issues to be enacted on the basis of majority voting. Early consequences of this move were new Directives on European works councils for transnational companies, on parental leave and, most recently, on the equal treatment of part-time and full-time workers (thus a response to some of the social consequences of the flexibility agenda). A directive to place EU-wide limits on working hours was forced through as a Health and Safety measure and hence applicable to Britain.

A new social dialogue?

These labour market regulations are probably the most important expression of 'social Europe'. (Since the New Labour administration which took office in Britain in 1997 signed up for the social protocol of the Maastricht Treaty, they are now universally applicable throughout the EU.) Once actual legislation on labour market issues was resumed, the social dialogue took on a new importance because employers' representatives were now aware that, in the absence of an agreement with trade union representatives, Parliament and Council could impose their own judgements in legally binding form. UNICE therefore signalled a new readiness for compromise with employee representatives.

There are other aspects to EU social policy but they are in general less important than its legislation on labour markets and conditions of employment. Thus the Social Fund, now subsumed in the 'structural funds', provides some resources for regional development, but the scale of this intervention is too limited to have a major impact on employment conditions except for a small number of regions on which intervention is concentrated.

There has been little EU activity in the field of social protection outside the general legal requirement, derived from the requirement of labour mobility within the EU, that 'national treatment' should be available to workers from other member states.

However, the 'Luxembourg' process, initiated in 1998, represents an interesting new departure in EU social policy. In essence the aim is to co-ordinate and supervise 'active' employment measures in the member states, without any major transfer of policy competence to EU level. Member states are committed to developing their active labour market interventions in favour of disadvantaged groups, especially the long-term unemployed. They report on these national developments which are then compared and measured against agreed 'benchmarks' such as a target of an offer of training or temporary work to each young unemployed worker before their spell of unemployment extends to six months. This is an innovative step in the transnational governance of EU labour markets in that it is designed on a network basis; the aim is not to establish a Europe-wide authority for labour market interventions, but to build a strong policy community which can connect national initiatives, spread best practice and start to lay down general standards. It may be through the growth of such policy communities rather than by directly federalist reforms that the EU dimension of labour market governance will develop in the near future.

A race to the bottom?

It is increasingly recognized that general economic interdependence is multiplying the spillover effects among national social models. Member countries are competing to attract investment and employment to their national territories and this leads to certain pressures to modify social governance structures. One extreme vision is of a generalized 'race to the bottom' where competitive pressures to reduce labour costs and to relax constraints in employment practice would tend to undermine the social models in all or many countries – this is the fear behind the famous theme of 'social dumping'. The vision is implausible because the various social models retain a great deal of functionality and each one has specific resources which it can mobilize in its own defence – such as the tradition of wide-ranging collective bargaining in Germany or the enduring legitimacy of strong state intervention in France. Nevertheless, these competitive pressures are real, and form one component of the constellation of factors (including many domestic economic and political developments) influencing changes in governance.

A federal social model?

It is equally implausible to envisage the emergence of a federal social model which would establish uniform patterns of labour market governance across the EU as a whole. This kind of prospect commands no political support and would be seen as weakening the link between national governance systems and the traditions and values that they reflect – the importance of solidarity in Scandinavia, for example, or the desire in Germany to protect family incomes and the established status of employees.

Nevertheless, interactions among national social models are bound to become more prominent and to involve all forms of governance. Market processes include competition for investment and finance, but also the diffusion of successful practices across national boundaries. Networks will include the Europe-wide policy communities referred to above and also the increasingly dense interactions which can be observed among national interest groups. And hierarchical authority will continue to be deployed, not to impose a common or uniform social model, but, as in the past, to lay down certain minimum standards in employment practice and even in some fields of social protection. The balance between these developments and the ability of network and/or hierarchical authoritative governance structures to respond to the failures of purely market structures are key questions for the emerging EU polity.

The changing framework

A final point to note here is that although the EU level has had a limited *direct* impact so far on the essentially national environment in which labour relations and associated welfare provision are determined, that may be about to change. The EU level is already changing the *framework* within which national policy is determined. It must do this, since even at the level of the most mundane economic activity the development of a Europe-wide economy of integrated trade, investment and migration has an impact on individual-country competitiveness, and hence on how it conducts its labour and social policies. The free movement of labour within the EU and migration, for instance, represent a challenge to the existing domestic arrangements. Additionally, the development of European companies with Europe-wide operations inevitably affects how they operationalize their labour strategies across the continent, and this again impacts on the frameworks of specific national economies.

As EMU develops this will once again increase the pressures for national adaptation to the macroeconomic implications of its operation – a single currency, single interest rate, no exchange rates. Thus the internal environment for the conduct of labour and welfare policies will increasingly have to take account of this new pan-European regulatory framework.

Summary

- In the context of the 'crisis' in the social Europe model new initiatives have emerged at the EU level.

- These are, however, only weakly represented in the face of still strong national reforms.

- The continuing robustness of these national systems also puts constraints on far-reaching and universalized pressures for change.

- We are unlikely to see a new federal EU social model emerging to compensate for the relative undoing of the old 'social Europe' model.

- However, the external environment of economic Europe is changing rapidly as the EU gathers more competencies over domestic economic management, which indirectly changes the framework for domestic social and labour policies.

8 Centralization, social corporatism and social pluralism

To return to the national level, which remains critical for the governance of labour markets in Europe, the importance of centralization for labour market governance must be stressed. As has been seen, the prevailing tendency in industrial relations over the last twenty years has been decentralizing – moving influence over wages and conditions toward the enterprise. However, this tendency has been contested both in theory and in practice. Some economists have suggested that centralized wage determination might produce more, not less, flexibility in the response of overall wage rates to variations in unemployment (Chapter 4). The argument depends on 'market failure' or externalities in decentralized labour markets. One source of such failure might be an 'insider/outsider' segmentation of the workforce which permits established workers to obtain wages above market-clearing levels at the expense of the unem-ployed. An encompassing agreement at national level might then allow such external effects to be internalized. This is a complex debate with no clear results. Some writers have stressed the co-ordination of wage determination rather than its centralization; this would amount to favouring network patterns of governance – linking up bargains in various sectors or regions – rather than hierarchical national structures as the best corrective to market inefficiencies.

In practice, it has become clear recently that the age of nationally agreed wage norms is by no means over. In particular, there has been concern in many countries that the advent of the single currency and the consequent inability to alter the national exchange rate might give rise to a serious loss of competitiveness and thus higher unemployment. In response, national 'social pacts' and 'social contracts' have been used – in the Netherlands, Ireland, Italy and elsewhere – to set limits to wage growth in return for concessions to unions in employment practice and social provision. These agreements are certainly lighter – less comprehensive and less constraining – than many centralized agreements have been in the past. But they indicate that there has been no complete triumph of the forces for market-led decentralization and depoliticization of European industrial relations. These complex relationships between the centralization and decentralization of wage bargaining mechanisms raise the general issue of the continued salience of social corporatism at the European level (Chapters 1 and 4).

The relationship between centralized wage bargaining and the political concept of 'corporatism' is very complex. Some economists use the two terms as synonyms but political scientists have used the expression 'corporatism' or 'neo-corporatism' to refer to the devolution of aspects of state power to organized private interests. The first characterization of Western European labour market regulation as corporatist was intended as a criticism of European polities: the aim was to contest the presentation of organized interest groups as 'pluralist' – by analogy with standard accounts of the USA – and to establish an element of continuity between contemporary European democracies and the traditionalist or authoritarian polities of the past. However, it was recognized that corporatist forms of governance today represent an innovation in that they amount to a means of introducing social control over governmental decisions and not simply, as in the past, a reinforcement of state control over society.

In the sphere of labour market governance the term 'social corporatism' is sometimes used to denote the presence of employee representatives in the governance structures concerned, alongside representatives of the employers (Chapter 3; Pekkarinen et al., 1992). (When only employer representatives are delegated authority over labour market governance, one might speak, by contrast, of 'conservative corporatism'.)

The key link between corporatism and labour market centralization lies in various forms of 'ergo omnes' clause; that is, on the fact that a centralized bargain agreed between employers' and employees' organizations becomes binding on all labour market actors, including those who do not belong to the organizations concerned. This practice is foreign to traditional British conceptions of free contract, but is the rule in Germany, France, Belgium, the Netherlands and Scandinavia. Clearly it amounts to a kind of state-sponsored monopoly – in this case a monopoly of representation. Although this kind of monopoly survives there is no doubt that it is being increasingly eroded: in more open and complex economies there is increasing scope for individual workers and employers to depart from prescriptive centralized agreements and these agreements themselves are becoming less ambitious. Indeed, it is probably true to say that the interaction of employers' and employees' organizations is becoming, belatedly, more *pluralist*. This does not mean that such organizations will cease to emphasize social questions, but it does suggest that they have to assert their social objectives more through *networking forms of governance* which link up a multiplicity of autonomous agents and less through the imposition of hierarchical constraints on individual behaviour. Thus the overall tendency of European labour market governance is toward what might be called 'social pluralism'.

Summary

- Complex relationships between centralization and decentralization characterize the contemporary reform of European wage bargaining mechanisms.

- This is having a profound impact on residual 'social corporatism' in Europe.

- There is a trend for this to be replaced by 'social pluralism'.

9 Conclusion

How can we assess the overall evolution of European forms of labour market governance, and of the European social models that they express? At the end of the 1970s, economic pressures led to a crisis of the European social models. The factors involved were not only macroeconomic (inflation, unemployment, public sector deficits) but also structural (increased differentiation of employee circumstances and of enterprise strategies).

This crisis led to a pattern of reform which at first sight seemed to threaten the very survival of the social models. Social protection regimes became less universal and less generous; industrial relations were decentralized and deregulated. Both developments reinforced market pressures on labour market agents and attenuated direct political influence over labour market outcomes. There certainly exists an influential neo-liberal stream of thought which advocates more reform in the same direction – toward, as it were, an Americanization of European labour markets.

However, there are reasons to believe that established governance mechanisms have more survival value than such a view allows. Both industrial relations and social protection regimes are rooted in national political cultures and continue to enjoy massive political legitimacy. The overwhelming majority of political forces are committed to the renewal of the social models rather than their dismantling.

Particularly impressive are some of the measures that have been used to recuperate the 'flexibility agenda' itself, for example to re-establish elements of social control over non-standard employment contracts or to reabsorb the socially excluded into the social protection system. In this context, decentralization of governance systems is accepted, but is subjected to significant constraints either by legislation or by framework agreements between employers and employees. The successful reduction of standard working weeks as a counterpart to more flexible working practices is one important expression of this tendency; so also is the increasingly systematic use of 'active' employment measures.

Similarly, although the economic development of the EU has certainly increased some of the pressures on national governance systems, there is also an important social dimension to European integration which works to underpin national social models.

Both national and Europe-wide developments exhibit a tendency to make more use of network relationships as a corrective to developments within labour markets and company hierarchies; centralized hierarchical control over employment practice, while it has certainly not disappeared, is less prominent than in the past. This new balance of governance mechanisms is necessitated by the growing complexity and differentiation of European economic and social systems. It implies a radical change in the functioning of the social models but need not imply the triumph of free markets over the values which these models express.

References

Coase, R. (1993) *The Nature of the Firm: Origins, Evolution and Development*, Oxford, OUP.

Esping-Andersen, G. (1990) *The Three Worlds of Welfare Capitalism*, Cambridge, Polity.

Giersch, H., Paqué, K.H. and Schmieding, H. (1992) *The Fading Miracle: Four Decades of Market Economy in Germany*, Cambridge, CUP.

Negrelli, S. (1997) 'Social pacts and flexibility: towards a new balance between macro and micro industrial relations: the Italian experience' in Fajertag, G. and Pochet, P. (eds) *Social Pacts in Europe*, Brussels, European Trade Union Institute/Observatorie Social Européan.

Pekkarinen, J., Pohjola, M. and Rowthorn, B. (1992) *Social Corporatism: A Superior Economic System?*, Oxford, Clarendon.

Regini, M. and Regalia, I. (1997) 'Employers, unions and the state: the resurgence of concertation in Italy?', *West European Politics*, vol.20, no.1, pp.210–30.

Sassoon, D. (1997) *Contemporary Italy: Economy, Society and Politics Since 1945*, London, Longman (second edition).

Soskice, D. (1990) 'Wage determination: the changing role of institutions in advanced industrialized countries', *Oxford Review of Economic Policy*, vol.6, no.4, pp.1–23.

Williamson, D.E. (1985) *The Economic Institutions of Capitalism*, New York, Collier Macmillan.

Further reading

Chasen, J. (ed.) (1997) *Social Insurance in Europe*, Bristol, Policy Press.

Crouch, C. and Streeck, W. (eds) (1997) *Political Economy of Modern Capitalism: Mapping Convergence and Diversity*, London, Sage.

Ferrera, M. and Rhodes, M. (eds) (2000) *Recasting European Welfare States*, London, Cass.

Hyman, R. and Femer, A. (eds) (1994) *New Frontiers in European Industrial Relations*, Oxford, Blackwell.

Hyman, R. and Femer, A. (eds) (1998) *Changing Industrial Relations in Europe*, Oxford, Blackwell.

Chapter 6
Governing European technology and innovation

Roberto Simonetti

1 Introduction

In the late 1980s Keith Pavitt and Parimar Patel, two researchers at the Science Policy Research Unit of the University of Sussex, published an academic article that was entitled significantly 'Is Western Europe losing the technological race?' (Patel and Pavitt, 1987). In their study they asked whether Europe had fallen so far behind the USA and Japan in the production of new technology that the gap was too wide to close. Since then, other studies that have analysed the technological activities of industrialized countries have confirmed that, although Europe is world leader in some areas of science and technology, the USA is home to radically new innovations in fast-growing markets and Japanese firms have the edge over Europe in many important technologies.

In particular, some studies have shown that Europe is lagging in various technologies, such as information and communication technologies (ICTs), which are associated with large increases in productivity (the output obtained for each unit of the inputs used in the process of production) and employment. Indeed, some economists argue that the cause of Europe's high rates of unemployment is to be found more in the structure of its technological and trade specialization than in the institutional structure of the labour markets. As we shall see, European countries tend to specialize in traditional sectors (which experience slow expansion or decline of output and employment) relative to Japan and the USA, in terms of both innovation and exports.

As the introduction of new technology is linked to the competitiveness of an economy and to increases in the quality of life it is important to understand the main issues in the governance of technology and innovation and, in particular, how European countries and institutions have tackled the governance of innovation over time.

To be sure, the introduction of new technology also has negative consequences and generates problems that society has to deal with. Two examples of the negative effects of technological change have been well known for a long time. During the industrial revolution the introduction of new machines generated unemployment as each new machine substituted for the work of many manual workers. Today, the demise of declining industries in some European regions, such as the North-West of England, still creates pockets of long-term unemployment. Moreover, the burning of fossil fuels such as coal or oil products, needed to operate the new machines, has generated much pollution and is associated with the process of global warming (Chapter 7).

The Austrian economist Joseph A. Schumpeter recognized the fact that industrial innovation both creates wealth and has a destructive effect on the economy, as firms that operate in old industries and use old methods of production are wiped out by innovative competitors. He coined the term 'creative destruction' to summarize the effect of innovation in the economy. In his opinion, the introduction of new goods and services and the creation of new markets were the prime engine of economic development. He recognized that some of the effects were undesirable and possibly unfair, but stressed that the main way to improve the wealth of the economy was to encourage the introduction of innovation. Today, economists and policy makers accept that even if innovation has some unpleasant effects (such as temporary unemployment and failure of firms) nations may not have much of a choice in the introduction of innovations because that is possibly the most important factor in international competitiveness.

Like all the other industrialized countries, European nations have for a long time designed and implemented many policies in support of science and technology. Public funding of scientific research and the establishment of the patent system, which protects the right of inventors from competitors who copy their patented new ideas, are just two examples of government policies designed to increase the scientific and technological knowledge in a country. More recently, European countries have also stepped up the degree of intra-European collaborations in science and technology within a number of programmes, some of which are managed by the European Commission.

This chapter aims to give a brief picture of the main issues that Europe currently faces in the field of science and technology, and to provide some theoretical tools to make sense of the rationale behind the governance of science and technology. The next two sections will illustrate the state of European technology, and will consider some historical developments that have led to the current situation.

Section 4 shows how the governance of technology is usually achieved through a mix of the three mechanisms of governance you have already met in this book: markets, regulation and networks. We shall also see that the concept of networks (or systems) is very relevant when we want to understand how innovation is governed. Many policy initiatives today are based on the notion that successful innovation is introduced when many different parts of the economy work well together as a system, and policy makers often talk about 'systems of innovation'.

Section 5 applies the notion of system of innovation to the European case and illustrates the development of cross-border European institutions aimed at the governance of innovation. As is the case in most of the issues in the social sciences, there is no easy conclusion on the best way of governing innovation, and many researchers and policy makers disagree on the best course of action. However, by the end of the chapter you should be familiar with the mechanisms involved in the governance of innovation and will have some knowledge of the European institutions that deal with the promotion of new technology so that you will be able to reach your own informed opinion about the best way Europe can govern science and technology.

2 Innovation in Europe: trends and developments

This section offers a snapshot of the innovative performance of European countries by viewing it under four headings. First, we look at the overall innovative efforts of Europe, irrespective of the nature of the activities undertaken and of their geographical distribution. Second, we consider the technological fields in which Europe has a relative advantage, namely the technologies in which Europe is specialized. Third, we illustrate the distribution of innovative activities within Europe. Finally, we introduce some issues that affect the innovation process, although traditionally they are not strictly considered as part of that process.

2.1 The overall innovative effort

Technological innovation, the introduction of new technology in the economy, is not easy to measure because it is a complex phenomenon that involves many different activities. A range of indicators of the technological activities of countries, firms and regions has been introduced over time to capture the various features of the innovation process. Among all indicators, the most used is the amount of resources invested in research and technological development (R & D) by business firms and government agencies. R & D is undoubtedly one of the primary sources of innovation, if not *the* major source. It includes the activities of scientists and engineers who aim both to improve knowledge in scientific and technological fields and to introduce new products and processes into the economic system. Therefore, the amount of resources devoted to R & D in, say, a country, offers a significant indication of the level of innovative activities in the country in question.

Figure 6.1 shows that European countries generally lag in the amount of expenditure devoted to non-defence R & D as a percentage of gross domestic product (GDP). The combined R & D expenditure as a percentage of GDP for the six European countries in the figure (Germany, France, Italy, the UK, Belgium and the Netherlands) is below the corresponding figure for both Japan and the USA in both the years considered. Moreover, the figure shows that, comparing 1993 with 1973, the gap between Europe and Japan is also increasing over time.

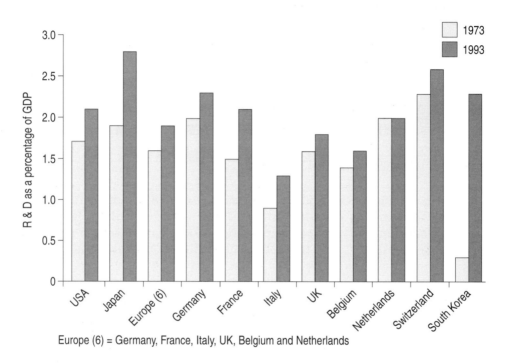

Europe (6) = Germany, France, Italy, UK, Belgium and Netherlands

Figure 6.1 Non-defence R & D as a percentage of GDP (estimates, selected years)

(derived from Fagerberg et al., 1999, p.5)

Concerns about the overall level of R & D expenditures in Europe were already expressed in the *White Paper on Growth, Competitiveness and Employment* published by the European Commission (Commission of European Communities, 1993). The paper reported an even bigger gap between Europe, meaning the European Community (EC) in 1991, and the other two major blocs, with the EC investing only 2 per cent of GDP in R & D compared with 2.8 per cent in the USA and 3 per cent in Japan. The paper also identified a bigger gap to be filled in the number of engineers and researchers – 4 out of 1,000 of the population in Europe compared to 8 and 9 out of 1,000 in the USA and Japan respectively.

These weaknesses are confirmed if we look at patent statistics (number of patents granted to residents in Europe) or trade in high-technology products, which are two other widely used indicators of the technological activities of a country.

2.2 The profile of technological and industrial specialization

The data on the overall innovative activities, on their own, only tell part of the story. We must also look at what European countries are particularly good at. A small amount of resources channelled toward the right areas could still represent a very good use of resources. In the European case, however, the patterns of technological and industrial specialization add to the existing concerns.

One way to analyse the pattern of technological specialization of a country is to examine how the country fares in the export of high-tech products. If the country's profile of trade specialization shows a good performance in high-tech products it means that the overall innovative investment of the country is specialized in high-tech areas, which are usually very beneficial to the rest of the economy.

Following work carried out by Pavitt (1984), it is possible to group industries according to the technological characteristics of the products and the sources of new technology.

- Industries included in the groups 'agricultural products and raw materials' and 'traditional industries', such as textiles, leather furniture and simple metal products, do not experience a significant rate of technological progress and rely on low-skilled labour. Innovation in these industries mainly occurs through new machines and components that are produced in other industries and used in the process of production.

- The 'specialized suppliers' group encompasses industries that produce machinery, components, instruments, and now, increasingly, software for a wide range of other industries. Innovation in these industries is often introduced by small and medium-sized enterprises (SMEs) and is important for innovation in downstream sectors, such as 'traditional' and some 'scale-intensive' industries.

- Industries in the 'scale-intensive' group, such as motor vehicles, rubber and consumer durables, are dominated by a few very large firms who exploit the significant economies of scale (see Box 6.1 overleaf) existing in the process of production.

- Industries in the 'science-based' group, which include drugs, computers, telecommunications and aerospace, rely directly on the output of R & D and academic research for the introduction of innovations. They include many of the ICT industries and are generally associated with increases in productivity and employment in the whole economy.

The share of exports in 'agricultural products and raw materials' in the total world trade has declined sharply, while the share of trade in 'science-based' industries has grown rapidly, as Figure 6.2 clearly shows. We go on now to consider this in the light of the EU's export shares in the various types of industry – and we shall see that it is bad news for Europe. Table 6.1 reports the share of exports of each of the four economic blocs – the EU, USA, Japan, and the newly industrialized countries (NICs) of Asia – for

Box 6.1   Economies of scale

Economies of scale exist when the average cost of a product (the cost of a unit of the goods produced) falls with the increase in number of the units produced.

The existence of large fixed costs is often the source of economies of scale. Fixed costs are those costs that do not depend on the number of units produced. They are usually due to large investment in capital equipment, such as large plants and machinery.

Large fixed investments have less effect on the cost of each unit of the product if they are spread over a large number of units. Hence, a large capital investment is often associated with economies of scale.

Economies of scale also have a dynamic aspect. The greater the number of units produced, the greater the opportunities to learn about the technology used in production through the process of 'learning by doing'. So, the greater the number of units produced the more the technology improves. This relationship between the cumulative output over time and the productivity of a plant is also known as the 'learning curve'.

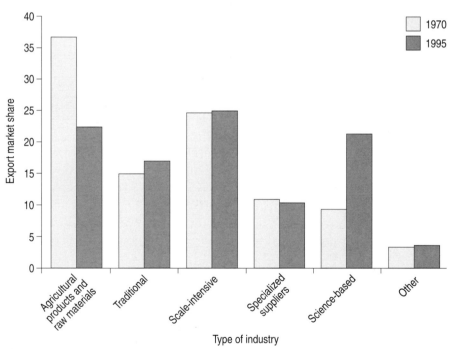

Figure 6.2 Commodity composition of world trade, 1970 and 1995 (derived from Fagerberg et al., 1999, p.10)

each group of industries for 1970 and 1995. European countries have improved their export shares only in 'agricultural products and raw materials' and were losing their relative strength especially in 'science-based' industries. They were only slightly declining in 'scale-intensive' industries.

Table 6.1 Export market shares (ratio of national exports to world total exports), 1970 and 1995

	Agricultural products and raw materials	
	1970	*1995*
EU 15	24.1	31.6
USA	13.1	11.0
Japan	1.2	1.4
Asian NICs	2.0	3.4
Total	40.4	47.4

	Traditional	
	1970	*1995*
EU 15	57.0	40.1
USA	7.4	6.7
Japan	9.3	3.2
Asian NICs	6.1	16.2
Total	79.8	66.2

	Scale-intensive	
	1970	*1995*
EU 15	55.7	47.3
USA	14.5	10.3
Japan	13.8	12.8
Asian NICs	1.0	8.7
Total	85.0	79.1

	Specialized suppliers	
	1970	*1995*
EU 15	61.2	47.6
USA	22.3	13.7
Japan	6.4	15.7
Asian NICs	9.3	8.8
Total	99.2	85.8

	Science-based	
	1970	*1995*
EU 15	48.6	33.8
USA	29.5	17.9
Japan	7.7	14.3
Asian NICs	1.0	17.8
Total	86.8	83.8

	Total	
	1970	*1995*
EU 15	44.6	39.6
USA	14.8	11.8
Japan	6.7	9.0
Asian NICs	2.1	10.8
Total	68.2	71.2

(derived from Fagerberg et al., 1999, p.12)

The data therefore show that, although there are some exceptions, the EU seems to be broadly specialized in the 'wrong' industries and technologies. This is especially true for ICTs (Information and Communication Technologies), in which European countries seem to be lagging substantially.

ICTs started as technologies for administrative purposes, such as payrolls, but they have now become so pervasive in almost all the functions of firms and the activities in society, that the opportunities they offer are abundant in many different spheres of activity. Many now talk about a new revolution – the information revolution – and the emergence of a 'new economy'. Whatever the terms used, there is widespread agreement that the development of strong capabilities in the ICTs is very important for the future prosperity of any industrialized country. Figure 6.3 shows the values of an index of technological specialization in ICTs for Europe, the USA and Japan.

The figure shows that Europe lags behind both the USA and Japan, and its specialization is also getting worse. In fact, the situation for Europe is even worse than the figure suggests, as the data employed underestimates the strength of the USA in ICTs. More data disaggregated by type of technology, but not reported here, indicates that Europe lags across virtually all the ICTs with the exception of telecommunications, in which various European countries have a positive specialization.

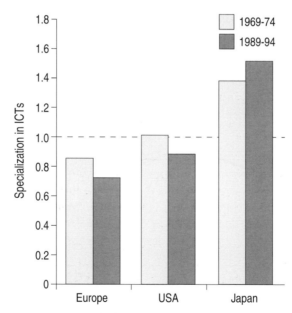

Figure 6.3 Index of technological specialization in ICTs for Europe, the USA and Japan, 1969–1974, 1989–1994

Note: Values above 1 indicate a positive specialization in ICTs while values below 1 indicate a negative specialization.

(derived from Dalum et al., 1999, p.117)

2.3   Unity and diversity in Europe

Important differences exist between member states in respect of Europe's technological specialization, as Figure 6.4 shows in the case of specialization in ICTs. The only two European countries with a positive specialization in ICTs are Ireland, because of inward FDI (foreign direct investment) from foreign multinationals active in ICTs, and the Netherlands, because it is home to the giant electronics corporation Philips. An analysis of trade data reveals similar differences.

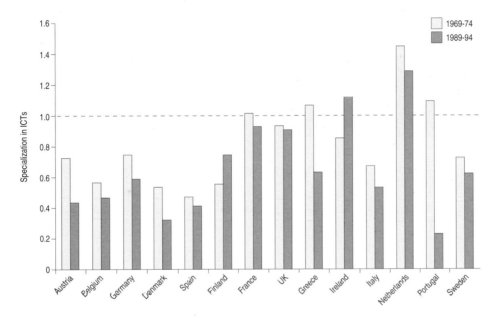

Figure 6.4   Index of technological specialization in ICTs by country in Europe, 1969–1974, 1989–1994

(derived from Dalum et al., 1999, p.117)

The very different level and profile of technological capabilities across European countries has, in fact, prompted the European Commission to promote social cohesion and less unequal distribution of technological capabilities within the EU. We discuss this further in Section 5.

The pattern of inequality that is observed at the country level is even more marked if we move to the regional level, with just a few regions responsible for most of the European R & D and innovative output.

Other issues

R & D expenditure, patents and trade in high-technology goods give us a picture of the scientific and technological potential of European countries, but are not the whole of the story. It is often reported that the European science and technology base does not rank second to, say, the Japanese one, but European firms find it difficult to translate knowledge into innovations that are successful on the market. Various reasons are often quoted for such failure, from the lack of a thriving entrepreneurial culture to the lack of adequate finance for new high-technology firms that are created to exploit new radical technologies. Moreover, it has also been suggested that large firms are often too powerful and that government policies do not pay enough attention to SMEs, which are very important actors in the regional economies.

Another important issue is the role of nations compared to that of institutions which extend beyond national boundaries, such as the EU. For example, what is, and what should be, the role of the EU in the governance of European innovation? What other significant cross-border initiatives exist?

Finally, given the much quoted process of globalization that is currently taking place in the world economy, we should ask ourselves what exactly the governance of European technology means when many European firms have set up research facilities abroad and foreign multinationals carry out research in Europe.

Summary

- Europe lags behind the USA and Japan in terms of overall innovative effort.

- Europe has a poor performance in most of the fast-growing 'science-based' technologies, especially ICTs, while it shows a good performance in 'agriculture and raw materials' and 'scale-intensive' industries.

- The strength and specialization of European science and technology varies a great deal across nations and regions.

- Other issues that impinge on the European strength in science and technology are the performance of financial institutions, the role of the European Commission in European science and technology, and the process of globalization.

3   Innovation in Europe: a historical perspective

The data presented in the previous section gives us an interesting snapshot of the current status of the technological activities of European countries, but does not tell us much about the factors that can help us understand the present situation. This section offers a different perspective on European innovation by looking at the lessons from history.

3.1   The early twentieth century

Due in part to its technological supremacy, the UK led the world economy until the end of the nineteenth century, and the other European countries followed in the process of industrialization. At the beginning of the twentieth century, however, the USA surpassed the UK in terms of output per person. Among the key factors behind the economic rise of the USA were the abundance of natural resources and the development of new technologies that were based on a new way of organizing the process of production and distribution of goods: mass production. A key component of the American technological success was the effective exploitation of economies of scale, which allowed American firms to produce large quantities of goods at very low prices.

For some authors, the emergence of scale-intensive production and of very large corporations represented a distinctive break from the previous model of industrialization and required compatible institutional structures in order to be effectively exploited. Scale-intensive production, for instance, requires a large market so that the high number of units produced can be sold and this means having many consumers with purchasing power. The USA had a large and expanding market at the time. The fragmentation of the European market, however, failed to adequately stimulate the growth of scale-intensive industries in Europe. The large size of the US market, combined with the scale-intensive technologies, encouraged the growth of huge corporations that led the American economic growth. The USA increasingly dominated the world economy until the middle of the century, when a process of convergence between industrialized countries started to take place, partly as a consequence of the end of the Second World War.

3.2   Post-Second World War

Since the 1950s, Europe has successfully caught up with the USA in many of the scale-intensive industries such as cars and domestic appliances, due in no small part to the efforts made to create a single European market with a size rivalling the American market in order to reap the benefits of economies of scale. In addition, the aftermath of the Second World War saw the diffusion of large-scale scientific and technological projects. The war had clearly shown the importance of being at the forefront of science and technology, and nuclear energy held many promises for the future model of industrialization.

The current European pattern of technological specialization indicated in Table 6.1 and Figures 6.1 and 6.3 above is partly the consequence of the economic events and the policies pursued in the decades after the Second World War. In those years, most of the European countries were catching up with the world leaders both economically and technologically. The process of catching up was mainly based on copying and assimilating existing technology from the USA. This is a task that does not require as much R & D as that needed to introduce completely new technology. In some European countries the investment in R & D was also subsidized by the state. These events can partially explain why European firms tend to invest less in R & D than their American counterparts, although it does not explain why Japanese firms invest such large amounts.

Policy makers at the time were also aware that the limited size of the national markets in Europe was limiting the opportunities offered by the well-developed scale-intensive technologies. The creation of the single market was seen as an important factor in the development of European scale-intensive industries. In 1988 the so-called Cecchini Report of the European Commission (see Box 2.2 of Chapter 2) estimated that the single market would produce a further 2.1 per cent economic growth just from the exploitation of economies of scale (Commission of European Communities, 1988).

The data on EU trade specialization, which we saw in Table 6.1, reflect the European effort in developing strong scale-intensive industries, in which Europe lost far less export market share than in the other manufacturing industries. The table also shows the effect of the development of the Common Agricultural Policy (CAP), which contributed to the European good performance in 'agricultural products and raw materials'.

While European efforts concentrated on the development of scale-intensive technology, science-based industries became gradually more important in terms of both economic growth and employment performance. ICTs began to emerge but most European countries missed the opportunity to gain an early lead in those new key technologies – with the exception of the field of telecommunications, in which both national and EU intervention have stimulated the creation of technological capabilities.

You will see below that European leaders acknowledge that ICTs are a key technology for the future prosperity of Europe, and the European Commission is currently placing a great emphasis on the development of the 'information society'.

Summary

- The economic rise of the USA until the second half of the twentieth century was largely due to the development of mass production, which occurred through an effective exploitation of scale-intensive technologies and the presence of a large internal market.

- In the second half of the twentieth century, European countries started catching up with the USA in scale-intensive technologies through technology transfer from the USA. In addition, the development of a single European market was perceived as an important factor in the stimulation of mass production in Europe.

- The emphasis on scale-intensive technology and agriculture in European industrial policy was partly responsible for the delay in the development of ICTs in Europe.

4   The governance of innovation

I have argued in the previous two sections that new technology has a key role in modern industrial economies and that Europe's performance in innovation lags behind the USA and Japan in important areas such as ICTs. In order to analyse the factors behind Europe's technological performance we need to establish a framework that allows us to understand and analyse how innovation is governed. In particular, we need to investigate how the three models of governance that you have met in this book help us to understand the governance of innovation. But before we do that we look briefly at the place of knowledge and skills in technological innovation.

4.1   Technology, knowledge and skills

Technological innovation is the introduction into the economy of new products or processes of production – new artefacts that embody new technological knowledge. In order to understand how technology is governed, however, it is more useful to concentrate on the *knowledge* that is required to create an artefact. Countries, regions and firms that possess advanced technological knowledge have important advantages in the introduction of new products or processes. So the problem in the governance of innovation is to find an effective way of promoting the creation of new technological knowledge and its diffusion within a country, region or firm. This, in turn, requires the understanding of the main features of technological knowledge.

Technology is often viewed as applied science. Indeed, scientific knowledge *is* a great input in the production of complex artefacts such as drugs or aircraft, but the idea of technology as applied science suggests that in order to produce an artefact it is only necessary to find the right type of *information*, for instance by reading a scientific journal. In some cases, however, science does not have much to do with the production of goods and services. For example, you can study all the scientific books in the world but will never be able to reproduce a beautiful piece of carpentry. In order to do that you need to be a skilled carpenter – you need *skills*. A skill is different from scientific knowledge because it cannot be passed on just like the sort of information gained through, say, a book: it is a particular type of knowledge, one that is *tacit*, not explicit, embodied in a person or even a group of persons. Some skills cannot be passed on at all, and in some cases people cannot even articulate what skills they have. Firms and other types of organizations can have skills (or 'tacit knowledge') that are embodied both in the people that form the organization and in the way those people interact and the procedures and routines they follow.

The key issue in the governance of innovation in a territory, therefore, is to find an effective way of promoting the creation and accumulation of public and tacit knowledge in the institutions of the territory. In practice, governance of innovation is achieved with a mix of the three models of governance: markets, regulatory order and networks.

4.2 Governing innovation: market system and regulatory order

We move on now to consider the pros and cons of market and regulatory systems and also see what happens when they are combined.

Market-led approaches

Supporters of the market system argue that markets are the best governance mechanism for innovation, for both theoretical and empirical reasons. Economists have shown that under certain conditions markets allocate the existing resources in the most efficient way, given the preferences of consumers and the technology available (Chapter 1). If this is true, then it is possible to argue that we could leave the allocation of resources for technological innovation to the market. In theory, the market, through the working of the price mechanism, would allocate the right amount of investment to innovation.

Indeed, privately owned firms do invest in R & D in order to gain profits and market share. In some industries, such as pharmaceuticals, computers and telecommunications, most of the innovations are introduced by privately owned profit-seeking firms, and firms know that their competitiveness depends on the accumulation of vital technological knowledge. The governance of technological knowledge through the market, however, is not without problems. The model of market that is used to neatly demonstrate the efficiency of markets is not always appropriate for all types of goods. In particular, technological knowledge is a good with some strange characteristics that make it difficult to allocate through a market system.

The introduction of technological innovation requires an investment in the creation and accumulation of new knowledge that is usually quite expensive and characterized by a high degree of *uncertainty* – most of the innovations that are the output of R & D are either technically or economically a failure. So innovative activity, because of its very nature involving the creation of something new, is subject to a very high rate of failure. The uncertainty associated with innovative activity acts as a deterrent to investment in innovative activities of private firms, who usually try to avoid risky ventures, and therefore spend less on innovation than they should.

In addition, the returns to investment in innovation are very uncertain because of the *public nature* of technological knowledge. Investment in new technology can lead to financial losses not only because of technical problems or because consumers do not like the new product, but also because competitors can often imitate successful new products without having to incur the initial investment associated with new technology. In other words, imitation may sometimes result in investors failing to appropriate the returns to their innovative investment.

Since investors know about the danger of imitation, they will not invest in new technologies that can be copied easily and the whole society misses out on the new technology. A pure market system that relies on private property and on the price mechanism to allocate resources will therefore fail to promote innovation. This argument, which emphasizes the public nature of technology (as information that is easily copied and transferred) is often invoked in support of a regulatory system of governance.

Regulatory approaches

One alternative option to governance through the market is to replace the market with a hierarchy, an administrative structure that does not respond to price incentives. This is not uncommon, especially as far as scientific research is concerned. Scientific research is mostly funded by governments because its output is mainly public information that anybody trained as a scientist can access and use. We have seen above, however, that technological knowledge is not only public information but also tacit knowledge that to a great extent remains privately owned by firms or individuals because it cannot be transferred. In this case, public funding is not necessary because market incentives are enough to stimulate investment in research activity. So government intervention is needed in those areas of technological knowledge where the public nature of such knowledge undermines the private incentives to invest in innovation or in very young technologies, especially when they are at such an early stage that commercial applications are far in the future and very uncertain.

An alternative to public funding to overcome the inadequacies of the market that lead to under-investment in technological innovation is to introduce a limitation to the freedom that economic agents have to copy and use new technology and ideas originally introduced by others. Intellectual property rights (such as copyrights and patents) have been introduced for this purpose. A patent grants a monopoly on the commercial exploitation of the patented invention to the holder. The technology patented can be licensed so that the patent holder can gain royalties from producers who use the technology described in the patent.

Mixed market and regulatory systems

Through the introduction of intellectual property rights the problem of the appropriation of the returns to innovative investment due to imitation is overcome, as technological knowledge that is public in nature becomes private and can be efficiently allocated through the market system. In this case, therefore, a regulatory system is mixed with the market in order to improve it.

Traditionally, science and technology policy has relied on the linear or 'technology-push' model of innovation, which is based on those two governance mechanisms. The model, shown in Figure 6.5, assumes that basic scientific research creates a pool of public knowledge which firms and individuals use to generate inventions that are usually produced and sold by firms. Since basic scientific research suffers greatly from the appropriability problem, most of it is usually publicly funded. The market then plays an important role in the subsequent stages of the process. So

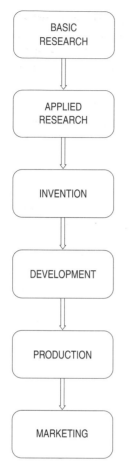

market and regulatory systems coexist: private firms invest in new technology in order to gain profits, basic scientific research is mainly supported by public funding, and governments enforce intellectual property rights (such as patents) by law.

The linear model, however, has two shortcomings. First, it neglects the role of important institutions other than firms, governments and formal research centres in the innovation process. These include universities, trade unions, the labour market and financial institutions. Successful innovations that are introduced on the market by firms are in fact ultimately the product of a whole system of institutions that have contributed to the innovation in various ways. Second, the technology-push model simplifies the innovation process too much by assuming that it occurs in a linear fashion. Important feedback takes place from production and from marketing and other contacts with customers to R & D. So, in recent years, academic scholars and policy makers have increasingly used the concept of 'system of innovation' to understand the innovative process.

Figure 6.5 The 'technology-push' linear process of innovation

(Simonetti, 1998, p.304)

4.3   Governing innovation: systems of innovation and networks

Today it is widely accepted that we should understand innovation in terms of a system of separate institutions that repeatedly interact, with feedbacks throughout the innovation process. Indeed, technology itself can be seen as a system. Final products are usually made up of components that can be very different in terms of the knowledge and skills required to produce them.

A firm that introduces an innovation needs to find all the pieces of knowledge it requires in order to succeed. Sometimes, components of a new product can be bought on the market. At other times the knowledge to produce them is publicly available. However, it is also possible that the innovating firm requires various new components that are innovations themselves and that the firm cannot produce. Indeed, many innovative firms buy important components from reliable *suppliers*. The role of suppliers in the introduction of innovations is often crucial because they have the skills (tacit knowledge) necessary to produce important new components for new products.

In many cases, *customers* also provide valuable inputs into the innovation process. For instance, the Italian company Bassano Grimeca, a world leader in the production of wheels and brakes for motor cycles, develops its new products in close collaboration with its customers, large companies such as Honda and Aprilia.

As noted earlier, the list of institutions involved in the introduction of new technology does not only include private firms. *Scientific institutions* such as universities and government laboratories are repositories of knowledge about scientific disciplines. They provide essential training for scientists and engineers in firms, and play an important role in the development of scientific instrumentation.

Since innovative investments are often substantial, very uncertain, and usually pay off only after a long time, efficient *financial institutions* that support innovation are essential actors in the development of new technology. The above discussion of the patent system also suggests that, besides funding R & D activities and ensuring a sufficient level of education, *governments* can do much to influence innovative activities by designing appropriate institutions. The list of institutions involved in the innovation process can also include trade associations, trade unions and so on. Figure 6.6 shows the structure of a system of innovation.

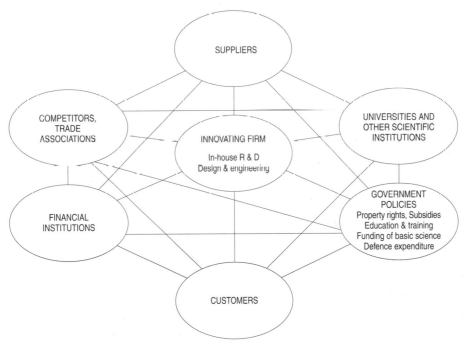

Figure 6.6 System of innovation
(Simonetti, 1998, p.317)

So, although innovation is often introduced by a private firm, it is ultimately the product of a system of institutions that are closely linked together by economic and social relationships. The various institutions have different skills and make different contributions to the innovation process. The notion of 'system of innovation' recognizes that tacit knowledge has an important role in the innovation process. If techno-logical knowledge were only public, a firm would be able either to buy some new components on the market or to gather all the necessary knowledge to introduce an innovation without having to refer to other organizations. Technology, however, is partly tacit and embodied in other organizations, so a single institution usually has to interact with other institutions in order to be able to use knowledge that it does not possess and that is not available publicly or on the market. If some of the relevant institutions are missing, not competent enough or cannot interact effectively, then the whole innovation process is in danger.

In addition, the interactions during the innovation process are far from linear. Innovative activities are constantly carried out to improve existing products and generate new ones, and feedbacks occur during the innovation process. Technological change, therefore, can be seen as an ongoing process of *accumulation of knowledge* by all the institutions included in the system of innovation. Each innovation is just a small step in the continuous advance of a technology, which co-evolves with the institutions that are part of the system.

Networks as a model of governance

The notion of system of innovation puts an emphasis on the interactions, or links, between the elements of a system. Only some of the interactions between the elements of the system are regulated by the price system or by a regulatory mechanism. In order to understand in depth how systems of innovation work, therefore, we have to go beyond the two traditional mechanisms of governance and use the model of governance through networks.

Chapter 1 defined the characteristics of governance through networks. Networks are groups of various elements that are linked together in some way; in our case, the elements are economic agents, that is individuals, organizations and various institutions. Governance through networks is used to describe those situations where networks spontaneously organize without any external intervention – they self-organize and reach some order. They differ from markets, which are also self-organizing, chiefly because the co-ordination is not achieved through the price mechanism as happens in markets. In networks, co-ordination is achieved informally through shared values, common culture, common interest and mutual trust.

Systems of innovations work using a mix of the three mechanisms of governance. They are located in market economies, where firms compete for customers in the market in order to make profits. Many relationships between firms and their suppliers, customers and financial intermediaries occur through the price mechanism, shrouded in the anonymity of markets. Systems are also shaped by government intervention, directly through funding of research or more generically through regulations such as the patent system. Another regulatory system that is important in systems of innovations is the internal form of organization of large firms; this influences which R & D projects are funded and what technologies are developed. Some of the relationships between the various elements of the system, however, are based on trust or on shared values or interest, and are reinforced by a common cultural background.

Illustrations of the 'networks of innovations' approach

Let us take the relationships between a firm that wants to introduce an innovation and its suppliers. In some cases, the firm can just purchase a part for its new product on the market. New products, however, often require new components whose performance can be crucial for the success of the final product. Moreover, some components have to be tailor-made in order to fit the specifications required by the innovating firm. In the example I mentioned above, the Italian company Bassano Grimeca often designs wheels and brake systems in association with its customer, the motorcycle company Aprilia (Box 6.2 overleaf).

Another example of non-market relationships that are important in systems of innovation are the links between universities and industrial firms. The nature of such links can be multifarious. For example, firms and universities co-operate in government-sponsored research pro- grammes, and scientists in firms are usually trained in universities and keep informal contacts with colleagues who still work in an academic environment. Informal networks of scientists who belong to the same discipline are important channels of transfer of knowledge across firms. Scientists who have studied together or simply share a common back- ground often offer valuable advice that helps solve bottlenecks in the innovation process.

The structure of the system and the importance of each type of institution in the innovation process varies according to the characteristics of the technology and of the demand. In some industries, scientific discoveries are an important source of innovation, while in others the learning generated in the interaction between the innovators and the users of new technology is more important. Suppliers of capital goods are a vital source of innovation in some industries. Besides institutional R & D activities, learning also takes place within the firm in other activities such as production, marketing, design and engineering, and informal contacts of technical staff with the staff of other institutions, including competing firms as well as universities, government research centres and consultants.

The idea that it is necessary to think about technology in terms of a system has recently been developed in different ways, depending on how each system is defined. Some of them emphasize the national dimension of systems and explore the importance of *national systems of innovation* for technology policy. Others define *technological systems* in terms of various factors – such as the subject area (for example, pharmaceuticals), the actors that are part of the system, and the institutional structure – and emphasize that the boundaries of the systems do not coincide with a country's boundaries. On the one hand, technological systems are more narrowly defined than national systems of innovation, as they refer to

Box 6.2   Successful networking – the case of Aprilia

Aprilia is a good example of how successful innovation requires a system of institutions – it is often referred to as a 'network firm'. This term refers to the fact that Aprilia does not manufacture the parts of its motorcycles, but it outsources their production to a wide network of suppliers (more than 200) with which it has a long-standing business relationship. The parts are developed together and produced by the suppliers; Aprilia then assembles the motorcycle and runs thorough quality checks to ensure that the product is of top quality. This is how Aprilia has managed to grow very fast and become a leader in motorcycling, reaching world fame through its victories in many world championships.

The case of Aprilia is an example of how non-price relationships are important for innovative firms. The firm has a long-standing relationship with a close number of suppliers that depends on much more than price. Collaboration in innovation is usually a very delicate matter because one party can exploit its partner by taking advantage of the knowledge received in the collaboration. One major problem with transactions that involve the transfer of knowledge is that it is extremely difficult to put a price on the knowledge that is transferred. Buyers can only judge how much they value the knowledge after they learn what the knowledge is, and at that stage they do not need to pay for it because they already possess it. The price mechanism breaks down and it is often necessary to establish long-term relationships that involve trust in order to encourage the transaction.

In the case of Aprilia, it is not by chance that the great majority of its suppliers are based in the same region, the North-East of Italy. The common culture and shared values have substantially contributed to the success of the network model of the firm, by making trust easier to build. Indeed, this model is not easily transferable to other areas where the social interactions are different, and the North-East of Italy is often quoted as a typical case where the social conditions make the emergence of networks relatively easy, as the large number of industrial districts in the region shows.

technologies rather than countries. On the other hand, the inclusion of multinational companies gives them an international dimension. Finally, systems of innovation have also been considered at the *regional* level. This is useful at least in some cases where many organizations that contribute to a system are concentrated in a geographical area, as happens in Silicon Valley with respect to information technology or in various industrial districts in Germany and the North of Italy.

We need to recognize, therefore, that it is not straightforward to define exactly where the boundaries of a system are, and it can also make sense to consider various overlapping systems of innovation. This issue is particularly important when we want to study innovation in Europe, because in addition to the national and sectoral dimensions we must also consider the European system of innovation.

Summary

- The governance of innovation should focus on the accumulation of technological knowledge in a country or region.

- There are two basic types of knowledge needed to produce a good or service: information which is publicly available and can be transferred and acquired easily; and tacit knowledge (also called skills or 'know-how'), which is embodied in persons and organizations.

- The standard argument in favour of markets states that the most efficient allocation of resources is achieved through governance by markets (that is, the price mechanism), so the market should allocate the right amount of resources to the production of new technology.

- Because technological knowledge is partly public and the returns to innovative investment cannot be fully appropriated by those who invest in the creation of new technology, leaving it to the market fails to mobilize enough resources for innovative activities. This is a market failure. Uncertainty about the results of innovative investment also discourages investment in new technology.

- The market failure argument concerning the creation of new technology justifies government intervention in the generation of new technology. Such intervention often takes the form of public funding of basic science, where the aim is to produce public knowledge that is an important input in the innovation process. In this case the market is replaced by a regulatory system.

- Another type of government intervention in the field of innovation is the establishment and enforcement of intellectual property rights, such as copyrights and patents. Patents transform the public side of technology into a private one so that inventors can earn the returns to their investment in new technology and, therefore, have an incentive to invest in innovative activities. This is an example of a regulatory system designed to make the market work more effectively.

- Traditionally, governance of innovation was based upon the linear technology-push model of innovation, which has been criticized because it neglects important causal links between the various sources of new technology, and focuses on the public aspect of technological knowledge, neglecting the role of tacit knowledge in the innovation process.

- A system composed of various institutions is needed to introduce new technology. A single organization does not usually have all the knowledge required to introduce an innovation.

- A system of innovation works effectively only if the institutions that are part of it communicate and interact effectively. The interactions between the elements of the system do not occur in a linear fashion.

- Systems of innovation can be defined at various levels: national, sectoral and regional.

- All three mechanisms of governance interact in systems of innovation: markets provide economic incentives to private firms to innovate; regulatory systems fund the bulk of basic scientific research and grant private rights to inventors in order to overcome the problems of uncertainty and appropriability; and governance through networks plays an important role in the systems because it enables and facilitates the flow of technological knowledge between elements of the system.

- Common culture, shared values and interests and trust contribute to the self-organization of networks.

5   The governance of innovation in Europe

Now that we have seen how the three governance mechanisms can help us understand the governance of innovation, we shall look at what role they play in the European system of innovation. This fifth section illustrates the history of institution building that supports innovation at the European level. In Section 6 we address the issue of whether there is a truly European system of innovation, or whether the governance of innovation in Europe is just the result of the aggregation of the innovation activities that are undertaken in the various European countries.

5.1   The institutions for the development of science and technology

There are currently a number of institutions at the European level that support the development of science and technology. Clearly, many different types of institution contribute to the introduction of innovations, from those that explicitly aim to promote science and technology, such as universities and R & D departments of private firms, to others that make it possible to translate technological knowledge into commercially viable goods and services, such as financial organizations and various labour market institutions. But the focus here is on those institutions and initiatives that are more closely related to the accumulation of scientific and technological knowledge in Europe. They can be classified into three groups according to their aims: scientific and technological research and development, diffusion of scientific and technological knowledge, and education and training of the workforce.

Within these three categories, there are institutions with diverse features that reflect the historical moment when they were established and their interaction both with national institutions and with each other. One particular dimension we are interested in is whether they contribute to the process of European integration by transferring 'sovereignty' to the European level, or just involve intergovernmental co-operation between autonomous national entities. First, we focus on scientific and technological research.

5.2   Collaborative scientific and technological research

European states started collaborating in the development of science and technology in the aftermath of the Second World War with the Euratom treaty, which aimed to create European capabilities in the production of energy using nuclear power – thought at the time to be the key energy source for the future. The treaty set up a body that transferred the co-ordination of the activities in this area to the European level, and established cross-border research facilities. These measures implied a substantial degree of sovereignty transferred to European level; indeed, some argue that the European Economic Community Treaty and the European Commission were a by-product of the Euratom Treaty.

The Euratom Treaty was to a large extent an example of the use of regulation as a mechanism of governance for science and technology. The European governments that initiated it did not trust the market as an effective model of governance of nuclear technology for various reasons, ranging from the usual market failure argument we saw above to the military relevance of nuclear technology. But Euratom did not manage to create a truly European division of labour in nuclear research, principally because of tensions between the interests of various member states that either were concerned about the military potential of nuclear technology or wanted to pursue the commercial opportunities independently. As a result, at the end of 1967 the plan for a European nuclear reactor was abandoned.

The next step in the history of the European system of innovation occurred in 1967 with the merger of the executive institutions of the Euratom, ECSC (European Coal and Steel Community) and EEC Treaties, to form the European Commission. The emphasis on integration and the transfer of sovereignty to the European level in the field of innovation was the subject of debate in the following years until the end of the 1970s. In those years, research in science and technology was mainly seen as part of broader policies for industrial objectives, such as the creation of the single market. As we saw from the data in Section 2, the emphasis was on the improvement of technology in scale-intensive industries.

One important initiative was the establishment of the COST Committee (European Co-operation in the field of Scientific and Technical Research) in 1970, which was involved in various projects with countries both inside and outside the EEC. A few years later, there was the start of a conscious attempt to create a science and technology policy approach at the European level, with a Council resolution in 1974 that recognized that a common science and technology policy would contribute to 'social progress, balanced economic expansion and an improvement in the quality of life'. Importantly, the resolution identified the need for co-ordination of national policies within Community institutions and for the joint implementation of projects of interest to the Community. This led to the establishment of CREST, the Committee for Scientific and Technological Research, and to support for the establishment of a European Science Foundation.

The influence of the European Commission grew in the following years, which saw it involved either directly or indirectly in various initiatives. The direct involvement of the European Commission centres on the framework programmes (FPs), which have become the main instrument for planning in science and technology in the EU. The Commission has also indirectly been involved in other programmes that include countries outside the EU, such as ESPRIT (the European Strategic Programme for Research and Development in Information Technology), which is the first significant endeavour to support the creation of European capabilities in ICTs. Given the generally weak performance of Europe in ICTs, the success of the programme, which is still ongoing, has been questioned. However, it is difficult to evaluate all the various indirect effects that large programmes such as ESPRIT have, and in any case ESPRIT is still an important step in the history of European science and technology policy because successive programmes have been designed using many of the same criteria, such as the 'shared-cost' approach to cross-border collaboration in R & D programmes.

In shared-cost projects various organizations, including private firms and universities, join forces and form consortia in order to carry out research projects that are largely funded by the EU. Shared-cost projects differ from concerted actions, in which the EU aims to co-ordinate policy initiatives of various member states without providing funding.

5.3   Competition and co-operation

ESPRIT can also be considered an important step in the construction of institutions in support of science and technology at the European level because it raised an issue that is still present in the current European policies, namely the tension between collaboration in scientific and technological activities and competition policy. The development of radically new technologies, as ICTs were in the 1980s, requires co-operation rather than competition between firms, given the problems about uncertainty – as we saw in Section 4, the commercial exploitation of very new technology is not only more uncertain, but also some time off in the future. Helping large firms to work together, however, opens the door to possible collusion and monopolistic practices that restrict competition without generating sufficient benefits to consumers. While ESPRIT has been designed to support commercially-oriented innovation, the initiatives of the European Commission had to take the constraints of competition policy more into account, and it was therefore necessary to define what type of research could be supported at the European level and into what types of collaboration firms would be allowed to enter.

The issue has been solved in the FPs by distinguishing between pre-competitive R & D and commercial R & D. In order for the R & D to be pre-competitive, the research must be 'far from the market'. This means that basic research is normally considered as pre-competitive and can be funded by public funds because its results are not usually goods and services that can be sold on the market. This is often the case with so-called 'generic' technologies, which can be put to use in very different industries when they are developed into commercially viable products. It has been noted, however, that some generic process technologies, such as the microprocessor, are not far from the market. What is more important is that some firms do patent the results of pre-competitive research in order to gain commercial advantage from the knowledge generated, even though no goods are produced. So the distinction is not as clear cut as it seems although it has been widely used in the various programmes (see Caracostas and Soete, 1997).

The early 1980s saw the birth of the FPs, which represent the main instrument of planning of research in the EU. The approach adopted in the first FP (1984–7) combined all three mechanisms of governance – market, regulation and networks – in the field of science and technology policy. Private profit-seeking firms are at the heart of European innovation policy: they are ultimately the organizations that will introduce the commercial innovation into the market. The establishment of a single European market also aims to facilitate the commercial exploitation of new technology.

5.4   Training and the creation of knowledge

Public funding for pre-competitive R & D, especially in basic scientific and technological research, is still motivated by market failure arguments. These funds, however, are not the main support to R & D that the European Commission provides. In the later FPs, the emphasis has shifted toward using the funds at the European level to promote the accumulation of knowledge in European people and organizations by facilitating the links between the various components of the European system of innovation. European science and technology policy, therefore, acknowledges the importance of networks as a governance structure and explicitly designs policies to improve the links between the different parts of the various research networks.

One clear example is the action taken at the European level in the area of training within the projects for COMETT (Community Action Programme in Education and Training for Technology), which started in 1986 and have promoted transnational co-operation between universities and industry on training in the field of technology. The COMETT programmes have used funds to bring together various types of institution, such as universities, firms and other relevant organizations, in consortia (University Enterprises Training Partnerships) that provide training at the regional or sectoral level. Other programmes in the fields of education and training, such as SOCRATES and LEONARDO, focus on the creation of partnerships and networks that give both trainers and trainees a common 'culture', which includes a common vision for the future development of various technologies.

5.5 Policies for the diffusion of knowledge and innovations

The development of a European approach to innovation was one of the objectives of the SPRINT programme (Strategic Programme for Innovation and Technology Transfer, 1989–94), which also set up support services for innovation in SMEs and channels of technology transfer. Although the initial emphasis in European industrial policy was toward the creation of the single market in order to favour the exploitation of economies of scale and scale-intensive technologies, increasingly the European Commission has paid attention to SMEs for various reasons.

- First, SMEs are the major component of the European industrial structure in terms of both number of firms and employment; since the 1980s they have also been the main source of job creation.

- Second, SMEs are important components of systems of innovation. Research suggests that areas where innovative SMEs thrive, such as industrial districts, seem to be able to retain competitive advantage and absorb new knowledge successfully. SMEs are embedded in the local economy and therefore are the ideal place for the accumulation of technological knowledge rather than in the increasingly footloose multinational corporations. Policies that aim to support the accumulation of knowledge in SMEs are more likely to be effective in terms of competitiveness and job creation in regional economies. Support for large multinationals, on the other hand, is important in cases where the development of new technologies requires the competencies and the financial strength that only huge firms have, but is risky because the economic returns and the accumulation of knowledge will not necessarily take place in Europe. Increasingly, European companies have acquired research facilities outside Europe, especially in the USA, through an intense activity of mergers and acquisitions in the 1980s and 1990s (Chapter 2).

- Third, the emergence of ICTs has changed the industrial landscape through the diffusion of flexible automation, which makes it possible for SMEs to compete successfully against very large companies.

The emphasis on SMEs has increased over the years and it is now very explicit in various initiatives of the European Commission. The BRITE-EURAM research programmes (Basic Research in Industrial Technologies for Europe and European Research on Advanced Materials), which began in the mid-1980s, have gradually emphasized the diffusion of new technologies to SMEs and the inclusion of SMEs in the European R & D initiatives among the objectives.

The inclusion of SMEs in the core of European research and the diffusion of advanced technological knowledge in SMEs are also strongly emphasized in recent FPs (for instance, FP V, 1998–2002). FP five is organized around twenty-three key actions grouped under four thematic programmes ('Quality of life and management of living resources', 'User-friendly information society', 'Competitive and sustainable growth', and 'Energy, environment and sustainable development'), and three horizontal programmes, one of which focuses on the 'Promotion of innovation and encouragement of participation of SMEs', the other two being 'Confirming the international role of Community research' and 'Improving human research potential and the socio-economic knowledge base'. Initiatives aimed at improving the technological capabilities of SMEs include: better information about the results of European R & D and best practice in industry; support for participation in European R & D projects; better access to finance, especially for new high-technology companies that need more venture capital; and an improved framework for intellectual property – currently the high cost of patent applications in Europe (about ten times more than in the USA) is an obstacle to innovation in SMEs who cannot afford them.

The Commission hopes that these measures will improve both the technological capabilities of SMEs and their rate of funding in European projects, which has been slightly declining from the second FP, as Figure 6.7 (overleaf) shows.

On the positive side, the figure shows that the share of funds that go to large firms has decreased. This confirms that the priorities of the European Commission have shifted from support to scale-intensive industries to promotion and reinforcement of links between various types of organizations, from firms of all sizes to universities and other research centres. In particular, universities (which are the majority of higher education institutions) have considerably increased their participation in FPs. This suggests that the university–industry links, which are at the heart of a technology policy based on the notion of systems of innovation, should improve in Europe over time.

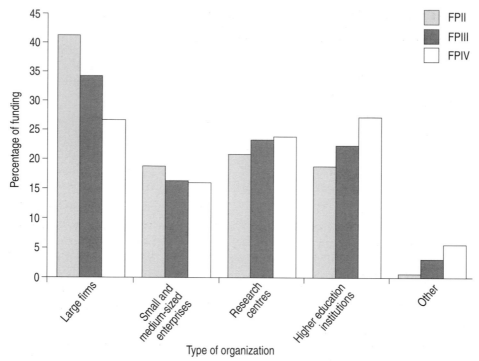

Figure 6.7 Distribution of funding in framework programmes (FPs) by type of organization – second, third and fourth FPs

(Geuna, 1999, p.371)

5.6 The increasing role of framework programmes

The improvement of university participation in European R & D programmes is not the only impact of R & D institutions at the European level. In particular, FPs have become increasingly influential in the landscape of European R & D in various ways. Over the years, the FPs have become more effective in shaping the research agenda in Europe. Increasingly, strategic areas have been defined more coherently with each other and with the other objectives of the European Commission. Following the Single European Act (SEA) and the Maastricht Treaty, for instance, 'social cohesion' has gained importance among the objectives in the various FPs (see also Chapter 5). The fourth FP has represented a step change both in terms of funds, as Table 6.2 shows, and in the way the programme is organized – along 'vertical' (or 'thematic' in the fifth FP) and 'horizontal' programmes. In the fourth FP there was a strong emphasis on the co-ordination of national efforts and industrial research policies, and a concentration on a limited number of key technologies that have a major impact on many branches of industry and society in general.

Further changes have been introduced in the fifth FP, not only because both ICTs and the environment have increased their importance, but also

Table 6.2   The five framework programmes

Programme	Duration	EU contribution (m ecu)
FP 1	1984–87	3,750
FP II	1987–91	5,396
FP III	1990–94	6,600
FP IV	1994–98	13,100
FP V	1998–2002	14,000

(Geuna, 1999, p.370)

(and mainly) because the whole programme now emphasizes the socio-economic *impact* of research for the European communities, including social cohesion. There is more emphasis on the application of the results of R & D on actions that are relevant to the communities, the diffusion of technologies, the improvement of the business environment (including financial services), the protection of innovators, training in new technologies, and the dissemination of information, especially to SMEs.

In spite of the efforts of the European Commission, however, some of the objectives are difficult to achieve. Among these, 'social cohesion' seems to be one of the most elusive objectives (Chapter 5). Various studies of the European research networks in the FPs, BRITE-EURAM and other programmes, as well as the analysis of university participation in European R & D programmes, have shown that capabilities are concentrated in a few regions and organizations, and that the programmes at the European level even tend to reinforce the existing concentration. There are a number of reasons for this outcome. For example, although the rules for the allocation of funds include preference to projects that involve participants from technologically less developed regions, the main criteria for the awards are related to the quality of the proposals, including the quality of the applicants. Only if the quality of the proposal is comparable with those from other regions are projects from less developed regions given preferential treatment. This means that applicants from more advanced regions tend to be more successful in attracting funds. Research has shown that most of the funds go to very few small geographical areas, and it is not easy to reverse this trend. Moreover, even when networks include participants from technologically less developed regions, the benefits from the R & D are usually greater for the most advanced partners because the absorption of technological knowledge is cumulative – the more knowledge there is already, the more it can absorb because of the better general understanding of the technology.

The difference between large technologically advanced countries and smaller less advanced ones also influences the way institutions at the European level have an impact on national institutions. Research has shown that the European agenda shapes policies in small lower-income countries fairly substantially while it does not have a great impact on R & D in large advanced countries where national science and technology policy is well established and thriving. This outcome occurs because in technologically less advanced countries the top scientists, who contribute to setting the national agenda, receive a relatively greater reward from taking part in European projects, given the domestic situation, than is the case in more advanced countries.

Summary

- During the second half of the twentieth century various institutions have been created at the European level to support science and technology, from Euratom to the recent framework programmes.

- European institutions differ in their origin, aims, features and the degree of sovereignty transferred from countries to European-level bodies. Policies for science and technology include funding of large research projects to reap economies of scale, and support for the diffusion of knowledge, education and training. Recently, emphasis has been put on the promotion of transnational collaborations in various fields in order to create a common European culture in research.

- Collaboration between private firms in the development of new technologies creates tensions with competition policy. This has been addressed by introducing the notion of pre-competitive (or far-from-the-market) R & D.

- National innovation policies are still important not only because of the principle of subsidiarity but also because the EU budget is only a small fraction of the whole research expenditure in Europe. The main aim of the EU is to co-ordinate national policies rather than replace them. The FPs have become the main instrument to achieve such co-ordination.

- The focus on quality of research creates a tendency to reinforce regional inequalities in the accumulation of technological knowledge. Policies designed to address this problem and increase cohesion have not been very successful so far.

6   Systems of innovation: European integration, national systems and globalization

The account just presented of the building of institutions for innovation at the European level suggests that a European system of innovation is now a reality in many ways. Increasingly, a number of European institutions play a significant role in the economic environment that

European companies face, and this influences the way they approach the introduction of new technology. The creation of the single market, the existence of the European Patent Office, the definition of common standards and regulations, and the existence of a number of projects that encourage and support the collaboration between European institutions in projects of scientific and technological nature are all examples of how the innovation process is shaped by factors that act at the European level to some extent.

Strategic decisions that influence the rate and direction of innovation in Europe are increasingly influenced by factors and institutions at the European level. Over the years there has been an increase in the number of innovative projects that involve transnational collaborations. Moreover, various schemes put in place by the European Commission have contributed to create a network of researchers for whom it is 'normal' to participate in projects at the European level. The fourth framework programme (FP IV), that was managed by the European Commission from 1994 to 1998, had an overall budget of 13,100 million ecu and it funded thousands of transnational collaborative projects with various types of organizations involved, such as private firms, universities, research centres and others. Other programmes, such as CERN (now the European Laboratory for Particle Physics), EUREKA and ESA (European Space Agency), have been running for years outside the jurisdiction of the European Commission. For 1998 to 2002 the fifth framework programme (FP V) is running with a budget of 14,000 million ecu.

The data presented in Section 2, however, show that European countries are very different both in terms of the overall amount of resources that they devote to innovation and in their technological areas of strength. This is due to their different histories and stages in the process of industrialization. It would be surprising if countries such as Greece and Portugal, which are still catching up with other European high-income countries in terms of GDP per capita and industrial base, did spend the same percentage of GDP on R & D, given that they mainly compete in resource-based and traditional sectors.

In addition, there are important differences between European countries and regions in aspects such as their industrial structure, the organization of their financial markets, the role of the state in the governance of technology and the organization of the labour markets. While Mediterranean regions tend to be more specialized in traditional industries, countries such as France, Germany and the UK are more active in science-based industries. Countries also differ in the importance that SMEs have in the economy. In the UK and the Netherlands a few large firms dominate the national economy, whereas in other countries, such as Italy and some areas of Germany, SMEs are very successful in competitive industrial districts.

The role of national institutions is also important when we consider R & D activities. The R & D budget of the EU only funds 4 per cent of the whole R & D expenditure in Europe. This percentage rises to just 10 per cent approximately when other European programmes are considered, leaving the greatest share of R & D to national organizations.

National systems of innovation are therefore still relevant in the European landscape, not least because the actions of the EU are subjected to the principle of subsidiarity, which limits their scope and influence. However, it could be argued that the influence of the R & D activities carried out at the European level also affects the initiatives designed and implemented at the national level, and there are institutions whose task is to co-ordinate the various national policies for science and technology. Indeed, the main aim of the European Commission is strategic, that is, to influence the objectives and the way research is carried out in Europe, rather than to add to the existing resources.

So the European system of innovation is made up of institutions and mechanisms that operate at different levels and interact in complex ways. Decisions that influence the European capabilities in science and technology are taken not only at the European, national and regional (in the case of industrial districts, for example) levels, but increasingly also at international level, where multinational companies are powerful agents that shape the agenda in many fields of science and technology.

Indeed, one important issue currently facing Europe relates to the increasing number of Europe-based multinationals that are setting up R & D facilities abroad, especially in the USA, mainly through the acquisition of foreign firms. Some academics and policy makers argue that this trend might lead to a weakening of the European system of innovation as tacit knowledge is accumulated outside Europe and European firms might decide in the long run to transfer their main R & D centres abroad. Others, however, see this trend, together with the rapidly increasing number of technological alliances and joint ventures with US and Japanese firms, as a positive development that enables European-based firms to keep abreast of global developments in science and technology and transfer important knowledge to Europe within the firms' structures.

Summary

- While national systems of innovation are still important, and profound differences still exist across European countries and regions, institutions at the European level increasingly influence the governance of innovation in Europe.

- The growing influence of multinational corporations in the world economy is influencing the structure of the European system of innovation, but there is no agreement on the effects that globalization has on the strength of European science and technology.

7   Conclusion

This chapter has outlined the major features of the European system of innovation, that is, the network of institutions that make a substantial contribution to the governance of innovation in Europe. Europe faces important challenges in the twenty-first century and new technology is generally considered one of the key factors that will determine its economic performance, including the level and quality of employment, and more generally the standard of living. In particular, we have seen that in spite of recent efforts Europe still lags behind the USA and Japan in many of the ICTs and in the overall level of resources committed to R & D.

Throughout the latter half of the twentieth century various institutions were created at the European level to improve the accumulation of scientific and technological knowledge, and in recent years the European Commission and the European Parliament have developed a more strategic approach to innovation policy that tries to direct the national R & D efforts toward some areas of priority identified at the European level.

The governance of innovation at the European level is managed through a mix of the three governance models we have met in this book. European governance of innovation starts from the assumption that innovation is mainly introduced by privately owned profit-seeking firms that face competition in world markets, and has traditionally used governance through regulation as a way of addressing market failures that derive from the public nature of scientific and technological knowledge. Increasingly in the last few years, however, policies that aim to improve the accumulation of technological knowledge have adopted a 'system approach' that focuses on the co-ordination and improvement of the links between the various institutions that are part of the European system of innovation, and on the creation of a European 'culture' about the innovation process.

While institutions at the European level play an increasingly important role in the European system of innovation, individual countries are still major players in science and technology policy and the European system of innovation should be understood as a mix of institutions that interact at various levels – European, national, regional and international. Indeed, European firms and countries face some new challenges and opportunities from recent trends that include the location outside Europe of R & D departments from European-based multinationals and the explosion in the number of technological alliances and joint ventures.

References

Caracostas, P. and Soete, L. (1997) 'The building of cross-border institutions in Europe: towards a European system of innovation?' in Edquist, C. (ed.) *Systems of Innovation: Technologies, Institutions and Organizations*, London, Pinter.

Commission of European Communities (1988) *The Costs of Non-Europe: Report of the Cecchini Committee,* Luxembourg, Office for Official Publications.

Commission of European Communities (1993) *White Paper on Growth, Competitiveness and Employment: The Challenges and Ways Forward into the Twenty-first Century,* COM(93) 700 final, December, Brussels, CEC.

Dalum, B., Freeman, C., Simonetti, R., von Tunzelmann, N. and Verspagen, B. (1999) 'Europe and the information and communication technologies revolution' in Fagerberg, J., Guerrieri, P. and Verspagen, B. (eds) *The Economic Challenge for Europe,* Cheltenham, Elgar.

Fagerberg, J., Guerrieri, P. and Verspagen, B. (1999) 'Europe – a long view' in Fagerberg, J., Guerrieri, P. and Verspagen, B. (eds) *The Economic Challenge for Europe,* Cheltenham, Elgar.

Geuna, A. (1999) 'Patterns of university research in Europe' in Gambardella, A. and Malerba, F. (eds) *The Organization of Economic Innovation in Europe,* Cambridge, Cambridge University Press.

Patel, P. and Pavitt, K. (1987) 'Is Western Europe losing the technological race?', *Research Policy,* no.16, pp.59–85.

Pavitt, K. (1984) 'Sectoral patterns of technical change: towards a taxonomy and a theory', *Research Policy,* no.13, pp.343–73.

Simonetti, R. (1998) 'Technological change' in Simonetti, R., Mackintosh, M., Costello, N., Dawson, G., Himmelweit, S., Trigg, A. and Wells, J. (eds) D319 *Understanding Economic Behaviour: Households, Firms and Markets,* Block 5, *Firms,* Milton Keynes, The Open University.

Further reading

Dent, C.M. (1997) *The European Economy: The Global Context,* London, Routledge. A longer and more detailed illustration of technology and innovation in Europe. See particularly Chapter 9.

Chesnais, F., Ietto-Gillies, G. and Simonetti, R. (eds) (2000) *European Integration and Global Corporate Strategies,* London, Routledge. The chapters in Part 2 examine the impact of globalization on technology and analyse European performance.

Nelson, R.R. (ed.) (1993) *National Innovation Systems: A Comparative Analysis,* Oxford, Oxford University Press. A comprehensive empirical study of various national systems of innovation.

Chapter 7
Environmental governance in the EU

Susan Baker

1   Introduction

This chapter examines environmental management in the European Union (EU). The traditional 'command and control' regulatory approach toward environmental management is increasingly being used alongside an emerging new governance approach toward dealing with the environment. The EU's commitment to the promotion of sustainable development provides the organizing framework within which the new governance patterns are emerging. We explore the relationship between these two approaches and the problems encountered by the EU in its efforts to adopt broader, more flexible ways of managing the environment.

The chapter is divided into seven main sections, beginning in Section 2 by asking why the EU manages the environment and why it is trying to make use of both regulation and the market to protect the environment. Section 3 explores the environment and the problems of governance, particularly within the multi-level policy-making structures of the EU. Section 4 examines in detail the emerging new governance patterns in the EU, in particular the use of the principle of partnership and shared responsibility to ground the new environmental management strategy. The promotion of sustainable development within the EU and the difficulties encountered at the member state level are the focus of Section 5. Section 6 deals with the problems of environmental governance within the context of EU moves to enlarge its membership into Eastern Europe. Section 7 deals briefly with the problems emerging with the adoption of the new governance approach. Finally, the conclusion draws together all the arguments.

2 Why manage Europe's environment: the roles of regulation and the market

Economic activity can give rise to negative environmental effects, including pollution. Without environmental management these effects have the potential to undermine the very resource base upon which future economic activity depends. Government intervention in environmental management is necessary in order to deal with the costs to society, including the health costs, that arise from this economic – especially industrial – activity. There is also the expectation that governments will act to protect society's interest in the face of pollution threats. As we shall see, there is some scope for the market to take account of pollution in its pricing levels. However, the market is not particularly effective in dealing with pollution costs.

Since the 1970s much of the intervention on behalf of the environment has taken place at the international level, as opposed to merely at the level of the nation state. This is because the transboundary nature of pollution (for example in relation to pollution in Europe's major river systems) and the fact that environmental problems are increasingly taking on a global significance (especially in relation to climate change) mean that the nation state is no longer the most appropriate level for environmental management. Within Europe, the major international actor regulating the environment is the EU.

2.1 Managing the environment: at what level?

The dynamic between EU and national level regulation

The process of European integration has meant that there has been a gradual shift from environmental decision making at the national, member state level to collective decision making at the EU level. The EU now has the power to exercise direct authority over member states in environmental matters. There has thus been a 'Europeanization' of national policy making, whereby national environmental policies have been forced to reflect this in accordance with EU regulations and norms. But, there has also been a 'nationalization' of European policy. The use of Directives by the EU imposed legal obligations upon member states regarding *objectives* and *timing*, but leaves the member states discretion over the *form* and *methods* used to achieve these objectives. The dynamic between Europeanization and nationalization is most noticeable in relation to areas that have traditionally been the subject of EU environmental policy, such as the industrial sector. However, other areas not traditionally receiving EU attention, such as land use planning, are increasingly being drawn into the EU policy remit.

However, while environmental policy has gained a great deal of legitimacy at the Union level, there is still tension between the commitment to continuous economic development and the aspiration to protect the environment. While the relationship between the economy and the environment is not necessarily always negative, as we shall see later, the EU has difficulties in reconciling, within its policies and funding programmes, its historical commitment to ensuring economic growth with its commitment to environmental protection (Baker, 1993). Similarly, at the member state level, environmental policy is not always implemented as thoroughly and effectively as is possible. This has given rise to an implementation deficit, which is discussed below.

Tackling environmental stress at EU sectoral level

There are many environmental problems that require the attention of policy makers in the EU. These include emissions of gases (especially of CO_2) into the air that are contributing to global climate change, waste, decreasing urban air quality and groundwater quality, habitat destruction and fragmentation, and the degradation of soil quality. The problems were highlighted in the European Environment Agency's Environmental Assessment Report (EEA, 1999). There are various sources of these environmental problems, particularly at the sectoral level. Focusing on the sectoral level is important because the EU is legally required to integrate environmental considerations into sectoral policies (in manufacturing industry, transport, tourism, agriculture and energy); this is known as 'sectoral policy integration'.

Ecological modernization in the industrial sector

In the last few decades, the industrial sector has made some progress in relation to pollution control and its response owes a great deal to the development by the EU of a strong environmental regulatory framework. The formation of a regulatory framework governing economic behaviour is mirrored across many EU policy areas, resulting in the claim that the EU acts as a 'regulatory state' (Majone, 1996). In relation to environmental policy, this framework has set acceptable standards for environmental (ambient) quality, including soil, air, noise and water.

In addition to responding to regulatory pressure, large companies have gradually realized that a sound natural resource base is a prerequisite for their continued development (CEC, 1995, p.3). In other words, some ecological modernization has taken place, where investment in the environment is seen as productive investment that may cut production costs, and open up or expand markets. Ecologically modernized manufacturing firms, for example, treat the environment not as a free resource, but rather as a factor of production that has to be priced. This leads manufacturers to adapt the production process so as to reduce the amounts of costly resource inputs that they use. Ecological modernization also helps the development of 'green proponents' within industry, which, in turn, have the potential to contribute to the acceptance of sound environmental norms across business practices more generally. However, in relation to small and medium-sized enterprises (SMEs) such environmental modernization has been very limited (CEC, 1996, pp.9–10).

The transport sector

Transport is a key source of environmental stress, particularly road transport. Despite this, the integration of environmental considerations into the EU's trans-European networks (TENs) has been 'piecemeal and slow' (CEC, 1994, p.17). TENs are the cornerstone of EU transport policy, which, in the context of the Single European Market (SEM), is aimed at physically linking Europe through a network of high quality roads. To date, legislation dealing with the negative environmental impact of road transport has been limited to technical improvements of vehicles (such as reduction of emissions and noise). However, the decision to complete the SEM was taken without consideration of its possible environmental consequences (Baker, 1997a). The SEM, for example, is expected to result in a multi-fold increase in transport use by encouraging a move away from localized production and consumption activities, and this is driving the large-scale transport infrastructure projects that are being funded through the TENs programme.

There are a number of challenges facing policy makers in their efforts to integrate environmental considerations into the transport sector. Currently, the impact of transport on the environment is evaluated through undertaking environmental impact assessments (EIAs), but these have proved unable to provide policy makers with clear guidelines for evaluating the environmental impact of TENs (CEC, 1994, p.17). A more intractable problem is that TENs, by facilitating the physical integration of Europe, are seen as playing a vital part in the deepening of the European integration process. In this case, the 'logic' of European integration is acting as a downward pressure on the environment. Transport policy has become the focus of considerable environmental opposition, at both the Union and member state levels (Climate Network Europe, 1995, p.6). This puts pressure on the Union to respond but, as we have seen, making an effective response is not easy.

The agricultural sector and the CAP

CAP-induced intensive agriculture has resulted in the pollution of the aquatic environment, altered natural habitats and reduced biodiversity across the EU (EEA, 1995b). Existing regulatory efforts to deal with the negative environmental impact of agricultural developments mostly consist of little more than ad hoc responses to particular problems.

Current efforts to integrate environmental considerations into agricultural policy are taking place in the context of Agenda 2000 (CEC, 1997). This links together proposals for changes in the CAP and the structural funds with the Eastern European enlargement of the EU (discussed below) and the framework for the medium-term budget of the Union. Agenda 2000 contains proposals to move the CAP away from an emphasis on production support and toward a more integrated rural policy. It does this by combining subsidies to farmers, which are decoupled from production, with rural environmental management and economic diversification measures (Ward, 1999, p.169).

The Agenda 2000 proposals for the reform of the CAP have the potential to bring positive environmental benefits by shifting from the current price support system to a direct payment system and by reducing price distortion. This reduction can lead to less intensive land use and a decrease in the use of polluting inputs. The integration of environmental considerations should, at least in principle, prove less difficult to achieve in this sector than in other sectors. This is because agriculture represents a policy area where the Union has the authority to intervene and effect substantial changes in farming practices and in production patterns. There is also real synergy between economic objectives and environmental protection: the necessity to reduce agricultural over-production corresponds to the environmental objective of reducing intensity of land use (*European Environment*, 1996, p.6).

The tourism sector

There is a similar potential for synergy between developmental objectives and environmental protection in relation to the tourism sector. This is because the development of tourism depends upon the protection of a high-quality natural resource base, including the landscape and bathing water. However, far from achieving such synergy, Europe's natural resources are under threat from the growth of tourism. Although this growth is partly led by consumer demand, it is also being driven by economic and political interests in the periphery, where the tourism sector is seen as providing an economic buffer against the competitive threat posed by the SEM. In addition, tourism is an economic activity that cuts across many different EU policies, including agriculture, transport and regional policy. This makes environmental policy co-ordination and integration very difficult to achieve (CEC, 1994).

2.2 Managing the environment: making use of multiple approaches

Traditionally the EU has used a 'command and control' approach toward environmental management. This has resulted in the build-up of almost 300 environmental directives by the EU which has gone some way toward reducing the negative environmental impacts of economic activity.

This approach is an example of a hierarchically driven attempt to regulate from the top down, and has given rise to the 'regulatory state' type of governance mentioned earlier. But in contrast to this, as we have seen, economic actors have also taken their own steps to deal with environmental problems, particularly pollution stemming from production activities. Ecological modernization within the industrial sector provides a good example, which is as much driven by *market-led* concerns as by the EU's regulatory order. The EU, especially the European Commission, has encouraged this sharing of responsibility. It forms part of a more flexible approach adopted by the Commission, grounded on the principle of partnership and shared responsibility. This approach encourages new forms of partnership between the private and public sectors, including the adoption of market-led solutions to environmental problems. The new approach is giving rise to a new form of environmental governance, which combines the traditional business of government (regulation) with new patterns of participatory governance (partnership and shared responsibility; the use of new policy tools). In many ways this new approach embodies the principles of self-organizing networks, as outlined in Chapters 1 and 6.

The rest of this chapter explores the developing relationship between the traditional business of government and new governance patterns in relation to environmental policy management. While primarily focusing on the EU, some attention is also paid to the member state level. We shall explore why businesses and firms are interested in sharing responsibility for environmental management. This involves uncovering the economic advantages of market-led solutions over the traditional hierarchical 'command and control' approach. We address the question of why the Commission is interested in utilizing a more flexible approach toward environmental management and what advantages it sees in this approach. We shall also examine what kind of relationship is developing between the regulatory order created by the EU and the market-led behaviour of economic actors. Can these approaches co-exist comfortably? Are there problems in reconciling one approach with the other? To answer these questions we begin by examining more fully the newly emerging patterns of environmental governance within the EU. This can help us explain the motivations of both regulators and economic actors in seeking to use a range of approaches toward environmental management.

Summary

- There is a great deal of negative pressure acting upon Europe's environment.

- Government intervention is necessary in order to address the negative environmental effects of economic activity.

- This has led to a Europeanization of environmental policy, with the role of the EU in environmental policy making taking on increased importance.

- Viewed from the sectoral level, far from there being a simple trade-off between environmental protection and economic development, the environment and the economy stand in a complex – at times antagonistic, at times complementary – relationship with each other.

- Within the EU, goal-directed intervention is being increasingly combined with a new pattern of governance. This makes use of the principle of partnership and shared responsibility and of new policy tools and instruments.

3 The environment and the problems of governance

We begin this section by asking what makes the task of environmental management particularly difficult. We then examine the difficulties presented by the multi-level governance structure of the EU.

3.1 The environment as a governance problem

The search for new approaches toward environmental management is driven, to a large degree, by the growing complexity of addressing environmental problems and the difficulties of finding efficient and effective public policy solutions to these problems. The growing complexity results from the growth of new environmental pressure groups, conflicts over the understanding of environmental issues, uncertainties and risks associated with economic policies, a loss of faith in scientific competencies and pronouncements, and the cross-cutting organizational and administrative difficulties encountered in bringing environmental and other issues together.

New governance initiatives

It is within the context of this problem of governability that new patterns of governance have emerged, which make use of co-regulation, co-steering, co-production and also new public/private partnerships. 'Governance' here means several things. First, the process of governing is no longer conducted exclusively by the state, but involves 'all those activities of social, political and administrative actors that ... guide, steer, control or manage society' (Kooiman, 1993, p.2). Second, the term governance also takes account of the fact that, within new governance processes, the relationship between states and non-state actors, such as environmental NGOs (non-governmental organizations), economic actors, and quasi-governmental agencies, is developing in non-hierarchical ways (Jachtenfuchs, 1997, p.4). In addition, as new governance patterns develop, there is a growing recognition of the mutual dependencies (or interdependencies) that exist between state and society, between the public and private sectors.

In short, as new governance patterns develop, society and the economic and political systems cease to be run, as it were, from the 'top down' by governments engaged in the traditional business of governing. Instead, a new model of governance is developing, where the boundaries between government and society are more diffuse and the lines between public and private responsibility are blurring. The process of governance stands, therefore, in contrast to the classic, state-centric, redistributive, command and control processes that form the traditional business of government (Hix, 1998, p.39). Instead, government, social and economic actors all take an active, negotiating, and learning-driven role in the process of governing. But this sets up tensions between the development of new patterns of governance at the EU level and the desire of member states to limit the EU's management of the environment to more traditional means.

3.2 Environmental management and the complexity of EU multi-level governance

The new patterns of governance that are emerging within the EU are highly complex, largely because of the bargaining and shifting alliances among the member states and between them and EU institutions. In formulating policy, differences can emerge within institutions and in particular within the Commission and its numerous Directorates-General (DGs).

Further, responsibility for the various stages of the policy process is fragmented: the Union plays a major role in policy formulation but has less direct control over the implementation stage, this being the job of the member states. The task of monitoring is also difficult, as the EU is reliant upon member states to provide it with information on policy achievements and success.

Regional and local authorities, pan-European interest groups such as the European Environmental Bureau (EEB), as well as national environmental and business interests, are also involved in policy making but to varying degrees. In addition, policy is not made by one institution in one sitting but takes place over a long period of negotiation and discussions through a variety of formal and informal channels. Interest groups, especially those representing industry, also play a role in shaping EU policy through the influence they exercise on the negotiating position of member states, the Commission, and individual Commissioners (Mazey and Richardson, 1995, pp.337–60). There is also a policy-making role for quasi-autonomous executive agencies such as the European Environment Agency.

In view of the complexity of its policy-making process, the EU has been characterized as a 'multi-level governance structure' (Marks, 1993, pp.391–410). This refers to the way that decision-making competencies are dispersed among national, supranational and sub-national (local and regional) actors, many of which are not public actors but private agents. In this interaction between state and private sector, informal contacts and networks help to define policy options. However, we also need to remember that the EU has been characterized as a 'regulatory state', that is, a political actor that lays down rules and regulations governing the ways in which the member states and economic actors manage the environment in a rather more traditional manner.

Summary

- Environmental management presents unique and highly complex problems for policy makers.

- There is a problem of governability with respect to environmental management that arises in part from this complexity, but also from a social critique that has undermined the belief in the capacity of government and expert advisers to protect the environment and society from pollution.

- This has led to a search for new patterns of governance.

- In the EU, the governance patterns that have emerged have done so within a complex, multi-level structure, where territorial and sectoral interests all play a role in shaping policy, albeit to varying degrees.

4 The emergence of new governance patterns in EU environmental management

In this section we look at the new governance patterns that are emerging in the EU. The combination of partnership and shared responsibility is an essential feature of the new governance patterns and we explore how this is being put into practice. Second, we examine the problems with the traditional hierarchical 'command and control' approach toward environmental management. This is followed by an exploration of the use of new instruments for environmental policy, using the Auto-Oil Programme as an example.

4.1 The right governance framework: making use of the principle of partnership and shared responsibility

The search for new governance patterns can be viewed as an attempt to find ways in which society can manage the interests of those concerned with environmental protection and those concerned with economic development. By involving different stakeholders in policy making it is easier to reach consensus about how to proceed in the complex business of managing the environment. In addition, reaching consensus between all the interested parties is important for achieving policy success. From the point of view of economic agents and actors, for example, unless they are participants in environmental decision making they may be unwilling to meet the costs of compliance. From the point of view of environmental actors, unless governments can find ways of including their concerns, there is a danger that significant sections of civil society will be excluded from having a say in shaping how society is managed. Such exclusion bodes ill for democratic practice.

To put this principle into practice the Commission has established new institutions, bodies and boards composed of representatives of different groups. They include consumer groups, environmental NGOs, business interest associations and economic actors (such as firms and trade unions), and economic development agencies. To varying degrees these partnerships are beginning to shape policy outcomes and deploy new tools for environmental policy.

4.2 Problems with the 'command and control' approach

The 'command and control' approach involves direct regulation, in which governments prescribe uniform environmental standards across large regions, mandate the abatement methods required to meet such standards, license production sites which adopt the required methods and assure compliance through monitoring and sanctions (Golub, 1998, p.2). The result of implementing such initiatives meant that the legislative capacity of the Union improved, quantified targets were set and there was an improvement in monitoring capacity.

The development of the EU's regulatory framework has largely been driven by a narrow, reactive approach to environmental management. But over time, weaknesses in this regulatory style have became apparent:

- There was the realization that unless stakeholders (such as firms and businesses) are involved in shaping policy, there is a strong possibility that compliance will be weak. Weak compliance gives rise to what is called the policy 'implementation deficit', which is discussed further below.

- Command and control approaches were also seen to lead to economic inefficiencies because they impose uniform reduction targets and technologies upon economic actors (such as industries) without taking account of the variable pollution abatement costs facing individual firms. They also stifle incentives to reduce emissions beyond mandated levels and do little to encourage firms to develop innovative pollution control technologies.

- There is the claim that regulatory bodies often develop close and dependent relationships with industry because of the latter's detailed knowledge of, and direct interest in, pollution activities and abatement options. Thus they allow polluters to 'capture' regulatory bodies, thereby shaping environmental policies in accordance with their own economic self-interest (see Golub, 1998, p.3).

Nevertheless, the shift from a command and control to a more consensus driven policy style is also driven by a more positive motive – the Union's adoption of the principle of sustainable development to guide policy. Sustainable development is not a blueprint for reconciling the economy and the environment. Rather, the promotion of sustainable development requires a process of social change within which solutions to the tensions between the economy and the environment can be elaborated. This is discussed more fully below.

4.3 Making use of new instruments for environment policy

In the light of the problems emerging with the command and control approach, by the mid-1990s a search had begun for new, more flexible and efficient policy instruments. The move from a predominately *legislative approach* to a more *voluntary approach* was also in keeping with the market-led ideology embedded in the SEM and the EU's white paper on growth, competitiveness and employment (CEC, 1993). The shift is also popular with governments because it is consistent with the continuing trend toward deregulation and re-regulation at the member state level (*Europe Environment*, 1994). Furthermore, the Commission hopes that making use of new instruments for environmental policy (NIEPs), as they are often known, will help alleviate the implementation deficit, because such tools have the advantage of shifting environmental responsibility onto mechanisms (the market) and agencies (for example, business interest associations) other than the EU or the nation state and its legislative powers.

New policy tools and instruments

New policy tools include fiscal tools (taxation), economic instruments to encourage the production and use of environmentally friendly processes and products, horizontal supporting measures (including information, education and research), and financial supporting measures (funds) and voluntary agreements. For simplicity, these tools can also be divided into *economic* and *'suasive'* instruments (Golub, 1998).

Economic instruments include several types of environmental taxes and charges, 'green tax' reforms, tradable pollution permit systems, government subsidies for environmental improvements and deposit/refund schemes. *'Suasive' instruments* include eco-labels, eco-audits and voluntary environmental agreements. These instruments give the market a new role in environmental management.

New instruments have several advantages. Industry groups are particularly keen because they may lighten the burden of regulation and thus help them to maintain competitiveness. Taxes and charges on pollution also provide firms with positive incentives to reduce pollution levels, because these reductions bring corresponding decreases in environmental taxation. Other instruments, such as eco-labels, allow firms to take advantage of growing consumer concerns about the environment and to sell their goods to the growing 'green consumer' markets. However, industry has shown some ambivalence toward the shift to new policy tools because of the uncertainty involved in their use and the costs they face in abandoning what is often a well understood regulatory approach over which they have considerable influence (Golub, 1998, p.7).

New tools are also considered to be less expensive for governments to manage, requiring less expenditure on implementation and monitoring. They can also provide governments with potentially lucrative sources of revenue. Furthermore, they have the potential to decrease regulatory capture and lend legitimacy to environmental policy by facilitating direct public involvement (for example, of consumers) with industry and regulatory agents. Some instruments, such as voluntary agreements, also have the advantage of facilitating closer co-operation, rather than confrontation, between government and industry.

Voluntary agreements

These agreements are being increasingly used across the member states, for example in relation to reduction in waste packaging and CO_2 emission levels, and to improve energy efficiency. Voluntary agreements are based on the assumption that behaviour can be changed through environmental consciousness raising. Actors are brought together, often by DG Environment, and are made aware of the effects of their behaviour on the environment. During this consultation and negotiation process a sense of responsibility is developed that leads (hopefully) to a voluntary agreement from the actors to change their behaviour. In practice, however, these agreements are often reached by industry and business interest associations when they are under the threat of legislative regulation, which is seen as potentially more costly.

Compared with regulations, voluntary agreements suffer less implementation difficulties, having the advantage of good compliance because they are self-regulating mechanisms. Two specific EU-wide voluntary environmental agreements are the eco-label scheme and the 'Eco-Management and Audit Scheme' (EMAS). The EU eco-label scheme uses a flower symbol, the 'EU Flower'. Similar labels exist within the member states, such as the 'White Swan' symbol used in Scandinavia and the German 'Blue Angel'. EMAS relies more on 'internalization' of environmental management within the firm and, as such, is a good example of a 'suasive' instrument. Companies that take part in EMAS have to establish an environmental protection system for a given production site and to conduct a systematic, periodic evaluation or audit of their environmental performance (Heyvaert, 1998, p.60).

Some concerns about the use of voluntary agreements for environmental policy have been raised. It has been argued that granting more decisional power concerning environmental protection and management to those who are also the environment's main assailants requires 'a considerable leap of faith' (Heyvaert, 1998, p.61). Moreover, self-regulating mechanisms, such as voluntary agreements, can be weak tools, as they tend to favour sectional interests over environmental ones and need to be backed up by sanctions. The EMAS in particular has been the subject of much criticism. There has been considerable disagreement over which experts (independent certifiers or a self-administering industrial body) ought to verify and certify industrial compliance with eco-audit standards.

Combined approaches

In practice, instead of relying upon either the command and control or the more market-led approaches, the EU frequently makes use of both approaches when trying to address particular environmental problems. The EU Auto-Oil Programme, described in Box 7.1 (overleaf), is a good example of current attempts to combine both the regulatory and voluntary approaches to environmental management. Exploring this Programme also shows us the problems that can arise with such efforts.

Assessing the Auto-Oil Programme

- The Auto-Oil Programme highlights the difficulties that stand in the way of trying to deal with the negative environmental impact of transport, especially when there are so many interests trying to have a say in shaping policy. At the European level, the Commission is subject to lobbying by both economic interests, including the oil and automobile industries, and environmental and consumer groups. The imbalance in resources between economic and environmental interests, with the oil industry in particular able to devote large amounts of personnel and finance to its campaign, gave economic actors the upper hand in this case.

- The Auto-Oil Programme shows that care must be taken in assuming that economic interests will always act in each other's favour and against the interests of environmental groups. Rather, alliances of interest groups should be seen as collaborations that are (temporarily) formed on the basis of pragmatic considerations. In the Auto-Oil case, the automobile industry formed an alliance with its traditional enemies, the environmental and consumer NGOs, because it saw this as potentially beneficial in a particular dispute it was having with the Commission and the oil companies.

Box 7.1   Combined approaches – the Auto-Oil Programme

In 1996 the Commission put forward proposals for an Auto-Oil Programme. The proposal contained three elements: a new directive on the quality of petrol and diesel fuels; a directive on measures against air pollution from motor vehicle emissions; and an outline for a broader, non-binding strategy for controlling atmospheric emissions from road transport. The proposals attempted to find the most cost-effective solutions to the problem of transport pollution in Europe. From the onset, the oil industry was particularly keen to influence the proposals, and committed considerable staff and financial resources to these efforts. When the proposed Programme was announced, it was initially praised by both the oil industry and automobile manufacturers. The Commission was also pleased with the close co-operation it had been able to build up with the oil and automobile industries. Others, however, were far from pleased.

Member state governments, NGOs and the European Parliament (EP) were not involved in the policy formulation; they were merely briefed on the results during the final stages of the negotiations. Not surprisingly, the Auto-Oil Programme came under fierce criticism from these groups. The EP saw the proposed directive on the quality of petrol and diesel fuels as too lenient and demanded that the directive on air pollution from cars set mandatory, not indicative, emission limits. They argued that consideration of the wider costs to society of transport pollution and the resultant ill health needed to be taken into account. The fiercest criticisms came from environmental and consumer groups such as the EEB, Transport and Environment and the *Bureau Européen des Consommateurs*. Member states were also critical, but with a clear north–south split. In the northern countries, especially the environmental leader states of Sweden, Germany and the Netherlands, there was particular concern that the proposed levels of benzene and sulphur in fuel were too high. Southern countries, including Spain, Greece and Portugal, stressed the potential cost implications for their domestic economies and consumers. France and Britain subsequently elected into power governments that put a strong emphasis on the need to curb pollution from road traffic.

As a result of these pressures, in 1997 the Commission put forward more stringent standards for a directive on fuels. But this modification was not acceptable to the EP, who held out for an even more stringent approach, especially in relation to mandatory limits for car emissions. As a result, the proposals are now the subject of conciliation talks between the EP and the Council. As time went on, the automobile industry also came to believe that the Commission's proposals were too lenient and that they favoured the interests of the oil industry. They believed that, by doing little to pressure the oil industry into developing reformulated fuel, the proposals could block environmentally friendly technological developments in car engine design. As a result, the industry took the unprecedented step of forming an alliance with Brussels-based environmental and consumer NGOs to lobby for stricter fuel standards. All of this put the Commission on the defensive. It retrospectively, but unsuccessfully, tried to legitimize its close co-operation with the car and oil industries at the expense of the governments of member states and the NGOs by pointing to the principle of shared responsibility in the Fifth Environmental Action Programme (5th EAP).

- We see that member states also command a great deal of power in relation to EU policy. Although they were not formally involved in the negotiations that led to the Auto-Oil Programme proposals, the less enthusiastic member states were able, at a later date, to shape policy (despite the fact that in the Auto-Oil case it was the environmental leader states which won out against the interests of the more laggardly ones). Thus member state governments still hold sway despite the growth of new governance patterns.

- The perils of making policy without adequate consultation are very evident here: the Commission ignored the input of both environmental and consumer stakeholders, it's own EP and the interests of the member states, only to find that the failure of appropriate consultation caused the Programme serious delays and difficulties. If any lesson is to be learned from the case of Auto-Oil it is that, in the environmental arena in particular, the inclusion of all stakeholders in policy making – not just economic ones – is vital to policy success. Public distrust of industry as self-proclaimed guardians of the environment remains high. This is especially so in the case of voluntary agreements, which are so often seen as pre-emptive moves on behalf of economic actors to avoid more stringent regulation, 'enabling industry to set the terms and simultaneously to demarcate the limits of environmental protection' (Heyvaert, 1998, p.62). In such cases of mistrust, widespread consultation is necessary.

- Our case shows us that while voluntary agreements and market-led solutions have their proponents within industry and within the Commission, and have a role to play in environmental management, other actors, including social stakeholders and member states, remain unhappy about leaving environmental management solely in the hands of economic actors.

4.4 Concerns about the growing use of new instruments

Many environmentalists oppose incentive schemes for pollution control (such as pollution permits) because such systems fail to stigmatize pollution as morally wrong. There is a danger that pollution becomes something to which you have a right if you can afford to pay for it (Dryzek, 1995, p.205). In addition, care must be taken to ensure that the trend within the Commission toward the reliance on market solutions to environmental problems takes account of *market failure*. Market failure is particularly acute in relation to public goods such as the environment, which means that regulation still has a major role to play in environmental protection in Europe. Concern has also been expressed about the possible distributional effect of the use of certain tools and, in particular, green taxes. However, little is actually known about the effectiveness of new instruments as pollution control measures and whether they in fact lead to a harnessing of market forces in favour of a cleaner environment.

Thus, new policy tools are not acceptable to all sectors of society and have been criticized by environmental NGOs. The European Environmental Bureau (EEB), an umbrella group representing over 120 environmental groups, has argued that, in the face of what it calls the move toward the 'privatization' of environmental protection at the European level, there is a need to preserve a strong legal framework to safeguard environment standards (EEB, 1996, p.6). The EEB is in effect articulating the growing public expectation that the state will protect society against environmental harm. In short, while new policy tools have a place in environmental management, there is still the need for a strong legislative framework governing environmental behaviour, a framework backed up by sanctions for non-compliance. Thus the 'shadow of hierarchy' still needs to fall over many new market-based or participatory governance mechanisms.

Summary

- The principle of partnership and shared responsibility has become the essential principle grounding the new environmental governance pattern emerging within the EU.

- New policy tools for environmental management can be divided into economic and 'suasive' instruments.

- Proponents of these new tools argue that a stronger reliance on market forces leads to more efficient management of the environment and can result in a higher degree of protection than that guaranteed under the traditional regulatory schemes. Making use of economic agents to drive market-led solutions to environmental problems has the advantage of helping compliance.

- However, opponents, especially environmentalists, have argued that it represents an attempt to privatize environmental management at the expense of maintaining public responsibility for environmental protection.

- In practice, the EU makes use of both approaches, as seen in the Auto-Oil Programme proposals.

5 Governance in practice: the promotion of sustainable development in the EU

The promotion of sustainable development requires strong state intervention, not least because containing economic activity within the limits of the environment's carrying capacity requires economic planning. This planning centres on controlling the market and gearing the economy toward achieving a set of environmental targets (Eckersley, 1995). But in order to promote sustainable development the EU has had to move beyond regulation and to draw upon both market tools and the principle of partnership and share responsibility. Thus, the promotion of sustainable development provides the organizing principle on which the utilization of the new governance approach toward environmental management is based.

5.1   Mechanisms for promoting sustainable development

The EU's Fifth Environmental Action Programme, *Towards Sustainability: A European Community Programme of Policy and Action in Relation to the Environment and Sustainable Development* (1992–97, ongoing) (CEC, 1992) provides the organizing framework for the change in policy orientation. It should be noted that in 1998, a new Action Plan aimed at setting priorities for the implementation of the 5th EAP was also adopted. Action programmes outline policy objectives, set priorities for action and provide the Commission with a framework within which new legislation on the environment can be formulated. The 5th EAP laid down that the promotion of sustainable development should be an overriding objective of EU environmental policy. Sustainable development is development that 'meets the needs of the present without compromising the ability of future generations to meet their own needs' (WCED, 1987, p.8). In practical terms the Union sees this to mean a commitment to:

- achieving sectoral policy integration;
- promoting partnership and shared responsibility for environmental management;
- broadening the range of policy instruments used to bring about effective environmental management;
- promoting sustainable consumption and production patterns;
- enhancing implementation and enforcement of existing regulations and legislation;
- strengthening the Union's international environmental role.

At a minimum, these objectives require that the Union develops a more proactive, preventative and integrated approach to environmental management (Baker, 1997a).

The Single European Act (in force in 1987) created a legal obligation upon the Union and its member states to integrate environmental considerations into other policies. This obligation was reinforced in Articles 130 (r) to (t) of the Maastricht Treaty and subsequently by the Treaty of Amsterdam. The promotion of sustainable development was also made a clear, legal obligation following the Treaty of Amsterdam (1997).

5.2   Early progress

A number of official reviews have been undertaken of the progress made by the Union in promoting sustainable development (CEC, 1994; CEC, 1995; CEC, 1996). At the general level, the lack of clarity in the term 'sustainable development' makes it difficult to measure progress. Furthermore, the 5th EAP has not always set clear implementation targets, having, for example, set no quantitative targets for the manufacturing sector. While the efficiency issue (maximizing the environmental benefits and minimizing the economic costs) has hardly been addressed (EEA, 1995a, p.2), up to the year 2000, appraisals have limited their focus to the effectiveness of measures (narrowly understood as 'how can the target be achieved?'). To add to these difficulties, action programmes such as the 5th EAP are non-binding framework documents and, as such, include no legal obligation on member states to report on their implementation.

Despite these evaluation difficulties, it has nevertheless been possible to reach a general consensus: that some decrease in the negative pressures exerted on the environment has been achieved, though this is of a limited nature.

More specifically, the reviews have found that within the Commission as a whole there is a general lack of environmental commitment. Furthermore, it is becoming evident that different DGs have competing or conflicting interests that may act as a barrier to promoting sustainable development and, more specifically, to achieving sectoral policy integration. The Regional Policy Directorate-General, for example, has an interest in promoting economic development in peripheral regions of the Union and may not be as concerned with the environmental impacts of their activities as the Environment Directorate-General would like them to be. Similarly, the Agriculture Directorate-General may well have interests that conflict with those of environmental organizations (Peters, 1996, p.65). The relative weakness of the Environment Directorate-General within the Commission in terms of both size and influence, is also of relevance. Evaluation reports have also found that the commitment to sustainable development 'varies considerably between and even within member states' (EEA, 1995a, p.17).

5.3   Using market-based instruments

The Commission has argued that making greater use of market-based instruments is the key to successful promotion of sustainable development. But tension has developed between this aim and the interests of member states. Precisely because they have the potential to diminish their role and influence, member states have been reluctant to allow the Union to make use of the full range of policy tools outlined in the 5th EAP, particularly to allow the Union to use fiscal tools. This is despite the fact that member states are themselves increasingly making use of these tools, as seen for example in the use of environmental charges and taxes in Denmark, Finland, the Netherlands and Sweden, albeit with mixed results. The lack of progress in the use of a Community CO_2 tax can be seen as a prime example of the way in which opposition by one or more member states can slow down or halt Commission attempts to ensure greater progress in the implementation of environmental policy (see Box 7.2). It is also a reminder of the political nature of decisions about whether or not to make use of market-led tools for environmental management.

Box 7.2 Market-based instruments – the carbon tax

The 1992 proposal by the Commission to introduce a carbon energy/ CO_2 tax was seen as an important example of the new reliance on market-based incentives. The tax was part of a set of packages put forward by the EU at the United Nations Conference on Environment and Development in Rio de Janeiro (the Earth Summit) to deal with global warming. The proposed tax rate was \$US3 per barrel of oil equivalent, with annual increases taking them to \$US10 a barrel after seven years. There was to be special treatment for energy-intensive industries and the revenues raised were to be used to offset other taxes. The tax was aimed at stimulating more efficient use of energy and helping to ensure a switch to fuels containing less or no carbon.

The proposal for a carbon tax was highly controversial. It was believed that it would hit some European sectors and companies harder than others, that it ran the risk of damaging European competitiveness and that it would not be neutral. There was also a concern that other industrialized countries might not take similar steps. Despite strong Commission backing and the support of the Netherlands, Luxembourg, Belgium, Denmark, Italy and Germany, the proposal became embroiled in political opposition and technical difficulties. The UK in particular refused to consider allowing such a tax to be imposed by the Union. The failure of the carbon tax proposal has acted as a blockage on the progress that has been made in expanding the range of policy instruments used by the Union. As a consequence, legislation remains the main approach to environmental management within the EU. In addition, the failure to introduce the tax has hampered EU efforts to meet the obligations incurred at the Earth Summit to deal with CO_2 emissions and to help deal with the problem of global warming. The lack of progress in the carbon energy/CO_2 tax can be seen as a prime example of the way in which opposition by one or more member states can influence EU environmental policy, and of the importance of governments even where other governance patterns exist.

The role of the member states in blocking Commission proposals for a carbon tax draws our attention to the differences between member states and to variations in response to the promotion of sustainable development at the sub-national level, including regional and local levels.

5.4 Implementing the commitment to sustainable development: the role of the member states

There is a great deal of evidence pointing to a large implementation deficit with respect to EU environmental policy. At the start of 1994, for example, nearly one-third of all environmental directives due for implementation at the end of 1988 were the subject of infringement proceedings initiated by the Commission (Butt Philips, 1998, p.268).

However, in fairness we need to recognize that many member states have proven to be highly committed to environmental protection, especially the so-called 'environmental leader' states of the Netherlands, Germany and Sweden (Andersen and Liefferink, 1997). However, among so-called environmental 'laggard' states, there is a continuation of the belief that environmental protection imposes limitations on economic activity. This belief is particularly prevalent among economically peripheral states, especially at the sub-national level (Baker, 1997b, pp.1–42). In so far as the economically weaker member states continue to feel vulnerable in the face of monetary union, the completion of the single market and Eastern European enlargement, their regional development priorities may well continue to favour economic over environmental goals.

Much has been written about the causes of the implementation deficit in environmental policy. It has been partly attributed to over-reliance upon the use of a legislative approach – Directives in particular – to regulate environmental behaviour (the 'command and control' approach). While establishing goals and timetables for action, these give member states a great deal of control over the form and method of implementation. Weaknesses within the legal and administrative systems of member states are also of relevance (see Jansen, et al., 1998, pp.300–5). It has been argued that an important factor is the presence of industrial competitors who act to achieve broad compliance – because it is in their economic interest to ensure that their competitors *also* pay the price of meeting environmental regulations and standards. On the other hand, when environmental legislation is largely related to activities within the confines of member states, and is not aimed at products or services that are sold or traded across national boundaries, implementation deficits are greater. This includes, for example, legislation relating to groundwater protection and the protection of wild birds (Macrory, 1996, p.11).

Highlighting the difference in response to environmental legislation in relation to tradable and non-tradable activities shows the important role that economic actors play as 'proponents' of environmental protection. Although their behaviour is not driven by environmental motives, achieving compliance through the involvement of economic actors is nonetheless making an important contribution to effective environmental management. Here the advantages of moving beyond the confrontational style that can characterize the 'command and control' approach become clear.

Summary

- The promotion of sustainable development provides the organizing framework for the shift to new governance patterns within the EU.

- EU efforts to promote sustainable development make use of both traditional practices of government, such as rule making and regulation setting, and of new governance methods to facilitate negotiation and agreements.

- Member states are not always willing to allow the EU to make use of market tools to manage the environment if it brings political costs.

- This was seen in member states' blockage of the proposed carbon tax, showing that environmental management decisions are made in a wider, political context and not just in the context of considerations of effectiveness and efficiency.

- To promote sustainable development, market-led solutions will have to act alongside the traditional, 'command and control', regulatory approach to managing Europe's environment.

6   The wider context: environmental governance in an enlarging EU

The EU is about to undergo profound change as it accepts new members from among the countries of the former Eastern bloc into its fold. Can sustainable development be promoted in this context?

6.1   Preparing for enlargement: benefits and costs

From an EU perspective, Eastern enlargement has the potential to bring positive environmental gains. First, managing the transition in Eastern Europe has given the Union a major say in shaping the emerging norms and practices in relation to environmental management in numerous countries in the region. Second, EU involvement has also contributed to a reduction in ecological stress in Europe as a whole and, in particular, in relation to transboundary pollution. Third, through the Phare restructuring programme and the Know-How Fund (see below), many EU firms have been able to export their environmentally-sensitive technical knowledge to Eastern Europe. This has enabled them to reap the rewards of the ecological modernization they underwent in the past.

But the process of learning is not all one-way. There is also increased recognition that many Eastern European states have gained skills and expertise that can also be beneficial to the West, as both the West and the East seek ways of dealing with the environmental damage brought by their respective forms of economic development. In particular, there is a lot that can be learned about nature conservation and forest management from Eastern Europe.

Preparation for enlargement makes policy reform, particularly of the CAP, urgent. This is to ensure that the EU can 'afford' the budgetary drain that new members would bring (see the discussion on Agenda 2000 above). Institutional reform is also necessary, to ensure that the EU can continue to govern effectively with so many new members (see Baker, 2000). In addition, in order to accommodate new members, the Union has to find ways to take account of the expansive physical scale and ecological diversity of the EU territories after enlargement. From an environmental point of view, this means that the Commission needs to ensure that it can continue to promote sustainable development while at the same time taking account of patterns of uneven development across the Union as a whole. The demands of many underdeveloped regions for EU funding to help their economic development will put strains on the EU's budget. Finally, enlargement, by increasing the number of environmental 'laggard' states within the Union, could act as a downward pressure on environmental policy in the future. In addition to posing challenges for the EU, preparation for membership also poses many challenges to the Eastern European countries.

6.2 Preparing for enlargement: requirements to be met by applicant countries

The main conduits through which the EU helps the new candidate countries prepare for membership are the Phare funding programme and the Know-How Fund. Through these, the EU has made available a (limited) range of funds and expertise to help countries meet the criteria for membership. This includes releasing some funding to help with environmental clean-up and, increasingly, to help strengthen environmental management institutional and administrative capacity, particularly in relation to monitoring and information gathering.

EU membership requires that new candidate countries take steps to approximate all of their environmental laws to that of the EU, that is, they have to adopt the *acquis communautaire* (the EU regulatory order). In relation to environmental policy, this means that they accept into their national law approximately 300 pieces of environmental legislation, mostly in the form of Directives. Through the adoption of the *acquis*, applicant countries are expected to meet certain EU norms (such as the promotion of sustainable development) and reach certain standards regarding environmental policy and its implementation, such as in relation to pollution levels, ambient quality standards and waste management.

However, the transition process is also bringing negative environmental consequences. New 'Western style' consumerism is bringing new environmental pressures, for example in relation to waste disposal and car pollution. These are pressures that have already been experienced by the West and for which adequate solutions have yet to be found. Furthermore, the economic shock of transition has done much to displace the centrality given to environmental concerns in the early days of transition. In addition, the improvement in ambient quality that accompanied the end of communism was as much due to the collapse of production in many of the large industrial enterprises that had been set up under the Communist regime as it was to improved environmental management. The danger with achieving ecological improvement through production collapse is that it neither enhances environmental management capacity nor does it contribute to policy learning. Indeed, there is a very real danger that lessons will not be learned at all and that, as economic upturn occurs, environmental degradation will begin to increase. Finally, as we see below, the marketization process, one of the cornerstones of transition, has brought renewed pressure on environmental administrators and has made the task of environmental monitoring more difficult.

6.3   Transition and the problem of environmental governance

Embedded in the EU Eastern enlargement process is also a problem of a more political nature. Despite the existence of mechanisms for mutual consultation, the relationship between Central and East European States (CEES) and the Union is an unequal one, with power skewed heavily in favour of the Union (Caddy, 1997, p.328). As a result, little has been done to promote public discussion on the political and economic conditions that the EU is laying down for application and membership or about the elements of pluralist democracy that potential membership is intended to encourage.

A new democratic deficit?

Tension is arising, for example, in relation to the introduction of sound environmental management practices and the necessity to ensure that ecological protection is not achieved at the expense of democratic practice. The ten new candidate countries have begun to bind their environmental policy into an EU legislative, monitoring and reportage framework that they have had no say in formulating. The adoption of EU environmental policy may bring greater ecological benefit than that obtained through previous practice and legislation, particularly in relation to implementation. However, what may be ecologically beneficial may not necessarily be good for the polity, that is, the adoption of the *acquis* may not make a contribution to the process of democratic consolidation. In the case of environmental policy, the adoption by Eastern European countries of the norms, legislation, standards and codes of practice that were the product of discourse, debate and compromise hammered out among political, social and economic actors from Western European member states is a profoundly undemocratic political act. In this respect, environmental politics in transition states bears similarities with the politics of environmental management under Communism: that is, it is largely driven by a top-down, legislative and regulatory approach that leaves little room for citizen participation and political dialogue.

In addition, the environmental dimensions of the Phare programme are weak and under-funded and both it and the Know-How Fund can be strongly criticized for channelling much of the actual funds involved to Western consultants, or 'experts'. The practice also carried the implicit message that Western agencies and expertise are 'superior' to those available within the East. Furthermore, Phare's prioritization of economic matters (privatization and marketization) over environmental matters has helped legitimize the long-standing practice (within both Western and Eastern Europe) of allowing economic considerations to take precedence over social and environmental goals (Baker and Jehlička, 1998). In addition, Phare-funded assistance has tended to reflect donor country priorities, such as transboundary pollution, providing further pressures to displace domestic environmental concerns. Decisions about how to allocate the limited funding available result in both ecological winners and losers. Having too many losers within Eastern European countries could undermine the public acceptance of transition.

The incorporation of countries from Eastern Europe into a wider EU framework of environmental regulation and management practices is shaping the way in which expressions of environmental concern are managed within the emerging political systems of transition states. The structure of environmental governance that has developed in the EU and which is being 'exported' to Eastern Europe involves the participation of organized interests in policy networks. Through the adoption of EU norms of environmental governance, the policy-making process in Eastern European countries is being opened up to environmental interests, at least in a tentative form in countries such as Hungary (Hanf and O'Toole, 1998). This is largely occurring through the establishment of mechanisms that facilitate the participation of (certain) environmental NGOs in the consultation stage of the policy process. But, while increased participation in policy making is seen as a necessity, it is not a sufficient condition to ground the democratic legitimacy of transition, nor of the system of environmental governance that the EU is helping to build in the transition states. This is because democratic legitimacy, as we have argued above, demands that issues of transparency (how decisions are actually reached and what the significance of consultation in this process actually is) and of accountability (whom these participating interests represent) be addressed.

Summary

- From an EU perspective, Eastern Enlargement has the potential to bring positive environmental gains.

- Enlargement also brings problems for the EU in relation to institutional reform and budgetary drain, and challenges it to find ways to economically integrate Eastern Europe without halting environmental progress.

- Preparation for membership, in particular the requirement to adopt the *acquis*, is doing little to help democratic consolidation in transition countries.

- New governance patterns are also being 'exported' to Eastern Europe, but the application of these patterns will not be sufficient to ground the democratic legitimacy of the transition process. The asymmetrical relationship between the EU and the new candidate countries throws the problem of the democratic legitimacy of environmental governance in transition states into sharp relief.

7   Problems with new patterns of environmental governance

The use of new tools for environmental policy, grounded in the principles of partnership and shared responsibility, has the potential to help the EU deal with its environmental policy deficit and the ever-deteriorating condition of Europe's physical environment. But the evolution of governance patterns has brought many difficulties and raises issues of importance for the practice of democratic politics.

7.1   The representative nature of participants

There can be tension between governance that involves public/private partnership and the responsibility that elected governments have to guard the wider public interest. In our Western political systems, democratic legitimacy requires that the wider interests of society, not just those of selected groups, be taken into account in policy making. In other words, when evaluating these new governance patterns, we have to ask: Who do these participating interests represent? If we elect political representatives to form governments and mandate them to engage in the business of government and then allow non-elected groups and interests to have a say in shaping policy, how can we ensure that the business of government remains democratic? In other words, if we have participation, how can we ensure that our policies are democratically formed and acceptable?

There are no easy solutions to this problem. If there is no participation, then government can be accused of not taking the interest of those it governs into account. Without participation we are also assuming that governments have the answer to the complex array of social, political and economic problems that arise in relation to managing the environment. As we have already argued, governments are no longer seen as the sole holders of solutions to the complex problems arising in today's society, nor do we accept that governments can be the sole agents of social change.

7.2 Accountability in democratic practice

Environmental governance is also about trying to ensure effectiveness and efficiency in policy delivery. On the one hand, governance patterns can help ensure successful policy outcomes, especially the compliance of economic actors. On the other hand, there remains the question of who is responsible for decision making when policy is formulated in complex networks and who is to blame when policy goes wrong? The classic notion of democratic accountability, which rests on the ideal of hierarchical control of administrators by elected politicians, has little applicability in the case of EU environmental policy. In the EU, environmental decision making is split between several layers of government and new governance structures and there is a blurring of divisions of responsibility arising from the involvement of EU, member states and non-governmental actors in policy making and implementation. Conventional methods of political accountability are now hard to apply to the EU because public administration in the EU is undertaken in diffuse policy networks rather than through top-down bureaucracies subject to the control of an elected political leadership. In addition, new governance patterns rely heavily upon informal political networks and, as a result, formal institutions are not always the real site of political initiatives.

7.3 Democratic legitimacy and governance

Viewed from one angle, the development of environmental governance uctures in the EU has had a democratizing influence upon the Union. incorporation of environmental considerations into EU policy has d in an opening up of the EU policy-making process (particularly at l of the Commission) to a broad range of interests. It has also given environmental NGOs a new conduit through which they can voice their concerns (via the Commission) and take legal action (via the European Court of Justice). Furthermore, by establishing policy networks and specific ad hoc bodies, it has helped to dismantle the centrality given to orthodox scientific expertise in shaping policy preferences.

But there are weaknesses in these developments that are, paradoxically, exposing the problems associated with the increased use of new governance processes for the democratic conduct of government. Participation is largely occurring through the establishment of mechanisms that facilitate the participation of (certain) environmental NGOs and economic interests in the policy process. But, as we have argued above, while increased participation in policy making is seen as a necessity, it is not a sufficient condition to ground the democratic legitimacy of the EU nor of the system of environmental governance that the EU is helping to build. This is because democratic legitimacy also requires that participating groups and interests be able to move beyond the narrow, vested interests that have, to date, motivated their involvement in policy making. Participatory democracy requires that participatory structures cease to be the forum for the articulation of narrow interests and become instead the opportunity for real dialogue among a wide range of social and economic groups.

Summary

- The (ongoing) development of environmental governance structures has had a democratizing influence upon the Union.

- However, the increasing use of new governance patterns still gives rise to problems concerning the representative nature of groups participating in policy negotiations and consultations. There is a need to ensure accountability in democratic practice when policy is formulated in complex networks and to ensure that participating groups do not use participatory structures merely as a forum for the articulation of narrow, vested interests. This behaviour can undermine the democratic legitimacy of governance structures.

8   Conclusion

In this chapter we have seen that there are many negative pressures ac on Europe's environment. Attempts to deal with these pressures ha to a Europeanization of environmental management, whereby the taken on an increasingly important role in regulating and shapi responses to environmental problems. This is especially so in pollution caused by industrial activity.

Traditionally the EU has managed the environment in a 'command and control' manner by acting as a 'regulatory state', establishing a regulatory framework for environmental policy and restricting the behaviour of economic actors. However, new governance patterns are emerging because of weaknesses inherent in the traditional approach. As a result, the goal-directed interventions typical of the EU environmental management strategies are increasingly taking place alongside a new governance approach. This new approach involves making use of new tools for environmental policy, grounded in the principle of partnership and shared responsibility. The promotion of sustainable development provides the organizing framework within which this new approach is situated.

Thus environmental management within the EU is characterized by a combination of participatory decision-making processes which lie side-by-side with a more traditional, regulatory approach. The development of new patterns of governance at the EU level is offering a way in which the old dichotomy between the state and the market can be overcome. This is because new governance patterns involve both state (as regulator) and markets (as solution provider) acting in a new alliance aimed at resolving the complex problems arising in relation to environmental management.

The chapter also showed that, while the EU is keen to utilize both regulatory and market-led solutions to environmental problems, member state governments are not always willing to allow the EU to use market tools to manage the environment if it brings political costs. Thus the development of new governance patterns is more advanced at the member state level than it is at the EU level. Member state reluctance to allow the EU to make full use of new tools for environmental policy was clearly seen in their blockage of Commission attempts to introduce a carbon tax. While a carbon tax was in keeping with the drive toward market solutions to environmental problems, in this case handing taxation powers over to the Union was politically unacceptable to some member states. This shows us the importance of understanding that decisions about how to manage the environment are made in a wider, political context and not just in the context of considerations of effectiveness and efficiency. It also points to the importance of taking account of the multi-level governance structure of the EU in our analysis.

However, the increasing use of new governance patterns raises concerns about the representative nature of groups participating in policy negotiations and consultations. There are also difficulties in how to ensure accountability in democratic practice when policy is formulated in complex networks, ensuring that groups do not simply pursue their own narrow, vested interests. In short, there is a need to protect the democratic legitimacy of new governance structures.

Thus, while the use of market-led solutions to environmental problems has an important role to play, these will have to act alongside the traditional 'command and control' regulatory approach to managing Europe's environment. The traditional approach is still needed if public authorities are to fulfil their public duty, if the problem of market failure is to be addressed and if society's trust in the political system is to be maintained. What is unclear, however, is how we can relate new governance patterns to the traditional practice of regulatory government, and do so in a way that can lead to both efficient *and* democratic environmental management within the EU.

References

Andersen, M.S. and Liefferink, D. (eds) (1997) *European Environmental Policy: The Pioneers*, Manchester, Manchester University Press.

Baker, S. (1993) 'The environmental policy of the European Community: a critical review', *Journal of International Relations*, vol.7, no.1, Summer, pp.8–29.

Baker, S. (1997a) 'The evolution of European Union environmental policy: from growth to sustainable development?' in Baker, S., Kousis, M., Richardson, D. and Young, S. (eds) *The Politics of Sustainable Development: Theory, Policy and Practice in the European Union*, London, Routledge.

Baker, S. (1997b) 'The theory and practice of sustainable development in EU perspective' in Baker, S., Kousis, M., Richardson, D. and Young, S. (eds) *The Politics of Sustainable Development: Theory, Policy and Practice in the European Union*, London, Routledge.

Baker, S. (2000) 'Between the devil and the deep blue sea: international obligations, Eastern enlargement and the promotion of sustainable development in the European Union', *Journal of Environmental Policy and Planning*, vol.2, pp.149–66.

Baker, S. and Jehlička, P. (1998) 'Dilemmas of transition: the environment, democracy and economic reform in East Central Europe – an introduction' in Baker, S. and Jehlička, P. (eds) *Dilemmas of Transition: Democracy, Economic Reform and the Environment in East Central Europe*, London, Frank Cass.

Butt Phillips, A. (1998) 'The European Union: environmental policy and the prospects for sustainable development' in Hanf, K. and Jansen, A-I. (eds) *Governance and Environment in Western Europe: Politics, Policy and Administration*, Harlow, Longman.

Caddy, J. (1997) 'Harmonization and asymmetry: environmental policy coordination between the European Union and Central Europe', *Journal of European Public Policy*, vol.3, no.3, pp.318–36.

CEC (Commission of the European Communities) (1992) *Towards Sustainability: A European Community Programme of Policy and Action in Relation to the Environment and Sustainable Development*, COM (92) 23 final, 11.

CEC (1993) 'White paper on growth, competitiveness, employment: the challenge and ways forward into the 21st century', *Bulletin of the European Communities*, Supplement 6/93.

CEC (1994) *Internal Review of Implementation of the European Community Programme of Policy and Action in Relation to the Environment and Sustainable Development 'Towards Sustainability'*, COM (94) 453 final.

CEC (1995) *Progress Report from the Commission on the Implementation of the European Community Programme of Policy and Action in Relation to the Environment and Sustainable Development 'Towards Sustainability'*, COM (95) 624 final.

CEC (1996) *Towards sustainability: Taking European Environment Policy into the 21st Century: A Summary of the European Commission's Progress Report and Action Plan on the Fifth Programme of Policy and Action in Relation to the Environment and Sustainable Development*, Luxembourg, Office for Official Publications of the European Community.

CEC (1997) *Agenda 2000: For a Stronger and Wider Union*, Brussels, CM-07-97-111-EN-C.

Climate Network Europe (1995) *Greening the Treaty II: Sustainable Development in a Democratic Union, Proposals for the 1996 Intergovernmental Conference*, Brussels, EEB.

Dryzek J. (1995) 'Democracy and environmental policy instruments' in Eckersley, R (ed.) *Markets, The State and the Environment: Towards Integration*, Basingstoke, Macmillan.

Eckersley, R. (ed.) (1995) 'Markets, the state and the environment: an overview' in Eckersley, R. (ed.) *Markets, The State and the Environment: Towards Integration*, Basingstoke, Macmillan.

EEA (European Environment Agency) (1995a) *Environment in the European Union, 1995: Report for the Review of the Fifth Environmental Action Programme*, edited by K. Wieringa, Copenhagen, EEA.

EEA (European Environment Agency) (1995b) *Europe's Environment: the Dobříš Assessment*, Copenhagen, EEA.

EEA (European Environment Agency) (1999) *Environment in the EU at the Turn of the Century*, Copenhagen, Environmental Assessment Report No.2.

EEB (European Environmental Bureau) (1996) *Memorandum to the Irish Presidency and the EU Member States*, Brussels, EEB.

Europe Environment (1994) 'Document: European Commission: voluntary approaches and sustainable development', no.445, December 20 supplement.

Europe Environment (1996) 'Document: European Commission: progress report on the Vth Environment Action Programme', no.469, January 23 supplement.

Golub, J. (1998) 'New instruments for environmental policy in the EU: introduction and overview' in Golub, J. (ed.) *New Instruments for Environmental Policy in the EU*, London, Routledge.

Hanf, K. and O'Toole, L.J. (1998) 'Hungary: political transformation and environmental challenge' in Baker, S. and Jehlička, P. (eds) *Dilemmas of*

Transition: Democracy, Economic Reform and the Environment in East Central Europe, London, Frank Cass.

Heyvaert, V. (1998) 'Access to information in a deregulated environment' in Collier, U. (ed.) *Deregulation in the European Union: Environmental Perspectives*, London, Routledge.

Hix, S. (1998) 'One study of the European Union 11: the "new governance" agenda and its rival', *Journal of European Public Policy*, vol.5, no.1, pp.38–65.

Jachtenfuchs, M. (1997) 'Democracy and governance in the European Union', European integration on-line papers, http://eiop.or.at/e10p/Texte/1997-002a.htm

Jansen, A.-I. and Hanf, K. (1998) 'Environmental challenges and institutional changes. An interpretation of the development of environmental policy in Western Europe' in Hanf, K. and Jansen, A.-I. (eds) *Governance and Environment in Western Europe: Politics, Policy and Administration*, Harlow, Longman.

Kooiman, J. (1993) 'Governance and governability: using complexity, dynamics and diversity' in Kooiman, J. (ed.) *Modern Governance: New Government–Society Interactions,* London, Sage.

Macrory, R. (1996) 'Community supervision in the field of the environment' in Somsen, H. (ed.) *Protecting the European Environment: Enforcing EU Environmental Law*, London, Blackstone Press.

Majone, G. (1996) *Regulating Europe,* London, Routledge.

Marks, G. (1993) 'Structural policy and multi-level governance in the EC' in Cafruny, A.W. and Rosenthal, G.G. (eds) *The Maastricht Debate and Beyond* in *The State of the European Community*, Vol.2, Harlow, Longman.

Mazey, S. and Richardson, J. (1995) 'Promiscuous policymaking: the European policy style?' in Rhodes, C. and Mazey, S. (eds) *Building a European Polity?* in *The State of the European Union*, Vol.3, London, Macmillan.

Peters, G. (1996) 'Agenda-setting in the European Union' in Richardson, J. (ed.) *European Union: Power and Policy-Making*, London, Routledge.

Ward, N. (1999) 'The 1999 reforms of the Common Agricultural Policy and the environment', *Environmental Politics*, vol.8, no.4, Winter, pp.168–73.

WCED (World Commission on Environment and Development) (1987) *Our Common Future*, Oxford, Oxford University Press.

Further reading

Baker, S., Kousis, M., Richardson, D. and Young, S. (eds) (1997) *The Politics of Sustainable Development: Theory, Policy and Practice in the European Union*, London, Routledge.

Collier, U. (ed.) (1998) *Deregulation in the European Union: Environmental Perspectives*, London, Routledge.

Eckersley, R. (ed.) (1995) *Markets, the State and the Environment: Towards Integration*, Basingstoke, Macmillan.

Golub, J. (ed.) (1998) *New Instruments for Environmental Policy in the EU*, London, Routledge.

Kohler-Koch, B. and Eising, R. (eds) (1999) *The Transformation of Governance in the European Union*, London, Routledge.

Kooiman, J. (ed.) (1993) *Modern Governance: New Government–Society Interactions*, London, Sage.

Chapter 8
Governing the EU economy as a whole

Christopher M. Dent

1 Introduction

While previous chapters have examined the governance of certain aspects of the European economy, this chapter considers its governance as a whole. Developments in the continued integration of the EU economy make this an ever more important topic as the European Union (EU) both broadens its membership and deepens its internalized economic linkages through projects such as Economic and Monetary Union (EMU). Both these integrational processes have extended the EU's sphere of influence across the European economic space to the extent that to many the 'EU' and 'European' economy are synonymous. As we shall discuss, EU citizens, firms, governments and other actors must pay increasing attention to economic decisions and developments that occur at the level of EU or European governance frameworks.

The overall aim of this chapter is to build up a picture of how the governance of these separate areas and actors adds up to a coherent system of governance for the European economy as a whole (or not, as the case may be) – termed the 'political economy of European integration' in Section 2. This involves an analysis of whether and how *EU policy* in particular is replacing *national policy* in the three key areas identified, so as to locate the sources of *political authority* over the economy as the integrative process evolves. A central analytical term used here is that of *pooled sovereignty,* which is defined in Section 2.

This chapter covers three broad areas:

- the general issue of European integration and economic governance;
- the new EU policy governance under EMU; and
- the connections between business systems and the governance of the European economic space.

In the first of these areas, we consider the political economy of European integration with particular reference to those actors with a stake in EU-level economic governance. Here we also discuss the costs and benefits stemming from the EU's pooled capacities of economic governance as well as examine certain aspects of where economic policy integration, co-operation and co-ordination has been advanced in Europe.

Regarding EMU, the role of the newly established European Central Bank in governing the 'Euroland' economy is considered. The implications for EU monetary and fiscal policies after the introduction of the euro receive special attention.

Our final area analyses how the different business systems affect the governance of the European economy. It also discusses the centripetal forces working toward the creation of a more homogenized European business system and the centrifugal forces working against it.

As with other chapters, the above themes are all discussed in the context of the market, regulatory order and self-organizing networks.

2   European integration and economic governance

As has been argued from the very beginning of this book, European economic integration has occurred through both *de facto* processes (integration driven by private business) and *de jure* processes (integration driven by public policy). Moreover, the former have a close association with market order governance and the latter with regulatory order governance. These twin forces have also often worked in accordance with one another through various modes of public/private sector co-operation and co-ordination, which themselves are closely associated with the structure of self-organizing networks. For example, business representatives played a prominent role in negotiations to establish the rules of the Single European Market (SEM). In EU industrial policy, policy makers have worked to organize strategic alliances between European firms in order to develop EU competitive advantages in high-technology sectors (see Chapter 6). Other instances of collaborative integration are examined in the chapter but more generally we shall discuss the links between deeper economic integration in the EU economy and the structures and processes of governance that have evolved with it; in other words, the extent to which the EU economy is governed as a whole.

2.1   The political economy of European integration

Previous chapters have shown how European integration in general has been shaped by a variety of economic, political and socio-cultural forces. Since its conception in the 1950s, the EU has maintained its position as the world's most sophisticated and advanced regional integration arrangement, providing a model for other aspirant regional groupings. From all perspectives, the EU can be understood as a complex multi-level system of governance, whereby various levels of authority, power and influence are wielded by both state and non-state actors with a stake in shaping both the current state and future direction of the EU's affairs. At the centre of this complexity lies the relationship between the EU institutions (such as the European Commission and the European Court of Justice) and the nation state governments that established them to manage the EU's pooled sovereignty.

For the purposes of this chapter, 'pooled economic sovereignty' expresses both the *de jure* legal status or location of economic power and the *de facto* operationalization of authority and the capacity to act in respect to this. Thus it is not quite the same as the strict notion of sovereignty deployed in discussions of political science where the emphasis is on the formal legal location of the ultimate authority to exercise coercive power (**Bromley, 2001a**). The definition of sovereignty used here is looser than this, merely expressing capacity to act with some authority that has effects; it is a more 'dispersed' form of sovereignty.

The politico-economic costs and benefits of pooled sovereignty are discussed later, but an important consequence of this arrangement has been the increased contestability of governance within the EU polity. This has primarily occurred through the creation of more centres and levels of political authority which in turn have provided actors from outside the mainstream public policy community (for example, firms and NGOs) with better opportunities to influence policy makers in the EU. Furthermore, the expansion of both the rules of EU governance and the number of game players have yielded various permutations of coalitions and conflicts between different actors.

For instance, the contest between different levels of EU political authority (central governments, local governments and EU institutions) over the governance of the European economy is largely determined by the location of the particular issue between the poles of intergovernmental and supranational competence (discussed in **Bromley, 2001b**). In some policy areas such as trade, competition and agriculture, the European Commission has considerable autonomy to take decisions without submitting proposals to the Council of Ministers. In these cases, it thus exercises degrees of *supranational executive competence* (although legislative competence lies with the Council of Ministers and European Parliament). In many other cases, however, decisions of EU economic governance derive from processes of *intergovernmental bargaining*, with EU institutions playing a more supportive, co-ordinative or arbitrative role. For example, in their 1999/2000 dispute over the intra-EU beef trade both the British and French governments sought rulings from the European Commission to support their respective national positions. In all these types of cases, however, the European Commission has often overstepped the mandates it is given by the Council of Ministers, the European Parliament and the national governments, leading to disputes and negotiations between the different levels and agencies.

While EU political authorities may appear to exercise direct governance over the European economy, their positions often reflect the interests of other actors. In the European political economy, EU-based firms represent a powerful constituency in this respect, not least because economic policies are increasingly formulated with their interests in mind. This trend is connected to the supposed shift from states to markets in the international economic system (and hence from regulatory order to other governance forms), whereby large European multinational firms in particular have developed considerable power and leverage over economic policy makers within Europe and beyond. In Europe, this has led to numerous 'marriages of convenience' between public policy officials and private sector representatives in seeking common economic objectives, such as improving industrial competitiveness. To some extent, this constitutes a move toward the self-organizing network paradigm.

At the same time, market forces have undermined certain forms of political control over the economy, and hence the effectiveness of economic policy itself. This is often attributed to globalization in which the growing economic interdependence of nation states, and hence the expanding commercial linkages and spillovers that connect them, has rendered independent policy governance within national economic boundaries increasingly difficult to achieve (Chapter 9). In matters of finance in particular, where economic globalization is the most advanced, the power of EU member state governments to conduct 'independent' policies has been seriously diminished (Chapters 2 and 4). As the 1992/93 Exchange Rate Mechanism (ERM) crisis demonstrated, not even the collective actions of powerful national governments can be assured of prevailing against global private-sector financiers. On the one hand, this correlates with the recent ascendance of market order in the international political economy. Yet we shall later discuss how a key purpose of the EU's EMU project is to reclaim some ground lost by political authorities in matters of European economic governance.

Extending the context of globalization, we need to consider how various actors not orginating from Europe also work within the EU's complex multi-level system of governance. For instance, American multinational firms long ensconced in Europe (such as Ford, IBM, Hoover) have proved effective lobbiers at different levels of EU economic policy making. Certain EU rules of economic governance must also comply with accords signed by EU member states or EU institutions in international organizations and regimes: World Trade Organization (WTO) rules and many aspects of EU trade policy; International Labour Organization (ILO) agreements and EU labour market regulations; and multilateral environmental agreements (such as the Montreal Protocol) and the EU's energy and environmental policies.

Hence we see the emergence of a complex mix of political authority operating at several levels combined with the influence of private business interests and set within the context of the growing internationalization of economic activity, as the main contours within which EU economic governance itself operates. In particular we have an experiment in 'pooled sovereignty' at the EU level, which it will be worth exploring in more detail.

2.2   Pooled capacities of EU economic governance: costs and benefits

In this sub-section we consider in more detail the politico-economic costs and benefits of pooled sovereignty in the context of governing the EU economy. Placing the notion of pooled 'economic sovereignty' in this context, it is perhaps more useful to talk of the pooled capacity of economic governance at the EU level. This relates to EU-level economic policies that entail the conferring of more localized political authority to 'higher' EU powers, be these to intergovernmental mechanisms or supranational agencies. The costs of pooling economic policy capacities are obvious: economic policies once managed exclusively by national governments are merged or co-ordinated at the EU level. With the SEM, this included a vast array of measures concerning the regulation of product, capital and labour markets (Chapter 2). As participants in the EMU project, EU economic ministries have been compelled to manage their monetary policies (for example, interest rate) in an increasingly co-ordinative fashion, thus subordinating the national economic interest to the general EU economic interest (Chapter 4). Indeed, this example of interdependent EU policy making can be linked back to EMU's precursor – the ERM – and its framework for exchange rate policy co-ordination that was first established in 1979.

In this debate on pooled policy capacity, the principle of *subsidiarity* is extremely important. Enshrined in the Maastricht Treaty, subsidiarity essentially commits the EU to devolve political authority to that level deemed most appropriate to deal with the particular problems or issues arising. It thus represents a 'check and balance' to the deferment of pooled capacity up to the EU level. The greater localization of economic policy capacity that it implies has been defended by both the EU's nationalist politicians and many local government authorities as a means to resist European integration. However, some local governments have welcomed the integrative pooled capacity trend because it has undermined the power of central governments over sub-state actors such as themselves. Moreover, the European economy can also be viewed as a patchwork of regional and sub-regional economies that have developed their own governance structures (**Anderson, 2001**). These are especially evident in more politically decentralized countries, such as Germany, where local governments exercise a much broader range of economic policies (for example, tax-raising powers) than their counterparts in politically centralized countries like France.

Nothwithstanding the need for localized governance in the European political economy, the benefits of pooled capacity can be exploited in various circumstances. In a general sense, EU-level policies can be increasingly legitimized as European economic integration itself deepens: single European markets and a single currency zone require unified economic policies to manage them. This not only relates to monetary or finance policies, but also to others like industrial and regional policies that manage certain aspects of the European economic space. As we shall see, from the start numerous EU-level policies have emerged and developed to help govern the European economy, and many of these are examined in the following section. The general rationalizing of policies at the EU level also helps avoid overlaps and a waste of policy resources between EU member states, and, moreover, can create important synergies between them. This will be illustrated in Section 2.3 where we examine EU competition, structural (regional, social, agricultural) and industrial policies.

More generally, for EU firms working increasingly across a more integrated European economic space, the creation of a more coherent EU economic policy space is especially important. This primarily relates to the commercial benefits yielded from a more unified regulatory environment and the opportunities for greater inter-firm co-operation presented by 'synergy-oriented' EU policies, the SEM being highly relevant to the former and industrial policy to the latter. Finally, the economic integration itself produces important dynamic benefits for firms and consumers that stem from reduced production and transaction costs, a more competitive dynamic between firms and hence lower prices. For example, the euro will lower the cost of doing business across the EU by removing the need to work in different currencies and simplifying inter-business transactions (Chapter 2).

In addition, unified economic policies have not only helped the better management of internal EU affairs but also those with its international trade partners and the international economic system in general. While this is discussed in more detail in Chapter 9, suffice to say here that common external policies (for example, on trade) have enabled EU authorities to more effectively govern the European economy in a generally more harmonious accord with the outside world than if strictly nationalist policies had prevailed. The elevation of EU-level policies also provides the means for securing the optimal absolute gains yielded from collaborative inter-state ventures, thus deflecting individual nation states from pursuing 'beggar-thy-neighbour' strategies based on achieving suboptimal relative gains against each other.

2.3   Economic policy integration, co-operation and co-ordination in the EU

A compressed history of EU-level policy reveals how its origins evolved from sectoral governance applied to selected industries under the ECSC regime (coal and steel industrial management) to the broad macroeconomic governance now experienced under the current EMU regime. In between, the EU's economic policy portfolio has developed to cover major areas such as social, employment, agricultural, environmental, energy, science and technology, industrial, transport, competition, trade (internal and external), and regional policies. These economic-related EU policies have thus provided an extended basis for EU-level governance over the European economy. We now examine three EU policy domains in some detail (to illustrate some of the above points) and consider the progressive way EU policy has displaced national policy as the focus of economic governance.

EU competition policy

The origins of this EU policy date back to 1962. Its objectives centred on promoting a dynamic competitive environment within the EU economy with the aim of enhancing both consumer welfare and techno-industrial advancement. Thus, operating and potential monopolies, cartels and other abuses of dominant market positions along with mergers, state aids to industry and additional forms of anti-competitive behaviour all come under the scrutiny of EU competition policy authorities located in DG Competition of the European Commission. Cartels of a European nature, which relate to any collusive behaviour between groups of companies to fix prices or control production to the detriment of trade between member states, are outlawed under Article 85 of the Maastricht Treaty. Firms that abuse their dominant positions in markets (for example, to organize predatory pricing or exclusive sales agreements) are liable to prosecution under Article 86.

Since the European Council's adoption of the Merger Regulation in December 1989, the European Commission has been conferred powers to scrutinize cross-border EU mergers before their completion to evaluate their net welfare effect. On this legal basis, it can block mergers completely or force modifications to the original merger arrangement so as to avoid a dominant market position arising. The key features of the Merger Regulation are outlined in Box 8.1.

Box 8.1 EU Merger Regulation

The criteria under which the Regulation can be applied are twofold:

- Where the worldwide turnover of the companies involved exceeds 5 billion euro.
- Where there is a 250 million euro turnover within the EU for at least two of the companies concerned, unless each undertaking derives more than two thirds of its EU-wide turnover within one member state only.

With regard to state aid, Articles 92–94 forbid public subsidies which potentially threaten competition in trade between member states. However, there are derogations, such as where the aid promotes EU-level industrial interests. Public financial support thus bestowed upon the Airbus Industrie consortium to assist its competitive struggles against Boeing, the American aerospace champion, has been permitted on these grounds.

Like many other economic-related policies, a major purpose of EU competition policy is to correct identifiable market failures in its associated domain of economic activity. This in turn entails implementing the necessary degree of regulatory order required to extract the full benefits from the dynamic workings of the market. In this case DG Competition has a specific responsibility for safeguarding the competitive dynamic of the single market. This is thus an example of a regulatory policy designed to enhance the operation of the market – in Chapter 1 this was termed a 'market correcting' policy.

EU structural policies: regional, social, agricultural

An important function of EU economic policy has been to assist European industry to respond to the pressures and opportunities created by structural change. Regional, social and agricultural policies formally comprise the set of structural policies with the common aim of promoting *economic and social cohesion within the EU*. Policy initiatives and development toward this end reflected the consensus to build a 'social Europe' alongside the 'business Europe' projects of the SEM and EMU (Chapter 5). Hence there is a strong human dimension to these policies in terms of labour market regulations and practices, human capital development and the protection or restoration of EU economic communities that have been adversely affected by profound structural change. This especially concerns those EU regions where structural decline in local industries has created high levels of unemployment and problems of labour mobility, both occupational and geographic. Not only does this apply to industrial sectors like steel and textiles (for example, East Asia is now the world's main centre for textile production and has played a significant part in the restructuring of the European textile industry), but also to agriculture, whose economic viability has been similarly undermined by competitive threats from outside the EU (Brown, 2001, Unit 2).

Regional policy

A central purpose of EU regional policy, which has been functioning since 1975, is to redress the core–periphery divides within the EU economy. The EU 'core' is characterized by its high-tech industrial development, superior infrastructure networks and a high income per capita demographic profile, and roughly stretches from South-East England to Northern Italy. The peripheral regions of the EU, which relate to its Atlantic and Mediterranean outskirts, tend to exhibit lower-tech industrial development, weaker infrastructure provision and a poorer demographic profile. Under the compensatory provisions of EU regional policy, the latter have received substantive financial support from various 'structural funds', mostly the European Regional Development Fund (ERDF), which provide for investment grants, employment grants, infrastructure development and other measures. Regional disparities in the EU can be found at a more micro-level and a number of smaller regions and urban areas (such as Merseyside in the UK) are eligible for EU regional policy assistance.

There are a number of important future challenges facing the EU's regional policy. For instance, EMU could have 'core-enhancing' effects where deeper capital market integration will allow capital to move more freely from low value-added, low-return locations (on the periphery of Europe) to high value-added, high-return regions (the core) of Europe (Chapter 2). Thus this process could exacerbate regional inequalities and require an enhanced regional policy initiative to combat it. There is also the EU's forthcoming eastern enlargement which will encompass a variety of relatively underdeveloped states (**Lewis, 2001**). Their membership will make them eligible for structural funds. This will naturally disadvantage the current EU periphery in subsequent allocations of the ERDF and other sources of financial support from Brussels (Chapter 6). Finally, the fact that the structural funds only represent 0.3 per cent of EU GDP, a low figure by most national comparisons, raises questions over how adequately the EU's structural difficulties can be managed, especially under the more integrative EMU regime. Thus the overall impact of EMU and enlargement may be greater diversity and inequality unless these structural funds can be increased.

Social policy

The broad objectives of EU social policy are to safeguard worker rights, improve the employability of EU workers and engender harmonious industrial relations (Chapter 5). Within the European Commission, DG Employment, Industrial Relations and Social Affairs is responsible for this EU policy domain. The European Social Fund (ESF) has been working to this end since its creation in 1960 but a formalized EU-level social policy was not established until 1974 under the first Social Action Programme (SAP). Recent policy developments have centred around the Social Chapter of the Maastricht Treaty and the EU's re-employment strategy.

The Social Chapter was to enshrine the 'Social Europe' principle in the Treaty, which introduced a range of labour market directives on issues such as working time rules, European Works Councils, parental leave and youth employees. With Europe's unemployment problem persisting into the 1990s, the EU sought to balance the Social Chapter's main emphasis on worker rights with a more proactive approach toward employment creation. Consequently, its re-employment strategy was developed over the 1994–1995 period leading to the introduction of an Employment Action Plan (EAP), with an agreement to concentrate structural funds on job-creation initiatives and a call for more labour market deregulation and re-regulation. More specifically, the EAP would introduce more 'active' labour market measures (such as training), press for less 'passive' measures (for example, unemployment benefit) and the reduction of non-wage labour costs, and target measures on the worst hit unemployed groups, typically the young and long-term unemployed (see Chapter 5). In essence, the EU's social policy has become its employment and social policy, which effectively prioritizes enhancing employability alongside, or even above, the protection of worker rights.

Agricultural policy

Although it too is a 'structural policy', the EU's Common Agricultural Policy (CAP) possesses a special distinctiveness. It is a 'common' EU policy that entails the conferring of policy competence to the supranational level (i.e. to the Commission), whereas comparatively independent regional and social policies are maintained at the member state level. The CAP also has a specific sectoral focus and has gained a certain notoriety, not least because it swallows approximately half of the annual EU budget (Brown, 2001). The governance of the EU's agriculture sector is also unique in that agriculture is as much concerned with maintaining the fabric of rural society as it is with rural business activity. Hence, there exists a strong extra-market dimension to CAP in the pursuit of its twin economic and sociocultural objectives. Taken together with the deep structural problems facing the sector, this helps explain why the EU's agricultural markets are so heavily regulated and governed.

The above points help explain why the CAP is one of the EU's most problematic policy domains. Many problems also stem from the diverse economic nature of the EU's agriculture sector. Contrast, for example, the UK's large scale and highly efficient grain producers of East Anglia with their micro-farm counterparts in certain Mediterranean parts of Europe like Greece. For some time, the UK has complained about the disproportionate distribution of CAP support given to the EU's most inefficient agricultural producers who receive by far the largest share of this. Establishing a common framework of policy governance is difficult with such a multifaceted policy domain in which various stakeholders seek influence. It is not just Europe's agricultural community that has a vested interest in CAP but also those communities with environmental regional development, animal welfare, consumer group and other interests at stake (Chapter 7). Moreover, major political tensions between EU member states over specific aspects of CAP frequently arise. A most recent example was the BSE issue and intra-EU beef trade whereby the UK, France and Germany were drawn into a bitter conflict on an agri-produce health and safety issue that began in the late 1990s.

EU industrial policy

From its antecedent ECSC roots, industrial policy has been a key policy domain for the EU, although a comprehensive multi-sector EU industrial policy (see Box 8.2) was not developed until the 1970s. Industry policies have traditionally been concerned with improving industrial competitiveness and the protection of those industries in structural decline. However, the legitimacy to uphold the latter has been increasingly contested in the era of globalization, freer markets and more open competition. Generally speaking, industry policies have a diffuse focus owing to their simultaneous preoccupation with cross-sectoral issues, such as technological improvement, and specific sectors especially those of a 'strategic' or high-tech character (such as aerospace and semiconductors). Thus, industrial policy governance requires a high degree of co-ordinative management with other policy domains, and

Box 8.2   EU industrial policy

The rationale for an EU-level industrial policy can be explained with reference to the following points.

- Unco-ordinated national policies may lead to the wasteful duplication of either scarce research and development (R & D) resources or of investments in productive assets where economies of scale are not separately attained. Hence, a co-ordinated industrial policy helps improve R & D and scale economy outcomes overall. A co-ordinated EU-level policy also helps reduce adverse spillover effects of national-level industrial policies – for example, state aid, that confers a domestic competitive advantage but at the expense of other EU firms.

- A common or a co-ordinated industrial policy in a large and expanding single market may yield a deeper impact on the economy than an isolated national policy, largely for reasons expressed in the point above.

- In an era of intensified global competition, EU firms need to work more closely within a unified industrial policy framework to improve their competitiveness in relation to their common non-EU rivals, especially those from North America and East Asia.

The following are the four key domains of EU industrial policy:

- *Promotion of intangible investment*
  This includes training, R & D, and the diffusion of information technologies and best industrial management practices throughout the EU economy.

- *Development of industrial co-operation*
  This involves various levels of strategic alliance between EU firms that create synergetic competitive benefits, the highest profile examples being the ESPRIT programme and the Airbus Industrie consortium. These represented EU-level industrial strategies to develop stronger capacities in the IT and aerospace sectors respectively.

- *Strengthening of competition*
  This entails harnessing the competitive dynamic of the single market to improve EU industrial performance, supported by improving the quality of regulation, the promotion of open instead of proprietary industrial standards, ensuring coherence between different EU policies that affect competition while monitoring their impact on competitiveness, and proposing necessary changes.

- *Modernization of the role of public authorities*
  An example is improving the regulatory framework in which they operate, assessing the future competitive challenges they face and improving their techno-industrial capabilities.

(Jovanovic, 1997; EC, 1994; and DG Industry's Communications and Industrial Competitiveness Policy Framework) developed links between industrial policy makers and representatives from the selected industry sectors (Chapter 6).

As with competition, regional and social policies, each EU member state maintains its own industrial policies to varying degrees of breadth and sophistication. France, with its *dirigiste* tradition, has operated a strong industrial policy, while in more liberal nation states such as the UK it has been relatively weak.

Member state industrial policy makers are supposed to work alongside DG Enterprise which co-ordinates regulatory and legislative activity in this field. This Commission office also runs its own separately funded EU-level policies and projects, and has specific responsibility for the steel industry under the ECSC framework. The core task for EU Industrial Policy, as set out in Article 130 of the Maastricht Treaty, is to improve the competitiveness of European industry through the pursuit of four main objectives:

- Speeding up industry's adjustment to structural changes.

- Encouraging an environment in which initiative can thrive and in which undertakings, particularly small and medium-sized enterprises (SMEs), can develop.

- Encouraging an environment favourable to co-operation between undertakings.

- Fostering a better exploitation of the results of innovation and of research and technological development which are of potential value to industry.

Policies aimed at promoting EU industrial competitiveness involve actions in two main categories:

- Those relating to the operation of markets, including regulations on market access and product specifications, trade policy and competition policy.

- Those concerning factors that affect industry's capacity to adapt to change, comprising: macroeconomic stability, accounting for the general public's expectations with regard to industry (for example, environment-friendly practices), and measures to promote intangible investments in areas such as technology and human resource development.

For reasons noted earlier, EU industry policy makers have increasingly withdrawn from sector-specific forms of subsidy-based or trade-protectionist support and now concentrate more on cross-sector modes of competitiveness promotion. This has entailed both DG Enterprise and national governments performing less of a centrally organizing or interventionist role in industrial development and more one of a facilitator and co-ordinator, for example, by focusing more on infrastructural provision with regard to technological and human resource development. Examples here would include establishing R & D laboratories and high-tech skills training programmes. In other words, industrial policy has become more concerned with context control (that is, creating the conducive environment in which industrial development can take place) rather than perpetrating direct control over industrial activities.

2.4 Adapting to change

In this section we have examined the broad relationship between European integration and economic governance. In particular, we have seen how a major benefit of the pooled capacity of EU economic governance is that EU-level market failures can be addressed. However, constructing EU-level regulatory orders and the operationalization of common EU policies also comes with certain costs. Aside from losses of national sovereignty over economic matters, advocates of market order further point to the dangers of installing a 'one size fits all' regulatory order across a diverse and expansive European economic space, making EU policies more prone to regulatory failure. Yet if the SEM is to work effectively then strengthened EU policies are required to enhance its market dynamics. This was discussed with respect to competition, where EU regulations aim to extract the welfare gains generated by SEM-improved competitive markets. Furthermore, as market conditions across Europe change, so do the structure and form of EU-level policies and their associated regulatory orders. As part of a 'third way' in EU-level economic governance, public and private sector representatives are forging new self-organizing network partnerships to confront the common challenges facing the European economy. These will be increasingly oriented by the deepening impact of EMU, the issue to which we now turn.

Summary

- The EU can be understood as a multi-level system of governance in which various actors (for example, governments, firms, citizens) seek to influence how a gelling EU economy is governed.

- The cost of relinquishing national policy sovereignty over economic matters to EU-level authorities is traded off against the benefits yielded from the more coherent EU policy approach required to manage an increasingly integrated European economy.

- EU economic policy integration, co-operation and co-ordination has evolved to cover a range of economic policies normally associated with those maintained by national governments.

3 Policy governance under EMU

The introduction of the euro in 1999 represented a major event in European economic history and had profound implications for the future governance of the EU economy. By sharing a common currency, the eleven original EMU member states committed themselves to pursuing a common monetary policy that would be managed by a new EU institution, the European Central Bank (ECB).

The history of EMU development is outlined in the Appendix to this chapter. While the ERM, the precursor to EMU, had forged a prior policy convergence on exchange rate and interest rate policies across the EU, the introduction of the euro heralded a significant step forward in pooling the capacity of economic governance within Europe. Given the combined geoeconomic weight of the euro-zone, it also brings significant ramifications for the international economic system: a more unified EU international finance policy can be anticipated and the euro has the potential to challenge the US dollar as the global standard currency of the twenty-first century. But it also opens up some additional governance problems internal to the EU, notably the relationship between the original eleven 'Euroland' economies who have signed up to EMU and those other EU economies that have chosen to stay out of the EMU project. Here we are likely to see a potentially unstable and 'shifting boundary' in the overall EU governance as countries move into (and possibly out of) full monetary union.

Let us first examine the role and nature of the ECB, which has been charged with managing the euro.

3.1   The European Central Bank (ECB)

The ECB is the most important EU institution to have been established in recent years, if not decades. It was created in May 1998 as an independent and federal-style central bank (see Box 8.3) based in Frankfurt to manage the EU single currency, the euro. Its inaugural President, Wim Duisenberg, leads an institution with the responsibility of running the monetary policy of the Euroland 11 (the EU 15 minus the UK, Sweden, Denmark and Greece – though Greece may join in the near future). Hence, it sets the interest rate, regulates the money supply and oversees the exchange rate of the large majority of EU member states that have committed themselves to EMU. Currency unions require a common monetary policy, given that exchange rates between participating countries become fixed and capital is free to move from one place to another within the union. The governance of monetary policy would effectively collapse if members were permitted to operate separate policy regimes. For example, if one member raised its interest rate above all others there would be no nominal impediments to massive flows of capital being rerouted to that member from elsewhere in the union. Investing firms will do this because they get a relatively higher interest rate return on their funds without facing the risk of a changing exchange rate (remember, these are fixed) affecting the relative value of that return. A central governing agency, like the ECB, is therefore required to preside over a common monetary policy for the group (recall the discussion in Chapter 1 on 'optimum currency areas').

As with EMU itself, the ECB carries forward the work of a precursor. The European Monetary Institute (EMI), set up in January 1994, prepared the way for the ECB by developing the procedures for strengthening co-operation between the central banks of EU member states and also monitored EMU convergence criteria during the post-Maastricht phase of the ERM (see Appendix). Member state central banks within Euroland were not closed down but reconstituted into the European System of Central Banks (ESCB) which forms the network of ECB subsidiaries operating in those individual countries.

Box 8.3 The constitution of the ECB

The ECB comprises an Executive Board of six members (the President included) appointed by the European Council for eight-year terms and a Governing Council which in turn consists of the Executive Board plus ESCB governors. Decisions taken by the ECB on monetary policy are determined by majority votes of the Governing Council and are subsequently implemented by the Executive Board. On non-ECB capital issues, this works on a 'one person, one vote' basis while on bank capital matters voting power is proportionate to the member states' subscribed capital (the 'working capital' used to help operate EU policy in areas such as foreign exchange reserve management) and no votes are conferred to the Executive Board. The ECB's subscribed capital is itself determined by an equal weighting of each member states' share of the population and GDP at market prices, averaged over the previous five years. In summary, the basic tasks of this governance system, as defined in Article 3 of the ESCB Statute, are to:

- define and implement the monetary policy of the Euroland 11,
- conduct foreign exchange operations,
- hold and manage the Euroland 11's official foreign reserves,
- promote the smooth operation of payment systems,
- contribute to the smooth conduct of policies pursued by the competent authorities, relating to the prudential supervision of credit institutions and the stability of the financial system.

The operation of the ECB

The ECB's independence means that national governments and other EU institutions have, in principle, no leverage over the day-to-day decisions made at Frankfurt. The institutional architects of the ECB – the Delors Committee and European Council – were at the time heavily influenced by economic literature that took a positive view toward central bank independence (Alesina and Summers, 1993; Healey, 1996). As Germany's central bank – the Bundesbank – had most successfully demonstrated in preceding decades, the decoupling of a country's political or electoral cycle from its economic cycle had proved an effective formula for price stability. By remaining autonomous from the political manipulations of governments seeking re-election by undertaking reflationary policies (such as lower interest rates, higher government spending), independent central banks are in theory able to pursue more economically rational monetary policies. It was no coincidence, then, that the ECB was closely modelled on the Bundesbank. Indeed, the ECB's prime objective, as stated in Article 105 of the Maastricht Treaty, is to maintain price stability: it pursues the medium-term target of keeping the Euroland-11's price index at below 2 per cent per annum. Like the Bundesbank, the ECB is not permitted to finance the budget deficits of national governments directly or take operational instructions from any political body.

Article 105 of the Maastricht Treaty also states that 'without prejudice to the objective of price stability, the ESCB shall support the general economic policies in the Community with a view to contributing to the achievement of the objectives of the Community as laid down in Article 2', where sustainable and non-inflationary growth, together with a high level of employment and social protection are among the stated aims. To some, these may present irreconcilable policy objectives as the pursuit of low inflation through maintaining austere monetary policies (such as high interest rates) may have an adverse impact on employment levels. Yet in the current climate of the global political economy, the ECB must primarily target inflation over employment to safeguard its credibility in the international finance community. Why is this necessary? We noted earlier the UK's 1992 currency crisis and how the power of financial speculators forced the British Government out of the ERM. Despite the UK Treasury taking extreme policy measures, such as raising interest rates from 10 per cent to 15 per cent in a few hours, the speculators had little faith in the Government's long term commitment to its ERM policy.

For its part, the ECB must moreover demonstrate its own commitment to maintaining low inflation in the EU economy as this creates the stable monetary environment that global financiers generally desire. Yet notwithstanding the seemingly resolute institutional and statutory arrangements for pursuing price stability, the ECB's Governing Council still includes representatives from EU member states with a high inflationary tradition, for instance Spain and Italy. This has lead to concerns of possible coalitions forming between certain Governing Council members who may press for a softer approach toward EU monetary policy. The alternative governance objective promoted by such coalitions would most likely be the pursuit of lower unemployment through expansionary monetary policies (see Chapters 2 and 4).

However, three main counter-factors make this scenario unlikely. First, coalitions of this kind would be matched against an even stronger coalition of 'low inflation' member states led by Germany. Second, the formation of 'soft policy' coalitions would rely on the existence of shared macroeconomic conditions (for example, high unemployment, an aligned business cycle out of sync with 'low inflation' countries) to provide the basis for this opposing stance. Nothwithstanding the high rates of unemployment that persist in many parts of the EU, the progression of economic and policy convergence toward EMU had created by the late 1990s a more cyclically aligned EU economy (Chapter 2). This means that interest rates set by the ECB should nominally fit the needs of all Euroland 11 members simultaneously – low interest rates in time of recession and high interest rates during a boom period when inflationary pressures require deflating. As Table 8.1 shows there was a remarkably small deviation between the low inflation rates of euro participants in the late 1990s, thus potentially allowing the ECB to pursue a low interest rate policy without causing significant inter-state tensions. Third, by signing up for the euro, EU member states are bound by the Maastricht Treaty to support the ECB's price stability objective. Therefore, even though an asymmetry of interests and sociocultural influences may persist within the euro membership, each participant is contractually obliged to uphold the ECB's anti-inflationary line. (During early 2001, however, the euro began to rise against other main currencies.)

Table 8.1 Macroeconomic indicators across the EU

	Inflation[1]		Interest rates[2]		Unemployment	
	1981–90	*1999*	*1981–90*	*1998*	*1981–90*	*1999*
EU 15	6.7	1.7	11.3	4.9	8.1	9.6
Euroland 11	6.5	1.5	11.2	4.7	9.1	10.5
Austria	3.6	1.6	8.1	4.7	3.4	4.3
Belgium	4.5	1.2	10.4	4.7	9.7	8.3
Finland	7.1	1.0	12.3	4.8	4.7	10.1
France	6.3	0.8	11.4	4.6	9.2	11.5
Germany	2.8	0.9	7.6	4.6	6.0	9.0
Ireland	7.0	4.0	12.6	4.8	14.7	6.0
Italy	10.6	2.1	15.0	4.8	8.8	12.2
Luxembourg	4.3	1.3	8.9	4.7	2.5	2.7
Netherlands	2.0	1.9	8.3	4.6	8.5	3.6
Portugal	17.5	3.3	18.8	5.0	7.0	4.7
Spain	9.4	2.2	14.3	4.8	18.5	17.3
Denmark	2.8	0.9	13.4	4.9	7.4	4.6
Greece	19.5	3.3	17.0	8.5	6.4	9.4
Sweden	7.7	1.2	12.3	5.0	2.6	7.8
UK	6.4	2.6	10.9	5.5	9.8	6.5

1 GDP deflator at market prices

2 Nominal long-term rates

(derived from *Eurostat* data)

The politics of ECB governance

The promotion of Euroland solidarity draws upon other imperatives. Historical experience has shown that new currencies require strong monetary policies at their launch to achieve a critical level of financial market confidence. This is extremely important as reputations regarding currencies and their supporting governance regimes are established from a very early stage. Hence, from the euro's outset the ECB needed to demonstrate its competence and resolve in order to provide it with a firm institutional platform. In addition, the euro and the ECB heralded the start of an important new macroeconomic governance regime within the EU. If other EU actors were to have faith in them, both needed to make a good first impression. However, the euro made a shaky start in the world's foreign exchange markets, almost falling to US dollar parity (it began at roughly 1:1.18) within a few months. By April 2000, the euro had experienced a 20 per cent depreciation since its formal launch in January 1999.

Figure 8.1   The euro's depreciation against the US$ January 1997 – July 2000

(*Datastream*, 2000)

Meanwhile, the ECB's credibility took an early knock from a heated intra-EU argument over the selection of the inaugural President, made worse by the fact that France and Germany were on opposing sides. As it transpired, a deal was struck, with Jean-Calude Trichet the incumbent Banque de France Governor replacing Wim Duisenberg (the Dutch President and favoured German candidate) halfway through the statutory eight-year Presidential term. The potential compromise on policy-making continuity caused by this premature shortening of the inaugural Presidential term could only have damaged the medium to long term market confidence in the euro. Moreover, the episode demonstrated how the ECB was at its very conception susceptible to high-level political interference despite official rhetoric to the contrary.

So although the ECB is supposed to be an autonomous decision-making body within the EU polity, it nevertheless complies to certain accountability mechanisms and procedures. For example, it is subject to audits under the jurisdiction of the European Court of Justice, while representatives from the President of the European Council and the European

Commission are allowed to attend meetings of the ECB Governing Council. Furthermore, the ECB must submit annual reports to both the European Parliament and ECOFIN (EU Committee of Economic and Finance Ministers) on its activities, and therefore comes under some form of political scrutiny. However, there are many who believe that the virtues of central bank independence have been overblown and that the ECB's accountability should be extensively broadened. This particularly relates to the EU's 'democratic deficit' problem, a matter to which we shall return. In their counter-independence thesis, Berman and McNamara (1999) argued that the most important prerequisite for combating inflation is a strong financial sector interested in price stability and willing to influence policy making to achieve this. By promoting institutional insularity in an alignment with the interests of financial markets, the EU political process risks further accusations of forsaking democratic accountability and transparency in the pursuit of bureaucratic and financial élite-determined economic objectives: put alternatively, a form of European-style 'crony capitalism'. This is important from the view of governance as it raises key questions regarding the concentration and distribution of power within the European political economy at the start of the twenty-first century.

The UK 'opt-out'

One of the EU's four major economies – the UK – was not an original EMU participant. The case for the British Government's initial reluctance reflected many of the potential risks facing EU member states in joining the euro zone. As previously mentioned, the UK economy had traditionally maintained a non-synchronous business cycle with continental Europe, thus making it prone to inappropriate monetary policy decisions made by the ECB, especially regarding interest rates. In addition, the asymmetries in the structural features of the UK's capital markets in relation to the continental norm remain pronounced. For example, owing to the high rate of home ownership and hence mortgage contracts in the UK, changes in interest rates have a larger and more rapid effect on aggregate demand than in most other parts of Europe (Pennant-Rea, 1997). This highlights the general governance problem of EMU in that what may be a suitable monetary policy for the EU economy as a whole can be simultaneously misaligned to the individual needs of many member state economies. Moreover, as Dornbusch et al. (1998) have argued, structural asymmetries in Europe's capital markets imply that even if all euro members were in business cycle synchronicity, the ECB's interest rate would have disproportionate effects across the EU economy owing to the different ways and degrees that interest rates affect both firms and households.

If nothing else, then, this particular 'opt-out' (and the absence of other EU members from monetary union) will present problems for governing the economic relationships between the two sets of economies. Something like a 'two-speed' or 'variable geometry' solution will have to be invented. As yet the nature of this is unclear.

3.2 The euro, monetary policy and fiscal policy

Perhaps the most difficult task of economic governance that confronts the ECB relates to the need to co-ordinate monetary policy with fiscal policy, the latter of which remains the executive competence of member state governments. The connections between monetary and fiscal policy are manifold. A key problem for the ECB is that the expansionary fiscal policies (lower taxes, higher public spending, deficit financing) of member states can cause significant inflationary pressures within the EU economy. This will generally depend on the degree of fiscal expansion, the combined weight of those member state economies that have embarked on these policies and their position in the business cycle. Regarding the latter, the attributive inflationary pressure will be attenuated if spare capacity exists in these economies, for example, during a recession. Let us examine why this is so in more detail. If firms are sitting on large amounts of unsold products, as is typical in a recession, then they are unlikely to raise prices to sell them even after a pick-up in consumer demand induced by the government injecting more money into the economy. The lesson here is that inflation is more likely when goods and services are in short supply.

What latitude, then, exists for EU member state governments to pursue independent fiscal policies? They are no longer able to finance budget deficits (public spending over and above tax revenue and other government incomes) by borrowing from their own central banks as in the past: the ESCB statutes do not permit this. However, EU governments are still able to issue and sell their own securities. These are usually short-term bills (for example, 90-day 'treasury' bills) or long-term bonds (such as the UK Government's 'gilts') which essentially are IOUs sold by the government to the private sector, which thereby finances government expenditures. In theory, heavily indebted members are now able to sell public debt under lower interest rate conditions than had previously been the case. Before EMU, such countries were compelled to offer relatively high interest rates on public sector securities to allow for the market's assessment of the foreign exchange risk associated with holding potentially weak currencies. For example, the Portuguese Government would have to offer a relatively high interest rate on its securities sold to its financiers owing to the escudo's susceptibility to depreciate over time.

This new situation, though, creates a so-called 'moral hazard' problem as the overall result of numerous members taking advantage of the weak and 'dispersed' feedback effects of fiscal extravagance under EMU will be cumulative upward pressure on the Euroland interest rate (because potential higher inflation rates require higher interest rates to combat them). To illustrate, a country like Portugal would have a strong incentive to maintain high levels of government spending if the subsequent dispersal of induced inflationary pressure occurred outside its national borders. Others may also take the same view and thus the inflationary pressure would build. Moreover, those members adhering to tight fiscal policies, and who thus carry a disproportionate share of the burdens created by their more freely-spending partners (in terms of higher inflation), will naturally wish to negotiate for fiscal convergence. They will want to develop a common fiscal policy to maintain the credibility of an overall low inflationary monetary policy.

Thus, given this potential for discordance between monetary policy and fiscal policy, some have argued that the ECB should be permitted to set *fiscal constraints* on member state governments so that it can pursue more effective anti-inflationary policies. During the mid-1990s, the German Government championed the 'Stability and Growth Pact' initiative which was designed to compel prospective EMU members into stricter fiscal discipline during the transition from the ERM to the EMU regime and beyond. This was formally accepted by the European Council at Amsterdam in 1997 which subsequently committed member states to 'adhere to the medium-term objective of budgetary positions close to balance or in surplus', and moreover led to the implementation of 'stability programmes' among the Euroland 11 which were commensurate with these fiscal aims. What implications did this carry for EU economic governance? The intention was not to formally extend the ECB's powers directly into the realm of fiscal policy management – the last remaining bastion of macroeconomic policy competence retained by Euroland 11 governments – but rather that a more holistic approach to EU economic policy governance was required with the introduction of the euro. A common monetary policy under the ECB's stewardship necessitated a closer co-ordination of fiscal policies between member states, even for those four initially outside the euro zone. Moreover, this process could be seen as an extension of the EMU convergence criteria arrangements into the euro period.

Yet, to many, this rationalization of EU economic policy governance exacerbated the EU's 'democratic deficit' problem, with particular regard to the political distance between the members of the ECB Governing Council and EU citizens. In their own member states, the latter can directly vote for elected governments that then preside over the nation's management of fiscal policy. Thus while we noted that the ECB currently possesses no *direct control* over national fiscal policy, it nevertheless wields considerable *indirect power*. Its general advocacy of fiscal restraint in the pursuit of price stability, widely supported by the private sector financial lobby, represents a powerful voice within the EU polity. Some of the ECB's monthly bulletins published in 1999 (especially the March and June issues) were severely critical of the decision to allow countries like Italy to overshoot its budget deficit target that year. Although the ECB's position subsequently softened (*European Voice*, 27 July 1999), partly owing to Rome's new commitment to narrow the deficit over the medium term, it demonstrated how seriously the institution took its position to bear down on any signs of fiscal laxity shown by culpable Euroland governments. Furthermore, there is a view that while EU member state governments retain their ability to issue public debt, the ECB's ability to fulfil its objective of price stability is fundamentally compromised. It was perhaps fortuitous that during the transition period the EU entered a low inflationary upswing in the business cycle with most member states in a proximate budget balance position, thus presenting largely non-inflationary fiscal circumstances for the ECB to deal with. These points notwithstanding, the fiscal implications of the euro will continue to be a key issue of EU economic governance well into the twenty-first century.

3.3   EMU, global markets and democracy

In this section we have discussed the euro's impact on the governance of the EU economy, particularly in regard to economic policy making. A number of other points are also worth raising. On the one hand, EMU is a means for consolidating the power of associated states into a bloc against an alignment of global market forces, and as such a reinforcement of EU-level regulatory order. The ECB is the representative agency of this bloc charged with the responsibility of upholding the integrity of the euro in times of both equanimity and volatility in the world's financial markets. As a consequence, the pooling of the Euroland 11's foreign exchange reserves into one central bank depository has strengthened the EU's monetary policy makers' ability to resist the speculative pressures within the global financial markets, although at the time of writing this had yet to be severely tested. On the other hand, the ECB's statutory independence and its acknowledged deference to the power of global finance are indicative of the relative weakening of political influence over the policy-making process, not just in Europe but elsewhere. This would hence indicate the growing relevance of market order governance in this economic domain.

Moreover, the new EU macroeconomic governance structure forged by the creation of the euro has shifted a considerable degree of power to a transnational élite community of central bankers (Germain, 2001). The extent to which this represents politically acceptable redistribution of governing power within Europe is a moot point. Yet EMU's centralization of regulatory order at the EU-level is unpalatable to a broad cross-section within the EU polity. This partly explains why some argue that the EU must eventually move toward economic and political union (EPU) in order to close the democratic deficit. This debate is likely to intensify the longer the ECB, other EU institutions and their associated élite policy networks, or self-organizing networks, are seen to set the parameters of member state's fiscal policies. However, if under the ECB/ESCB's governance the EU's traditionally high rate of unemployment dramatically falls then the pressure for EPU will be considerably mitigated.

Summary

- The key to managing the Euroland 11's monetary policy involves the ECB operating to maintain price stability (i.e. low inflation) as its primary policy objective.

- Problems with managing an EU monetary policy stem from various factors like the differences in the business cycles and financial market structures of member state economies which makes a 'one size fits all' EU interest rate policy difficult to sustain. In addition, there are likely to be problems of adjustment for those countries used to monetary laxity that now find they must comply with the ECB's more disciplined monetary stance.

- The many linkages between monetary and fiscal policy may require EU member states to pool their fiscal policy capacity more at the EU level, thus leading to more co-ordinated and even common EU policies on taxation and public expenditure.

4   Business systems and governance in the EU

Thus far, we have considered economic governance of the EU economy from a mostly public policy and macroeconomic perspective. This has been important given the *de jure* driven processes that have forged the EU into the integrated political and economic entity that it is today. However, we must also examine how the existence of different European business systems affects the governance of the region's economy. In contrast to what has preceded, this relates more to a private sector and microeconomic study of the European economy. We must first establish what the term 'business system' refers to. In many ways, a business system characterizes the very nature of an economy as it relates to the complex of interacting and interlocking factors, including markets, institutions, network relationships and sociocultural determinants, that broadly determine how business activity is organized and conducted. Thus, the application of regulatory order and market order, as well as self-organizing networks, is highly relevant to any analysis of business systems. A closely associated term to 'business system' is that of 'corporate governance', which particularly relates to the way in which companies themselves are governed (see Chapter 3 in particular).

Many of Europe's 'business systems' have evolved in distinct capitalist cultures that are nation specific, although many common factors between different systems can be identified leading some analysts to construct systemic subgroups as a result. In addition to overviewing these systems, this section will focus on the forces working for and against the creation of a more homogenized European business system. This will relate specifically to the various economic, political and sociocultural factors interacting at the local, national, regional and global levels. We shall see how much of this debate is closely related to the new regimes of pan-EU governance introduced with the euro. So although in this section we primarily study more private sector and microeconomic developments in the governance of the European economy, these have an interface with many aspects of EU public policy discussed earlier.

4.1   Subgroups of European business systems: market-oriented and network-oriented

This section uses two basic business system frameworks for its analysis:

- the 'Anglo-American market-based system', and
- the 'regulatory/network-based system', which is divided into two sub-systems – the 'Germanic' (Germany, Switzerland, Austria, Benelux, Scandinavia) and the 'Latin' (France, Italy, Spain, Greece).

Characteristics of these systems are shown in Tables 8.2 and 8.3, and are primarily taken from Rhodes and Apeldoorn's (1998) important work on the transformation of European corporate governance. Indeed, much of this section draws upon their analysis of this subject. Market-oriented business systems are synonymous with the Anglo-American system, where the UK economy and its firms, alongside a powerful set of EU-operating, American-owned but 'European insider' multinationals, are the major players.

Note that 'regulatory order' and 'network order' are combined in this analysis so the *two* basic distinctions used here incorporate the *three* 'governance mechanisms' deployed separately elsewhere in this book. These are then compared to the 'market order' of the Anglo-American business system. This division is a function of the particular way Rhodes and Apeldoorn categorize their systems, which does not coincide exactly with the one used in this book. However, there is a clear affinity between the two approaches which makes the Rhodes and Apeldoorn one used here particularly appropriate for our purposes. The two approaches use the same conceptual terminology, though they categorize things slightly differently. Rhodes and Apeldoorn's argument would presumably be that the regulatory order and self-organizing network order overlap a good deal in the case of these business systems (see also Chapter 10). Note also how the basic division of forms of capitalism used here – between 'Anglo-American' and 'regulatory/network' variants – corresponds closely to a similar division used in Chapter 1, between 'decentralized capitalism' and 'organized capitalism'.

Let us now discuss these tables under the two basic divisional headings they involve, which act as a frameworking device for the following analysis.

Table 8.2 Characteristics of market and regulatory/network-oriented systems: corporate governance

Corporate features	Market-oriented	Regulatory/network-oriented[1]	
	Anglo-American	Germanic	Latin
Employee influence	limited; Japanese FDI promoted shop-floor collaboration, 1980s/1990s	extensive, through works councils on organization of work and training	strong shop-floor influence until early 1980s; now minimal
Role of banks	banks play a minimal role in corporate ownership	universal; banks play an important role in corporate finance and control	bank holdings and participation in France and Spain only
Role of stock exchange	strong role in corporate finance; 70 per cent of top 100 companies in UK listed	publicly listed corporate firms limited; stock exchanges small	stock exchanges relatively underdeveloped; closed ownership
Shareholder sovereignty	widely dispersed share ownership; dividends prioritized	number of freely traded shares limited; dividends less prioritized	shareholder sovereignty recognized but shareholders' rights restricted
Family-controlled firms	general separation of equity ownership and management control	family ownership important in small and medium-sized firms	family ownership and control extensive, exercised through holdings
Market for corporate control	scope for hostile takeovers 'corrects' management failure	takeovers restricted; managers under direct stakeholder influence	takeovers restricted; little external challenge to management
Management boards	one-tier board system: includes executive and non-executive managers	two-tier board system: supervisory and executive responsibilities separate	administrative board combines supervisory and executive duties
Managerial labour market	incentives (for example, stock options) align management with shareholders	performance-linked compensation limited: 'equality' important	incentives more important (for example, stock options in France)

1 Based on Rhodes and van Apeldoorn (1998) with an amendment to their 'network-oriented' designation (changed to 'regulatory/network-oriented' for the purposes of this book).

Table 8.3 Characteristics of market and regulatory network-oriented systems: external environment

Institutional context	Market-oriented	Regulatory/network-oriented[1]	
	Anglo-American	Germanic	Latin
Role of the state	shift toward a minimal state since the 1980s	a regulatory state rather than interventionist state	extensive public ownership (now declining)
Co-operation between social partners	conflictual until the 1980s; now minimal contact (Ireland maintains corporatism)	extensive at the national level until late 1960s; revived in the 1980s/1990s	social pacts in Italy and Portugal in 1980s/1990s; problematic in Spain and Greece
Labour organization	union membership high till 1980s; fragmented organization	union membership density high; strong centralized unions	union membership density generally low; significant decline outside public sector
Education and training	fragmented training system; poor skills provision	high level of participation in vocational and professional training	lower levels of participation in fragmented training systems
Labour market flexibility	poor internal flexibility owing to poor skills; high external flexibility	high skills allow internal flexibility; external flexibility more restricted	lower internal flexibility (lower skills); external flexibility also restricted
National innovation system	low levels of R&D; weak regional innovation support system	higher levels of R&D; regionalized innovation support systems	France excepted, R&D national and regional support weak
Finance for innovative small firms	explosion of venture capital companies, but regionally concentrated	venture capital weak; access to regional banks for small firm finance	venture capital weak; access to regional banks for small firm finance

1 Based on Rhodes and van Apeldoorn (1998) with an amendment to their 'network-oriented' designation (changed to 'regulatory/network-oriented' for the purposes of this book).

The Anglo-American market-based business system

In essence, the Anglo-American model is based on the axioms of individual success, short-term financial results, minimalist government involvement, shareholder sovereignty and 'finance' rather than 'production' being the predominant interest in corporate affairs and structures. More specifically, product and factor markets must be permitted to operate freely with the intention of exerting competitive discipline upon business managers and workers. Thus, Anglo-American values espouse economic deregulation and liberalization, with the market as the organizing (or disorganizing) principle prevailing in economic society. Managerial incentive structures are capital market based, for instance, originating from hostile takeover threats derived from poorly performing share prices, or from performance-related bonuses conferred from appreciating share prices. This systemic feature is buttressed by large institutional shareholders (investment funds, pension funds and insurance companies) and their fund managers who are under an incentive structure compulsion to produce short-term results from stock-exchange transactions, thus quickly discarding stocks and shares that do not 'perform' well. In the UK this is clearly seen in the workings of the City of London, Europe's most prominent financial centre. Labour market flexibility is another key characteristic providing a competitive cost advantage, although this is offset by comparatively low levels of education and training that result from a deregulating state and low social solidarity found in 'individual-based' Anglo-American societies.

Mainland European regulatory and network business systems

As noted above, Europe's regulatory/network-oriented business systems can be broadly divided into their Germanic and Latin subdivisions. The axioms of collective achievement, long-term profit objectives, corporatist state–business relations, 'stakeholder sovereignty' and a more balanced power alignment between finance and production in the corporate boardroom and wider business community are found in both subdivisions, although they are stronger in Germanic business systems. These are also more communitarian in nature in that their organization relies more on 'contractual' governance principles found within their company networks. This can be illustrated by the interlocking patterns of share-ownership within these networks, thus connecting different firms – including associated banks – together into more collaborative, longer-term-relationships (Chapter 3). In Latin business systems, family-run firms and networks providing similar linkages are best exemplified in the industrial districts of 'Third Italy' (Chapter 6). Hence, both regulatory/network-oriented systems lack the decoupling of company management and ownership found in the Anglo-American model where highly developed stock markets have enhanced the powers of shareholder governance. The closer alignment between industry and finance in network-oriented business systems allows the provision of 'patient capital' willing to wait for returns to accrue in the longer-term – especially in the Germanic variant – while regulatory order usually prevails over the market as the organizing principle of economic society. Invariably, then, the state plays a more proactive role in regulatory/network-oriented systems, either by creating a conducive regulatory environment (Germanic) or by more direct state involvement in industry (Latin). While strong stakeholder partnerships between employer and employee found in many European network-oriented systems have generated competitive advantages, their highly regulated labour markets are the cause of critical rigidities and cost uncompetitiveness.

Some comparative issues

There are a number of important points that should be made regarding such categorization of Europe's business systems. From one perspective, the Germanic and Latin sub-divisions may appear to be an exercise in convenient analytical compartmentalization that obscures the important differences in national and even sub-national capitalist cultures across the region covered earlier in this text (for example, in Chapter 5). Nevertheless, it is equally important to highlight their common factors especially in the context of discussions concerning the emergence of more integrated European business systems. From another perspective, the geographical spread of the systemic subgroups analysed would initially suggest a marginalization of the Anglo-American system, being primarily championed by the UK only. However, our next discussion considers how the axioms of this system, allied with the forces of globalization, have laid siege to Europe's continental business systems.

4.2 Toward a more homogenized European business system: forces for convergence

During the 1990s, a predominant thesis arose propounding that European and other models of capitalism were being transformed by the irresistible forces of globalization-driven, neo-liberal convergence in which the market-oriented 'Anglo-American' business system was emerging as the norm. The association between globalization and the Anglo-American model can be broadly explained by the latter's reliance on liberalized, deregulated markets – a requisite for transnational capital operations – and the fact that the most powerful advocates of the former originate from, or are located within, Anglo-American societies (USA, UK and other English-speaking countries). Globalization's nurturing of cross-border economic interdependence and transnational linkages in general has brought greater pressure to bear on national business systems and cultures through the permeable effects that these 'globalizing' (that is, world integrative) processes introduce. Multinational firms lie at the centre of this phenomenon through their international expansions of finance capital, direct investments abroad, share ownership and managerial culture. In order to operate effectively in their global economic space, multinationals seek to remove national barriers to the cross-border flow of trade, investment and finance as these barriers raise costs and impede access to markets and resources. International organizations too, in their advocacy of economic liberalism (such as the WTO in trade, the IMF in finance), have helped underwrite these globalizing processes by providing the multilateral rules by which they are nominally safeguarded, or at least can be legitimized.

Despite being home to diverse business cultures, as we shall examine later, the EU's susceptibility to the homogenizing forces of globalization is relatively high. Regional economic interdependence in Western Europe is more advanced than anywhere else in the world, and hence extensive interpenetrations and linkages exist between its national economies. The EU is the world's largest overseas investor and host to inward foreign investment, with the pan-European strategies of various multinationals forging dense webs of cross-border production, distribution and service linkages across the regional economy (Chapter 2). The transmission mechanisms for the conveyance of corporate practices within the EU are therefore well developed. Furthermore, as key members of international economic organizations the EU and its member states have supported the development of, and subsequently complied with, their agendas for economic liberalization. The SEM programme could even be said to have provided some form of template for the expanding remit of the WTO's trade agenda (see Chapter 9).

It should also be noted that both EU market integration and EU policy integration have had mutually reinforcing effects, creating the firmer basis for a common European corporate space. With EMU, both capital market restructuring in preparation for the euro, and the enhanced capital market integration it brings, work significantly toward this end.

> When Europe's leaders met at Maastricht in 1991, the last thing they intended was that monetary union should be a vehicle for spreading Anglo-[American] capitalism. But that will be the most dramatic effect of a single currency ... There will be more equities and corporate bonds. And as it grows, the capital market will exert its influence on all other sectors of the European economy. It will increase the pressure on companies to perform. Pursuit of shareholder value, hostile take-overs and better corporate governance – all will become increasingly prominent features of the European landscape.
>
> (The Lex Column, *Financial Times*, 30 March 1998)

Leading up to the euro's implementation, the member state's pursuit of the EMU convergence criteria committed Europe's policy élites still further to the neo-liberal economic agenda. Arguably, this will be consolidated by the ECB and its policy networks as we discussed in relation to the more disciplined environment in which EU fiscal policies are now formulated.

In addition to the anticipated impact of EMU argued above, other developments in Europe's financial sector and capital markets may also produce convergence effects. In recent times, regulatory and network-oriented business systems have increasingly accommodated the market-oriented, Anglo-American model's feature of channelling capital flows to corporations through the institutional investors mentioned earlier. This can be mostly attributed to the expansion of funded pensions across continental Europe in response to the region's demographic ageing problem, which in turn has provided institutional investors with deeper inroads into French, German and other network-oriented corporate governance structures (Morin, 2000; Jürgens et al., 2000). What do we mean by this? As the magnitude of pension scheme contributions in the EU increase, so will the consolidated holdings of institutional investors to invest across Europe's stock markets. The higher the number of network-oriented firms in continental Europe that 'list' their shares on these stock-markets (that is, make them available to purchase), the greater the opportunity for pension fund managers to secure degrees of ownership and therefore control over these companies, consequently leading to changes in the ways in which they are run. In addition, the increasing number of continental European companies seeking stock-market 'listing' or 'quotation' will also link managerial incentive-structures more to share-price performance criteria – a feature of the market-oriented system. For example, Deutsche Bank, Daimler Benz and many other German companies had introduced stock option schemes for senior management by the late 1990s (*Financial Times*, 14 January 1998).

Furthermore, various privatization programmes implemented in continental Europe from the late 1980s onwards – which themselves were indicative of the shift from the mixed economy to the regulated market economy paradigm in Europe – allowed bigger injected doses of Anglo-American capitalism into the region's network-oriented business systems. This has occurred through large American and British institutional investors purchasing shares in newly privatized continental European enterprises. The general liberalization of European capital markets during the 1990s had a similar effect with the general penetration of global capital further internationalizing Europe's national capitalist systems. In another development, the regional expansion of foreign financial service companies within the single market has not only underpinned capital market integration in Europe but has also strengthened the position of 'finance' over 'production' in the European political economy, thus leading to a deeper infiltration of Anglo-American business culture. This has particularly related to the growing presence of American institutional investors, consultancy firms and credit agencies in the EU. As a consequence of the above developments, there has been growing support for greater shareholder sovereignty in these systems, thus posing a challenge to the stakeholder sovereignty principle and the interlocking network relationships that are core features of many continental business systems.

Finally, as an addendum to this section, in April 2000 a decision was taken by the London and Frankfurt stock exchanges to merge into one system based on the mutualized competitive advantages it would confer.

This may prove to be an important cornerstone on which a more homogenized European business system may be built in the future.

4.3   Against a homogenized European business system: forces for divergence

While the globalization-related forces of neo-liberal convergence have brought considerable pressure to bear on Europe's regulatory/network-oriented business systems, there nevertheless persists a powerful alignment of counter-pressures at the domestic level. In general terms, this mainly relates to embedded institutional and sociocultural determinants that underpin the various corporate governance structures found across the EU economy. Moreover, there exists a reluctance amongst Europe's national élites to forsake aspects of business systems that have proved successful in the past, and as Rhodes and Apeldoorn (1998) argue: 'the efficiency and competitiveness of economies are linked to the microstructures of industries and firms whose incentives to use different organizational forms are shaped by particular national regulator policies: continued competitiveness will depend on adjustment rather than abandonment of those structures and policies' (p.418). How can we illustrate what they mean by this? It was noted earlier how the state plays a more proactive role in a regulatory/network-oriented system. In both variants, this can take the form of competitiveness-promoting policies where both the state and firms work in partnership with each other to improve the nation's techno-industrial capacities. While the tools of enhancing competitiveness may change, as observed in EU industrial policy, the essential key objectives have not. According to these arguments, the aforementioned pressures may therefore only lead to a partial rather than wholesale accommodation of the market-oriented, Anglo-American model in Europe.

Let us examine the centrifugal forces against homogenization in more specific detail, taking first the governance networks of stakeholder relations found in Germanic and Latin business systems. While the integrity of interlocking share ownership within the company groups (for example, German *konzerns*) has generally weakened, for reasons discussed earlier, they have retained much of their inbuilt resistance to hostile takeovers and the intrusions of institutional investors. Similarly, in Italy the more or less continued balance of interlocking vested interests between large family-run firms, such as Fiat, and their associated financial holding companies is indicative of the prevailing networked relations that still characterize many Latin business systems. In finance, despite the local financial infrastructure of network-oriented systems coming under siege from internationalized finance capital, the importance of retaining this infrastructure is recognized by policy élites, especially owing to their support of small and medium-sized enterprises (SMEs). In industrial relations, centralized bargaining systems persist in most Germanic business systems, with the importance of high-trust relations between employer and employee still valued over the low-trust alternative offered by the Anglo-American model (Chapter 5).

During the implementation period of the SEM programme, there was much discussion regarding the development of a uniform system of corporate governance in the EU. Advocates of harmonization based their arguments on the need for lower transaction costs and the avoidance of damaging competitions between member states over such matters as attracting foreign capital and investment. However, subsequent directives (for example, on company statutes and laws) aimed at regulating the European corporate space have been frequently obstructed or compromised by member state governments and other national-level barriers. As Fligstein and Mara-Drita (1996) contend, the regulation of property rights and competition is more critical to a state's capacity of economic governance than the rules of exchange (for example, trade and investment flows), and it is the liberalization of the latter rather than the former that was far more significantly achieved under the SEM programme.

Consequently, various institutional and political impediments originating at the national level have mitigated against the adoption of a singular European capitalist culture and model. These factors further explain the various regulatory gaps and inconsistencies within the European corporate space, as the responsibility for domestic market regulation remains largely in the hands of member state governments, despite the European Commission largely presiding over the governance of international economic exchange within the EU. To illustrate: while the Second Banking Directive of 1989 permitted banks to offer their services to the customers of other EU locations, the responsibility for regulating financial institutions was retained by home governments. The 1988 Capital Movements Directive also allowed for a national diversity of rules to be maintained, resulting in the continued fragmentation of the EU's insurance and pension services markets. Similar scenarios exist with respect to bankruptcy laws and the governance of equity markets across Europe. However, other directives, such as those on investment services (1996) and capital adequacy (1996) have introduced common European rules and standards of governance into the region's financial practices. The overhaul of Europe's stock exchanges, involving the introduction of greater transparency, openness to foreign investors and wider provision of financial products, has also propagated greater convergence in Europe's business systems.

4.4   Finding the balance

In this section, we have broadly considered the forces working for and against the creation of a more homogenized European business system. In one sense, it is a question of how these different systems can accommodate the forces of global capitalism without compromising the competitive advantages of each business system. In Europe, this is particularly complex given the strongly defined nature of these systems on the one hand and the high degree of regional economic interdependence – itself driven by formidable globalizing forces – on the other. The growing multinationalization of the EU economy has simultaneously brought more pressure for integrated markets and a common regulatory order in the region, and furthermore greater transnational interlinking of different national business systems. Whatever transpires in the future European economic space, the business systems contained within it will continue to shape both its broad environment and its orders of governance.

Summary

- The Anglo-American 'market-oriented' business system has gained increasing salience around the world. To some extent this can be explained by the association between economic globalizing forces and their reliance on liberalized, deregulated markets – virtues championed by the Anglo-American system.

- Extensive inter-penetrations and linkages between different EU national economies which have evolved through deepening European business integration, may lead to a dominant, EU-wide business system emerging in the future.

- The euro could create a more coagulated European economic space, and therefore a stronger possibility of the above trend emerging.

- However, embedded sociocultural, institutional and relational factors may prove impervious to both internal and external pressures to change. National governments still retain important regulatory capacities in key areas that shape corporate governance practices (for example, property rights, competition) and in many 'regulatory/network-oriented' business systems the advantages of maintaining close institutionalized links between firms and state authorities are still deemed important.

5   Conclusion

In this chapter, we have discussed the extent to which the EU or European economy is governed as a whole. This has entailed an analysis of key EU-level common economic policies, deepening EU policy governance under EMU, and Europe's business systems. In addition to exploring the viability of pan-EU economic governance, we have also discussed in some cases whether it is an appropriate pursuit given the varied nature of the European economic space. Yet the deepening regional integration of the EU economy, principally via the SEM and EMU projects, has required EU policy makers to increasingly address the pan-EU economic governance issue. However, this is not simply a technocratic challenge but also a political one as a coagulating European economic space develops at a faster rate than its political counterpart. We saw how this will become increasingly relevant as the EU manages a euro-based economy and economic society. In our study of Europe's business systems, we examined the respective cases for and against a more homogenized European business system emerging in the twenty-first century. It was argued that the integrational processes and developments studied here, as well as other factors, may eventually create a more uniform system by which European business is governed. Yet it was also proposed that a diverse range of nationally-embedded sociocultural, institutional and relational factors evident across the European economic space will continue to hinder the realization of such a system. In sum, we have seen that there exist important choices regarding whether to proceed with a structure of regulatory order, market order or self-organizing networks in the governance of the whole EU economy. This multifaceted conundrum is likely to keep analysts of EU economics busy for some considerable time yet.

Appendix
From Maastricht to the euro

1991 Maastricht Treaty on European Union

Plans for EMU based on the 1989 Delors Plan. Single currency envisaged by as early as 1997 or by 1999 at latest between the majority of EU members.

Convergence criteria targets based on the Delors Plan to be pursued, comprising:

- *Price stability*: An average rate of inflation that does not exceed by more than 1.5 per cent that of the three best performing member states.

- *Interest rates*: An average nominal long-term interest rate that does not exceed by more than 2 per cent that of the three best performing member states in terms of price stability.

- *Exchange rates*: Participation in the ERM's normal bands without devaluations from the beginning of EMU's Stage 3 (that is, at least two years).

- *Budget deficits*: A government budget deficit of less than 3 per cent of GDP under sustainable conditions.

- *National debt*: A government national debt of less than 60 per cent of GDP.

Other economic policy co-ordination measures included.

Both the UK and Denmark negotiate an 'opt out' of the final (single currency) stage of EMU.

1992 Portugal enters the ERM at wide band rate in April. By the end of September, the UK and Italy forced to drop out of the ERM. Other currencies come under severe pressure in the foreign-exchange markets. The Spanish peseta and the Portuguese escudo devalue later on that year.

1993 Devaluation of the Irish punt in February and the peseta and escudo in May. In August, the ERM implodes owing to renewed speculative pressure. The ERM is recast with a 15 per cent band set for participating members as a defensive move to salvage the system. Maastricht Treaty finally ratified in all members states by November.

1994 All remaining members of the ERM manage to stay within the new bands.

1995 On accession, Austria decides to join the ERM but Sweden and Finland do not. Further devaluations of the peseta and the escudo in March. At the Madrid Summit in December, EU leaders decide upon the name 'euro' for the future single currency.

1996 Some EU member states begin to move to narrower ERM bands.

1997 At the European Council meeting in Amsterdam, EU leaders agree to adopt the 'Stability and Growth Pact', and thus commit EMU participants to mutual fiscal discipline. The Asian financial crisis brings disruption to international currency markets, although intra-EU currency movements remain relatively stable.

1998 EU decides on which member states will proceed from the ERM to the euro. The UK and Denmark decide to remain outside Euroland for the meantime in accordance with their Maastricht Treaty 'opt out' protocols. Greece and Sweden fail to meet EMU 'convergence criteria', leaving eleven members to adopt the single currency. The European Central Bank (ECB) is established in May.

1999 **Introduction of the euro**

The euro is introduced on 1 January 1999 but it will take until July 2002 before the full adoption is completed. Exchange rates between the eleven Euroland member states become essentially fixed. Prices in Euroland are shown in both euros and 'euro expressions' (that is, national currencies that remain in circulation until 2002). ERM 2 established between Euroland and non-euro member states but the UK and Sweden remain outside this arrangement.

2000 The euro experiences a 20 per cent devaluation in its first year of trading on the currency markets.

2001 Target date by which Greece hopes to join Euroland.

2002 Euro notes and coins become the legal tender in Euroland.

References

Alesina, A. and Summers, L. (1993) 'Central bank independence and macroeconomic performance: some comparative evidence', *Journal of Money, Credit and Banking*, vol.25, pp.151–62.

Anderson, J. (2001) 'The rise of regions and regionalization in western Europe' in Guibernau, M. (ed.) *Governing European Diversity*, London, Sage/The Open University.

Berman, S. and McNamara, K.R. (1999) 'Bank on democracy: why central banks need public oversight', *Foreign Affairs*, vol.78, no.2, pp.2–8.

Bromley, S.J. (2001a) 'The nation state in the European Union' in Bromley, S.J. (ed.) *Governing the European Union*, London, Sage/ The Open University.

Bromley, S.J. (ed.) (2001b) *Governing the European Union*, London, Sage/The Open University.

Brown, W. (2001) 'Food Fights: Europe and Agriculture', DD200 *Governing Europe, Module 1: Introduction*, Milton Keynes, The Open University.

Dornbusch, R., Favero, C. and Giavazzi, F. (1998) *EMU: Prospects and Challenges for the Euro*, Oxford, Blackwell.

EC (1994) *Growth, Competitiveness, Employment: The Challenges and Ways Forward into the 21st Century*, Luxembourg, Office for Official Publications of the European Communities.

Fligstein, N. and Mara-Drita, I. (1996) 'How to make a market: reflections on the attempt to create a single market in the European Community', *American Journal of Sociology*, vol.102, no.1, pp.1–33.

Germain, R.D. (2001) 'The European Central Bank and the problem of authority', *Journal of European Public Policy*, forthcoming.

Healey, N. (1996) 'What price central bank independence?', *The Review of Policy Issues*, vol.2, pp.3–14.

Jovanovic, M.N. (1997) *European Economic Integration: Limits and Prospects*, London, Routledge.

Jürgens, V., Maumann, K. and Rupp. J. (2000) 'Shareholder value in an adverse environment: the German case', *Economy and Society*, vol.29, no.1, pp.54–79.

Lewis, P. (2001) 'The enlargement of the European Union' in Bromley, S.J. (ed.) *Governing the European Union*, London, Sage/ The Open University.

Morin, F. (2000) 'A transformation in the French model of shareholding and management', *Economy and Society*, vol.29, no.1, pp.36–53.

Pennant-Rea, R. (ed.) (1997) *The Ostrich and the EMU*, London, Centre for Economic Policy Research.

Rhodes, M. and van Apeldoorn, B. (1998) 'Capital unbound? The transformation of European corporate governance', *Journal of European Public Policy*, vol.5, no.3, pp.406–27.

Further reading

Berman, S. and McNamara, K.R. (1999) 'Bank on democracy: why central banks need public oversight', *Foreign Affairs*, vol.78, no.2, pp.2–8.

Jovanovic, M.N. (1997) *European Economic Integration: Limits and Prospects*, London, Routledge.

Pennant-Rea, R. (ed.) (1997) *The Ostrich and the EMU*, London, Centre for Economic Policy Research.

Rhodes, M. and van Apeldoorn, B. (1998) 'Capital unbound? The transformation of European corporate governance', *Journal of European Public Policy*, vol.5, no.3, pp.406–27.

Scharpf. F. (1999) *Governing in Europe: Effective and Democratic?*, Oxford, OUP.

Chapter 9
The EU and international economic governance

Simon Bromley

1   Introduction

Since the end of the Second World War, and in particular since the Bretton Woods Conference of 1944, there has been a remarkable explosion of international economic governance. Moreover, despite the passing of those political and international conditions which originally made the Bretton Woods arrangements possible, the governance of the international economy has become ever more extensive in its coverage, both geographically and functionally, and reaches ever more deeply into national economies and national policy making. Within the overall architecture of contemporary international economic governance the European Union (EU) plays a very particular role. On the one hand, the EU represents the most far-reaching and radical attempt to reconfigure economic governance above the level of the nation state yet seen. On the other hand, the EU and its member states are contributing components of the wider framework of international economic governance provided by the major states in the Organization for Economic Co-operation and Development (OECD) and by the main multilateral institutions, such as the International Monetary Fund (IMF) and the General Agreement on Tariffs and Trade (GATT) and its successor the World Trade Organization (WTO). What are the distinctive features of the EU's model of international economic governance within the Union? How does the EU seek to govern the external economic relations among its member states? And how does this model of economic governance relate to the wider frameworks governing the world economy? What impact does it have outside the Union, and how do wider forces impact on governance within the EU? These are the questions addressed in this chapter.

2   Size and importance of the EU

These questions are important not only for an understanding of the EU itself, but also for the wider international framework of economic governance. One reason for this is simply the quantitative importance of the EU economic space within the world economy as a whole. As we saw in Chapter 2, the EU represents a major force in the world economy. Taken together, the member states of the EU account for more than one-fifth of world GDP and one-sixth of world trade (excluding intra-European trade). This makes the EU economy roughly the same size as that of the USA and more than twice as large as the Japanese economy (IMF, 1997). Just under one-third of world trade is denominated in EU currencies (compared with nearly one-half in US dollars), and EU currencies account for one-quarter of global foreign exchange reserves (compared with over one-half by the US dollar). Considered as single units, then, the USA and the EU are roughly equivalent powers in the world economy, even if the dollar has a bigger international role than European currencies (including now the euro). Another reason why the EU model of international economic governance matters is that it represents a *qualitatively* distinct pattern which, some analysts have suggested, might provide a model for other regions of the world (see Box 9.1). Among and between its member states the EU's contribution to international economic governance is highly distinctive compared with, say, the relations of governance found in North America or the Asia-Pacific region. Uniquely, EU states have agreed to pool or share elements of their economic sovereignty and to be bound by a common legal order in important areas of international economic governance.

Box 9.1   Challenges to and from the EU

The EU is the crucible of reform in the world today. Over the next decade and beyond, Europe will be the first among the major industrial powers to grapple with the challenges of the twenty first century:

- how to redefine national sovereignty as individual nations surrender economic autonomy;

- how to mesh different cultures with different priorities and different decision-making processes;

- how to deregulate separate national economic regimes and to induce competition among national monopolies;

- how to establish transnational incentives to promote innovation and technological advance without sacrificing the benefits from, or being captive to, laissez-faire economics.

Europe is poised to be the global economy's next great growth engine, pulling along the collapsing economies of Eastern Europe and the moribund economies of Africa, South Asia and parts of Latin America. But a united Europe will also reorder the globe's economic priorities. Europe has suddenly become a focal point for investment and trade. And it poses a threat to US pre-eminence in the global economy – a challenge that surpasses even that of Japan.

(C. Michael Aho (Senior International Economist at Prudential Securities Inc.) *Columbia Journal of World Business*, fall 1994, quoted in Meier, 1998, p.239)

The subject of international economic governance is huge, ranging from the regulation of trade, investment and finance, through to questions of development and the environment, to issues relating to the regulation of things like international migration. As well as operating in the GATT/WTO and the IMF, the EU has:

- *Association agreements* with: the European Economic Area (Iceland, Liechtenstein and Norway) and Central and Eastern Europe (Bulgaria, the Czech Republic, Estonia, Hungary, Latvia, Lithuania, Poland, Romania, Slovakia, Slovenia); the Mediterranean – Turkey (customs union), and Cyprus and Malta (association agreements); Israel (free trade agreement); Egypt, Jordan, Morocco, Tunisia (Euro-Mediterranean accords); and Algeria, Lebanon and Syria.

- *Partnership and co-operation agreements* with: Armenia, Azerbaijan, Belarus, Georgia, Kazakhstan, Kyrghyzstan, Moldova, Russia, Ukraine, Uzbekistan.

- *Trade, co-operation, framework agreements* with: Europe – Albania, Switzerland (free trade agreement); North and South America: Canada, Argentina, Brazil, Chile, Mexico, Paraguay, Uruguay; Andean Pact, Central America, Mercosur (interregional agreements); Middle East and Asia – Gulf Co-operation Council (interregional agreement); ASEAN (interregional agreement); China; Bangladesh, India, Nepal, Pakistan, Sri Lanka; Republic of Korea; Vietnam; Cambodia, Laos; Australia, New Zealand; and South Africa.

- *Lomé Convention* (involving seventy African, Caribbean and Pacific states).

We cannot hope to cover everything here. Instead, we focus on the international governance of trade and money, and in particular on the patterns of international economic governance established between the developed capitalist economies of the North. There are two reasons for this choice of focus:

- first, trade, money and trade-related investment policies are the areas of international economic governance in which the EU has the greatest degree of competence in relation to the member states;

- second, the vast bulk of the EU's economic relations with the rest of the world is accounted for by its relations with North America and Japan, and collectively these three groups of economies dominate the rest of the world economy.

We start by situating the EU in relation to the wider framework of international economic governance. This involves asking why there is a need for economic governance at the international level, looking at the role of the Bretton Woods Institutions (BWIs) and the relation of the EU to these. In doing so, we consider the changing trade relations between the EU and the other members of the international trading order as well as some of the reasons for trade conflicts; and we shall examine some of the implications of Economic and Monetary Union (EMU) and the arrival of common currency in Euroland for the wider international monetary system. Once we have sketched some of the architecture of international economic governance and the place of the EU within this (Sections 4 and 5), we turn to consider the impact of international economic governance on international economic integration and ask what kinds of institutions and principles make up international governance, both within the EU and between the EU and the rest of the world (Section 5). We conclude with some reflections on the implications of the EU's distinctive model of international economic governance for the wider international system beyond Europe.

Summary

- The EU is a large 'continental economy' on a par with the USA.

- It represents a unique experiment in economic governance which will have a major impact on international relations.

3   International economic governance and the BWIs

Perhaps the most important reason why international economic governance matters is that it helps to shape the pattern of economic activity within and between national economies. Different forms of international economic governance give rise to different patterns of economic activity within the world economy. We shall define international economic governance as the attempt to regulate or shape the processes and structures of economic interaction among national economies in the wider international system. In this respect, it is worth noting that contemporary international economic governance takes place in an international system characterized by a highly interdependent international economy and a formally ungoverned state system: it is 'a decentralized system that involves decisions by households and firms within each nation, national governments, regional organizations [such as the EU], multinational corporations and international agencies [such as the International Monetary Fund or the World Trade Organization]. There is no central decision mechanism' (Meier, 1998, p.418).

3.1   Domestic governance

Notwithstanding the fact that there is no central decision-making mechanism for international governance, there is still a high level of governance in the international economy. At the national level, the efficient working of a market economy presupposes certain political conditions. At a minimum these include: the definition and enforcement of property rights; the correction of important market failures; a stable monetary order; and a taxation system that enables the state to extract sufficient resources to cover its own activities. More generally, states not only help to constitute markets by providing these political preconditions, but they also intervene at a microeconomic level to regulate the conditions under which market agents are able to trade, invest and raise finance within the national economy. And finally, states seek to manage their national economies at the macroeconomic level, especially through monetary and fiscal policies, in order to achieve overall economic objectives relating to: the growth of output and employment; inflation; the internal and external balances of savings and investment; and social objectives relating to the distribution of income, wealth and welfare. In short, nation states play an important role in *constituting, regulating, managing* and *supplementing* the workings of markets within national economies.

3.2   International co-operation and governance

National economies, and the nation states which help to constitute, regulate, manage and supplement them, do not live in isolation from one another. On the contrary, national economies interact with one another through, at a microeconomic level, flows of trade, investment and finance, and through international markets for goods and services, factors of production and finance. Economic actors and processes cross national borders on an increasingly large scale, tying national economies together in dense and complex networks of interdependence and transnational linkages. And because of these linkages macroeconomic policy in one country can have important consequences in another. To what extent, then, does this international economic interaction require political regulation and management at either the microeconomic or the macroeconomic level? Do the workings of international markets need to be supplemented by other social objectives? And to the extent that economic activity between and across national economies does presuppose any such measures, how can they be provided in a decentralized, sometimes competitive and sometimes co-operative, system of sovereign nation states? Economic theory suggests that there are considerable gains to be had from co-operation that facilitates international economic integration (see Box 9.2 overleaf), but how is this organized?

Many analysts argue that the major institutions of international economic governance, the Bretton Woods Institutions (BWIs), are important because they allow states to co-operate with one another and to realize the gains of an increasingly open and integrated international economy. The BWIs enable states to provide public goods for the international economy in the form of an open, rule-based trading system, a stable system of international money and payments, and a framework for the management of international investment and finance (see Box 9.3 on

> # Box 9.2   The economics of co-operation
>
> The theory of comparative advantage says that the economic welfare of all countries improves if they make trade among themselves easier. Different patterns of absolute and comparative advantage in the production of goods and services among countries provide the basis for mutually beneficial trade.
>
> In general, economic theory suggests that the freer the trade among countries the more their joint welfare will be enhanced. International flows of factors of production and finance can also be thought of as a form of trade, since flows of labour (international migration) represent a trade of labour for goods and services, capital flows (international borrowing and lending) are a trade of current for future consumption, and financial flows (stocks and bonds, etc.) are trades in assets to diversify risk and smooth income. Again, general economic theory says that trade in the factors of production between national economies increases welfare. Finally, consider the case of national macroeconomic policies. In an interdependent international economy the effects of national macroeconomic decisions are transmitted through international markets to other countries. The effects of one country's policies spill over into the economies of others. Government policies toward interest rates, the exchange rate and fiscal policy have consequences beyond their national borders. Just as in the case of interaction between the goods and factor markets of different countries, in theory there are considerable efficiency gains for states if they can co-operate to co-ordinate their respective macroeconomic policies.
>
> In sum, economic theory teaches us that there are potential gains from co-operation in the field of trade and investment as well as in the co-ordination of macroeconomic policy.

page 276). Indeed, some analysts maintain that: the charters of the BWIs amount to an increasingly comprehensive framework for the core of international monetary, trade and investment issues; the BWIs provide international forums within which policy is made; the BWIs have responsibilities for the governance of money, trade and investment on an international basis; and the BWIs have regulatory powers over increasing areas of national policy on these matters.

As a broad generalization, it is true to say that since the end of the Second World War and the formation of the BWIs, inter-state policy and rule making has increasingly taken an institutionalized and legal form. Compared to the imperial economic rivalries of the late nineteenth and early twentieth centuries and the competitive and eventually violent conduct of foreign economic policy in the inter-war years, the post-war world witnessed a remarkable growth of law-based, highly institutionalized regulation and management of the international economy. At first this was confined to the Northern states of Western Europe, North America and Japan, but it has gradually come to include more and more states from the South as well as the states in transition of the former Eastern bloc. Most states in the system are now members of the BWIs and these institutions are increasingly recognized as providing the framework for the development of international economic law. (This is perhaps surprising in so far as the BWIs were initially set up under US leadership – not to say dominance – and they were very much a set of rich country clubs.) To be sure, states retain their economic sovereignty under international economic law to determine the form of their national engagement with the international economy, including how they respond to the policies of other states, but their rights and duties have been redefined such that while a state may still legislate nationally as it sees fit, it will be held to account by other states for its obligations under international law.

Under strong leadership from the USA, the leading capitalist countries (together with some developing states) established the BWIs as the main framework of international economic governance. It is difficult to overstate the economic dominance of the USA immediately after the Second World War. In 1948 the US economy accounted for about 45 per cent of total global industrial production, and its real GDP was nearly twice that of the UK, Germany, France and Japan combined. The US share of world gold reserves is variously estimated to have stood at between 60 per cent and 75 per cent of the world total. Combined with its political and military power and its containment of Soviet influence, these resources gave the USA enormous leverage in shaping the post-war international order in the capitalist world. This leverage enabled the USA to push for the creation of a series of international 'public goods' and to enlist the support of others in this endeavour.

The basic idea was to establish a set of arrangements for governing the international economy that would steer a middle course between surrendering national policy choices to the dictates of the international economy, on the one side, and pursuing national autonomy without regard to its international consequences, on the other. The experiences of the late nineteenth century and the first half of the twentieth century (worldwide economic crises, highly politicized economic rivalries and warfare) indicated that a balance between national autonomy and international responsibility had to be struck.

More specifically, the thinking behind the BWIs was that national autonomy was to be exercised collectively and on a reciprocal basis. National autonomy was desirable so that countries could pursue policies that satisfied their domestic political constituents, particularly policies of full employment and increased welfare protection. But international responsibility was equally important, since the inter-war years had demonstrated that an uncontrolled pursuit of national autonomy was self-defeating.

Box 9.3   The Bretton Woods Institutions

The International Monetary Fund (*IMF*) was established to achieve exchange rate stability in a multilateral payments system in which all the major currencies would be convertible against one another for trade, to provide short-term financial assistance for countries experiencing balance of payments problems, and to act as a consultative organization on matters of international monetary and financial policy. It represented an attempt to combine a binding international framework with a significant degree of national independence in matters of monetary and fiscal policy. The *International Bank for Reconstruction and Development (IBRD)*, popularly known as the *World Bank*, was set up to support investment in countries recovering from war and in need of development. (After 1949 most of its activities were directed to what was then called the 'developing' world in the South.) And finally, it was intended that there would be an International Trade Organization (ITO) to oversee not only the reduction of trade barriers 'but also private foreign investment, intergovernmental commodity agreements, and restrictive international business practices' (Meier, 1998, p.421). This proposal never passed the US Senate and the more limited *General Agreement on Tariffs and Trade (GATT)* was established in its place to serve as a forum for a rules-based, multilateral reduction in trade barriers and to oversee the settlement of trade disputes. The *World Trade Organization (WTO)* created by the Uruguay Round of the GATT now has a remit similar to that of the ITO at its conception.

Both the IMF and the GATT were conceived as multilateral institutions. That is, they were to be open to all states willing to sign up to their purposes, while their rules and procedures were to apply equally to all member states.

The IMF's basic procedures were:

- members linked their currencies to gold at fixed exchange rates;
- these rates could only be changed to correct a 'fundamental disequilibrium';
- reserves for the defence of a member's exchange rate could be supplemented by the IMF's resources, resources which were obtained from the quotas of the member states;
- the size of a member's quota was determined by the size of its economy; voting rights in decision making roughly reflected quotas; important decisions require 85 per cent of the votes; and
- members' drawing rights are subject to conditionality after an initial automatic entitlement.

The main principles of the GATT were:

- the most favoured nation (MFN) clause which says that a right to trade granted to any one member has to be granted unconditionally to all;

- reciprocity, namely the idea that states should engage in mutual reduction of trade barriers; and

- a prohibition on non-tariff barriers to trade, with a preference for the transparency of tariffs if trade is to be restricted.

Apart from the USA, few of the major trading countries were ready to move toward the full convertibility of their currencies for trade until after a long phase of post-war reconstruction. In fact, the IMF only ever functioned in something like the manner originally intended between 1958 and 1971. The GATT was more successful, beginning with a series of tariff-reducing agreements as early as 1947 and an expanding membership that accounted for more than 80 per cent of world trade as early as 1960.

Summary

- Economic relations between the advanced capitalist countries since the Second World War have been characterized by a form of governance in which there is no single, centralized decision-making mechanism, but in which the BWIs play a major role in setting the basic framework for international trade and monetary relations.

- This framework was an attempt to balance the need to allow scope for national autonomy in the choice of economic policies against the need for international responsibility in order to avoid damaging conflicts and rivalries.

4   The EU and the architecture of international economic governance

Against this background, where and how does the EU fit into the pattern of international economic governance provided by the BWIs?

4.1   The EU and the BWIs

Prior to the establishment of the EEC in 1958, the member states were all individual members of the IMF and the GATT. Legally and formally, this position has been maintained as the EEC has expanded and evolved into the EU and as the GATT has become the WTO: the EU itself is not a member, a 'contracting party', of either the IMF or the WTO – formal membership of these multilateral organizations is confined to states. The formation of the EEC coincided more or less with the final moves toward currency convertibility among the major trading economies, at a time when conditions were ripe for a significant liberalization of world trade. Post-war reconstruction and stable, non-inflationary growth seemed to have been established. The major economies of Western Europe (and Japan) now had the capacity to earn sufficient US dollars on export markets to feel confident that currency and trade liberalization would advance their interests. The USA had encouraged European integration from the outset of post-war reconstruction, making Marshall Plan aid conditional on (West) European co-operation, and it looked favourably upon the creation of the EEC (Chapter 1).

The Treaty of Rome (1957) aimed to create a customs union (a combination of internal free trade based on the four freedoms – discussed in Chapter 2 – and a common external tariff) as well as a range of common policies on agriculture, energy, transport and competition, together with limited fiscal transfers for regional development. Moreover, the Treaties of Paris and Rome set down the pattern of governance for the EU, a combination of intergovernmental and supra-national decision making under a common legal framework. With the formation of the customs union in the EEC (substantially completed by 1968), the member states no longer had national trade policies. In their place, the Community developed a Common Commercial Policy (CCP), such that the member states acted as one in concluding trade agreements with others, whether bilateral agreements with specific countries or multilateral deals under the auspices of the GATT/WTO. Thus, although the EU is not a contracting party to the WTO, 'by virtue of its member states' treaty obligations to act as one in the international trade arena (an obligation that yields solid political and economic advantages), it is in effect "a *de facto* WTO member"' (Dinan, 1999, p.489). (Since the EU had no competence in the sphere of monetary and exchange rate policy until the development of EMU at the end of the 1990s, the formation of the EEC did not have significant implications for its member states' relations with the IMF.)

The CCP is part of the Community pillar of the EU and, as such, responsibility for the conduct of the CCP is shared among the Commission, the Council of Ministers and the European Parliament. Piening (1997) describes the general balance of power as follows:

> [The Commission has] the independent right to make recommendations to the Council on the agreements it believes to be necessary, but before it can act it needs the Council's go-ahead in the form of a negotiating directive ... When negotiations are complete, the Commission can initial the agreement, but the Council concludes it on the basis of a majority vote ... Even during the negotiations themselves, the Commission is overseen by a [Committee] of top trade officials from the member states.

> (Piening, 1997, p.26)

The EU is also able to enter into 'trade and co-operation' agreements. Often having free trade as a long-term objective, trade and co-operation agreements generally involve trade preferences as well as assistance from the EU and, since the 1980s, they may also have attached to them political conditions relating to human rights and democracy. For these kinds of agreements (for example the 'partnership' agreements signed with countries of the former Soviet Union), the European Parliament is involved under the consent procedure and the Council operates according to unanimity if the agreement covers a field for which unanimity is required within the EU. Finally, the EU is empowered to conclude 'association' agreements, based on Article 310 (Ex. 238), which states that: 'The Community may conclude with one or more states or international organizations agreements establishing an association involving reciprocal rights and obligations, common action and reciprocal procedure'. The conclusion of association agreements requires both the involvement of the European Parliament under the assent procedure (giving it the right of veto) and unanimity in the Council of Ministers.

This partial transfer of competence over commercial policy from the member states to the Community pillar has not been unproblematic, however. There is an obvious tension between the EU's right of initiative and its role in negotiating on the Community's behalf, on the one side, and the authorization, oversight and sanctioning of this role by the Council of Ministers, on the other. Most obviously, overall competence in the field of trade has shifted dramatically from member states to EU institutions: as a consequence of the development of the CCP, the EU presents a Common External Tariff to the rest of the world; quantitative restrictions on imports, import quotas, passed from member states to the EU with the completion of the single market programme following the SEA (1986); anti-dumping measures are administered by the Commission, in accordance with the GATT/WTO rules; and the Commission has attempted to acquire competence for negotiating voluntary export restraints (VERs) from the member states. And as we have seen, the Commission and the European Parliament have a significant role in the conclusion of trade and co-operation agreements and association agreements.

Less obviously, the extent of the EU's competence has proved controversial as the international trade agenda itself has changed. When the CCP was originally formulated: trade policy was essentially about 'at-the-border' tariffs and national quota restrictions on imports; trade in agriculture was largely excluded from the framework and disciplines of the GATT; trade and investment issues were not closely linked; there was little trade in services; and trade was not generally seen as related to such issues as the protection of the environment or to labour standards and human rights. In short, trade policy was not high on the political agenda and the further liberalization of trade in manufactured goods seemed to be a fairly straightforward affair, something that member states could safely delegate to the Commission. We will see below (Section 4.2) that all of this has now changed in ways that were not foreseen.

Many of the most significant changes to the agenda of international trade negotiations and to the political significance of trade were highlighted by the negotiations of the Uruguay Round of the GATT (1986/94) and the establishment of the WTO. In fact, during the Uruguay Round member states questioned the Commission's competence to negotiate on their behalf in relation to the new trade issues of services and trade-related intellectual property matters (TRIPs). (Since responsibility for competition and investment policy was already within the Community pillar, trade-related investment matters, TRIMs, were less sensitive.) In response to this challenge to its competence the Commission sought a ruling from the European Court of Justice (ECJ), and the Court ruled (in Opinion 1/94) that responsibility for negotiating services and intellectual property agreements is shared between the EU and its member states. Subsequently, during the Intergovernmental Conference (IGC) leading up to the Treaty of Amsterdam (1997), the Commission argued for services and TRIPs to come under the remit of Article 133 (Ex. 113), the basis of the CCP, but the member states refused – though the Treaty did make provision for such a change in the future if the member states are unanimous. Similarly, the member states turned down a request from the European Parliament for a greater role in the negotiation of the CCP. In other words, as the political salience of trade policy increased, the member states were careful to keep control of the new trade issues at an intergovernmental level, rather than ceding control to the more supra-national elements of the EU.

4.2   The EU and the governance of trade

Almost as soon as the EEC was established, there were concerns that the formation of a customs union might be more trade diverting than trade creating and that the EEC might abuse its strong position in world markets to rig trade in its favour (Chapter 2). In theory, a large trading bloc can use a tariff to limit both its imports and exports, lowering the price of the former and raising the price of the latter, thereby improving its terms of trade. If this terms-of-trade effect is larger than the losses that arise from the distortions to production and consumption, an 'optimal tariff' can increase overall welfare inside the bloc at the expense of outsiders. This assumes that trading partners do not retaliate with tariffs of their own. Thus an optimal tariff is a potential weapon against small trading partners but not against other large trading blocs. In any case, to forestall such an eventuality the USA took the lead in pushing for two multilateral rounds of trade negotiations in the GATT, the Dillon Round (1961/2) and the Kennedy Round (1964/7). Thereafter, tariffs served less and less as barriers to trade in manufactures, and the focus of attention shifted to non-tariff barriers created by 'behind-the-border' measures. These were first addressed on a serious basis in the Tokyo Round of the GATT (1973/9).

The new trade agenda has raised the temperature of trade negotiations between the EU and its outside trading partners. Although the USA was concerned about the possibilities of trade protectionism with the formation of the EEC, on balance European integration has represented an economic opportunity for the US economy rather than a threat. We noted above that the formation of the EEC coincided with the final moves toward the convertibility of European currencies against the dollar. One important result of this was that US multinational corporations (MNCs) increased their investment in Europe. For the US economy, overseas production by MNCs – not exports – became a much more important means of penetrating overseas markets. By the early 1970s, when the stock of US foreign investment still accounted for just over one-half of all foreign investment, the value of production by US affiliates abroad was some four times that of US total exports. Where the US led, Western Europe and Japan followed, as real wages in these areas began to catch up with those in the USA, undermining their export competitiveness, and as European and Japanese firms achieved the necessary scale to contemplate an international presence.

We can say, then, that the integration of the world economy has been driven as much by foreign investment as it has by trade (see Box 9.4). Indeed, in the mid-1980s, the value produced by MNCs outside their domestic markets was greater than the value of world trade, and a significant proportion of world trade (estimates vary from about one-quarter to two-fifths) is closely linked to foreign direct investment (FDI). The growth of regional integration in the world economy, not only in the EU but also in the North American Free Trade Area (NAFTA), encompassing the USA, Canada and Mexico, as well as various schemes for integration in the Asia-Pacific region (most notably, Asia-Pacific Economic Co-operation, APEC), is 'motivated by the desire to facilitate international investment and the operations of multinational firms as much as the desire to promote trade' (Lawrence, 1996, p.17).

Box 9.4 Giovanni Agnelli, former chairman of Fiat, on European integration

The current unity of Western Europe is not so much the result of a Utopian dream as it is the political recognition of economic reality: the reality of global markets, the reality of economic interdependence and the reality of competitive pressures – all of which make co-operation essential.

The reason that the project has continued to progress and defy the odds against it is that it does not depend entirely on political goodwill; [it] was born for sound economic reasons and those forces continue to be its engine ... Entrepreneurs and corporations are keeping the pressure on politicians to transcend considerations of local and national interest. We believe that European unity is our best hope for stimulating growth and technological innovation, and for remaining an influential presence in the world.

(quoted in Meier, 1998, p.236)

For the USA in particular, integration in Europe has given rise to what the US economist Hufbauer has called 'Opportunity Europe'. Writing in the late 1990s, Meier noted that: 'The stock of US direct investment in the EU has risen much more than the value of American exports to the EU. Sales of US-owned affiliates within the EU have in recent years amounted to eight to ten times the value of exports from the USA to the EU. Moreover, a third of American exports to Europe already go to US-owned affiliates' (1998, p.252). These FDI linkages serve as a counterbalance to any tendencies toward trade rivalry between the major regions of the world economy.

Nevertheless, there are various unresolved issues in transatlantic economic integration which relate both to trade and investment. (See Box 9.5 for background and definitions of the features of economic governance discussed below.) To begin with, the EU and its trading partners sometimes have a different understanding of 'reciprocity' in trade negotiations. The EU interprets reciprocity to mean *national treatment* plus effective access to foreign markets. But how is 'effective access' to be defined once the principal barriers to trade and investment are no longer at-the-border tariffs but behind-the-border measures? Next, the EU and its major trading partners do not have *common standards* on issues relating to health, safety and the environment, nor do they as yet operate on the basis of mutual recognition of each other's standards. That is to say, market integration between the member states of the EU has gone much further than between the EU and the USA and Japan. A related question concerns rules of origin and local content. For the purposes of the single market the EU has defined what is to count as an EU product or service if it is produced by, say, a Japanese MNC operating in Europe. These rules can serve to restrict trade and discriminate between EU and foreign goods and services. And finally, there is considerable debate on how far public procurement, government spending on goods and services, should be opened to foreign competition, especially given that this activity often has a public service component related to issues of national culture and welfare objectives.

Box 9.5   Types of international economic governance

At-the-border measures include tariffs and quotas for trade, capital controls for flows of investment and finance and immigration policies to regulate flows of labour. *Behind-the-border* measures include any law or policy, whether microeconomic, macroeconomic or welfare-oriented, which seeks to constitute, regulate, manage or supplement the workings of the domestic economy of a nation state. Complete national autonomy involves states having the unilateral right to decide their own at-the-border and behind-the-border measures. And under international economic law, 'economic sovereignty' means that states have the right to determine the use of their permanent resources, to choose their own economic system, and to decide how to engage with the international economy. At the same time, however, states have

certain duties under international economic law to the wider international community. In practice, national autonomy is exercised
collectively and *reciprocally*. States retain the right to determine their
own rules and policies at the national level but exercise this right in
free negotiation with other states, seeking reciprocal forms of co-
ordination and co-operation when they can. Broadly speaking, it is
possible to identify six main types of international economic governance arrived at on this basis. These are:

- *National treatment,* where states reciprocally open their economies to
  trade and investment with foreigners but once foreign goods and
  services have crossed the border they are treated no less favourably
  than goods and services originating in the 'host' country. Rules and
  policies in different 'host' countries may differ and therefore there
  will be market competition among different national economies.

- *Mutual recognition*, involving agreement between two or more states
  on a bilateral, regional or multilateral basis, where foreign standards
  are recognized alongside national standards and where market
  competition is allowed to guide the economic process.

- *Common standards*, adopted on a bilateral, regional or multilateral
  basis, where states mutually agree to adopt the same set of rules and
  policies as each other and to implement and enforce these in their
  respective national jurisdictions.

- *Monitored decentralization,* where states enter into macroeconomic
  policy undertakings with one another but are nationally responsible
  for the implementation of policy, subject to joint surveillance by a
  collective body.

- *Intergovernmental co-ordination*, involving jointly designed mutual
  adjustments of national macroeconomic policies but still with
  national implementation, subject to joint surveillance by a collective body.

- *Quasi-federal shared, or pooled, sovereignty,* which involves continuous, regular bargaining and joint, centralized decision making
  within a common legal order.

The *most favoured nation (MFN)* principle states that, at the border, a
good or service coming from a given economic partner is treated no
less favourably than the same good or service coming from any other
country. Within the GATT/WTO, unconditional MFN is the norm.

Taken together, the MFN principle and national treatment are called
'non-discrimination'. As they were originally conceived, the BWIs
allowed for a significant degree of national autonomy in behind-the-
border measures as long as at-the-border measures were non-discriminatory. Further integration requires a move beyond national treatment
and MFN principles. Among relations between the member states of
the EU there are significant elements of mutual recognition, common
standards, monitored decentralization and intergovernmental co-ordination. Uniquely, the EU has also developed elements of quasi-
federalist governance in relation to trade, common policies and money.

If national and international markets function efficiently, then national treatment combined with free trade maximizes efficiency and accountability, assuming that national policies accurately reflect citizens' preferences. This combination has been called 'shallow integration' and, together with the MFN principle, it has been an important part of the framework of international governance developed since the end of the Second World War. In particular, it has provided the basis for much of the expansion of trade between different national economies. However, national treatment still erects barriers to international trade (and investment), since it fragments the international economy into distinct national economic spaces defined by a particular framework of rules and policies. Thus, even if states agree to remove all their at-the-border restrictions, to adopt completely free trade on an MFN basis, foreign firms still have to adapt to different national rules and policies behind the border in order to do business in another state. This fact alone may give domestic firms a considerable advantage in their 'home' market and thereby limit the potential gains from trade.

For this reason closer market integration for the exchange of goods and services often requires something more than national treatment and being open to trade. In principle, there are two main ways of moving beyond national treatment: the first and simplest is mutual recognition; the second and more demanding is the development of common standards. Under mutual recognition, countries agree to trade and invest with one another on the basis that a good or service that can be marketed in one country can be legitimately marketed in another. Each country recognizes the other's rules and standards alongside and as equivalent to its own. This has been the basis of the completion of the internal market within the EU under the Single European Act (1986). In many instances, mutual recognition is an efficient and relatively simple way of deepening market integration. The main advantage of mutual recognition is that governments are spared the task of harmonizing previously discrepant rules and standards. The interaction of firms and consumers in the market will determine the patterns of specialization and trade. By the same token, the disadvantage of mutual recognition is that it presupposes that the states generally trust one another's standards. Where this is not the case, and where states fear that market competition might allow lower standards to drive out higher ones, then they may insist on harmonization around minimum common standards. In so far as the EU has had to develop *new* rules and standards for the single market, say in the area of environmental protection, it has generally adopted the minimum common standards approach. Common standards are particularly appropriate when there are significant externalities associated with the economic activity concerned. When common standards apply a floor is placed under the market and the impact of regulatory competition between different national frameworks is thereby limited.

4.3 The political economy of international trade

Traditional theories of trade based on differences in relative labour productivities and factor endowments suggest that a country or trade bloc will benefit from liberalizing its trade even if its trading partners do not reciprocate. Yet we noted above that the GATT was based on the notion of multilateral reciprocity, specifically the GATT/WTO negotiations are based on the idea of 'first difference reciprocity' where it is the proportional changes to tariffs that are bargained over. Politicians often talk as if exports are good and imports, especially subsidized (or 'dumped') imports, are bad. But why would a country need export earnings if not to pay for imports, and why should it care if foreign governments are prepared to subsidize its consumption? More generally, if trade is a positive-sum issue, in which all parties benefit, why is there so much opposition to free trade? Why is it so common for politicians to speak of trade as if it were a competition between nations, rather than firms, portraying it as a constant-sum process, in which one country's gain is another's loss? To an economist, this kind of talk sounds perilously close to nonsense.

There are two economic answers to these questions as well as a political one and they are all relevant and important for understanding why trade has become such a political issue. In the first place, unless the process of market adjustment to new trading conditions is complete and rapid it will create both winners and losers, even as it increases overall welfare. The owners of resources specific to sectors that are displaced by import competition may be unable to find alternative employment for their resources. And, since in the long-run we are all dead (as Keynes famously observed), some people may suffer real and permanent welfare losses from increased trade. Moreover, trade can alter the distribution of income between such groups as the owners of capital and labour, or between different categories of labour (for example, the skilled and the unskilled). Even when all benefit, some will do better than others. If trade has these kinds of consequences, it is perhaps not surprising that states are unable to leave it wholly to the market.

In the second place, an increasing amount of trade between the advanced capitalist countries is not based on the traditional sources of comparative advantage, but is intra-industry trade based on oligopolistic competition, economies of scale in production and product differentiation among consumers. In these circumstances, comparative advantage can become a dynamic attribute of successful economies, in which success breeds success in a process of cumulative causation, and countries may gain an advantage at the expense of others by virtue of being first in the field. By the same token, countries may be unwilling to see a domestic industry succumb to import competition if its presence creates significant positive externalities for the rest of the national economy. These considerations have given rise to the debate about *strategic* trade, the idea that states can actively improve their trading position at the expense of their 'rivals' by promoting strategic industries.

These economic arguments feed into an important set of political considerations. Krugman (1992) has called the logic of international trade negotiations 'GATT-think', a mindset which believes that:

exports are good;
imports are bad; and
other things being equal, an equal increase in imports and exports is good.

On the basis of GATT-think, country A will open its markets to imports from country B, if its exports gain access to the markets of country B. It is as if trade negotiators were negotiating on behalf of *producers* not *consumers*, since exports are 'good' for export producers and imports are 'bad' for import-competing producers. According to the economic theory of trade, (old or new) GATT-think is, as Krugman somewhat unkindly says, 'nonsense' – but it makes very good political sense. It makes political sense partly because of the real world complications noted above – namely, that adjustment to trade is slow and imperfect and that trade has distributional consequences – and also because producers find it easier to organize and press their case than consumers. There are far fewer producers affected by trade than consumers; information about gains and losses is immediately apparent to producers but difficult to gather for consumers; and producers are well organized in unions, industries and trade associations, whereas consumers are generally poorly organized. All of these make it much more likely that producer interests will be voiced in the political sphere and that consumer interests will be easily overlooked or neglected.

For these kinds of reasons, the pursuit of freer trade may run into strong political opposition. Indeed, during the 1980s, many politicians in the USA and the EU began to question the open, rule-based, non-discriminatory system embodied in the GATT. Particular concern was focused on the rise of the Japanese economy and its astonishing trading successes. These were said to arise from the pursuit of strategic trade by the Japanese government, and producers in the USA and Europe claimed that 'unfair' trading practices were driving them from their traditional markets. Between 1951 and 1971 US industrial production increased 122 per cent (an annual rate of 4.0 per cent) and its GDP rose 90.3 per cent (3.2 per cent per annum), whereas industrial production in Japan increased 1,092 per cent (12.4 per cent per annum) and overall GDP rose by 453 per cent (8.5 per cent per annum). In the context of a general slowing of growth in the world economy and the monetary and exchange rate instabilities that followed the breakdown of the IMF-based fixed exchange rate system in 1971 (see below Section 4.4), these changes had considerable impact.

In this context, the Uruguay Round of the GATT negotiations was especially important (see Box 9.6). The upshot of this new trade agenda

Box 9.6   The Uruguay Round and the WTO

The Uruguay Round had four main objectives:

- First, to extend GATT disciplines to cover trade in agricultural products and services (the GATT had traditionally been concerned with manufactured goods).

- Second, to move toward freer trade in those areas where the advanced countries had traditionally restricted imports from the South, especially textiles.

- Third, to examine new issues relating to trade that required deeper integration involving behind-the-border measures such as the protection of intellectual property rights and aspects of foreign investment related to trade.

- Fourth, to strengthen the institutional basis of trade negotiations, establishing a degree of surveillance over national trade policy (policy review) and an independent adjudication and dispute settlement procedure.

Prior to the Uruguay Round, the most obvious abuses under the GATT were that developing countries used Article XVIII(b) to impose trade restrictions to support the balance of payments and to protect national industries, while the advanced countries excluded agriculture from the GATT framework, introduced the multi-fibre agreement (MFA) to limit textile imports, and resorted to the inaccurately named 'voluntary' export restraints (VERs) to circumvent Article XIX on nondiscrimination.

The bargain that was eventually struck involved the surrender of the license permitted under Article XVIII(b) by the developing countries (including, in relation to the new issues of services, intellectual property rights and investment) in return for a commitment by the advanced countries to liberalize agriculture, dismantle the MFA and accept Article XIX disciplines with regard to nondiscrimination. (The detailed outcome was complicated by the fact that not all states signed up to all aspects of the final agreement and the timetable for implementing agreed changes varied according to the economic status of the country concerned.) In addition, the agreement resulted in the formation of the WTO to oversee world trade issues, to provide a forum for future trade negotiations, and to serve as an independent means of adjudicating and arbitrating on trade disputes between its member states.

was that trade negotiations no longer focused solely or even primarily on 'at-the-border' issues, questions of tariffs and quotas, but were increasingly concerned with 'behind-the-border' aspects of domestic policy, potentially impacting on most aspects of public policy. This meant not only that questions of trade policy now went beyond national treatment to include issues of mutual recognition and common standards but also that trade policy became a much larger political issue and something that began to engage the concern of consumers as well as producers. 'Shallow integration – removing border barriers and providing for national treatment – does not necessarily create integrated markets. [As] intraindustry trade increases, behind-the-border barriers ... inevitably become the focus of attention' (Lawrence, 1996, p.59–60). In short, trade became an important political issue.

Equally important from the perspective of the EU was the inclusion of agriculture within the GATT/WTO framework. Apart from agriculture, the EU has not conformed to the naive predictions of the theory of optimal tariffs. It has certainly pursued protectionist policies in relation to specific industries (for example, cars, steel and textiles) but overall it has pursued trade liberalization for manufactured goods. Summarizing the consequences of EU policy for its international trade down to the completion of the single market programme in the early 1990s, Lawrence has concluded that:

> the data support the argument that Europe's industrial trading relationships with the rest of the world have grown at the same time as its internal trade has flourished. ...The GATT rules and process ... have been critical in providing outsiders with the means to mitigate some of the trade diversion effects. ...The EC's choice of trying to thwart market pressures in sectors such as agriculture, steel, and coal led to a Europe that was more protectionist to the outside world. And the Community's efforts to wrest control of external voluntary export restraint (VER) policies away from individual countries has probably also led to more protection for the Community as a whole. Similarly, the availability of anti-dumping rules (administered by the Commission) has permitted producers one-stop shopping for protection that might have been more difficult to achieve in markets that were more fragmented ... Market conforming measures, however, have had the opposite effect – leading to increased trade opportunities both internally and externally. European disciplines on states aids and other measures that favour domestic producers provide benefits for all who compete within Europe. Similarly, the achievement of common standards reduces costs for all who wish to sell in the market.
>
> (Lawrence, 1996, pp.59–61)

In the case of agriculture, however, it has been a different story. The Common Agricultural Policy (CAP) has, of course, been the largest single common policy of the EU and prior to the Uruguay Round agricultural trade never came under the GATT disciplines. In contrast to the EU's generally open engagement with the international trading system, Lawrence says (somewhat diplomatically) that 'evidence of trade diversion is more apparent in agriculture' (1996, p.59). Indeed, conflict between the USA and the EU over bringing agricultural trade into the

GATT framework nearly sank the Uruguay Round at one point in the negotiations, and the CAP is a continuing source of irritation to US trade officials and a cause of significant transatlantic trade tensions.

What is at stake in many of these debates is the purpose of market integration inside the EU. On the one hand, there is a neo-liberal view that European competitiveness requires continental solutions: 'that market forces should operate on a continental basis, that competition policy should be tough, and mutual recognition should introduce competition between regulatory regimes' (Lawrence, 1996, p.61). On the other hand, there is a more interventionist strand of thinking, which argues 'that intervention and rules should operate on a continental basis, that industrial policies should promote European competitors (rather than enforce competition), and Europe-wide regulatory, agricultural, and social policies should temper the effects of the market' (Lawrence, 1996, p.61).

4.4   The EU, international money and EMU

We noted above that the member states of the EU are also members of the IMF and that the Fund was designed to oversee a fixed exchange rate regime of international payments among the major trading currencies. Between 1958 and 1971 this system operated quite successfully and currency convertibility and stability provided an environment in which international trade and investment could rapidly expand. However, the international monetary system contained two serious design flaws.

The first problem was that the system was unbalanced. Effectively, it was a dollar standard. The idea was to rule out devaluation as a response to balance of payments deficits (except in the most persistent cases) and to finance temporary deficits from the IMF. Deficit countries were still expected to deflate their economies to restore equilibrium to their balance of payments. This created a system-wide problem: if countries deflated their economies to eradicate their payments deficits, the surplus countries would also see their surpluses fall. If surplus countries sought to recoup their position either by devaluation or deflation, then in turn the problem would reappear in the weaker economies. The system as a whole had an inherent deflationary bias. In practice, this bias was overcome because the largest economy in the world, the USA, was willing to run a persistent balance of payments deficit.

As early as 1960 it was pointed out that there were also limits to how far this policy could be consistently maintained (Triffin, 1960). By 1961, the value of overseas dollar holdings exceeded that of the US gold and foreign exchange reserves, thereby undermining long-term confidence in the value of the dollar. For a while this did not matter too much: the USA benefited from having its currency circulate as international money; the inflationary impact of dollar surpluses on domestic inflation in Western Europe and Japan was limited; the new surplus countries (above all, West

Germany and Japan) were reluctant to see their currencies serve as international money alongside the US dollar; and the USA guaranteed the military security of Western Europe and Japan and could therefore expect a certain degree of co-operation in the international management of the dollar standard. After a time, however, the USA found the system too much of a constraint on its national autonomy. In 1971, President Nixon unilaterally ended the system by abrogating the commitment to exchange dollars for gold, devaluing the dollar and refusing to guarantee its future value. Despite two years of negotiations over the nature of the international monetary order (1971–1973), the fixed exchange rate regime was finished.

The second problem with the original design was that it made no provision for the re-emergence of private international financial markets:

> Until the beginning of the 1960s, domestic financial markets tended to be protected from external competition by capital and exchange restrictions introduced to limit the destablizing impact of short-term cross-border flows of private capital ... international capital transactions were still dominated by official operations effected outside of financial markets ... Private-sector finance was still dominated by traditional domestic banking activity and was subject to government controls.
>
> (Padoa-Schioppa and Saccomanni, 1994, p.238).

From the late 1960s onwards, however, private markets rapidly developed in payments services, capital flows and bank-based financial intermediation. The IMF had no responsibility for, or control over, these developments. The result was a significant erosion of the ability of governments to manage the exchange rate regime through buying and selling their foreign exchange reserves, since foreign exchange trans-actions in private markets soon overwhelmed public interventions. The state-led international monetary system overseen by the IMF was replaced by a market-led system.

Against this background, the schemes for monetary co-operation in Europe that have now culminated in the project of EMU and the introduction of a single currency can be seen as attempts to find a new basis of stability for international money on a regional rather than a global basis. Just as the member states pooled their national rights to make trade policy in the CCP, so EMU involves a pooling of authority in relation to monetary and exchange rate policies. As yet, the wider international implications of the single currency are far from clear but they are potentially very significant indeed.

If nations are to trade with one another and to lend and borrow from each other, then there must be a form of money that private and public actors can use for their international transactions. Countries have their own national currencies for all domestic transactions, but for trade and factor movements across national borders there must be some form of international money. Moreover, since nation states have traditionally claimed an exclusive right to issue the national currency and control its use through a Central Bank, the international circulation of a national currency is a directly political issue. Economically speaking, money has three functions: it is a medium of exchange, a unit of account and a store of value. The international payments regime determines how these functions are performed for transactions between national economies. It is not necessary for a single currency to perform all these functions and a range of national currencies can serve as international money. However, historically only a few currencies have performed the full range of money functions in the international economy and these are often called *key* currencies. As we have seen, after the Second World War the dollar was the key currency.

One important issue for the EU is the extent to which the private sector will come to use the euro as a key currency and, then, the degree to which this will be supported or resisted by the public authorities, the European System of Central Banks (ESCB). Currently, the ESCB has price stability *within* Euroland as its priority (Chapters 4 and 8) and the EU has not adopted a specific policy toward the international – that is, external to Euroland – role of the new currency. However, according to the Treaty of Maastricht:

> In the absence of an exchange rate system in relation to one or more non-Community currencies ... the Council, acting by a qualified majority either on a recommendation from the Commission and after consulting the ECB, or on a recommendation from the ECB, may formulate general orientations for exchange rate policy in relation to these currencies. These general orientations shall be without prejudice to the primary objective of the ECB to maintain price stability.

In cases of serious exchange rate misalignment in the past, the three major trading and investment blocs (the USA, Japan and Western Europe) have attempted to manage their exchange rates. For example, the Plaza Agreement (1985) and the Louvre Agreement (1987) sought to devalue the US dollar against both the Deutschmark and the Japanese yen. In practice, such arrangements can only work by signalling policy changes, especially in relation to interest rate movements.

The problem in this context is that the policies required to pursue price stability *within* the EU might be in conflict with a particular target for the exchange rate of the euro against other currencies (see Table 9.1). For this reason, some analysts see the Maastricht provisions as flawed and in 1999, after initial squabbles between the ECB and the Council, there was 'an agreement to desist from exchange rate orientations except under 'exceptional circumstances' (Eijffinger and de Haan, 2000, p.180). (But who is to define what counts as 'exceptional circumstances', especially given that this agreement is not part of the Treaty and could in principle be revoked by the Council of Ministers?) In late 2000, for example, growing international concern about the falling value of the euro, expressed in particular by the IMF, led to international action to support the currency. These interventions drew attention to the fact that the management of the euro is not and cannot simply be an internal matter for the EU (Chapters, 2, 4 and 8). Inevitably, it will also carry international responsibilities. How the EU discharges these responsibilities and how it does (or doesn't) co-operate on these matters with the USA, Japan and the IMF remains to be seen.

Table 9.1 Conflicts between the ECB's internal and external monetary policies

Monetary policies – internal	Monetary policies – external	
	ECB's exchange rate policy aimed at appreciation *of euro*	ECB's exchange rate policy aimed at depreciation *of euro*
ECB's restrictive money supply policy (overshooting of monetary target and/or expected inflation)	*no* conflict: internally and externally higher European money market interest rates	*possible* conflict: internally higher, but externally lower European money market interest rate
ECB's expansionary money supply policy (undershooting of monetary target and/or expected inflation)	*possible* conflict: internally lower, but externally higher European money market interest rate	*no* conflict: internally and externally lower European money market interest rate

(Eijffinger and de Haan, 2000, Table 7.5, p.175)

Two possible developments have received some attention. First, the major currency blocs in the world economy (the USA, Euroland and Japan) might agree to a greater degree of monitored decentralization for their monetary and exchange rate policies. This would involve not so much questions of rules and regulations, standards which *private* transactions must meet, but rather the management of *public* policy by governments, especially macroeconomic policy. In the case of monitored decentralization, governments commit themselves to follow a particular policy, to provide information on the conduct of that policy to a central body and to allow that body to report to other members the results of its surveillance. For example, under the terms of membership of the IMF, governments are already obliged to conduct their exchange rate policies in certain ways relating to transparency and fair dealing, they must provide the IMF with regular and detailed information about their foreign exchange transactions and reserves and this information is made available to other members of the Fund and its governing bodies. Failure to comply not only attracts censure but can lead to various penalties. (At the limit, for gross violation of obligations to the Fund, a state can be suspended from membership.)

Second, and more ambitiously, Euroland, the USA and Japan might move toward intergovernmental co-ordination. This is an extension of monitored decentralization, since it not only presupposes monitoring or surveillance of national policy by others, but it seeks specifically co-ordinated changes to policy among a number of states. For example, a country with a persistent current account surplus may agree to undertake a fiscal expansion to increase domestic demand and imports if another country with a persistent deficit agrees to a domestic contraction aimed at shifting resources to the tradeable sector. These kinds of policy alignments are demanding, not only because of the technical and practical difficulties involved, but also because countries may stand to loose a great deal if they keep their side of the bargain while others fail to reciprocate. In this sort of eventuality it may be better to stick with an unsatisfactory status quo than risk an even worse outcome.

Within Euroland, member states are already engaged in monitored decentralization – as in the requirements for joining EMU and the rules of the stability pact, and intergovernmental co-ordination has gone as far as the quasi-federal making of common policies in relation to the new currency. How far these can be extended to relations *between* the EU and the other regions of the world economy remains to be seen. But in principle there is no reason why greater co-operation over monetary policy and exchange rates could not be agreed between the major currency regions and subject to IMF surveillance.

Summary

- Within the basic framework of international governance, the EU constitutes a highly distinctive model of governance among its member states, since it has gone far beyond the non-discriminatory national treatment required of members of the BWIs to include common standards and policies, mutual recognition, monitored decentralization and intergovernmental co-ordination based on a quasi-federal sharing of sovereignty in joint decision-making under a common legal framework.

- Despite some tensions between the protectionist and interventionist aspects of the EU's economic governance, especially in relation to agriculture, and the interests of its external trading partners, the EU has on balance contributed to the liberal direction of international economic governance overseen by the GATT/WTO.

- The 1980s and 1990s have seen a widening of the international trade agenda in the context of a more unstable international monetary order. This has served to raise the political salience of trade (and trade related investment) issues between both the EU and its trading partners and public opinion. In turn, this has created some tensions within the EU between the competence of the Commission and the member states over trade matters.

- With the breakdown of the Bretton Woods framework for international monetary stability in the 1970s, the EU embarked on various schemes of monetary co-operation, eventually leading to the adoption of a single currency by most member states. A single currency for Euroland injects a new element into the international monetary order, where previously the US dollar has been the almost unchallenged key currency. How relations between the euro and the dollar will be managed, if at all, is as yet unclear but under existing IMF obligations it is unlikely that the EU will be able to escape a degree of international responsibility for the value of its currency.

5 International economic governance and international economic integration

We noted above that states have economic sovereignty under inter-national economic law, they are constitutionally independent and equal before the law. This is merely the economic parallel of their more general sovereignty under public international law. But we also saw that states tend to exercise their sovereign rights collectively and reciprocally. To be sure, many states have exercised complete national autonomy over some highly limited areas of policy but the unilateral exercise of autonomy, without regard to the actions of other states and making no attempt to co-ordinate and co-operate in areas of mutual benefit, is not a serious principle for the conduct of international economic governance. Put bluntly, complete national autonomy and an inter-national economy cannot coexist. In fact, despite much contemporary rhetoric about the 'loss' of national autonomy in the contemporary international or global economy, it has rarely been tried and for very good reason. The only states that have ever taken the idea at all seriously have either disengaged from the world economy to a considerable extent or been sufficiently powerful to impose their national decisions on their economic 'partners'. The first of these options has resulted in economic catastrophe and the second is scarcely to be recommended on democratic grounds.

Rather, states generally retain their sovereign rights to national decision making but choose to exercise this in common with other states, seeking reciprocal action on the basis of national treatment, mutual recognition, common standards, monitored decentralization and intergovernmental co-ordination. (In the case of the EU, of course, this process has gone even further, to include the pooling or sharing of sovereignty in some areas.) The obvious reason why states co-operate is that there are net gains from doing so.

The real question, then, becomes not so much why states co-operate, but how they realize these potential gains. Given that the networks of trade, investment and payments in the international economy are shared by many states, the decisions taken by any given state in relation to its domestic and at-the-border measures, as well as the conduct of macroeconomic policy, will typically depend on what other states do. One way of thinking about the benefits of co-operation among states is to regard them as a kind of public good for the international economy. But the market, in this case the system of sovereign states, is notorious for under-provision of public goods: each individual contributor only receives a small share of the gain its actions produce, while non-contributors get an equal share of the total benefits. If all potential contributors reason in this way, then the public good will not be provided. Individual rational action will result in a collectively irrational outcome. Of course, within a nation state the government can provide the public good and then use its authority or its coercive powers to raise the necessary taxes to pay for it, thereby overcoming this particular kind of market failure.

At the level of the inter-state system, however, there is no overriding coercive authority with the power to implement and enforce collectively beneficial patterns of co-operation. Analysis suggests that in these latter circumstances, co-operation is most likely to be successful when the number of participants is small, information about the relevant course of action is precise, interaction among the states concerned is easy and regular, and cheats or defectors are easily detected and punished. For these reasons states may establish specific institutions to organize their co-operation. Where they exist, such international regimes may help states to co-operate with one another to common ends, co-ordinate their policies and even undertake joint collaboration, by providing a focus around which expectations can converge, an arena for information sharing and learning, a means of reducing the costs of negotiating and bargaining, and a way of making their commitments to one another credible by identifying defectors. It is precisely these kinds of factors that have been at work in the *de facto* and increasingly *de jure* integration in the economic space of the EU.

5.1 Institutions and principles for international economic governance

The kinds of international institutions, and especially the principles by which these institutions operate, will often help to determine the extent of economic integration that states can achieve. We have identified a spectrum of international co-operation running from national treatment plus MFN (non-discrimination), through mutual recognition, common standards, monitored decentralization and intergovernmental co-ordination, to the quasi-federal pooling or sharing of economic sovereignty. And we have also seen that the principles governing such interaction can range from neo-liberal ideas about negative integration and market-making regulations to more interventionist philosophies based on a significant role for the state in regulating, managing and supplementing market outcomes in pursuit of social objectives. This conflict of principles runs through debates about the nature of international economic law.

We noted above that international economic law (IEL) is part of the law among states and that one of its central principles is that of the state's economic sovereignty. However, the purpose of IEL is not solely or even primarily to regulate interaction between *states*, but rather to facilitate and regulate the private interactions of market agents and processes across national borders. Thus whereas public international law in general 'is based on the state and the notion of sovereignty', some have argued that the core principle of IEL:

> is based on the dictates of comparative advantage, on promoting individual cross border exchanges and specialisation ... Accordingly, IEL (particularly International Trade Law) is defined as being concerned with those State measures that are taken at the border, or internally, that inhibit the operation of the comparative advantage (specialisation and voluntary exchange) to function effectively. International economic law is concerned with eliminating cross-border impediments.
>
> (Qureshi, 1999, pp.9–10)

This 'comparative advantage model' of IEL certainly captures important aspects of reality. But it has not gone unchallenged. While it is undoubtedly the case that IEL can be seen as the legal regulation of a liberal international and transnational economic order, it remains the case that its principal subjects and objects are states, notwithstanding the increasing legal standing of international economic organizations and private agents under IEL. Traditionally, the formation and implementation of states' foreign economic policies, like the sphere of foreign policy more generally, were not subject to extensive constitutional or legal procedures. Moreover, domestic legal systems have not traditionally recognized the *trans*national economic rights for individuals, that is, rights associated with a liberal international economic order. And, as we argued above (Section 4.2), there are good reasons for thinking that in formulating their foreign economic policies liberal democratic states won't be concerned simply with maximizing their economic welfare, let alone worldwide economic welfare. In the comparative advantage model of IEL, 'the theory of comparative advantage is considered to have been embraced by the international economic community in an absolute form and released into the system without any restrictions' (Qureshi, 1999, p.11). This is probably not the case: the 'state model' of IEL, which sees it as a creation of and bearing the imprint of states and the inter-state system, remains relevant for a full understanding of the legal regulation of the international economy.

There has certainly been a merging of domestic legal systems and international law, the foreign economic policy making of states has been increasingly subject to legal regulation, and private actors have gained transnational rights in some contexts, especially under the framework of Community law in the EU. Indeed, in this respect the EU is unique since its foreign economic policy making is highly institutionalized and large elements of it operate under a precisely defined legal constitution which is binding on its members. No other form of international economic governance has this kind of authority. It is true that the WTO has a quasi-judicial dispute settlement procedure, but the international law relating to trade does not have the solidity and authority within the national legal systems of the WTO members that the community legal order commands within the member states of the Union. The IMF also generates 'soft' law and informal interpretations of its Articles of Agreement in the field of international monetary policy, but only the Articles themselves and their formal interpretation are legally binding on member states. And, neither the WTO nor the IMF have the *legislative* capacity to generate new law that the Community pillar of the EU possesses.

Within this expanding corpus of law (European and international) the balance between the dictates of comparative advantage and the interests of states in determining its content remains an issue that is politically contested by a range of different actors. Nevertheless, within the EU as well as outside in the wider framework of IEL, a fundamentally important feature of the contemporary international economic order is that it is to a considerable extent a *law-bound* order which exhibits a very high degree of compliance. That is to say, IEL is not simply a body of rules for regulating and managing the international economic order, it also constitutes a form or process of decision making in which legal principles and procedures are combined with political negotiation and bargaining. International economic law may not have the solidity and authority of European economic law but it is fundamentally the same kind of order, rather than a completely different type of governance. And it is the growing solidity of these arrangements that has led some analysts to speak of a constitution for international economic governance based on the charters of the principal multilateral institutions – the IMF and the WTO.

What might such an order of governance look like and where does the EU's distinctive contribution to international economic governance fit in relation to it? The choice between the various governance mechanisms for the international economy is both an economic and a political question. Economic theory does provide some general principles for determining the appropriate scale and scope of governance mechanisms, but they do not give rise to any clear-cut answers. Lawrence (1996) summarizes the basic principles well as follows:

> On the one hand, to realize scale economies and
> internalization, the scope of governance should be increased.
> On the other hand, to realize a more precise matching of tastes
> and choices and enhance accountability, governance should be

localized ... as global interdependence increases, so too do the pressures for common rules and institutions at supranational levels. At the same time, however, as incomes increase, the scope for exercising different preferences also increases.

(Lawrence, 1996, pp.8 and 30)

These kinds of consideration can inform political decisions about governance mechanisms but they cannot determine them because international policy problems usually involve many different actors with conflicting interests, competing objectives that may not be commensurable with one another and indeterminate and intangible outcomes. In these circumstances, what is needed is not simply an analysis of the most efficient means to a given end but rather a decision about how decisions will be made and by whom. What principles will guide decision making and what are the limits of the jurisdiction of different organizations – firms, states, regional bodies like the EU, and the wider multilateral forums? These kinds of decisions are irreducibly political choices since they involve competing 'ends'.

The nature and extent of international economic integration can be significantly affected by how, where and by whom these issues are resolved. In this context, Rodrik (2000) posed the question: How far will international economic integration go? He notes that there is a series of political dilemmas associated with national sovereignty in regard to economic policy making, the international integration of national economies through trade and investment, and the ability of liberal democracies to choose between meaningful alternatives in the field of economic policy. What Rodrik calls the 'Bretton Woods compromise' sought to balance a degree of economic sovereignty, allowing for meaningful choices of economic policy at the national level, against a commitment to remove 'at-the-border' barriers to trade and non-discriminatory treatment of foreign goods and services: 'The essence of the Bretton Woods-GATT regime was that countries were free to dance to their own tune as long as they removed a number of border restrictions to trade and generally did not discriminate among their trade partners' (Rodrik, 2000, p.183).

This regime has also been called 'embedded liberalism' (Ruggie, 1982) and 'shallow integration' (Lawrence, 1996). Collective, reciprocal co-operation facilitates the competition between different national economies with their own distinctive patterns of public policy.

We have seen above that the international trade agenda under the WTO has now moved well beyond its original, limited GATT framework and that the re-emergence of private international finance has undermined the effectiveness of national controls over capital flows. Both of these developments have contributed to a more market-oriented, some would say neo-liberal, definition of international economic governance. In these circumstances, Rodrik contends that the 'price of maintaining national jurisdictional sovereignty is that politics have to be exercised over a much narrower domain' (Rodrik, 2000, p.182). Friedman (1999) has called this the 'golden straightjacket', because it involves constraining national policy choices within a range that is acceptable to international or global market forces. It embraces integrated international markets and national sovereignty at the price of forfeiting meaningful autonomy. If this trend were to continue, the content of IEL would increasingly come to resemble the 'comparative advantage' model.

But both in Europe and elsewhere there is considerable concern that the current agendas of the WTO and the IMF represent a US-inspired version of the golden straightjacket. In this scenario, states would remain formally sovereign but their scope for meaningful choices over economic policy, the degree of national autonomy in policy making, will be limited by ever wider and deeper international economic integration conducted under neo-liberal rules overseen by multilateral institutions. In part, the development of international economic governance within the EU can be understood as an attempt to escape this golden straightjacket by resorting to federalism on a *regional* basis not a global one. Within the economic space of the EU, international economic governance has gone far beyond non-discriminatory national treatment to embrace mutual recognition and common standards and policies, organized under a quasi-federal political and legal order. Moreover, despite the free market orientation of the single market, EU governance also serves wider social objectives relating to welfare and environmental concerns. The content of European economic law therefore bears the imprint of state interests as well as the dictates of comparative advantage.

Extending this kind of logic to the global level is one of the future scenarios envisaged by Rodrik, in the form of global federalism: 'Under global federalism, politics need not, and would not shrink: it would relocate to the global level' (Rodrik, 2000, p.183). In this scenario, states give up national sovereignty in order to re-regulate the international economy at a higher level, autonomy in the field of policy making is re-established at the price of having to formulate and implement such regulations collectively with other states. Could the WTO and the IMF become the vehicles for such a development and, if so, what kinds of principles would organize decision making? (Collectively, the member states of the EU have the largest single voice in both the IMF and the WTO.) Or does the experience of the EU demonstrate that the regional level is a more appropriate site for substantive decision making? Perhaps neo-liberalism is the lowest common denominator of large numbers of states and that to achieve the highest common factor requires smaller groupings. Arguably the future success or otherwise of the EU will play a major role in determining how international economic governance moves between these alternatives.

Summary

- Although there is no centralized body to legislate for international economic governance, states co-operate with one another because there are benefits from doing so. In order to facilitate co-operation, states establish institutions and agree principles to guide their collective decision making. There are differences and conflicts over both the appropriate institutions for international economic governance and the principles by which they should operate. Nevertheless, international economic governance within the EU and in the wider Bretton Woods system operates in a framework of law.

- One important conflict over the principles of governance relates to the content of international law. Should the law serve the interests of the market and market actors as conceived in neo-liberal terms or do states have the right to impose non-market outcomes? Both elements can be found but the principle subjects and objects of international law are states, notwithstanding the growth of legal rights for market actors.

- The consolidation of international economic governance as *law* and the authority of that law has gone much further *within* the EU, in the framework of European economic law developed by the Community pillar, than in the wider multilateral institutions governing trade (the WTO) and money (the IMF). This is what makes the EU so distinctive as a system of international economic governance: it has developed a significant degree of quasi-federal shared economic sovereignty under a common legal order for its trade and monetary affairs (as well as for its common policies within the EU).

- Changes to the international economic environment have moved beyond the 'shallow integration' envisaged by the BWIs. Within Europe, these changes have produced a much deeper form of integration involved in developing common 'behind-the-border' policies. How far the EU's experience can provide a model for international economic governance beyond Europe, for the wider world, remains an open question.

6 Conclusion

Clearly, the depth of economic integration achieved within the EU is considerably greater than that between the EU, on the one side, and its major trading partners in North America and East Asia, on the other. As we have seen, considered as a system of international economic governance, the EU is unique. But I have argued that the wider framework of international law organized around the main multilateral institutions – the IMF and the WTO – is a similar kind of governance, even if the solidity and authority of this law is much less secure than the corpus of European law.

One possible future is that other regions in the world will develop their own distinctive patterns of integration, with their own particular substantive laws and policies, perhaps on the basis of NAFTA and APEC. And just as the development of the EU's own distinctive style of international economic governance has been for the most part compatible with the more limited, if wider, frameworks set by the GATT/WTO and the IMF, so might be the governance of these other regional groupings. Alternatively, the WTO and the IMF might themselves become the vehicles for deeper integration. Or there might be some mix of these two options.

The other possibility is that mechanisms of international economic governance will fail as they did in the late nineteenth and early twentieth centuries and in the years between the two World Wars of the twentieth century. If that were to happen, it would almost certainly curtail, if not reverse, the degree of international economic integration that has characterized the advanced capitalist world since the end of the Second World War and that has been one of the main props of a generally remarkable rise in economic output and improvement in living standards.

Either way, the future development of international economic governance, and the role played by the EU within this, will have a major bearing on the fortunes not only of those living in Europe but on much of the rest of the world as well.

References

Dinan, D. (1999) *Ever Closer Community*, London, Macmillan.

Eijffinger, S. and de Haan, J. (2000) *European Monetary and Fiscal Policy*, Oxford, OUP.

Friedman, T. (1999) *The Lexus and the Olive Tree*, London, HarperCollins.

IMF (1997) *World Economic Outlook*, October, Washington, DC, International Monetary Fund.

Krugman, P. (1992) 'Does the new trade theory require a new trade policy', *The World Economy*, vol.15, no.4, July, pp.423–41.

Lawrence, R. (1996) *Regionalism, Multilateralism and Deeper Integration*, Washington, DC, Brookings Institution.

Meier, G. (1998) *The International Environment for Business*, Oxford, OUP.

Padoa-Schioppa, T. and Saccomanni, F. (1994) 'Managing a market-led global financial system' in Kenen, P. (ed.) *Managing the World Economy*, Washington, DC, Institute for International Economics.

Piening, C. (1997) *Global Europe*, London, Lynne Rienner.

Qureshi, A. (1999) *International Economic Law*, London, Sweet and Maxwell.

Rodrik, D. (2000) 'How far will international economic integration go?', *The Journal of Economic Perspectives*, vol.14, no.1, pp.177–86.

Ruggie, J. (1982) 'International regimes, transactions, and change: embedded liberalism in the post-war economic order', *International Organization*, vol.36 pp.379–415.

Triffin, R. (1960) *Gold and the Dollar Crisis*, New Haven, Yale University Press.

Further reading

Lawrence, R. (1996) *Regionalism, Multilateralism and Deeper Integration*, Washington, DC, Brookings Institution.

Meier, G. (1998) *The International Environment for Business*, Oxford, OUP.

Nugent, N. (1999) *The Government and Politics of the European Union*, London, Macmillan.

Reinicke, W.H. (1998) *Global Public Policy*, Washington, DC, Brookings Institution.

Chapter 10
Governing the European economy: reviewing the issues

Grahame Thompson

1 Introduction

This chapter takes a broad look at the themes and issues that have arisen and been discussed through the book. It is not a comprehensive review but concentrates just on the main thematic issues and does not always identify the exact chapters where these issues were originally discussed, although it should be clear where the issues were first posed and analysed in the chapters. The main objective of this short concluding chapter is to underline the key features of European economic governance and to chart the evolving character of the relationships between the national economies and the supranational forces and organizations that have established a variety of pan-European governance structures over the post-Second World War period.

2 Forms of governance and their relationship

We look first at the central issue addressed in the book: the nature of European economic governance. The chapters have shown how the three frameworks through which governance can be organized – regulation, the market and self-organizing networks – constitute a rich and complex mix of governance techniques and mechanisms. The relationship between these three approaches was represented in the opening chapter as three 'analytical torches' that each shone a particular beam of light onto the object of analysis, illuminating all or part of it. The emerging issue was which of these analytical focuses was best able to explain the characteristics of European economic governance in the most effective way.

The chapters have concentrated on the two main governance models, regulation and the market. Broadly speaking, it has been these two approaches that have marked out the terms of discussion for the trajectory for economic Europe over the post-Second World War period.

They make both a positive and an analytical claim on how European economic governance *actually operates* and a normative claim on how it *should operate*. These two approaches embody both a 'neutral' analytical style of reasoning, and a style that involves value judgements about what is best and most effective in producing favoured outcomes. The categories of 'regulatory order' and 'market order' are not then simply abstract and formal analytical devices, but also ideological ones. They carry with them deeply held beliefs about how the economy should be organized and governed.

What is said here about regulation and the market – that they embody deeply held belief systems as well as operating as analytical devices – is also true of networks. Although as mechanisms of governance these have been less distinctively specified in the chapters, where they have appeared as central to the debate they have also involved value judgements on their worth and appropriateness. This in part explains why there is such an intense debate and dispute over the trajectory for European economic governance. The chapters have amply demonstrated how sharp and conflictual this debate and struggle has become. Differences of view involve not only macroeconomic management and the operation of the European Central Bank, for instance, but also how environmental governance is organized, how corporate governance could be reformed, and how labour markets should be made to work.

Returning for a moment to the way such debate was characterized in the opening chapter, Figure 1.6 from that chapter is reproduced here (Figure 10.1) as the basis for a discussion of what the nature of economic Europe looked like at the turn of the twenty-first century.

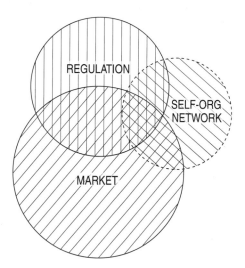

Figure 10.1 The governance approaches compared

The market is given the largest 'spotlight' in Figure 10.1, because it seemed to be the most robust and extensive mechanism organizing economic activities in the latter part of the twentieth century. Regulation is also important, and is given a large space. Self-organizing networks is more difficult to pin down analytically, and it is given a smaller role and a less distinct boundary because of this (indicated by a broken line).

One obvious question that arises in respect to Figure 10.1 is whether these spaces and boundaries are the appropriate ones. Do they indicate the real position with any accuracy? In addition, they seem rather 'static'; we have noted earlier that this could be the picture at the turn of the twenty-first century, but would it have been an accurate one in, say, 1950? This poses the issue of the *evolution* of the governance mechanism in respect to Europe over the post-war period. Let us explore some possibilities and discuss their likely importance as explanatory devices.

First, it could be argued that the regulatory order has been much more important than indicated by Figure 10.1. This relates to the way *de jure* integration was not only a key early approach to re-organizing the European economy after the Second World War, but has remained a central governance approach ever since. It is embodied in the successive moves by the EEC and the EU in advancing the momentum of economic integration through the various treaties that have marked post-Second World War European development. There can be little doubt that the European Commission, as the embodiment of EU governance, represents a formidable regulatory institution. But backing it up are the various other public institutions of European governance, like the Council of Ministers, the European System of Central Banks (ESCB), and the array of more functional institutions that organize particular parts of *de jure* Europe. And this formidable array of organizations is supplemented by all the parallel national public institutions in each of the member states. It may be, then, that an 'organized capitalism' with a strong 'regulatory order' continues to dominate economic Europe, and that this completely eclipses the other governance mechanisms. Such a possibility is portrayed in Figure 10.2.

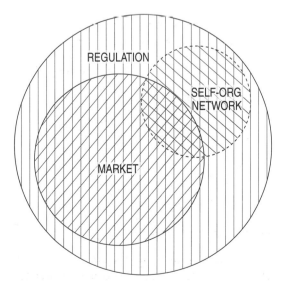

Figure 10.2 Regulation as the dominant governance model

From Figure 10.2 we see that regulation *encompasses* both the market and self-organizing networks. The latter two are no more than secondary forms of activity, completely dominated by bureaucratic regulation and management. In effect, of course, this is the argument of those who are ideologically opposed to European integration of the EU type. They suggest that the EU represents nothing more than an over-regulated and thoroughly bureaucratized nightmare, one that stifles the individual initiative that would be provided by a more market-driven system (and possibly, even, one driven by networks).

This line of argument provides us with a way of characterizing an altogether different scenario for the operation of economic Europe, one that is already completely driven by market forces, and where regulation is on the retreat or completely eclipsed. This is the scenario depicted in Figure 10.3.

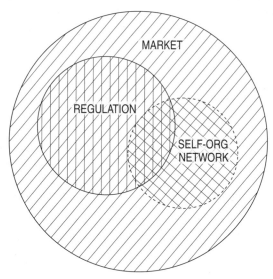

Figure 10.3 The market as the dominant governance model

In this case it is the market that rules the economic organization of Europe, broadly operating through the plethora of *de facto* private economic initiatives that are integrating Europe. Thus the growth of intra-European trade, economic investment and migration have established what is for all intents and purposes a completely market-driven European system. This is aided by the way that the public authorities are adopting 'market friendly' policies for integration ('market making' deregulation, as Scharpf, 1999, puts it) which are enhancing the dominating effect of already powerful market forces. The 'neo-liberal' policy agenda that has swept Europe, as discussed in many of the chapters above, represents the key feature in this move.

Perhaps we should also consider the third alternative that emerges: namely the possibility that self-organizing networks are hegemonic in European economic governance, eclipsing regulation and markets in turn. Although this seems fanciful, it may not be quite so unlikely as it first appears. For one thing it rather depends upon how one defines 'networks'. Couldn't they *include* markets and regulatory institutions? Couldn't we extend the notion of networks to consider market organization as a big network, for instance – after all, it depends heavily on informal connections which also build on trust (such as those involved in contracts not completely specified) and loyalty (such as brand identification)? A similar case can be proffered for public institutions, which also rely for their operation on informal contacts and personalized relationships, and which again engender trust and loyalty.

But perhaps this is to extend the definition of networks just too far. If they were to be defined as operating like this then they would become so ubiquitous that they would lose their specificity, and we would lose any analytical ability to discriminate between different forms of social organization. If networks are arguably everywhere and explain every-thing, then they cannot be anywhere specific nor can they explain anything in particular. (But we should acknowledge that networks are sometimes conceived in this all-encompassing manner.)

Even if one does not wish to extend the domain of networks in this way but rather keep to a narrower definition as outlined in Chapter 1, they still remain an important 'lubricant' of the economic mechanism and of the formation of public policy. Recall the way this was discussed in Chapter 7, for example, as a key mechanism for governance in respect to the formation and organization of environmental governance. This involved not only networks in the traditional sense, but all sorts of semi-autonomous partnership agreements and other innovative, rather 'informal', configurations of pressure groups and interests. In many ways these take on the characteristics of more traditional networks.

This type of analysis could be extended to the more formal and central mechanisms of institutional governance, like the ESCB, or even the Council of Ministers. These institutional mechanisms, as well as relying upon traditional modes of regulatory and hierarchical organization, also contain a large degree of informality and élite networking. They must do this if they are to operate pragmatically with the necessary degree of flexibility and discretion. Not everything can be dealt with formally and by rule-governed procedures.

Nevertheless, this is not to argue that we could sensibly construct a similar figure to that of Figure 10.2 or 10.3, this time giving networks the all-encompassing governance role. This would probably be to exaggerate the real significance of network governance beyond what is credible in modern Europe. But a system dominated by either a regulatory order or a market order does remain a feasible one. The situations depicted in Figures 10.2 and 10.3 are possible scenarios for the overall governance of economic Europe at the turn of the twenty-first century. Certainly, the tone of the analysis arising from the chapters could be compatible with one that suggests there has been a *move* from the situation depicted in Figure 10.2 toward that shown in Figure 10.3; that is, from one where regulation was the typical mode of governance directly after the Second World War to one where the market rules relatively unambiguously as we turn the century. This signals the pressures that have built up in economic

Europe over this period to abandon overt regulatory management of economic activity *against the grain of the market*, and to move instead toward either minimal regulation (deregulation, privatization, liberalization) or a stance on regulatory management that encourages market solutions and commercial managerialism (regulation *with the grain of the market*).

That said, we should not necessarily accept this as the single most important message emerging from the analysis of the chapters of this book, though it is a strong and feasible one. An alternative would be to go back to something like our Figure 10.1 situation, where all three modes of governance are still clearly represented and in play, but see them as operating in a somewhat unstable and fluid combination with one another. There is no single dominant governance mechanism, though the shape and extent of the three would have moved over the period, and the relationships between them would have altered. We might accept that, since economic Europe is a *capitalist system* (whether 'organized' or 'decentralized' – Chapter 1), it would be *very unlikely* if the market form of organization was not the most important one, albeit tempered by the other two. So we might feel comfortable with this as being the largest 'spotlight' on economic Europe, even in the 1950s. And we might also feel comfortable with the fact that the spotlight of the market model has spread over the period 1950–2000, and that of the regulatory model has shrunk somewhat (with the network model falling somewhere in between, though this may also have grown in importance from small beginnings relative to regulation and even the market).

What is clear is that there is no definitive answer. It would be foolish to pretend that there is a clear and unambiguous message emanating from the chapters as a whole. Indeed, we are left with a number of possible conclusions on this issue, some of the terms of which have been outlined here.

But a final point before moving on is to revisit the issue of governance altogether. The above analysis has discussed the market in two broad, and not altogether consistent, ways. It has used it, first as a form of economic organization, and second as a mode of governance. But you will remember from Chapter 1 that the market is not really an overt mode of governance at all. If we mean by governance the explicit and conscious attempt to establish and maintain order *by design*, then the market does not claim to do this. Indeed – and by contrast – while it claims to establish order it does so not by conscious design but by the 'natural' operation of the 'guiding hand' offered by decentralized price formation and competitive advantage. A market order, then, could be said to 'govern' in the sense that it produces ordered outcomes, but not in the same way as a regulatory order does or a self-organizing network does. These distinctions should be borne in mind when using the three analytical approaches embodied in the figures discussed above. In the final analysis, there is not much that can be done about this. It is a fact of theoretical life that there always remains some ambiguity in any attempt to bring systematicity and coherence to bear on the real complexity of social and economic life.

3   The national and the supranational

A second main theme that arises from the chapters is the relationship between national and supranational governance mechanisms. In respect to this, where does the real centre of gravity lie in relation to the economic governance of Europe? Clearly, we have seen how there seems to have been a steady progress toward more and more governance functions being ceded to the EU level and away from the national level.

But this has perhaps been less of a steady evolution than it might at first appear; it has gone ahead very much in 'fits and starts'. There have been periods of rapid forward movement followed by periods of stagnation and slow advance. Many of the periods of quickened pace have arisen as a reaction to external, international events beyond the control of the EU states (for instance: concern about complete US economic dominance immediately after the War; the break up of the Bretton Woods system of semi-fixed exchange rates in the early 1970s, quickly followed by the oil price shocks of the mid-1970s; and the emergence of Japan and the East Asian economies as formidable economic competitors in the 1980s). The sense of a loss of *national* control over these and other events among the key European states was, at least in part, one of the main driving forces for them to seek salvation in the creation of a much larger and more powerful economic entity. They ceded power at the national level (though somewhat reluctantly at times) in order to regain it at the EU level. National governments might have given up some aspects of national economic sovereignty at the domestic level, but they did so in an attempt to gain collective power or economic sovereignty at the EU level.

But note how this is formulated. National governments are deemed not to have abandoned completely their desire to exercise economic sovereignty by ceding it to the supranational EU level; they have tried to *retain* it or *regain* it by these means, but now exercised under a collective umbrella. Thus there is a *complex relationship* operating here between the national and the EU level, one not easily captured by a simple mechanism of the *transfer* of capacities from one level to another.

Of course, this way of putting things presumes that there was no effective way for the individual European governments to have continued to exercise their powers singly in order to govern their national economies. Those opposed to the EU would challenge this. They argue that it is still possible, for example, for the individual European powers to conduct their own monetary and fiscal policies, without having to pass these to the EU with EMU. They reject the idea that 'economic sovereignty' has in effect been clawed away from individual national governments by 'international events' beyond their control, very much against their will and with little that those governments can do about it. They continue to believe in the possibility for much more to be retained at the domestic level, and for effective economic policy still to be exercised there.

In addition, of course, this 'counter sentiment' against the EU has another aspect to it. Many of those opposed to the 'ceding of sovereignty' do not wish the EU to exercise such powers because they are ideologically opposed to what they see as the over-regulated and thoroughly bureaucratized nature of the EU (as suggested above). They would rather see much more 'left to the market' to decide, and would favour the establishment of a less interventionist and less regulatory environment for the conduct of European economic activity.

What is made of these arguments is really a matter for individual judgement based upon analyses such as those offered by the preceding chapters. It is probably fair to say – perhaps undeniable – that there has been a major shift away from the national arena toward the supranational one in respect to the economic governance of Europe.

But it is also worth considering another possibility, that membership of the EU has fostered *sub-national* economic initiatives as well. The EU has been particularly concerned to foster 'regional development', which has often taken a sub-national form (this is most obviously the case with respect to regional and structural funds, and in the case of innovation and technology policy, for instance). Here the effect of the development of the competencies of the EU in economic matters may have shifted the focus of economic governance not 'upwards' from the national level to the EU level but 'downwards', from the national level toward the local or regional level.

Clearly, there have been multiple initiatives in governance matters that involve these considerations, both macro and micro in character. Again, complex results have followed, and it is perhaps too early to say exactly what are the consequences for the overall mix of 'levels' on governance (supranational, national, regional, local). In addition, this *varies* enormously across Europe, depending upon the different initial starting points in respect to the already existing relationships between local, national and forms of supranational or transnational governance (see **Anderson, 2001**).

It is in respect to this issue that we can also point to the *resistances* that have emerged to any attempt to undermine national economic sovereignties. Such resistances are not just the expressions of an overt political opposition to the project of 'economic Europe', but also those that arise because of the deeply embedded *national practices* of economic management and the *nationally based character* of economic activity and economic relationships. This relates then, in part at least, to the differences in the forms of capitalism found in Europe, an issue first broached in Chapter 1. In that chapter a basic configurative difference between a broad continental style of 'organized capitalism' was contrasted with the Anglo-American style of 'decentralized capitalism'. These two styles of capitalism were argued to have offered the main alternative imagery of the characteristics of economic Europe and to be in some respect in competition with one another in defining the future trajectory for economic Europe. Echoes of the way these types of capitalism operated to organize economic governance were exemplified in many of the chapters that followed (particularly in Chapters 3, 4, 5 and 8) In some cases this required the elaboration and extension of the styles of capitalism used in the analyses, to expand the number of different forms and their variety (as was noted in Chapter 5).

The point of raising this now is to indicate the way in which these very different forms of capitalism often operate 'naturally' to stall the programme of constructing a common or harmonized economic governance system at the EU level. The deeply embedded national features of these different relationships and mechanisms serves to frustrate any attempt to install either a common economic logic for the whole of Europe, or a programme of either *de jure* regulation or even the construction of an integrated common market through private *de facto* means.

4   The reasons for integration: political or economic?

A related theme to those already outlined arises for the issue of the imperatives that have driven the integrative project called 'economic Europe'. What has been the logic behind European integration? We have seen above how both *de jure* and *de facto* processes have been involved, but has there been a more all-encompassing objective? Supposing we accept the key role that *de jure* integration has played, thereby focusing on the political role of integration. Under what ideological or philosophical imagery was the EU project established and fostered?

Clearly, a key early consideration here was the political attempt to solve the problem of Europe as perceived in the immediate post-Second World War period, namely to prevent any further conflict on the continent and in particular to lock Germany and France together as a central condition for the prevention of such conflict. So, we can claim that at least one of the major reasons for the development of the EU economy was a political one. This might signal the continued importance of the political imperatives for European economic integration, with the EU remaining, above all, a political project – some would say a political project to construct a federal Europe. And if this were the case, then the integrative project of economic Europe would merely be a secondary adjunct to this overarching political agenda for integration.

On the other hand, we might view this in more pragmatic terms, as suggested earlier. Here there would be no overriding and consistent political project but rather a series of ad hoc and often reactive moves to strengthen European integration in the face of perceived economic threats from outside. In this case the economic imperative for integration might come more to the fore, and we could argue that Europe, rather hesitantly, might have stumbled along the road to economic union, sometimes almost unknowingly, or certainly without foreseeing the complete consequences of each individual move. The development of economic Europe came about almost by chance and without any overriding imperative.

5 The place of Europe in the wider world

The final broad theme to highlight in this review concerns the way that the evolving European economic space is fitting into the international system of governance. This was explicitly raised in Chapter 9, but it is clearly implicated in many other chapters as well. Indeed, as was indicated above the whole formation and evolution of the EU cannot be divorced from the international context in which Europe found itself throughout the post-war period.

The post-Second World War international governance of economic matters was fundamentally shaped by the outcome of the Bretton Woods conference in 1944. This established the familiar institutions of that governance, the World Bank: the IMF, and the GATT mechanism for the conduct of international trade negotiations (replaced by the WTO in 1995). In addition, this conference set up the semi-fixed exchange rate mechanism between the main international currencies that lasted until the early 1970s (semi-fixed because it allowed countries to alter their exchange rates vis-à-vis the US dollar only under exceptional circumstances – when their exchange rates were deemed to be fundamentally misaligned – and only with the agreement of the IMF). The collapse of this exchange rate regime in 1972/3 plunged the international economy into some turmoil. It eventually led to a regime of flexible exchange rates, at least among the main world economic powers.

We have already noted that these events in the 1970s were one stimulus for the EU to consider various forms of exchange rate management among the countries of the EU (the EMS and the ERM), and eventually a full economic and monetary union. These mechanisms were designed to add some stability to the EU framework of internal economic integration, and to provide a counterbalance to the international role of the US dollar. It was thought that a precondition for full economic integration was a stable exchange rate regime for the EU currencies.

Through its own internal integration process – the moves of which have been analysed at length throughout this book – the EU has gained a significant role in the contemporary regime of international governance. Its major status as an independent economic player, alongside the USA and Japan, secured for the EU a key voice in the conduct of international economic negotiations, in whatever forum was involved. In many ways the EU has found it easier to conduct these external negotiations than it has the internal negotiations over its own future. Brokering agreement among the EU members has been easier where external matters were concerned, while they have remained fractious and difficult in the case of the internal dynamic of its integration process.

The key economies in the international system are the USA (along with its NAFTA allies – Canada and Mexico), the EU and Japan. These are sometimes summed up as the 'Triad'. This Triad accounted for some 60 per cent of FDI flows and 70 per cent of trade flows within the global economy in the late 1990s. The USA and the EU were about the same size in terms of GDP, with Japan about one third smaller. Together they accounted for 75 per cent of world output in 1996. All these figures indicate the formidable importance of these three players for the future of the international system, and the relationships among them for the conduct of international economic governance.

As the East Asian economic crisis unfolded in the very late 1990s, and Japan's own dynamic growth also faltered during that period, the role of Japan has faded somewhat in the Triad (perhaps only temporarily). These events also served to shift the focus of attention away from the Pacific Ocean as the central arena for economic activity, and back toward the Atlantic Ocean. They turned attention toward the relationship between the USA and the EU, and in particular to the relationship between the US dollar and the EU euro. There can be little doubt that the US economy still acts as the engine that drives the international economy, so the management and health of the US economy remains crucial to the future of the global system as well.

What the advent of EMU could do is to establish another equally large continental-sized economy, one that could act as a real counterbalance to the power of the USA in the international system. In many ways this was prefigured in the relationship between the dollar and the euro at the turn of the twenty-first century. The introduction of the euro, far from making the international exchange rate system more stable, initially led to greater instability as the euro plunged against the dollar, and this instability is likely to continue to be the case. We shall probably see large fluctuations between the dollar and the euro, oscillating one way or another as economic fortune and sentiment fluctuate in each economy. Until the advent of the euro there was only one real 'safe haven' into which short-term investment and long term capital could flow if things got uncomfortable for international investors. That safe haven was the US dollar. Now there are potentially two such safe havens: the US dollar and the EU euro. Thus, as economic events change between these two economic blocs, even quite small changes in perception and expectations could trigger very rapid and large exchange rate fluctuations between the two currencies as money moves out of one and into the other. In the coming decades the key to the conduct of international economic governance, and with it the key to the prosperity of the global economy, will be how the relationship between the dollar and the euro is managed. This threatens to become the dominant issue in international economic governance for the first part of the twenty-first century. In this respect what happens to the euro, and how the USA and the EU think about their respective roles in the international system, could largely shape the international economic fortunes of the early part of the twenty-first century.

References

Anderson, J. (2001) 'The rise of regions and regionalism in Western Europe' in Guibernau, M. (ed.) *Governing European Diversity*, London, Sage/The Open University.

Scharpf, F. (1999) *Governing in Europe*, Oxford, OUP.

Index

Acknowledgements

Grateful acknowledgement is made to the following sources for permission to reproduce material in this book.

Figures

Figure 2.1: 'Chapter V: Developed Countries', pp. 154, 156, World Investment Report 1998: Trends and Determinants, United Nations Publication; *Figure 2.2:* European Union: Inflation and General Government Balance, p. 66, (1997), World Economic Outlook, October 1997, International Monetary Fund; *Figure 2.3:* Issues in the current conjuncture, p. 39, (1997), World Economic Outlook, Selected Advanced Economics: Employment and Unemployment, October 1997, International Monetary Fund; *Figure 4.1:* Allsop, C. *et.al.* (1990) 'Wage determination: the changing role of institutions in advanced industrialized counties', vol. 6, no. 4, Oxford Review of Economic Policy, Reproduced by permission of Oxford University Press.

Tables

Table 3.1: Fleming, S, 'How the web works for a top trio', p. 45, (2000) Evening Standard, Business Day, Evening Standard Newspaper, Solo Syndication Limited; *Tables 4.1, 4.2, 4.3:* Extracts taken from 'Economic growth in selected economics, 1960–1997', no. 67, © OECD 2000; *Table 4.4:* Extract taken from Forder, J. and Menon, A. (1998) 'Should unemployment convergence precede monetary union?', The European Union and National Macroeconomic Policy, Taylor and Francis Books Limited; *Table 6.1:* Fagerberg, J. *et.al.* (1999) 'Europe – a long view', The Economic Challenge for Europe Adapting to Innovation Based Growth, Ch. 1, Edward Elgar Publishing Limited; *Table 6.2:* Gambardella, A. and Malerba, F. (1999) The Organization of Economic Innovation in Europe, Cambridge University Press; *Table 8.1:* © European Communities, 1995–2000; *Tables 8.2, 8.3:* Rhodes, M. and van Apeldoorn, B. eds. (1998) 'Capital unbound? The transformation of European corporate governance', vol. 5, Journal of European Public Policy; *Table 9.1:* Eijffinger, S. and de Haan, J. (2000) 'Chapter 7, EMU and international policy – co-ordination', European Monetary and Fiscal Policy, by permission of Oxford University Press; *Table 9.1:* Eijffinger, S. and de Haan, J. 'EMU and international policy co-ordination', (2000) Ch. 7, European Monetary and Fiscal Policy, by permission of Oxford University Press.

Photograph

Page 130: © European Commission Audiovisual Library.

Every effort has been made to trace all the copyright owners, but if any has been inadvertently overlooked, the publishers will be pleased to make the necessary arrangements at the first opportunity.